Autistic spectrum disorders

Fondazione Pierfranco e Luisa Mariani ONLUS
viale Bianca Maria 28
20129 Milan, Italy

Telephone: +39 02 795458
Fax: +39 02 76009582
Publications Coordinator: Valeria Basilico
e-mail: publications@fondazione-mariani.org
www.fondazione-mariani.org

Autistic spectrum disorders

Edited by
D. Riva and I. Rapin

Mariani Foundation Paediatric Neurology Series: 14
Series Editor: Maria Majno

John Libbey EUROTEXT

ISSN 0969-0301
ISBN 2-7420-0590-0

Cover illustration: "Siesta", oil by Walter Lazzaro.
The kind permission of the Lazzaro by Corsi Gallery is gratefully acknowledged.

Published by

Éditions John Libbey Eurotext
127, avenue de la République, 92120 Montrouge, France.
Tél.: 33 (0)1 46 73 06 60; Fax: 33 (0)1 40 84 09 99
e-mail: contact@jle.com
http//www.jle.com

Contents

Autistic spectrum disorders, D. Riva and I. Rapin (eds.)

Chapter 1

Autistic spectrum disorders: an overview

Isabelle Rapin

The Saul R. Korey Department of Neurology, the Department of Pediatrics, and the Rose F. Kennedy Center for Research in Mental Retardation and Human Development, Albert Einstein College of Medicine, 1300 Morris Park Avenue, Bronx, NY 10461, USA
rapin@aecom.yu.edu

Summary

The autistic spectrum disorders (autism) or pervasive developmental disorders (PDDs) are developmental disorders of the immature brain that affect sociability, language and imagination, and behavioural and mental flexibility. Changing diagnostic criteria and heightened awareness of professionals and parents account for the perceived marked increase in prevalence. Autism has many aetiologies, some environmental, most genetic, although single-gene defects are individually rare. The meagre neuropathological information points to subtle neuronal developmental abnormalities in multiple brain areas. Routine neuroimaging rarely detects clinically significant abnormalities. Electroencephalography occasionally reveals unsuspected epileptiform activity, especially during slow wave sleep. Event related potentials, and morphometric and functional magnetic resonance imaging, have little current clinical relevance but are powerful research tools for understanding neuropathophysiology. Drugs are not curative but may alleviate some troublesome behaviours. In a recent double-blind study in children, risperidone showed modest efficacy on irritability and overall behaviour. The cause of the autistic/language regression between 18 and 24 months in about a third of children is not understood. It is not attributable to measles/mumps/rubella immunization. Medical investigation must be targeted at attempting to define an aetiology, especially for the rare treatable medical condition. Outcome is unpredictable at preschool except in the face of demonstrably severe brain pathology or profound global retardation. Parents need reliable information about genetic risk and appropriate interventions, and to be warned of the many unproven treatment suggestions offered. The most effective intervention is early education to circumvent deficits and target behavioural and communication needs. Some degree of improvement is expected in virtually all children.

Definitions

Autism, like dementia, is a behaviourally defined disorder of the brain, but a developmental disorder of the immature brain. No matter what their level of intellectual ability or other handicaps, anyone who has deficits in the following three behavioural domains is on the autistic spectrum. The three domains are first, social skill, empathy, and insight into others' minds; second, verbal and non-verbal communication and imagination; and third, cognitive and behavioural flexibility. Persons with autism are distributed along a bell-shaped curve because of the very broad range of severity of their symptomatology. As is the case for height, weight, and many other human characteristics and measures, diagnostic consensus is excellent for prototypic cases at the centre of the distribution. Diagnostic consensus is not as good at the mild end of the spectrum in view of the lack of a dichotomous cut-off between normality and pathology, especially as mild autism is likely to overlap with other disorders such as developmental language disorders, obsessive/compulsive disorder (OCD), Tourette syndrome, and others. At the other severe end of the spectrum, there is frank disagreement between those who insist that in order to diagnose autism it has to be out of proportion to the degree of mental retardation, and those who hold that, as there are no exclusion criteria for a diagnosis of autism, the more diffuse the brain dysfunction, the more likely it is, statistically, to disrupt complex neural networks and thus cause both severe mental retardation and autistic symptomatology.

DSM-IV (American Psychiatric Association, 2000) and ICD-10 (World Health Organization, 1992) divide autism or pervasive developmental disorder (PDD) into subtypes on the basis of age and the number and distribution of clinically handicapping symptoms in the three behavioural domains affected by autism:

(1) *Autistic disorder*, prototypic autism and the more severe subtype. It requires endorsement in all three behavioural domains, with endorsement of at least six of the 12 behavioural descriptors provided.
(2) *Asperger syndrome* applies to high-functioning individuals who are not mentally retarded (IQ of at least 70) and who spoke at the expected age, yet have serious social deficits and rigidity.
(3) *Disintegrative disorder* refers to children who regress and become autistic after completely normal early development, including speaking in sentences.
(4) *Pervasive Developmental Disorder-Not Otherwise Specified* (PDD-NOS) is used for children who are on the spectrum but do not fulfil criteria for the other three subtypes.

Rett syndrome, still listed as a fifth subtype of autism, is no longer defined on behavioural grounds as it is aetiologically defined in the majority but not all girls by mutations of the *MECP2* gene on chromosome Xq28 (Amir *et al.*, 1999).

Prevalence of autism and causal controversies

There is a current impression that autism has become much more prevalent than was the case just a decade ago. Indeed a recent American population survey in the children of Atlanta, Georgia yielded a figure of 3.1/1000 for autistic disorder and 3.4/1000 for autistic spectrum disorder (ASD) (the estimate of Asperger and PDD-NOS cases was considered to be an underestimate) (Yeargin-Allsopp *et al.*, 2003), compared to earlier prevalence estimates of 4/10,000. This has raised questions about such potential environmental causes or triggers as toxins from industrial dumps (Bertrand *et al.*, 2001), or nefarious effects from vaccines, especially the measles/mumps/rubella (MMR) vaccine. Vaccines have been implicated on two totally disparate grounds: either because they contained trace amounts of the preservative ethyl mercury (thimerosal) (Bernard *et al.*, 2001), or because of persistent infection of the gut and leucocytes by the attenuated measles vaccine virus (Kawashima *et al.*, 2000) suspected of rendering the gut leaky to small toxic molecules capable of entering the brain. In particular, MMR immunization has been blamed, without direct evidence, as a cause for the autistic regression which is most likely to coincide in time with the administration of this vaccine (Shinnar *et al.*, 2001; Kidd, 2002). Large, competent epidemiological studies have provided no support for these suspicions (Bertrand *et al.*, 2001; Madsen *et al.*, 2002; Fombonne & Cook 2003). The apparent increase in the prevalence of autism seems to be a function of better educated professionals who now identify much milder cases of ASD – in other words to changing diagnostic criteria – rather than to a true increase (Fombonne, 2003). Although it may be the case that what is inherited in some cases is atypical susceptibility to environmental influences because of genetic immunological or neurotransmitter vulnerability, this has yet to be demonstrated rigorously (Korvatska *et al.*, 2002). By the same token, perinatal insults that do not result in overt neurological abnormalities are unlikely aetiological candidates, despite some evidence that they may contribute to the severity of the autistic symptomatology in some children (Gillberg & Coleman, 2000).

Biologic basis of autism

Aetiologies

Because autism is a behaviourally defined condition like dementia, there is no biological diagnostic test to confirm the diagnosis. Autism has many different acquired and non-acquired causes (Gillberg & Coleman, 2000). Twin and family studies, together with cytogenetic abnormalities in a non-negligible proportion of affected individuals, provide definitive evidence for genetics as the major aetiology. However, less than complete concordance between monozygotic (MZ) twins and, in some cases, disparity in severity between MZ twins concordant for ASD indicate that autism has non-genetic causes or influences as well. Recurrence rates of less than 10 per cent within sibships and an increased risk for other developmental disorders in the families of affected persons indicate that single gene defects are less frequent causes of autism than polygenic influences (Bailey *et al.*, 1995; Risch *et al.*, 1999; Pickles *et al.*, 2000, Muhle *et al.*, 2004). The strong preponderance of autism in males is unexplained but much more plausibly genetic than environmental.

Neuropathology

Information about the neuropathological basis of autism is meagre and is very likely unrepresentative of its whole range of pathologies. Descriptions of the neuropathology of autism are currently limited to less than 60 cases worldwide, and only the most recent reports used state of the art technology. In fact, it is only following the demonstration in 1985 that neuronal cell bodies in the cerebellum and limbic system were smaller and axodendritic connections in the neuropil less complex than in control brains (Bauman & Kemper, 1985; Kemper & Bauman, 1998) that the neuropathological study of autism started in earnest. Discovery of similar findings in the minicolumns, which are the developmental and computational units of the neocortex, had to await the development of sophisticated computer programs that could be applied to microscopy (Casanova *et al.*, 2002).

Neuroimaging

Various investigators have reported that a disproportionate number of children with ASD have head circumferences that exceed norms (Rapin, 1996; Woodhouse *et al.*, 1996) and necropsies have shown a similar trend for brain weight (Courchesne *et al.*, 1999). Morphometric neuroimaging of the brain indicates that it is the volume of the white matter that is disproportionately large in children (Herbert *et al.*, 2003). A very recent study suggests that, on average, the rate of brain growth is accelerated during infancy and then slows down excessively, so that adults are not megalencephalic (Courchesne *et al.*, 1999; Courchesne *et al.*, 2003). Relative smallness of a number of brain regions has also been described in some of individuals, but thus far no clinically useful or pathognomonic pattern has emerged. Functional imaging has been applied to study the living brain, mostly to cooperative older children and adults. For example it shows that individuals with autism preferentially scan the mouth rather than the eyes and therefore are likely to miss clues of emotion (Klin *et al.*, 2002). Thus it has the potential to identify circuits that are dysfunctional in autism and shed light on its pathophysiology, but is still in the early stages of its application.

Electrophysiology

The electroencephalogram (EEG) of some 20 per cent of children with autism is abnormal and may show epileptiform activity even in some who do not have clinical epilepsy (Tuchman & Rapin, 1997). By adolescence about a third of the children will have experienced at least two unprovoked seizures. Again, not surprisingly, it is those with mental retardation or overt motor deficits who are at highest risk for epilepsy (Tuchman *et al.*, 1991b). Autism is also associated with atypical event related potentials (Steinschneider & Dunn, 2002), but full understanding of the significance of the described abnormalities will require much more work.

Neuropharmacology

What little is known of the neurochemical basis of autism arises in large part from the effects of the psychotropic drugs given empirically in attempts to control some of the more troublesome behaviours such as aggression, self injury, inattention, perseveration, and obsessive-compulsive tendencies (Posey & McDougle, 2001). The effectiveness of these drugs is attributed to modulation of the amounts of neurotransmitters at the synapse, notably serotonin but also dopamine, and probably norepinephrine, acetylcholine, and perhaps others. The effects of psychotropic drugs on neurotransmitters are not limited to one of many different neurotransmitter receptors; thus neurotransmitter effects on cells may be indirect, and a neurotransmitter may have both agonist and antagonist influences on the release of other neurotransmitters. No wonder that none of the drugs has entirely selective or predictable behavioural benefits, that drug effectiveness may change with time and dosage and differ among individuals, and that more or less serious undesirable side effects are frequent. It is important to stress that no drug cures autism, and that none acts directly on the social, communicative, or cognitive deficits at the core of autism.

The dopamine antagonist haloperidol was the first and may still be the most effective agent to improve the core symptoms of autism, but its use is limited by sedative and serious motor side effects (Campbell *et al.*, 1992). In the 1990s, specific serotonin reuptake inhibitors (SSRIs) and α_2-noradrenergic agonists were found to have beneficial behavioural effects for some individuals, although very few state-of-the-art trials were carried out, especially in children (Tsai, 1999). There is some clinical evidence that SSRIs have a place in alleviating the obsessive tendencies of some high-functioning individuals on the autistic spectrum (Scahill & Koenig, 1999) Imaging studies suggest that the maturation of serotonin systems differs in autism (Chugani *et al.*, 1997; Chugani *et al.*, 1999). Recent research has begun to consider whether there is evidence for altered acetylcholine activity in autism (Perry *et al.*, 2001), with an eye to the limited beneficial role of cholinergic drugs in Alzheimer disease. The neuropeptide oxytocin has also came under scrutiny because it has been shown to modulate sociability in experimental animals and to be somewhat lowered in some children with autism (Green *et al.*, 2001).

A double-blind placebo-controlled study of the effects of risperidone in children with autism was published in 2002 (McCracken *et al.*, 2002). The effectiveness of risperidone is attributed to its dual influence on serotonin and to a lesser degree on dopamine receptors. The major effect was on irritability, with suggestive improvement on a global functional autistic rating scale. This encouraging 8-week study will need to be replicated and parents made aware that risperidone is no panacaea and that pharmacological intervention needs to target specific troublesome behaviours. Because of the potential toxicity of the potent psychotropic drugs available thus far, the ratio of hoped for benefits for the particular individual to the safety and potential side effects of drugs must be considered before prescribing them.

Autistic language regression

About one of three parents report that their child had regressed but that there had been no loss of motor skills (Tuchman *et al.*, 1991a). Regression was most likely to have occurred between 18 and 24 months of age and to have been so insidious as to have passed unnoticed. All too often, if consulted at all, their physician reassured the parents until the child became completely non-verbal and the loss of sociability and interest in toys and imaginative play was undeniable.

The reality of the regression, which professionals tended to question at first – at least in some children – has been documented by videotapes of the child's behaviour before the reported regression compared with that after it. Exceptionally, a very severe regression may occur in an older child who was fully verbal and normal in every way; it is to these cases of later regression that the term 'disintegrative disorder' applies (Catalano, 1998; Fombonne, 2002).

To date, the cause of regression in toddlers and older children alike is unknown. Understandably, parents have attempted to identify a cause for it. Some ascribe it to an antecedent non-specific infectious illness or to an immunization; others to a seizure; and others to a psychological stress like an absence of the mother, a move to a new house, or the birth of a younger sibling (Kurita *et al.*, 1992; Shinnar *et al.*, 2001). It is in children with so called 'regressive autism' that environmental influences, notably MMR vaccine, have come under suspicion. The most common age at regression coincides in time with a period of frequent non-specific illnesses in toddlers, and with the administration of multiple immunizations. This coincidence is probably a major factor in the attribution of the regression to either immunological or infectious influences, or to toxicity from mercury in vaccines, none of which has been confirmed by rigorous research.

Epilepsy, either clinical or subclinical, became a suspect by analogy with the language regression that defines the syndrome of acquired epileptic aphasia (Landau–Kleffner syndrome) (Landau & Kleffner, 1957), and by the observation that EEG epileptiform activity is activated during slow sleep in both syndromes (Jayakar & Seshia, 1991; Tuchman & Rapin, 2002). The high frequency of epilepsy by adolescence, and infantile spasms as a precursor of autism in some children, have contributed to raising the possibility that subclinical epilepsy might exist and be responsible for the regression in some preschool children with autism. There is no evidence thus far, however, that children whose parents report the typical toddler regression are at higher risk for epilepsy than those who did not regress. The course of the regression is a prolonged plateau, typically lasting a number of months, sometimes longer, usually followed by some improvement in both language and behaviour, although not to normalcy. Prognosis in disintegrative disorder is worse and many children are left permanently demented and quite often epileptic. The course of the regression makes it clear that it does not denote a progressive degenerative disease of the brain, which must be considered of course, especially in disintegrative disorder.

There is no empirically based evidence to recommend a specific treatment for children whose language regresses with or without autism (Tuchman & Rapin, 2002). There are anecdotal reports of improvement following the administration of spike suppressant anticonvulsants, notably benzodiazepines, ACTH or steroids, intravenous immunoglobulin, or perhaps even surgery if seizures are intractable. Because regression is so poorly understood, and in view of its unpredictable course and of the expected improvement even in untreated children, a consensus on how to evaluate children who regress and what treatment to offer has not been achieved.

Course and predictors of outcome

Even though autism is a lifelong trait, its course is improvement with early, intensive, appropriate intervention that addresses both the behavioural and communicative deficits of young children (National Research Council, 2001). The strongest predictor of outcome is the severity of the mental retardation (Stevens *et al.*, 2000), ostensibly because it is a powerful surrogate for the extent and location of the underlying brain dysfunction. Although some half to two thirds of individuals with autism have full scale IQs below 70, cognition is not a defining feature as autism also occurs in very bright persons (Baron-Cohen *et al.*, 2001). Even gifted individuals typically have more uneven cognitive profiles than average. In retarded persons, the verbal IQ (VIQ) tends to be inferior to the performance IQ (PIQ), and rote memory and non-verbal spatial reasoning are often disproportionately high, which means that the full scale IQ smears high and low subtest scores and is less than informative (Goldstein *et al.*, 2001). In persons with average or better than average full scale IQs there may be no verbal/performance disparity, or the VIQ may be higher than the PIQ; this type of individual often does not have the delayed onset of expressive language that is the presenting complaint of many parents of toddlers with ASD and is thus likely to fulfil criteria for Asperger syndrome (Goldstein *et al.*, 2001). Keep in mind that children with Asperger syndrome and those with mild PDD-NOS may not be identified until the escalating social demands of mid-childhood or adolescence bring their social ineptitude and inadequate organizational skills to light, although their families and peers have probably long been aware that they are ‘different’. The least severely affected may weather childhood with minimal or no assistance and it not until adulthood that some identify themselves (Baron-Cohen *et al.*, 2001).

Although, as just stated, overall intelligence is the best predictor of outcome it does not always guarantee the ability to function independently in adulthood, as it is communicative ability and social skill that ultimately determine adaptability and employability. Therefore early, effective, and sustained educational intervention that addresses deficits in these behavioural domains is critical. Even if there is no ‘cure’ for autism, many children experience significant improvement, and the quality of life of even those who will not achieve independence and of their families can be substantially enhanced.

Evaluation and intervention

The family history and history of early development with specific questions regarding sociability, language, imaginative and reciprocal play, rigidity, narrowness of interests, repetitive behaviours, and in some cases epilepsy generally provide a strong suspicion of the diagnosis and some potential clues regarding aetiology (Filipek *et al.*, 2000). Some goals of the physical and neurodevelopmental evaluation are to uncover any evidence for a specific genetic condition, such as tuberous sclerosis, that mandates medical intervention, and to identify signs pointing to the dysfunction of particular brain systems like the cerebellar, sensorimotor, language, or other pathways. Clinicians should be able to tell parents confidently whether or not their child is on the autistic spectrum and to give them an idea of the severity of the developmental problem. If the clinicians are uncertain whether or not the child is on the spectrum, they are obligated to state their suspicion unambiguously and point out that, in borderline cases, it is further maturation and, especially, response to intervention that will clarify the diagnosis in time. Clinicians also need to stress that in young children the current level of functioning is not a reliable predictor of eventual attainment unless there is incontrovertible evidence for severe brain maldevelopment and very severe global retardation.

As part of the initial evaluation, physicians must inform parents of the recurrence risk in future children because, even if it is less than 10 per cent when autism has no obvious cause, this risk is still significant. They need to plan medical evaluations such as a hearing test in any child with defective or no speech, and a prolonged sleep EEG if there is a history of regression or a suspicion of epilepsy to look for a potentially treatable subclinical disorder (Filipek *et al.*, 2000). The yield of brain imaging is negligible if the neurological examination has raised no suspicion of a diagnosable intracranial process. They must refer appropriate children promptly to a geneticist or other specialist as indicated. This limited clinically targeted evaluation contrasts with the systematic and much more extensive genetic/metabolic, immunological, imaging, and electrophysiological studies justified in the context of a formal research study, the goal of which is to advance knowledge about autism.

Physicians need to stress the limited efficacy of drug treatment and that the most effective intervention by far for ASD is individualized, intensive, early intervention (National Research Council, 2001). The goal of referral to a psychologist and speech pathologist is to pinpoint current interventional needs. These evaluations are generally required for admission to a remedial program; it is important to remind parents that estimates of cognitive and language ability in preschool children have little predictive value, and that there is no one educational intervention that is appropriate for every child on the spectrum. Most parents will need professional help in selecting the one that best suits their child's particular current needs, but that it may need to be altered in the future. Finally, it is important to warn parents about well meaning but ineffective and often expensive interventions, some of which are touted on the Internet. The physician needs to schedule a revisit as parents will require time to digest the enormous amount of information they have been given before they can ask questions relevant to their particular needs. It is very helpful if a physician who knows the disorder well follows children on the autistic spectrum prospectively so as to interpret and supplement information offered by the many teachers and therapists who will enter the life of the child's family.

Conclusions

Now that autism is finally under the limelight of both the research and educational communities, the need is clear for research into both its biological basis and the relative effectiveness of the various interventions currently being offered without proof of efficacy. Because autism has so many disparate causes, some of which, like genetics, are not likely to be directly addressable, research into prevention needs to focus on and identify potentially avoidable environmental triggers and susceptibility to these nefarious influences. Advancies in the understanding of the neural pathophysiology of autism are most likely to elucidate contributing factors like epilepsy, potential immune problems, and altered neurotransmission. Pharmacologists need to be challenged to devise more effective drugs that can influence aberrant behaviours and ameliorate the course of the disorder. It is research into pathophysiology that will illuminate the basis of such troublesome behaviours as stereotypies, aberrant responses to sensory stimuli, self injury, gaze avoidance, excessive anxiety, distractibility, and others that are the focus of so much current educational effort. Enhanced understanding of the ontogeny of the complex social skills of humans will provide educators with better honed tools to address core deficits of autism. In industrialized countries society is now financially swamped with the costs of responding to desperate parents' ever escalating demands for intensive interventions for their children with autism. It is encouraging that therapists and educators are starting to mount the rigorous interventional research that is crucial to both stemming the overwhelming tide of interventions of dubious effectiveness and devising more specific, more efficacious, and more economical substitutes.

References

American Psychiatric Association (2000): *Diagnostic and statistical manual of mental disorders, 4th ed., text revision: DSM IV-TR*, pp. 69–84. Washington, D.C.: American Psychiatric Association.

Amir, R.E., van den Veyver, I.B., Wan, M., Tran, C.Q., Francke, U. & Zoghbi, H.Y. (1999): Rett syndrome is caused by mutations in X-linked *MECP2*, encoding methyl-CpG-binding protein. *Nat. Genet.* **23**, 185–188.

Bailey, A., Le Couteur, A., Gottesman, I., Bolton, P., Simonoff, E., Yuzda, E. & Rutter, M. (1995): Autism as a strongly genetic disorder: evidence from a British twin study. *Psychol. Med.* **1**, 63–77.

Baron-Cohen, S., Wheelwright, S., Skinner, R., Martin, J. & Clubley, E. (2001): The Autism-Spectrum Quotient (AQ): evidence from Asperger syndrome/high-functioning autism, males and females, scientists and mathematicians. *J. Autism Dev. Disord.* **31**, 5–17.

Bauman, M.L. & Kemper, T.L. (1985): Histoanatomic observations of the brain in early infantile autism. *Neurology* **35**, 866–874.

Bernard, S., Enayati, A., Redwood, L., Roger, H. & Binstock, T. (2001): Autism: a novel form of mercury poisoning. *Med. Hypoth.* **56**, 462–471.

Bertrand, J., Mars, A., Boyle, C., Bove, F., Yeargin-Allsopp, M. & Decoufle, P. (2001): Prevalence of autism in a United States population: the Brick Township, New Jersey, investigation. *Pediatrics* **108**, 1155–1161.

Campbell, M., Small, A.M., Anderson, L.T., Malone, R.P. & Locascio, J.J. (1992): Pharmacotherapy in autism. In: *Neurobiology of infantile autism*, eds. H. Naruse & E.M. Ornitz, pp. 235–243. Amsterdam: Excerpta Medica.

Casanova, M.F., Buxhoeveden, D.P., Switala, A.E. & Roy, E. (2002): Minicolumnar pathology in autism. *Neurology* **58**, 428–432.

Catalano, R.A. (1998): *When autism strikes: families cope with childhood disintegrative disorder*. New York: Plenum Press.

Chugani, D.C., Muzik, O., Rothermel, R., Behen, M., Chakraborty, P., Mangner, T., da Silva, E.A. & Chugani, H.T. (1997): Altered serotonin synthesis in the dentatothalamocortical pathway in autistic boys. *Ann. Neurol.* **42**, 666–669.

Chugani, D.C., Muzik, O., Behen, M., Rothermel, R., Janisse, J.J., Lee, J. & Chugani, H.T. (1999): Developmental changes in brain serotonin synthesis capacity in autistic and nonautistic children. *Ann. Neurol.* **45**, 287–295.

Courchesne, E., Muller, R.A. & Saitoh, O. (1999): Brain weight in autism: normal in the majority of cases, megalencephalic in rare cases. *Neurology* **52**, 1057–1059.

Courchesne, E., Carper, R. & Akshoomoff, N. (2003): Evidence of brain overgrowth in the first year of life in autism. *JAMA* **290**, 337–344.

Filipek, P.A., Accardo, P.J., Ashwal, S., Baranek, G.T., Cook, E.H., Dawson, G., Gordon, B., Gravel, J.S., Johnson C.P., Kallen, R.J., Levy, S.E., Minshew, N.J., Ozonoff, S., Prizant, B., Rapin, I., Rogers, S.J., Stone, W.L., Teplin, S., Tuchman, R.F. & Volkmar, F.R. (2000): Practice parameter: screening and diagnosis of autism: report of the Quality Standards Subcommittee of the American Academy of Neurology and the Child Neurology Society. *Neurology* **55**, 468–479.

Fombonne, E. (2002): Prevalence of childhood disintegrative disorder. *Autism* **6**, 149–157.

Fombonne, E. (2003): Epidemiological surveys of autism and other pervasive developmental disorders: an update. *J. Autism Dev. Disord.* **33**, 365–382.

Fombonne, E. & Cook, E.H. (2003): MMR and autistic enterocolitis: consistent epidemiological failure to find an association. *Mol. Psychiatry* **8**, 133–134.

Gillberg, C. & Coleman, M. (2000): *The biology of the autistic syndromes*, 3rd ed. London: MacKeith Press.

Goldstein, G., Beers, S.R., Siegel, D.J. & Minshew, N.J. (2001): A comparison of WAIS-R profiles in adults with high-functioning autism or differing subtypes of learning disability. *Appl. Neuropsychol.* **8**, 148–154.

Green, L.A., Fein, D., Modahl, C., Feinstein, C., Waterhouse, L. & Morris, M. (2001): Oxytocin and autistic disorder: alterations in peptide forms. *Biol. Psychiatry* **50**, 609–613.

Herbert, M.R., Ziegler, D.A., Deutsch, C.K., O'Brien, L.M., Lange, N., Bakardjiev, A., Hodgson, J., Adrien, K.T., Steele, S., Makris, N., Kennedy, D., Harris, G.J. & Caviness, V.S. (2003): Dissociations of cerebral cortex, subcortical and cerebral white matter volumes in autistic boys. *Brain* **126**, 1182–1192.

Jayakar, P.B. & Seshia, S.S. (1991): Electrical status epilepticus during slow-wave sleep: a review. *J. Clin. Neurophysiol.* **3**, 299–311.

Kawashima, H., Mori, T., Kashiwagi, Y., Takekuma, K., Hoshika, A. & Wakefield, A. (2000): Detection and sequencing of measles virus from peripheral mononuclear cells from patients with inflammatory bowel disease and autism. *Dig. Dis. Sci.* **45**, 723–729.

Kemper, T.L. & Bauman, M. (1998): Neuropathology of infantile autism. *J. Neuropathol. Exp. Neurol.* **57**, 645–652.

Kidd, P.M. (2002): Autism, an extreme challenge to integrative medicine. Part 1. The knowledge base. *Altern. Med. Rev.* **7**, 292–316.

Klin, A., Jones, W., Schultz, R., Volkmar, F. & Cohen, D. (2002): Visual fixation patterns during viewing of naturalistic social situations as predictors of social competence in individuals with autism. *Arch. Gen. Psychiatry* **59**, 809–816.

Korvatska, E., Van de, W.J., Anders, T.F. & Gershwin, M.E. (2002): Genetic and immunologic considerations in autism. *Neurobiol. Dis.* **9**, 107–125.

Kurita, H., Kita, M. & Miyake, Y. (1992): A comparative study of development and symptoms among disintegrative psychosis and infantile autism with and without speech loss. *J. Autism Dev. Disord.* **22**, 175–188.

Landau, W.M. & Kleffner, F.R. (1957): Syndrome of acquired aphasia with convulsive disorder in children. *Neurology* **7**, 523–530.

Madsen, K.M., Hviid, A., Vestergaard, M., Schendel, D., Wohlfahrt, J., Thorsen, P., Olsen, J. & Melbye, M. (2002): A population-based study of measles, mumps, and rubella vaccination and autism. *N. Engl. J. Med.* **347**, 1477–1482.

McCracken, J.T., McGough, J., Shah, B., Cronin, P., Hong, D., Aman, M.G., Arnold, L.E., Lindsay, R., Nash, P., Hollway, J., McDougle, C.J., Posey, D., Swiezy, N., Kohn, A., Scahill, L., Martin, A., Koenig, K., Volkmar, F., Carroll, D., Lancor, A., Tierney, E., Ghuman, J., Gonzalez, N.M., Grados, M., Vitiello, B., Ritz, L., Davies, M., Robinson, J. & McMahon, D. (2002): Risperidone in children with autism and serious behavioral problems. *N. Engl. J. Med.* **347**, 314–321.

Muhle, R., Trentacoste, S.V. & Rapin, I. (2004): The genetics of autism. *Pediatrics* **113**, e472-e486.

National Research Council (2001): *Educating children with autism*. Washington DC: National Academy Press.

Perry, E.K., Lee, M.L., Martin-Ruiz, C.M., Court, J.A., Volsen, S.G., Merrit, J., Folly, E., Iversen, P.E., Bauman, M.L., Perry, R.H. & Wenk, G.L. (2001): Cholinergic activity in autism: abnormalities in the cerebral cortex and basal forebrain. *Am. J. Psychiatry* **158**, 1058–1066.

Pickles, A., Starr, E., Kazak, S., Bolton, P., Papanikolaou, K., Bailey, A., Goodman, R. & Rutter, M. (2000): Variable expression of the autism broader phenotype: findings from extended pedigrees. *J. Child Psychol. Psychiatry* **41**, 491–502.

Posey, D.J. & McDougle, C.J. (2001): Pharmacotherapeutic management of autism. *Expert Opin. Pharmacother.* **2**, 587–600.

Rapin, I. (1996): Neurological examination. In: *Preschool children with inadequate communication: developmental language disorder, autism, low IQ*, ed. I. Rapin, pp. 98–122. London: MacKeith Press.

Risch, N., Spiker, D., Lotspeich, L., Nouri, N., Hinds, D., Hallmayer, J., Kalaydjieva, L., McCague, P., Dimicelli, S., Pitts, T. *et al.* (1999): A genomic screen of autism: evidence for a multilocus etiology. *Am. J. Hum. Genet.* **65**, 493–507.

Scahill, L. & Koenig, K. (1999): Pharmacotherapy in children and adolescents with pervasive developmental disorders. *J. Child Adolesc. Psychiatr. Nurs.* **12**, 41–43.

Shinnar, S., Rapin, I., Arnold, S., Tuchman, R.F., Shulman, L., Ballaban-Gil, K., Maw, M., Deuel, R.K. & Volkmar, F.R. (2001): Language regression in childhood. *Pediatr. Neurol.* **24**, 185–191.

Steinschneider, M. & Dunn, M. (2002): Electrophysiology in developmental neuropsychology. In: *Child neuropsychology*, 2nd ed., eds. S. Segalowitz & I. Rapin, vol. 8, part I, pp. 91–146. Amsterdam: Elsevier Science.

Stevens, M.C., Fein, D.A., Dunn, M., Allen, D., Waterhouse, L.H., Feinstein, C. & Rapin, I. (2000): Subgroups of children with autism by cluster analysis: a longitudinal examination. *J. Am. Acad. Child Adolesc. Psychiatry* **39**, 346–352.

Tsai, L.Y. (1999): Psychopharmacology in autism. *Psychosom. Med.* **61**, 651–665.

Tuchman, R.F. & Rapin, I. (1997): Regression in pervasive developmental disorders: seizures and epileptiform EEG correlates. *Pediatrics* **99**, 560–566.

Tuchman, R.F. & Rapin, I. (2002): Epilepsy in autism. *Lancet Neurol.* **1**, 352–358.

Tuchman, R.F., Rapin, I. & Shinnar, S. (1991a): Autistic and dysphasic children. I. Clinical characteristics. *Pediatrics* **88**, 1211–1218.

Tuchman, R.F., Rapin, I. & Shinnar, S. (1991b): Autistic and dysphasic children. II. Epilepsy. *Pediatrics* **88**, 1219–1225.

Woodhouse, W., Bailey, A., Rutter, M., Bolton, P., Baird, G. & Le Couteur, A. (1996): Head circumference in autism and other pervasive developmental disorders. *J. Child Psychol. Psychiatry* **37**, 665–671.

World Health Organization (1992): *The ICD-10 classification of mental and behavioural disorders. Clinical descriptions and diagnostic guidelines*, 10th ed. Geneva: World Health Organization.

Yeargin-Allsopp, M., Rice, C., Karapurkar, T., Doernberg, N., Boyle, C. & Murphy, C. (2003): Prevalence of autism in a US metropolitan area. *JAMA* **289**, 49–55.

Autistic spectrum disorders, D. Riva and I. Rapin (eds.)
© 2005 John Libbey Eurotext, pp. 11–17.

Chapter 2

Genetic considerations in autism

Paolo Curatolo, Barbara Manzi, Simona Pennacchia and Maria Cristina Porfirio

Department of Neurosciences, Paediatric Neurology Unit, Tor Vergata University of Rome, Via Montpellier 1, 00133 Rome, Italy
Curatolo@uniroma2.it

Summary

Autism is a complex, behaviourally defined, disorder characterized by impairments in three behavioural domains: 1) social interaction; 2) language, communication, and imaginative play; and 3) range of interests and activities. Aetiological research shows autism as a syndrome with multiple genetic and non-genetic causes. Epigenetic factors and exposure to environmental modifiers may contribute to variable expression of autism-related traits. The identity and number of genes involved remain unknown. Several studies began to focus primarily on defining the genetic mechanisms involved. The identification of chromosomal abnormalities and Mendelian syndromes among individuals with autism, in conjunction with data from genome screens and candidate-gene studies, has helped to refine the view of the complex genetics that underlie autism spectrum conditions. Future clinically usefull insights and potential medications depend on identifying these genes and elucidating the influences of their products on brain development and physiology.

Historical background

Autistic disorder is a behavioural syndrome beginning before the age of 3 years and lasting over the whole lifetime. It is characterized by impairment in communication, impaired social interactions, and repetitive interests and behaviour. In the first report describing autism, Kanner (1943) postulated that it was an inborn disorder, yet for many years little attention was paid to possible genetic factors because it was so uncommon to have two autistic children in the same family (some two per cent of cases in the reports reviewed by Smalley *et al.*, 1988). Early chromosome studies also failed to reveal any abnormalities. However, even a two per cent rate of autism in siblings means a huge increase in relative risk compared with the general-population. The first systematic, general-population based twin study, by Folstein & Rutter (1977), provided evidence of a strong genetic component. Furthermore, discovery of the fragile X anomaly led to investigations with findings suggesting that a substantial minority of autistic individuals had this anomaly (Blomquist *et al.*, 1985). This led to major research interest in the association, as well as to a renewal of interest in other chromosome anomalies that might be associated with autism (Gillberg & Wahlstrom, 1985). Clinical investigations brought growing awareness that some children with autism were affected by single gene medical disorders showing a Mendelian pattern of inheritance (Folstein & Rutter, 1988; Folstein & Piven, 1991).

Mechanism of inheritance

Autism is aetiologically heterogeneous. Known medical conditions are implicated in perhaps 20–25 per cent of cases, the strongest associations being with tuberous sclerosis and the fragile X syndrome. Family and twin studies show evidence of a substantial genetic predisposition in most idiopathic cases.

The frequency of autism is much higher in the siblings of children with autism (two to six per cent) than in the general population, but the strongest evidence for the heritability of autism comes from twin studies. Monozygotic twins have been shown to have a higher concordance rate than dizygotic twins in several studies.

In a review by Smalley *et al.* (1988), pooled estimates were 61 per cent concordance rate for monozygotic (MZ) twins *versus* nine per cent for dizygotic (DZ) twins, giving a DZ/MZ ratio of 0.14. In a 1989 twin study by Steffenburg *et al.*, the concordance rate in MZ twins was 91 per cent, *versus* 0 per cent in DZ twins. Bailey *et al.* (1995) reported that 60 per cent of MZ twins were concordant for autism, *versus* 0 per cent of DZ twins. When a broad definition of the autistic spectrum was used, there was a 92 per cent concordance rate for MZ twins compared with only 10 per cent for DZ twins, giving a DZ/MZ ratio of 0.11. This suggested a heritability of autism of 91–93 per cent. The fact that the concordance rate does not reach 100 per cent in monozygotic twins is in favour of some participation by environmental factors. This interaction of genetic factors and the environment corresponds to most complex human diseases.

The genetic studies indicate that autism is a genetically heterogeneous polygenic disorder caused by the additive and epistatic effect of many different genes, each with a small effect and with some showing maternal or paternal imprinting, plus a modest environmental component. While many dozens of genes may contribute to the autism phenotype, a given individual may only need to inherit a subset of these to develop autism.

The 4:1 male to female ratio for autism suggest that affected females may require a higher degree of genetic loading to develop the disorder than males. It is not known why there is a preponderance of males with autism. It is possible that one of many susceptibility genes is present on the X chromosome. This could result in a complex X linked pattern of inheritance in which heterozygous females with a susceptibility variant are at less risk than homozygous males with a susceptibility variant that is one of many genes related to autism risk. Another intriguing possibility is that there may be a gene on the X chromosome that is only expressed if inherited from the father. This would place all males at higher risk when other susceptibility factors are present.

Although altered secretion of the androgens is not a common feature of autism (Tordjman *et al.*, 1995), it has been suggested that autism may arise as the result of exposure to high concentrations of prenatal testosterone.

Chromosome abnormalities in autism

There are several approaches that can be used in searching for genes involved in complex diseases. One of these is to find *de novo* chromosomal aberrations in patients and to suppose that such aberrations – corresponding to translocations or duplications-deletions – disrupt genes or regulating regions involved in the aetiology of the disease. The frequency of such anomalies in the autistic population can be estimated to be about three per cent, but unfortunately many chromosomes have been found to be abnormal. The most common specific genetic causes of autism yet identified are abnormalities of the 15q11–q13 region. Deletions of this region lead to either Angelman syndrome or Prader-Willi syndrome, depending on whether the deletion is from the maternal chromosome (Angelman syndrome) or the paternal chromosome (Prader-Willi syndrome). Both of these disorders are associated with syndromal characteristics that should lead to their identification. Both of them may be caused by having two otherwise normal chromosomes (uniparental disomy). If a patient gets two otherwise normal chromosomes from their father, they are 'missing' their mother's 15q11–q13 region (as well as the whole chromosome) and have Angelman syndrome. Angelman syndrome has been associated with autism.

Individual candidate genes

Various genome-wide linkage studies have been published. As is typical of the use of linkage analysis for traits that are polygenic with many genes involved, some of the results were in agreement while most were not. Most of the agreement concerned signals on chromosome 7q,on 2q, 16p *(Fig. 1)*. The following is a review of some of the more likely candidate genes and preliminary results with some association studies.

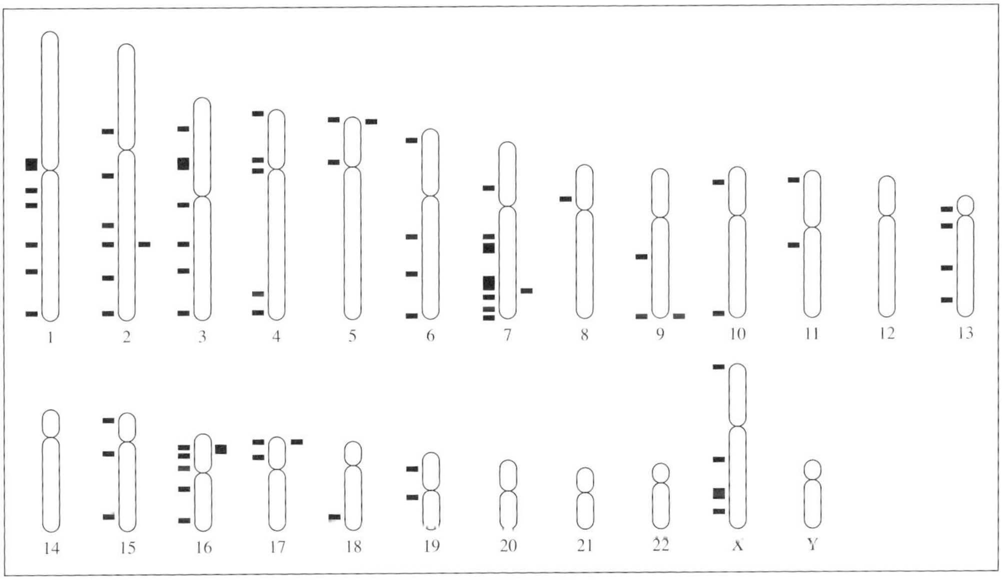

Fig. 1. Genome screen for loci that predispose to autism spectrum disorders. The most consistent signals are on chromosome 7q,2q and 16p. (Modified from Folstein & Rosen-Sheidley, 2001.)

Chromosome 7q

The most consistent linkage finding has been the presence of a signal at the chromosome 7q31–q35 area. The 7q31 locus may have a general influence on specific language impairment (SLI). Fisher *et al.* (1998) identified a locus on 7q31 that segregated with a severe speech and language disorder (SPCH1) in a large three generation pedigree. The trait segregated as autosomal dominant. There is considerable evidence for a gene on chromosome 7q31 that plays a role in the development of autism. Therefore SLI and autism are likely to share one or more genes in common.

Several groups have been looking closely at 7q22–31 because the region has been implicated in various genome screens. *Reelin* gene is expressed in this region and it has been identified in an autism association study. Moreover Hong *et al.* (2000) identified splicing mutations in *Reelin* gene that cause autosomal recessive lissencephaly – an abnormality of neuron migration.

Chromosome 2

Using a sample of autism-affected relative pairs restricted to those with a delayed onset (< 36 months) of phrase speech, Buxbaum *et al.* (2001) identified a locus on chromosome 2q with a LOD score of 2.99. The chromosome 2 result is the highest multipoint maximum LOD score generated to date in an autism genome screen; it is supported by reported nominal linkage of 0.64 by Philippe *et al.* (1999) and by IMGSAC (2001).

Defects in neurotransmitters

Defects in serotonin, dopamine, norepinephrine glutamate/NMDA, GABA, and opioids have all been described in autism. Defects in the amygdala, especially in relation to problems with social interaction, have been proposed in autism, and some neurotransmitters involved in autism are well represented in this structure.

Serotonin

Serotonin plays a role in many of the behaviours associated with autism, including obsessions and compulsion, mood disorders, aggression, anxiety, impulsivity, and disorders of sleep and social interaction. One of the most highly replicated biological findings is the presence of a raised level of platelet serotonin in approximately one third of autistic subjects. Using ^{11}C-methyl-L-tryptophan and positron emission tomography, Chugani *et al.* (1999) showed that in normal children, serotonin-synthesizing capacity was more than 200 per cent that of adult levels up to the age of 5, and then declined. The decline was earlier in girls than in boys. By contrast, in autistic children serotonin-synthesizing capacity increased gradually between the ages of 2 and 15 and then declined towards adult levels, and there were no sex differences. They concluded that humans undergo a period of high brain serotonin-synthesizing capacity during childhood and that this developmental process is disrupted in autistic children. These results suggest that serotonin genes, and especially the serotonin transporter genes, are important candidate genes in autism.

Adenosine deaminase (ADA)

ADA plays a role in purine metabolism, immune responses, and peptidase activity. Deficiency of ADA activity gives rise to severe combined immunodeficiency (SCID). In the normal population, two alleles have been observed: ADA1 and ADA2. The second allele is associated with a decrease of 20 per cent in enzymatic activity and is the less common allele in the normal healthy European population, with a frequency of approximately six per cent.

Recently two groups (De Luca *et al.*, 1999; Persico *et al.*, 2000; Bottini *et al.*, 2001) have independently reported an association at the population level between the common adenosine deaminase biochemical polymorphism (ADA1) and autism. This result suggests that there could be linkage disequilibrium between ADA1 polymorphism and a causative polymorphism located in its vicinity. To assess whether the ADA association actually encompasses the ADA1 biochemical polymorphism, our group examined three ADA polymerase chain reaction polymorphisms in relation to autism, using pairwise measures of linkage disequilibrium in a sample of 48 autistic Italian children. Our results support the hypothesis that inside the ADA structural gene only the biochemical polymorphism (ADA1) confers susceptibility to autism. In view of the role of ADA in the normal development and function of both the nervous system and the immune system, the observed association of the less active ADA1 allele with autism justifies a specific function of the ADA gene in the pathology of autism. These investigations may benefit from biochemical explorations of purine metabolism in autistic patients.

Tuberous sclerosis

Tuberous sclerosis complex (TSC) is a rare dominant genetic disease caused by mutations of two functionally related genes, TSC1 and TSC2. Autistic disorder is common in TSC. Different studies have shown that three to four per cent of autistic subjects may have TSC. Conversely, studies of TSC patients have identified much higher rates of autism, ranging from 17 per cent to as high as 61 per cent. Curatolo and coworkers (2001) identified autism in six of 23 patients (26 per cent) with TSC. On the other hand, among individuals with autistic disorder the rate of TSC ranges from one per cent to three per cent, which is an increase of about 120-fold compared with the general population. This makes TSC the most common monogenic disease encountered in autistic patients. Several screens for autistic disorder have recently been completed (Lamb *et al.*, 2005; Yonan *et al.*, 2003; Shao *et al.*, 2002; IMGSAC, 2001; Buxbaum *et al.*, 2001; Risch *et al.*, 1999; Philippe *et al.*, 1999; IMGSAC, 1998). Besides seven other chromosomes (1, 2, 4, 7, 10, 19, 22), a region on chromosome 16p between the markers D16S418 (16p13.2) and D16S3114 (16p13.3) shows a significant linkage to autistic disorder, with a maximum LOD score of 1.51. Philippe *et al.* (1999) carried out a genome-wide screen with 264 microsatellites markers in 51 multiplex families, using non-parametric linkage methods. Eleven regions gave nominal *P* values of 0.05 or lower. One of these regions overlapped with regions on chromosomes 16p identified by the first genome-wide scan of autism.

Besides the linkage analysis in multiplex families, the existence of a susceptibility locus for autistic disorder on 16p13 is supported by other observations. Hebebrand *et al.* (1994) reported the case of a patient with autistic disorder and a partial duplication of 16p13, and another case of autism associated with a microduplication of 16p13 has been found by Philippe *et al.* (1999). Moreover, autism occurs in a number of patients with tuberous sclerosis, and about half the cases of TSC are caused by mutations within the TSC2 gene mapping on chromosome 16p13 (Curatolo *et al.*, 2001; The European Chromosome 16 Tuberous Sclerosis Consortium, 1993). Comorbidity of autism with epilepsy, attention deficit-hyperactivity disorder, mental retardation, and Tourette syndrome confirms the involvement of this region. In fact, each of these disorders had susceptibility genes in the 16p region (Hebebrand *et al.*, 1994; Daniels *et al.*, 2001; Smalley *et al.*, 2002).

Our recent study (Curatolo *et al.*, 2003) compared polymorphism allele frequency distributions between affected probands and unaffected control subjects for D16S291 and D16S407. We described a marginal association between the marker D16S502 (mapping 16p13.2) and autism. D16S502 polymorphism may be in linkage disequilibrium with an unidentified functional gene. Our result is the first obtained in an Italian population using an association study and seems to be in line with the relation between the 16p13 region and autism previously identified using genome screening and linkage analysis.

Future directions

The linkage findings are consistent with a great deal of genetic heterogeneity in a true polygenic trait, with most of the genes accounting for less than three per cent of the variance. Attempts to identify the causative genes in autism using linkage techniques, such as sibling pair analysis, have been largely unsuccessful. Case-control association studies are likely to be the single most powerful methods of identifying the genes involved in autism, but parent-child trios will be necessary to test for preferential transmission from the maternal or paternal side.

Because of the great genetic heterogeneity of autism, 100 different gene variants may be involved in all autistic subjects. However, of these only 10 to 20 may be causative in a given individual. Techniques that examine genes one at a time are unlikely to identify the genes involved. With the current ability to test to many genes simultaneously in a single tube or array, autistic subjects could easily be screened for the entire set of identified relevant genes. This would show which genes and which combinations of genes are involved in a given subject. This in turn could allow treatment to be tailored for each individual, based on the genetic profile.

References

Bailey, A., Le Couteur, A., Gottesman, I., Bolton, P., Simonoff, E., Yuzda, E. & Rutter, M. (1995): Autism as a strongly genetic disorder: evidence from a British twin study. *Psychol. Med.* **25**, 63–77.

Blomquist, H.K., Bohman, M., Edvinsson, S.O., Gillberg, C., Gustavson, K.H., Holmgren, G. & Wahlstrom, J. (1985): Frequency of the fragile X syndrome in infantile autism. A Swedish multicenter study. *Clin. Genet.* **27**, 113–117.

Bottini, N., De Luca, D., Saccucci, P., Fiumara, A., Elia, M., Porfirio, M.C., Lucarelli, P. & Curatolo, P. (2001): Autism: evidence of association with adenosine deaminase genetic polymorphism. *Neurogenetics* **3**, 111–113.

Buxbaum, J.D., Silverman, J.M., Smith, C.J., Kilifarski, M., Reichert, J., Hollander, E., Lawlor, B.A., Fitzgerald, M., Greenberg, D.A. & Davis, K.L. (2001): Evidence for a susceptibility gene for autism on chromosome 2 and for genetic heterogeneity. *Am. J. Hum. Genet.* **68**, 1514–1520.

Chugani, D.C., Muzik, O., Behen, M., Rothermel, R., Janisse, J.J., Lee, J. & Chugani, H.T. (1999): Developmental changes in brain serotonin synthesis capacity in autistic and nonautistic children. *Ann. Neurol.* **45**, 287–295.

Curatolo, P., Verdecchia, M. & Bombardieri, R. (2001): Vigabatrin for tuberous sclerosis complex. *Brain Dev.* **23** (suppl. 7), 649–653.

Curatolo, P. (2003): *Tuberous sclerosis complex: from basic science to clinical phenotypes*. Cambridge, UK: Cambridge University Press.

Daniels, R.J., Peden, J.F., Lloyd, C., Horsley, S.W., Clark, K., Tufarelli, C., Kearney, L., Buckle, V.J., Doggett, N.A., Flint, J. & Higgs, D.R. (2001): Sequence, structure and pathology of the fully annotated terminal 2 Mb of the short arm of human chromosome 16. *Hum. Mol. Genet.* **10**, 339–352.

De Luca, D., Lucarelli, P., Bottini, N., Porfirio, C. & Curatolo, P. (1999): Adenosine deaminase polymorphism in autism. *J. Child Neurol.* **14**, 323–324.

The European Chromosome 16 Tuberous Sclerosis Consortium (1993): Identification and characterization of the tuberous sclerosis gene on chromosome 16. *Cell* **75**, 1305–1315.

Fisher, S.E., Vargha-Khadem, F., Watkins, K.E., Monaco, A.P. & Pembrey, M.E. (1998): Localisation of a gene implicated in a severe speech and language disorder. *Nat. Genet.* **18**, 168–170.

Folstein, S. & Rutter, M. (1977): Infantile autism: a genetic study of 21 twin pairs. *J. Child. Psychol. Psychiatry* **18**, 297–321.

Folstein, S.E. & Rutter, M.L. (1988): Autism: familial aggregation and genetic implications. *J. Autism Dev. Disord.* **18**, 3–30.

Folstein, S.E. & Piven, J. (1991): Etiology of autism: genetic influences. *Pediatrics* **87**, 767–773.

Folstein, S.E. & Rosen-Sheidley, B. (2001): Genetics of autism: complex aetiology for a heterogeneous disorder. *Nat. Rev. Genet.* **2**, 943–955.

Gillberg, C. & Wahlstrom, J. (1985): Chromosome abnormalities in infantile autism and other childhood psychoses: a population study of 66 cases. *Dev. Med. Child Neurol.* **27**, 293–304.

Hebebrand, J., Martin, M., Korner, J., Roitzheim, B., de Braganca, K., Werner, W. & Remschmidt, H. (1994): Partial trisomy 16p in an adolescent with autistic disorder and Tourette's syndrome. *Am. J. Med. Genet.* **54**, 268–270.

Hong, S.E., Shugart, Y.Y., Huang, D.T., Shahwan, S.A., Grant, P.E., Hourihane, J.O., Martin, N.D. & Walsh, C.A. (2000): Autosomal recessive lissencephaly with cerebellar hypoplasia is associated with human RELN mutations. *Nat. Genet.* **26**, 93–96.

International Molecular Genetic Study of Autism Consortium (IMGSAC) (1998): A full genome screen for autism with evidence for linkage to a region on chromosome 7q. *Hum. Mol. Genet.* **7** (suppl. 3), 571–578.

International Molecular Genetic Study of Autism Consortium (IMGSAC) (2001): A genomewide screen for autism: strong evidence for linkage to chromosomes 2q, 7q and 16p. *Am. J. Hum. Genet.* **69** (suppl. 3), 570–581.

Kanner, L. (1943): Autistic disturbances of affective contact. *Nervous Child* **2**, 217–250.

Lamb, J.A., Barnby, G., Bonora, E., Sykes, N., Bacchelli, E., Blasi, F., Maestrini, E., Broxholme, J., Tzenova, J., Weeks, D., Bailey, A.J., Monaco, A.P. & The International Molecular Genetic Study of Autism Consortium (IMGSAC) (2005): Analysis of IMGSAC autism susceptibility loci: evidence for sex limited and parent of origin specific effects. *J. Med. Genet.* **42**, 132–137.

Persico, A.M., Militerni, R., Bravaccio, C., Schneider, C., Melmed, R., Trillo, S., Montecchi, F., Palermo, M., Pascucci, T., Pugliesi-Allegra, S., Reichelt K.-L., Conciatori, M., Baldi, A. & Keller, F. (2000): Adenosine deaminase alleles and autistic disorder: case-control and family-based association studies. *Am. J. Med. Genet.* **96**, 784–790.

Philippe, A., Martinez, M., Guilloud-Bataille, M., Gillberg, C., Rastam, M., Sponheim, E., Coleman, M., Zappella, M., Aschauer, H., Van Maldergem, L., Penet, C., Feingold, J., Brice, A., Leboyer, M. & van Malldergerme, L. (1999): Genome-wide scan for autism susceptibility genes. Paris Autism Research International Sibpair Study. *Hum. Mol. Genet.* **8**, 805–12.

Risch, N., Spiker, D., Lotspeich, L., Nouri, N., Hinds, D. *et al.* (1999): A genomic screen of autism: evidence for a multilocus aetiology. *Am. J. Hum. Genet.* **65**, 493–507.

Shao, Y., Wolpert, C.M., Raiford, K.L., Menold, M.M., Donnelly, S.L., Ravan, S.A. *et al.* (2002): Genomic screen and follow-up analysis for autistic disorder. *Am. J. Med. Genet.* **114**, 99–105.

Smalley, S.L., Asarnow, R.F. & Spence, M.A. (1988): Autism and genetics. A decade of research. *Arch. Gen. Psychiatry* **45**, 953–961.

Smalley, S.L., Kustanovich, V., Minassian, S.L., Stone, J.L., Ogdie, M.N., McGough, J.J., McCracken, J.T., MacPhie, I.L., Francks, C., Fisher, S.E., Cantor, R.M., Monaco, A.P. & Nelson, S.F. (2002): Genetic linkage of attention-deficit/hyperactivity disorder on chromosome 16p13, in a region implicated in autism. *Am. J. Hum. Genet.* **71**, 959–963.

Steffenburg, S., Gillberg, C., Hellgren, L., Andersson, L., Gillberg, I.C., Jakobsson, G. & Bohman, M. (1989): A twin study of autism in Denmark, Finland, Iceland, Norway and Sweden. *J. Child Psychol. Psychiatry* **30**, 405–416.

Tordjman, S., Anderson, G.M., McBride, P.A., Hertzig, M.E., Snow, M.E., Hall, L.M., Ferrari, P. & Cohen, D.J. (1995): Plasma androgens in autism. *J. Autism Dev. Disord.* **25**, 295–304.

Yoman, A.L., Alarcon, M., Cheng, R., Magnusson, P.K. *et al.* (2003): A genomewide screen of 345 families for autism-susceptibility loci. *Am. J. Hum. Genet.* **73**, 886–897.

Autistic spectrum disorders, D. Riva and I. Rapin (eds.)

Chapter 3

Autism and dysmorphic-genetic syndromes with mental retardation: clinical aspects

Chiara Pantaleoni, Stefano D'Arrigo and Michela Marzaroli

Developmental Neurology Division, National Neurologic Institute 'C. Besta', via Celoria 11, 20133 Milan, Italy
pantaleoni@istituto-besta.it

Summary

'Disorders of the autistic spectrum' is the term commonly used to describe the vast group of syndromes symptomatically associated with autism. We speak of 'dual syndromes' when patients with autism also have a second syndrome, that is a pathology originally described in non-autistic subjects. In addition to the large number of adult psychiatric disorders and the group of neurocutaneous syndromes, dysmorphic-genetic syndromes represent the most common example of dual syndrome. We selected several patients referred to the Developmental Neurology Division of the Istituto Neurologico 'C. Besta' with dysmorphic-genetic syndrome and mental retardation who were identified as having an autistic disorder and we analysed the clinical characteristics of these syndromes, carrying out a detailed analysis on the behavioural phenotypes involved.
Our clinical experience leads us to believe that patients with dual syndrome often have a form of atypical autism, in that they lack one of the three diagnostic criteria according to the DSM-IV. We believe there is a far from negligible association between pervasive developmental disorder and genetic syndromes. As a consequence, the child neuropsychiatrist must not fail to assess autistic patients from a 'dysmorphological' standpoint, with a view to identify any suspect elements that might suggest a concomitant genetic syndrome.

Introduction

'Disorders of the autistic spectrum' is the term commonly used to describe the vast group of syndromes symptomatically associated with autism (Filipek *et al.*, 1999). In fact, a far from negligible percentage of autistic subjects have a concomitant medical condition, though there is no consensus between the various more recent studies, which have estimated that this applies to anywhere between 7 and 37 per cent of cases (Gillberg & Coleman, 1996). We speak of 'dual syndromes' when patients with autism also have a second syndrome – that is, a pathology originally described in non-autistic subjects which, in the majority of cases reported, does not include an autistic type of behaviour (Barton & Volkmar, 1998). As we can see from the literature, however, almost all dysmorphic-genetic syndromes present an autistic behavioural phenotype in isolated cases at least (Wassink *et al.*, 2001).

In addition to the large number of adult psychiatric disorders in which the onset may be delayed in autistic subjects (schizophrenia, bipolar disorder, depression) and the group of neurocutaneous syndromes (including tuberous sclerosis, neurofibromatosis, Ito's hypomelanosis), dysmorphic-genetic syndromes represent the most common example of dual syndrome (Gillberg, 1998).

In the strictly neurological context, it is worth emphasizing that children suffering from specific malformations of the central nervous system (posterior fossa, temporomesial structures) may often have autistic disorders, and the same can be said of children suffering from prenatal or perinatal damage. In addition, autistic behaviour may be seen, though rarely, in patients suffering from metabolic-degenerative conditions, in which case other neurological signs and symptoms may also be involved, which will facilitate the diagnostic process.

Methods

Among the patients referred to the Developmental Neurology Division of the Istituto Neurologico 'C. Besta', we selected several with dysmorphic-genetic syndrome and mental retardation who were identified as having an autistic disorder. We then analysed the clinical characteristics of these syndromes, carrying out a detailed analysis on the behavioural phenotypes involved.

Results

Fragile X syndrome

Fragile X syndrome is caused by a mutation on chromosome X (X q27.3) in the FMR1 gene (fragile X mental retardation 1). This mutation is associated with CGG triplet expansion, which leads to an FMR1 protein production deficiency (Oostra & Willemsen, 2002). The FMR1 gene is the only gene currently known to be associated with fragile X syndrome. Genetic tests for gene mutations generally identify the number of triplet repetitions and this number is conventionally used to classify the FMR1 alleles as follows:

(a) *normal alleles*: the range of triplets falls between 5 and 44; these alleles are transmitted with no changes in the number of triplets;
(b) *intermediate alleles*: the range of triplets falls between 45 and 58; these alleles are transmitted with a potential, but usually occasional, slight variation in the number of triplets;
(c) *alleles with pre-mutation*: the range of triplets falls between 59 and 200: females in this group are considered at risk of affected offspring, due to a potential for expansion in the number of triplets;
(d) *alleles with full mutation*: the number of triplets exceeds 200 (Song *et al.*, 2003).

There is a clear genotypic-phenotypic correlation in fragile X syndrome. In male patients (hemizygotes) with complete mutation, the prepubertal clinical picture is characterized by psychomotor retardation, mainly in the language areas, and craniofacial dysmorphisms, including elongated face, prominent forehead, large ears, and prominent jaw. The mental retardation is moderate (IQ 30 to 50) and often associated with behavioural disorders – for example, hypersensitivity to sensorial stimuli, hyperactivity, stereotypia (hand flapping, hand biting), shifting gaze, and social anxiety. Some patients have some or all of the symptoms of autism: in a series of 27 children with a diagnosis of fragile X syndrome, Rogers *et al.* (2001) found the criteria for a diagnosis of autism in eight per cent of cases. In various studies, the incidence of fragile X syndrome in autistic patients is reportedly between 2.5 and 6.0 per cent. Although several symptom features are very similar to the symptoms of autism, an important behavioural difference is detectable in these children – that is, the ability of patients with fragile X syndrome to recognize the emotional expressions of the human face (an ability severely lacking in autistic patients), which has proved to be much the same as in the general population; hence the tendency of children with fragile X syndrome to preserve adequate preferential relations with their caregivers.

In the postpubertal period, evident phenotypic traits include macrocrania, strabismus, macroorchidism, and articular hyperextensibility. The cognitive deficit persists and the behavioural signs observable include an exacerbated hyperactivity, social anxiety, obsessive-compulsive disorder, and in the more severe cases psychotic symptoms (Hatton *et al.*, 2002).

The heterozygous females with complete mutation show similar physical and behavioural features, but of milder degree (Hessl *et al.*, 2001). Patients with premutation generally have a normal appearance and intellectual faculties. Some have mild intellectual or behavioural disorders (learning difficulties, social anxiety).

Female carriers of premutation may have early menopause, while an ataxic syndrome has been detected in males with late-onset tremor.

Angelman syndrome

Angelman syndrome is associated with a DNA anomaly at the site q11.2–13 on chromosome 15. This may be a microdeletion or a paternal uniparental disomy (that is, both the alleles at this specific location on chromosome 15 are inherited from the father). It may also be caused by a defect of the imprinting centre or of the gene UBE3A (Nurmi *et al.*, 2001). In 20 per cent of cases, no genetic anomaly is demonstrated and the diagnosis is clinical. The prevalence of this disorder is estimated to be 1/12,000. From the clinical standpoint, patients have severe psychomotor retardation, ataxic syndrome, and language disorders (mainly affecting the expressive sphere). They also always have a frank behavioural disorder: these children are defined as 'happy puppets', because of their typical apparently cheerful behaviour, excitability, hyperactivity, and short attention span, associated with stereotypical movements such as 'hand fluttering'. More than 80 per cent of patients also have acquired microcephaly, epilepsy, and a typical electroencephalographic pattern (with slow high voltage frontal and occipital anomalies in the waking state with eyes open).

Less common signs (in 20 to 80 per cent of cases) include a flat occiput, strabismus, macrostomia with gaps between the teeth, prominent jaw, and hypopigmentation of the skin and eyes.

From the behavioural standpoint, patients may be hypersensitive to heat and attracted to water, or they may have a sleeping disorder characterized by little need for sleep and disrupted sleeping/waking rhythms. It is well known that some behavioural aspects of this syndrome perfectly satisfy two of the three essential diagnostic criteria for autistic disorder according to the DSM-IV classification – that is, stereotyped behaviour and impaired communication (Steffenburg *et al.*, 1996), whereas reciprocal social interaction appears to be relatively well preserved in these children, who seek relations with others. In their report on the differential diagnosis of this syndrome, Williams *et al.* (2001) claimed that patients with a clinical diagnosis of Angelman syndrome but proving negative in laboratory tests designed to identify the four currently known types of genetic anomaly should be considered as suffering from Pervasive Developmental Disorder-Not Otherwise Specified (PDD-NOS) according to the DSM-IV criteria. In fact they noted, after evaluating these patients longitudinally, that the phenotypic characteristics of the syndrome became milder over the years, while the behavioural disorder became more evident.

Smith-Magenis syndrome

Smith-Magenis syndrome is caused by an interstitial deletion of the short arm of chromosome 17 (17p11.2). The prevalence of this disease is estimated to be 1/25,000. The somatic phenotype of the syndrome varies in relation to the patient's age: in early infancy (0–3 years), the facial dysmorphic traits are very mild and the face has a characteristic 'cherub-like' appearance, with prominent, fleshy cheeks, upslanting palpebral fissures, a flat bridged nose, and micrognathia. The shape of the mouth is also typical, with the upper lip shaped like a Cupid's bow and a pronounced philtrum. During childhood (3–10 years), the facial appearance becomes more coarse and 'Down-like', owing to hypotonia of the facial musculature, brachycephaly, a flattened face, and a short flared nose. Over 10 years of age, the facial features are even more characteristic owing to facial hypoplasia, with a wide jaw and prognathism (Greenberg *et al.*, 1996). The cognitive phenotype is characterized by a highly variable degree of mental retardation: some cases have been described with borderline IQs and others with severely deficient IQs. Expressive language disturbance is a prevalent sign. The behavioural phenotype is strongly characteristic, with maladjusted behaviour (such as self-destructiveness, impulsiveness, fits of rage, and onychotillomania) associated with stereotyped behaviour (typically self-hugging, but also shaking of the trunk and repeated non-finalized object displacement, for example 'object spinning'). Both Udwin *et al.* (2001), in a study on approximately 50 patients, and Willekens *et al.* (2000), in a study on a series of just three patients, independently found highly demanding and dependent behavioural traits in relation to both family members and strangers: this correlation typically distinguishes the syndrome from classic autism.

Inversion-duplication of chromosome 15 syndrome

This syndrome, which is caused by the inversion-duplication of chromosome 15 (inv-dup 15), is a genetic condition diagnosed in the majority of cases with the standard karyotype, characterized by psychomotor retardation varying from mild to severe, hypotonia, ataxic syndrome, and dyspraxia. Many patients have epilepsy, with myoclonal or atonic generalized or focal seizures; these patients are also somewhat resistant to pharmacological antiepileptic treatment. Not all patients have seizures, but even in those without seizures the EEG typically shows generalized fast rhythms and focal bilateral paroxysms (Buoni *et al.*, 2000). Patients have some, albeit mild, dysmorphic features – for example, a flat bridged nose with flared nostrils, downslanting palpebral fissures, micrognathia, low set ears, and a flat occiput. Their behavioural phenotype is characteristically of the autistic type. In a recent study (Borgatti *et al.*, 2001), six patients with inv-dup 15 syndrome were examined: two met the diagnostic criteria for a typical autistic disorder, while a diagnosis of PDD-NOS was established in the other four cases, according to DSM-IV criteria, as these patients had severe social interaction and communication difficulties but no repetitive or stereotyped behaviour traits had been observed or reported.

Other syndromes

We now describe certain behavioural characteristics peculiar to several syndromes that can occur in clinical practice in association with autism – that is, Rett syndrome (which DSM-IV places in the group of pervasive developmental disorders) and the Sotos, Cohen, and Noonan syndromes, which in our clinical experience we have observed as dual syndromes. For these syndromes, details are only provided on certain aspects that seem significant for our present purpose, while the reader can refer to the specific literature for a more exhaustive description of the conditions.

Rett syndrome

Rett syndrome is a genetic condition in which different mutations of the gene MECP2 on chromosome X have been identified. This syndrome usually, but not always, affects the female sex and in its classic form it has a typically autistic behavioural phenotype (Mount *et al.*, 2003). What is noteworthy in these patients from the phenotypic standpoint is their gentle, dreamy expression. They have a significantly characteristic laugh that follows a circadian rhythm (occurring mainly in the evenings) and is clearly distinct from the laugh of patients with Angelman syndrome, which is virtually constant throughout the day.

Sotos syndrome

Sotos syndrome is characterized by rapid somatic growth, particularly evident in the first 5 years of life. These children have macrodolichocephalism, prominent forehead, high hairline, downslanting eyes, and prognathism. Their bone age is typically, though not necessarily, older than their chronological age. Patients may be cognitively adequate or have an intellectual deficit varying from mild to severe. From the behavioural standpoint, they may have phobias, sleep disorders, hyperphagia, and aggressiveness. Morrow *et al.* (1990) described a case of autistic disorder in association with Sotos syndrome. In approximately 50 per cent of patients, a genetic anomaly (point deletion or mutation) is detected on the long arm of chromosome 5 (5q35).

Cohen syndrome

Howlin (2001) established a diagnosis of autism in 19 of 33 patients with Cohen syndrome, a condition characterized by low birth weight, microcephaly, and psychomotor retardation of variable degree, from mild to severe. Patients have jaw hypoplasia, large ears, prominent upper incisors, slender fingers, trunk obesity, and scoliosis. They may also have neutropenia and a chorioretinal dystrophy or optic atrophy.

Noonan syndrome

Another relatively frequent syndrome is called Noonan syndrome, which is known to have a prevalence of 1/2000 and is characterized by short stature, pterygium colli, low hairline, epicanthus, low set and misshapen ears, and micrognathia, associated in 50 to 80 per cent of cases with congenital cardiopathy and frequently with pulmonary stenosis. Patients are often cognitively adequate, or they may present a mild to moderate deficit. They have behavioural disorders, such as sleeping disturbance, aggressiveness, and anxiety, and an association with autism has been reported (Ghaziuddin *et al.*, 1994).

Comment

For some time now, the problem of dual syndromes has been the subject of discussion among numerous investigators concerned with autism and dysmorphic-genetic syndromes. In a recent report, Gillberg & Coleman (1996) examined the seven published studies on the topic of medical conditions associated with autism (Wing & Gould, 1979; Gillberg, 1984; Burd *et al.*, 1987;

Bryson *et al.*, 1988; Cialdella & Mamelle, 1989; Ritvo *et al.*, 1990; Steffenburg, 1991). They found this association in the autistic population in a mean 24 per cent of cases (range 11 to 37 per cent). The difference depended, according to Gillberg, on the accuracy of the diagnostic work-up performed. From Gillberg's study, we extrapolated the average proportion of associated dysmorphic-genetic symptoms, which amounted to 13.6 per cent. Among these studies, we also analysed the ones that differentiated between pervasive developmental disorder (PDD) of autistic type and PDD-NOS (Wing & Gould, 1979; Gillberg, 1984; Burd *et al.*, 1987; Steffenburg, 1991): the cases of medical conditions associated with PDD of autistic type amounted to 28 per cent (dysmorphic-genetic syndromes accounted for 15.7 per cent), as opposed to 30 per cent (12.5 per cent dysmorphic-genetic syndromes) for PDD-NOS. As emphasized by the investigators in these studies, there are therefore apparently no significant differences between the two groups; the only study that detected a higher frequency of association for PDD-NOS (53 per cent *versus* 29 per cent for PDD of autistic type) was by Burd *et al.* (1987) of North Dakota. Our experience, albeit with the drawbacks of a limited case series, seems to be more consistent with Burd's findings.

Our clinical experience leads us to believe that patients with dual syndrome often have a form of atypical autism, in that they lack one of the three diagnostic criteria according to the DSM-IV. No significant differences emerged in Gillberg's study (1996) for the gender variable, but as regards intellectual level, associated medical conditions were more common in patients with moderate to severe mental retardation than in the mildly retarded cases.

In agreement with published data, we believe there is a far from negligible association between PDD and genetic syndromes. As a consequence, the child neuropsychiatrist (the first specialist called upon to deal with behavioural problems) must not fail to assess autistic patients from a 'dysmorphological' standpoint, with a view to identify any suspect elements that might suggest a concomitant genetic syndrome.

In assessing the child, it is thus always essential to consider the auxological variables, not only seeking any major malformations but also taking care to avoid overlooking apparently 'minor' features. Along with the fundamental tests (EEG, MRI), we should also include a standard karyotype for 'preliminary screening', following up with molecular investigations for fragile X syndrome in males and relying on the contribution of clinical genetics, where necessary, for any 'Gastaltic' diagnosis or specific tests.

We are also convinced that the clinical geneticist needs to consider a potential associated behavioural disorder in patients with dysmorphic syndrome: this has to be clearly described and clinically defined, and that is why we believe it is indispensable to have a neuropsychiatric assessment, in addition to providing indications on therapeutic-rehabilitative measures. Moreover, we should not disregard the possibility of the neuropsychiatrist being involved in the diagnostic approach work-up as well: behavioural disorders, and autism in particular, may not only be associated with other syndromes; they may even be the symptom of a more complex neurological disease, of metabolic-degenerative type, for instance.

Conclusion

In conclusion, we wish to emphasize that, although they represent only a small proportion of all cases of autism, dual syndromes could contribute important information to studies on the genetic causes of this disorder (Andres, 2002; Volkmar & Pauls, 2003). We must bear in mind that two of the genetic regions identified in linkage studies on autistic patients' families have been found situated near the site of a gene responsible for tuberous sclerosis on chromosome 16, and of the gene responsible for neurofibromatosis on chromosome 17 (International Molecular Genetic Study of Autism Consortium, 2001).

References

Andres, C. (2002): Molecular genetics and animal models in autistic disorders. *Brain Res. Bull.* **57**, 109–119.

Barton, M. & Volkmar, F. (1998): How commonly are known medical conditions associated with autism? *J. Autism Dev. Disord.* **28**, 273–278.

Borgatti, R., Piccinelli, P., Passoni, D., Dalprà, L., Mozzo, M., Micheli, R., Gagliardi, C. & Balottin, U. (2001): Relationship between clinical and genetic features in 'inverted-duplicated chromosome 15' patients. *Pediatr. Neurol.* **24**, 111–116.

Bryson, S.E., Clark, B.S. & Smith, I.M. (1988): First report of a Canadian epidemiological study of autistic syndromes. *J. Child Psychol. Psychiatry* **29**, 433–445.

Buoni, S., Sorrentino, L., Farnetani, M.A., Pucci, L. & Fois, A. (2000): The syndrome of Inv Dup (15): clinical, electroencephalographic, and imaging findings. *J. Child Neurol.* **15**, 380–385.

Burd, L., Fisher, W. & Kerbeshian, J. (1987): A prevalence study of pervasive developmental disorders in North Dakota. *J. Am. Acad. Child Adolesc. Psychiatry* **26**, 704–710.

Cialdella, P. & Mamelle, N. (1989): An epidemiological study of infantile autism in a French department (Rhone): a research note. *J. Child Psychol. Psychiatry* **30**, 165–175.

Filipek, P.A., Accardo, P.J., Baranek, G.T., Cook, E.H., Dawson, G., Gordon, B., Gravel, J.S., Johnson, C.P., Kallen, R.J., Levy, S.E., Minshew, N.J., Prizant, B.M., Rapin, I., Rogers, S.J., Stone, W., Teplin, S., Tuchman, R. & Volkmar, F.R. (1999): The screening and diagnosis of autistic spectrum disorders. *J. Autism Dev. Disord.* **29**, 439–484.

Ghaziuddin, M., Bolyard, B. & Alessi, N. (1994): Autistic disorder in Noonan syndrome. *J. Intellect. Disabil. Res.* **38**, 67–72.

Gillberg, C. (1984): Infantile autism and other childhood psychoses in a Swedish urban region. Epidemiological aspects. *J. Child Psychol. Psychiatry* **25**, 35–43.

Gillberg, C. & Coleman, M. (1996): Autism and medical disorders: a review of the literature. *Dev. Med. Child Neurol.* **38**, 191–202.

Gillberg, C. (1998): Chromosomal disorders and autism. *J. Autism Dev. Disord.* **28**, 415–425.

Greenberg, F., Lewis, R.A., Potocki, L., Glaze, D., Parke, J., Killian, J., Murpha, M.A., Williamson, D., Brown, F., Dutton, R., McCluggage, C., Friedman, E., Sulek, M. & Lupski, J.R. (1996): Multi-disciplinary clinical study of Smith-Magenis syndrome (deletion 17p11.2): *Am. J. Med. Genet.* **62**, 247–254.

Hatton, H.H., Hooper, S.R., Bailey, D.B., Skinner, M.L., Sullivan, K.M. & Wheeler, A. (2002): Problem behaviour in boys with fragile X syndrome. *Am. J. Med. Genet.* **108**, 105–116.

Hessl, D., Dyer-Fiedman, J., Glaser, B., Wisbeck, J., Barajas, R.G., Taylor, A. & Reiss, A.L. (2001): The influence of environmental and genetic factors on behaviour problems and autistic symptoms in boys and girls with fragile X syndrome. *Pediatrics* **108**, E88.

Howlin, P. (2001): Autistic features in Cohen syndrome: a preliminary report. *Dev. Med. Child Neurol.* **43**, 692–696.

International Molecular Genetic Study of Autism Consortium. (2001): A genome-wide screen for autism: strong evidence for linkage to chromosome 2q, 7q, and 16p. *Am. J. Hum. Genet.* **69**, 570–581.

Morrow, J.D., Whitman, B.Y. & Accardo, P.J. (1990): Autistic disorder in Sotos syndrome: a case report. *Eur. J. Pediatr.* **149**, 567–569.

Mount, R.H., Charman, T., Hastings, R.P., Reilly, S. & Cass, H. (2003): Features of autism in Rett syndrome and severe mental retardation. *J. Autism Dev. Disord.* **33**, 435–442.

Nurmi, E.L., Bradford, Y., Chen, Y., Hall, J., Arnone, B., Gardiner, M.B., Hutcheson, H.B., Gilbert, J.R., Pericak-Vance, M.A., Copeland-Yates, S.A., Michaelis, R.C., Wassink, T.H., Santangelo, S.L., Sheffield, V.C., Piven, J., Folstein S.E., Haines, J.L. & Sutcliffe, J.S. (2001): Linkage disequilibrium at the Angelman syndrome gene UBE3A in autism families. *Genomics* **77**, 105–113.

Oostra, B.A. & Willemsen, R. (2002): The X chromosome and fragile X mental retardation. *Cytogenet. Genome Res.* **99**, 257–264.

Ritvo, E.R., Mason-Brothers, A., Freeman, B.J., Pingrre, C., Jenson, W.R., McMahon, W.M., Petersen, P.B., Jorde, L.B., Mo, A. & Ritvo, A. (1990): The UCLA-University of Utah epidemiologic survey of autism: the etiologic role of rare diseases. *Am. J. Psychiatry* **147**, 1614–1621.

Rogers, S.J., Wehner, D.E. & Hagerman, R. (2001): The behavioral phenotype in fragile X: symptoms of autism in very young children with fragile X syndrome, idiopathic autism, and other developmental disorders. *J. Dev. Behav. Pediatr.* **22**, 409–417.

Song, F.J., Barton, P., Sleightholme, V., Yao, G.L. & Fry-Smith, A. (2003): Screening for fragile X syndrome: a literature review and modelling study. *Health Technol. Assess.* **7**, 1–106.

Steffenburg, S. (1991): Neuropsychiatric assessment of children with autism: a population-based study. *Dev. Med. Child Neurol.* **33**, 495–511.

Steffenburg, S., Gillberg, C.L., Steffenburg, U. & Kyllerman, M. (1996): Autism in Angelman syndrome: a population-based study. *Pediatr. Neurol.* **14**, 131–136.

Udwin, O., Webber, C. & Horn, I. (2001): Abilities and attainment in Smith-Magenis syndrome. *Dev. Med. Child Neurol.* **43**, 823–828.

Volkmar, F.R. & Pauls, D. (2003): Autism. *Lancet* **362**, 1133–1141.

Wassink, T.H., Piven, J. & Patil, S.R. (2001): Chromosomal abnormalities in a clinic sample of individuals with autistic disorder. *Psychiatr. Genet.* **11**, 57–63.

Willekens, D., De Cock, P. & Fryns, J.P. (2000): Three young children with Smith-Magenis syndrome: their distinct, recognisable behavioural phenotype as the most important clinical symptom. *Genet. Couns.* **11**, 103–110.

Williams, C.A., Lossie, A. & Driscoll, D. (2001): Angelman syndrome: mimicking conditions and phenotypes. *Am. J. Med. Genet.* **101**, 59–64.

Wing, L. & Gould, J. (1979): Severe impairments of social interaction and associated abnormalities in children: epidemiology and classification. *J. Autism Dev. Disord.* **9**, 11–29.

Autistic spectrum disorders, D. Riva and I. Rapin (eds.)

Chapter 4

Autistic phase in Rett syndrome

SakkuBai Naidu and Genila Bibat

The Kennedy Krieger Institute, Department of Neurogenetics, The Johns Hopkins University, Departments of Neurology and Pediatrics, 707 North Broadway, Baltimore, MD 21205, USA
naidu@kennedykrieger.org

Summary

The clinical variability of Rett syndrome, associated with mutations in the MeCP2 gene, ranges from classical to asymptomatic females, and in males there may be none of the diagnostic features considered pathognomonic in females. Multiple factors contribute to this variability. Compared with mutations towards the carboxyl-terminus, mutations closer to the amino-terminus, before amino acid 255, lead to severe clinical manifestations such as inability to walk, severe dysphagia, and urinary organic acid abnormalities. However, there appears to be no correlation between severity and mutation type missense *vs* nonsense. Despite the importance of mutation location for clinical severity, the widely varying severity within the same mutation suggests that in females X inactivation also plays a role in determining the phenotype.

We propose that stages 1 and 2 of the disease reflect failure of time-linked expression of MeCP2 in cerebellar neurons, as noted in Purkinje and granule cells of wild-type mouse and rat. This, in association with the recent observation that MeCP2 protein plays a definite role in repressing the BDNF gene, has opened new areas of investigation and understanding of the transient age-specific autistic-like behaviour, and motor and cognitive dysfunction seen in stages 1 and 2 of this disease.

Introduction

The neurological manifestations of Rett syndrome consist of microcephaly, seizures, severe mental retardation, respiratory irregularities, and stereotyped behaviours. The four clinical stages of Rett syndrome are now well known (Rett, 1966; Hagberg *et al.*, 1983; Naidu, 1997). Mutations in the MeCP2 gene located at chromosome Xq28 region (Sirianni *et al.*, 1998; Xiang *et al.*, 1998; Amir *et al.*, 1999) are seen in over 80 per cent of patients with these clinical signs. It is known that Rett syndrome differs from other neurodegenerative disorders in not having a progressive downhill course leading to death; but instead a short period of regression in infancy and early childhood referred to as stages 1 and 2. This regression is characterized by developmental arrest, lack of gain in language skills, and transient autistic-like behaviours consisting of poor eye contact, reduced sleep, and irritability. Subsequently, there is recovery of social interaction, with amelioration of these symptoms and stabilization of the clinical progression leading to stages 3 and 4.

Neither the biological basis for the early stages of the disease nor the entire function of MeCP2 is completely understood as yet, apart from its role as a transcription repressor (Meehan *et al.*, 1992; Nan *et al.*, 1997; Nan *et al.*, 1998; Bird & Wolffe, 1999). More recently, a new isoform of MeCP2 was identified called MeCP2B, which has higher expression in brain than the previously described form now called MeCP2A. (Mnatzakanian *et al.*, 2004). Mutations in MeCP2B appear to be causative of the neurological manifestations of Rett syndrome. The clinical stages and variability in Rett syndrome are the outcome of diverse factors, most importantly the spatial temporal expression of MeCP2 in brain (Shahbazian *et al.*, 2002), the type of MeCP2 mutation, X inactivation status (Hoffbuhr *et al.*, 2002), and the genetic background of the individual. Environmental influences on normal and abnormal MeCP2 function are unknown. Skewed X inactivation (XCI) has been shown to occur in many asymptomatic to atypical cases of patients with known mutations in the MeCP2 gene (De Bona *et al.*, 2000; Hoffbuhr *et al.*, 2001; Bienvenu *et al.*, 2002; Zappella *et al.*, 2003).

There is increasing expression of MeCP2 in neurons as they become more differentiated, suggesting that it plays a role in launching or maintaining neuronal maturation (Akbarian *et al.*, 2001; Shahbazian *et al.*, 2002; Jung *et al.*, 2003). This notion is also well supported by *in vivo* analysis of the olfactory system showing that MeCP2 is expressed in postmitotic neurons when synaptic connections are about to be made (Cohen *et al.*, 2003; Matarazzo *et al.*, 2004). The observation in a simple neurological system such as the olfactory system demonstrates that MeCP2 deficiency serves a critical function in neuronal cell biology mediating the final stages of neuronal development, which then delays the terminal differentiation of olfactory neurons.

It is unclear as to how many genes are subject to MeCP2 repression. The recognition of MeCP2 as a repressor of brain-derived neurotrophic factors (BDNF) has provided considerable insight and explanation of findings such as increases in CSF and brain glutamate levels (Pan *et al.*, 1999; Riikonen, 2003), and NMDA and AMPA receptors by Blue *et al.* (1999a). It is known that BDNF modulates long-term potentiation (LTP) by binding to TrkB receptors on postsynaptic neurons, which in turn open sodium and calcium channels of the glutamate NMDA and AMPA receptors accounting for the increased receptor levels reported by Blue *et al.*, (Manabe, 2002). The recent discovery of a loss of imprinting in Rett syndrome lymphoblasts of maternally expressed Dlx5 gene that regulates production of enzymes synthesizing γ-amino butyric acid (GABA), provides a plausible explanation for both the autistic phases and the seizures resulting from altered GABAergic neurons (Horike *et al.*, 2005). GABA receptor subunit genes have been implicated in autistic disorder (DeLorey *et al.*, 1998; Martin *et al.*, 2000; Menold *et al.*, 2001; Buxbaum *et al.*, 2002).

Explaining the autistic phase of Rett syndrome

The significant change in behaviour, designated as stage 2 in the natural history of the disease, occurs in the previously apathetic, developmentally marginal, hypotonic infant (stage 1), swiftly bringing medical attention between the ages of 10 months and 2 years (Hagberg & Witt-Engerström, 1986; Trevathan & Naidu, 1988). Although many studies have pointed to striking developmental irregularities in early infancy, most importantly the deceleration of head growth beginning from 2 to 4 months of life, many of the subtle signs of developmental lag or abnormal posturing are underplayed or unrecognized until stage 2 (Naidu *et al.*, 1986; Nomura & Segawa, 1990; Kerr, 1995; Leonard & Bower, 1998). The child with Rett syndrome is symptomatic at birth, but as there are no overt signs such as seizures or irritability, little concern arises. Because stage 2 of the disease brings about noticeable behavioural and clinical changes – including the onset of seizures, autistic-like features, failed language development, tremulousness, sleep disturbance, and irritability – this leads to consideration of autism or a neurodegenerative process, resulting in many biochemical and neuroimaging tests.

Bauman & Kemper (1991) demonstrated diffuse alterations in neuronal morphology, suggesting that the changes caused by MeCP2 abnormalities are not cell autonomous. Changes in neuronal size and shortened dendritic length in Rett syndrome (Armstrong, 2002) have also been demonstrated in autistic brains by Raymond *et al.*, 1996. A simplified inferior olivary nucleus in the postmortem brain stem of Rett syndrome females is noted (Bauman *et al.*, 1995), indicating prenatal onset of modified and disrupted neuronal architecture. The inferior olive is intimately connected to deep cerebellar nuclei and Purkinje cells, which in turn directly or indirectly influence medullary, pontine, midbrain, and cortical activity. These prenatal deficits in the brain stem and the deeper layers of the cortex (Shahbazian *et al.*, 2002) presumably contribute to the behavioural changes seen in stage 1.

That the head circumference is normal at birth is of interest. However, because of the demand for postnatal dendritic arborization and activity dependent synaptic proliferation and pruning, early deceleration of head growth ensues owing to an inability of MeCP2 deficient neurons to differentiate and mature. This is in contrast to autism, where most cases have enlarged head circumference (Deutsch & Joseph, 2003).

The expression of MeCP2 in rodent cerebellar Purkinje cells by the first postnatal week, and in granule cells by the fourth postnatal week, reported by Johnston *et al.* (2003), occurs during a critical period when synaptic connections are being established among cerebellar neurons, from cerebellar neurons to brain stem structures, and ultimately to cerebral cortical regions. The timing of postnatal MeCP2 expression in Purkinje and cerebellar granule cells suggests a link between this process and the increasing neuromotor and behavioural changes that manifest in stages 1 and 2 of Rett syndrome. The cerebellum is known to play a critical role in language, motor, and cognitive development (Raymand *et al.*, 1996; Middleton & Strick, 2001; Gebhart *et al.*, 2002), and has been shown to be one of the important sites of pathology in autism (Townsend *et al.*, 1999; Pierce & Courchesne, 2001; Townsend *et al.*, 2001; Allen & Courchesne, 2003). Autistic subjects demonstrate visual spatial attention deficits, multisensory modulation defects, arrested language development, and stereotyped behaviours much like Rett syndrome subjects, particularly in stage 2 (Kern, 2002). Therefore, the postnatal apathy, hypotonia, and autistic phase of stages 1 and 2 might reflect an age-sensitive epoch of MeCP2 malfunction in cerebellar Purkinje and granule cells, within the complex cerebellar circuitry, that would normally influence cortical and brain stem motor and cognitive activities during this period (Pinto *et al.*, 2003). This failure of MeCP2 expression in granule and Purkinje cells, added to the cortical neuronal abnormalities in Rett syndrome, would reflect the change from stage 1 to the precipitous shift in the clinical manifestations of stage 2 (Dum & Strick, 2003). The aberrant overexpression of glutamate/NMDA (N-methyl-D-aspartate) receptors also noted in the frontal cortex in this younger age group (Blue *et al.*, 1999b) would augment the encephalopathic clinical state in stage 2. The excitotoxicity caused by an upsurge of NMDA receptors in the developing brain (McDonald & Johnston, 1990) would indeed be a trigger for abnormal electroencephalograms and ictal activity in stage 2, which subsides with age when the NMDA receptors are reduced in number (Blue *et al.*, 1999b). Such neuronal hyperexcitability affecting cerebellar granule, mossy fibre, and Purkinje cell synapses (Ward *et al.*, 2000) could account for the tremulousness and gait disturbance that become obvious in stage 2.

Discussion

The Rett syndrome phenotype has a course marked by a bewildering clinical deterioration in infancy, termed stage 2, that resembles autism. The underpinnings of this phase of the disease have been poorly understood, as it differs from other degenerative processes of the nervous system, a schematic representation of which is shown in *Fig. 1*. Interestingly, Bauman *et al.* (1995) reported that the inferior olivary nucleus in the postmortem brain stem of Rett syndrome girls was simplified, suggestive of early changes in a brain stem structure that has important links between the cerebellum and cortical thalamic pathways. The morphological changes suggested abnormalities occurring before 32 weeks' gestation, because the normal undulations of the inferior olivary nucleus develop between 28 and 32 weeks (Friede, 1989). Similar involvement of cortical neurons could account for stage 1 of early infancy in Rett syndrome.

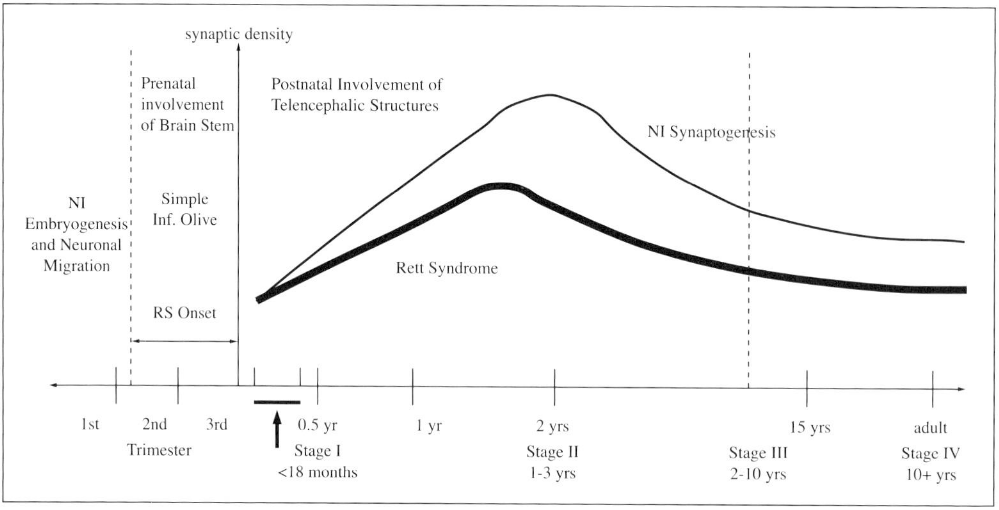

Fig. 1. Rett syndrome vs *normal: schematic representation of aberrant brain development and clinical correlation.*

The collective clinical and pathological changes observed in stage 2 – namely, the pathognomonic clinical features, autoradiographic evidence of transient increased glutamate/NMDA receptors in postmortem brain of young Rett syndrome patients, functional mitochondrial abnormalities (Naidu *et al.*, 2003), and period of postnatal MeCP2 expression in wild-type murine cerebellar granule cells (Johnston *et al.*, 2003) – suggest a time-sensitive impact of MeCP2 dysfunction on cortical and cerebellar neurons, resulting in stage-specific postnatal clinical signs and symptoms resembling autism. An NMDA receptor dependent activation of cAMP responsive element binding protein (CREB) is an important transcription factor for cell differentiation, required for survival of cerebellar granule cells (Monti *et al.*, 2002; Petralia *et al.*, 2002). An overexpression of NMDA/glutamate receptors (Blue *et al.*, 1999b) may also be an attempt to increase neuronal viability. Such well intended increases in NMDA receptors could cause excitotoxic injury and have an adverse effect on differentiating neurons in postnatal cerebellum. In addition, NMDA receptor activation increases intracellular free calcium, resulting in calcium loading of mitochondria that would increase oxidative damage to these vulnerable cells (Ward *et al.*, 2000). Alternatively, in view of the systemic nature of the mitochondrial abnormalities, downregulation of mitochondrial function could be a specific effect of MeCP2 dysfunction. According to the Hennebery hypothesis, such impairment of mitochondrial function would increase the likelihood of NMDA mediated neuronal injury (Henneberry, 1989). Regardless of whether mitochondrial dysfunction is a primary or a secondary consequence of impaired MeCP2 activity, the presence of mitochondrial abnormalities in the more severely affected Rett syndrome patients has important implications for therapy in those identified in the early stages. Conversely, it is important to recognize that some patients with primary mitochondrial disease (and normal MeCP2) regress in a manner that closely parallels stage 2 of Rett syndrome. This seems to be especially common in children with mild form of mitochondrial complex I deficiency. However, such children with primary mitochondrial defects usually do not lose purposeful hand use as in Rett syndrome.

Understanding the time course and biological basis of these age-specific effects, as they relate to the ontogenetic expression of MeCP2 and clinical stages of Rett syndrome, is essential to provide appropriate medical management. Recent reports of cyclooxygenase-2 inhibition in the rescue of cerebellar granule cells from glutamate-mediated cell death, and contributions of transplanted bone marrow and embryonic cerebellar cells in regeneration of cerebellar cells and their connections are provocative (Tolbert & Heckroth, 1998; Kaemmerer & Low, 1999; Rossi *et al.*, 2002; Strauss & Marini, 2002; Weimann *et al.*, 2003).

A significant degree of clinical variability in the severity of the autistic phase could result from non-random XCI patterns, where favouring the normal X chromosome would result in unaffected or minimally affected carrier females. Some of these atypical Rett syndrome individuals were identified because of a recurrence of Rett syndrome in their offspring (Wan *et al.*, 1999; Couvert *et al.*, 2001; Villard *et al.*, 2001; Dotti *et al.*, 2002; Hoffbuhr *et al.*, 2002). Individuals with germ line mosaicism would be asymptomatic but capable of transmitting the disease and, unfortunately, difficult to identify, as other tissues may not reflect the mutation (Amir *et al.*, 2000; Villard *et al.*, 2001). Thus, when a child with a mutation in MeCP2 has been identified, it is important to consider prenatal testing for subsequent pregnancies in the mother, even when a mutation in MeCP2 is not identified in her DNA (Singer & Naidu, 2001; Armstrong *et al.*, 2002).

References

Akbarian, S., Chen, R.Z., Gribnau, J., Rasmussen, T.P., Fong, H., Jaenisch, R. & Jones, E.G. (2001): Expression pattern of the Rett syndrome gene MeCP2 in primate prefrontal cortex. *Neurobiol. Dis.* **8**, 784–791.

Allen, G. & Courchesne, E. (2003): Differential effects of developmental cerebellar abnormality on cognitive and motor functions in the cerebellum: an fMRI study of autism. *Am. J. Psychiatry* **160**, 262–273.

Amir, R.E., van den Veyver, I.B., Wan, M., Tran, C.Q., Francke, U. & Zoghbi, H.Y. (1999): Rett syndrome is caused by mutations in X-linked MeCP2, encoding methyl-CpG-binding protein 2. *Nat. Genet.* **23**, 185–188.

Amir, R.E., van den Veyver, I.B., Schultz, R., Malicki, D.M., Tran, C.Q., Dahle, E.J., Philippi, A., Timar, L., Percy, A.K., Motil, K.J. *et al.* (2000): Influence of mutation type and X chromosome inactivation on Rett syndrome phenotypes. *Ann. Neurol.* **47**, 670–679.

Armstrong, D.D. (2002): Neuropathology of Rett syndrome. *Ment. Retard. Dev. Disabil. Res. Rev.* **8**, 72–76.

Armstrong, J., Aibar, E., Pineda, M., Perez, M.M., Gean, E., Carrera, M., Casas, C., Martinez, F. & Monros, E. (2002): Prenatal diagnosis in Rett syndrome. *Fetal Diagn. Ther.* **17**, 200–204.

Bauman, M.L. & Kemper, T.L. (1991): The neuropathology of Rett syndrome is pervasive throughout the brain. *Neurology* **41**, 306a.

Bauman, M.L., Kemper, T.L. & Arin, D.M. (1995): Microscopic observations of the brain in Rett syndrome. *Neuropediatrics* **26**, 105–108.

Bienvenu, T., Villard, L., De Roux, N., Bourdon, V., Fontes, M., Beldjord, C., Tardieu, M., Jonveaux, P. & Chelly, J. (2002): Spectrum of MECP2 mutations in Rett syndrome. *Genet. Test.* **6**, 1–6.

Bird, A.P. & Wolffe, A.P. (1999): Methylation-induced repression – belts, braces, and chromatin. *Cell* **99**, 451–454.

Blue, M.E., Naidu, S. & Johnston, M.V. (1999a): Altered development of glutamate and GABA receptors in the basal ganglia of girls with Rett syndrome. *Exp. Neurol.* **156**, 345–352.

Blue, M.E., Naidu, S. & Johnston, M.V. (1999b): Development of amino acid receptors in frontal cortex from girls with Rett syndrome. *Ann. Neurol.* **45**, 541–545.

Buxbaum, J.D., Silverman, J.M., Smith, C.J., Greenberg, D.A., Kilifarski, M., Reichert, J., Cook, E.H., Fang, Y., Song, C.Y. & Vitale, R. (2002): Association between a GABRB3 polymorphism and autism. *Mol. Psychiatry* **7**, 311–316.

Cohen, D.R., Matarazzo, V., Palmer, A.M., Tu, Y., Jeon, O.H., Pevsner, J. & Ronnett, G.V. (2003): Expression of MeCP2 in olfactory receptor neurons is developmentally regulated and occurs before synaptogenesis. *Mol. Cell. Neurosci.* **22**, 417–429.

Couvert, P., Bienvenu, T., Aquaviva, C., Poirier, K., Moraine, C., Gendrot, C., Verloes, A., Andres, C., LeFevre, A.C., Souville, I., Steffann, J., des Portes, V., Ropers, H.H., Ynbtema, H.G., Fryns, J.P., Briault, S., Chelly, J. & Cherif, B. (2001): MeCP2 is highly mutated in X-linked mental retardation. *Hum. Mol. Genet.* **10**, 941–946.

De Bona, C., Zappella, M., Hayek, G., Meloni, I., Vitelli, F., Bruttini, M., Cusano, R., Loffredo, P., Longo, I. & Renieri, A. (2000): Preserved speech variant is allelic of classic Rett syndrome. *Eur. J. Hum. Genet.* **8**, 325–330.

DeLorey, T.M., Handforth, A., Anagnostaras, S.G., Homanics, G.E., Minassian, B.A., Asatourian, A., Fanselow, M.S., Delgado-Escueta, A., Ellison, G.D. & Olsen, R.W. (1998): Mice lacking the beta3 subunit of the GABAA receptor have the epilepsy phenotype and many of the behavioral characteristics of Angelman syndrome. *J. Neurosci.* 18, 8505–8514.

Deutsch, C.K. & Joseph, R.M. (2003): Brief report: cognitive correlates of enlarged head circumference in children with autism. *J. Autism Dev. Disord.* **33**, 209–215.

Dotti, M.T., Orrico, A., De Stefano, N., Battisti, C., Sicurelli, F., Severi, S., Lam, C.W., Galli, L., Sorrentino, V. & Federico, A. (2002): A Rett syndrome MECP2 mutation that causes mental retardation in men. *Neurology* **58**, 226–230.

Dum, R.P. & Strick, P.L. (2003): An unfolded map of the cerebellar dentate nucleus and its projections to the cerebral cortex. *J. Neurophysiol.* **89**, 634–639.

Friede, R.L. (1989): *Developmental neuropathology*, pp. 372–373. Berlin, Springer Verlag.

Gebhart, A.L., Petersen, S.E. & Thach, W.T. (2002): Role of the posterolateral cerebellum in language. *Ann. N.Y. Acad. Sci.* **978**, 318–333.

Hagberg, B., Aicardi, J., Dias, K. & Ramos, O. (1983): A progressive syndrome of autism, dementia, ataxia, and loss of purposeful hand use in girls: Rett syndrome – report of 35 cases. *Ann. Neurol.* **14**, 471–479.

Hagberg, B. & Witt-Engerström, I. (1986): Rett syndrome: a suggested staging system for describing impairment profile with increasing age towards adolesence. *Am. J. Med. Genet.* **24**, 47–59.

Henneberry, R.C. (1989): The role of neuronal energy in the neurotoxicity of excitatory amino acids. *Neurobiol. Aging* **10**, 611–613; discussion 618–620.

Hoffbuhr, K., Devaney, J.M., LaFleur, B., Sirianni, N., Scacheri, C., Giron, J., Schuette, J., Innis, J., Marino, M., Philippart, M., Narayanan, V., Umansky, R., Kronn, D., Hoffman, E.P. & Naidu, S. (2001): MeCP2 mutations in children with and without the phenotype of Rett syndrome. *Neurology* 56, 1486–1495.

Hoffbuhr, K.C., Moses, L.M., Jerdonek, M.A., Naidu, S. & Hoffman, E.P. (2002): Associations between meCP2 mutations, X-chromosome inactivation, and phenotype. *Ment. Retard. Dev. Disabil. Res. Rev.* **8**, 99–105.

Horike, S.I., Cai, S., Miyano, M., Cheng, J.F. & Kohwi-Shigematsu, T. (2005): Loss of silent-chromatin looping and impaired imprinting of DLX5 in Rett syndrome. *Nat. Genet.* **37**, 31–40.

Johnston, M.V., Mullaney, B. & Blue, M.E. (2003): Neurobiology of Rett syndrome. *J. Child. Neurol.* **18**, 688–692.

Jung, B.P., Jugloff, D.G., Zhang, G., Logan, R., Brown, S. & Eubanks, J.H. (2003): The expression of methyl CpG binding factor MeCP2 correlates with cellular differentiation in the developing rat brain and in cultured cells. *J. Neurobiol.* **55**, 86–96.

Kaemmerer, W.F. & Low, W.C. (1999): Cerebellar allografts survive and transiently alleviate ataxia in a transgenic model of spinocerebellar ataxia type-1. *Exp. Neurol.* **158**, 301–311.

Kern, J.K. (2002): The possible role of the cerebellum in autism/PDD: disruption of a multisensory feedback loop. *Med. Hypotheses* **59**, 255–260.

Kerr, A.M. (1995): Early clinical signs in the Rett disorder. *Neuropediatrics* **26**, 67–71.

Leonard, H. & Bower, C. (1998): Is the girl with Rett syndrome normal at birth? *Dev. Med. Child Neurol.* **40**, 115–121.

Manabe, T. (2002): Does BDNF have pre- or postsynaptic targets? *Science* **295**, 1651–1653.

Martin, E.R., Menold, M.M., Wolpert, C.M., Bass, M.P., Donnelly, S.L., Ravan, S.A., Zimmerman, A., Gilbert, J.R., Vance, J.M., Maddox, L.O., Wright, H.H., Abramson, R.K., DeLong, G.R., Cuccaro, M.L. & Pericak-Vance, M.A. (2000): Analysis of linkage disequilibrium in gamma-aminobutyric acid receptor subunit genes in autistic disorder. *Am. J. Med. Genet.* **96**, 43–48.

Matarazzo, V., Cohen, D., Palmer, A.M., Simpson, P.J., Khokhar, B., Pan, S.J. & Ronnett, G.V. (2004): The transcriptional repressor MeCP2 regulates terminal neuronal differentiation. *Mol. Cell. Neurosci.* **27**, 44–58.

McDonald, J.W. & Johnston, M.V. (1990): Physiological and pathological roles of excitatory amino acids during central nervous system development. *Brain Res.* **15**, 41–70.

Meehan, R.R., Lewis, J.D. & Bird, A.P. (1992): Characterization of MeCP2, a vertebrate DNA binding protein with affinity for methylated DNA. *Nucleic Acids Res.* **20**, 5085–5092.

Menold, M.M., Shao, Y., Wolpert, C.M., Donnelly, S.L., Raiford, K.L., Martin, E.R., Ravan, S.A., Abramson, R.K., Wright, H.H., Delong, G.R., Cuccaro, M.L., Pericak-Vance, M.A. & Gilbert, J.R. (2001): Association analysis of chromosome 15 GABAA receptor subunit genes in autistic disorder. *J. Neurogenet.* **15**, 245–259.

Middleton, F.A. & Strick, P.L. (2001): Cerebellar projections to the prefrontal cortex of the primate. *J. Neurosci.* **21**, 700–712.

Mnatzakanian, G.N., Lohi, H., Munteanu, I., Alfred, S.E., Yamada, T., MacLeod, P.J., Jones, J.R., Scherer, S.W., Schanen, N.C., Friez, M.J., Vincent, J.B. & Minassian, B.A. (2004): A previously unidentified MECP2 open reading frame defines a new protein isoform relevant to Rett syndrome. *Nat. Genet.* 36, 339–341.

Monti, B., Marri, L. & Contestabile, A. (2002): NMDA receptor-dependent CREB activation in survival of cerebellar granule cells during *in vivo* and *in vitro* development. *Eur. J. Neurosci.* **16**, 1490–1498.

Naidu, S. (1997): Rett syndrome: a disorder affecting early brain growth. *Ann. Neurol.* **42**, 3–10.

Naidu, S., Murphy, M., Moser, H.W. & Rett, A. (1986): Rett syndrome: natural history in 70 cases. *Am. J. Med. Genet.* **24**, 61–72.

Naidu, S., Bibat, G., Kratz, L., Kelley, R.I., Pevsner, J., Hoffman, E., Cuffari, C., Rohde, C., Blue, M.E. & Johnston, M.V. (2003): Clinical variability in Rett syndrome. *J. Child. Neurol.* **18**, 662–668.

Nan, X., Campoy, F.J. & Bird, A. (1997): MeCP2 is a transcriptional repressor with abundant binding sites in genomic chromatin. *Cell* **88**, 471–481.

Nan, X., Ng, H.H., Johnson, C.A., Laherty, C.D., Turner, B.M., Eisenman, R.N. & Bird, A. (1998): Transcriptional repression by the methyl-CpG-binding protein MeCP2 involves a histone deacetylase complex. *Nature* **393**, 386–389.

Nomura, Y. & Segawa, M. (1990): Clinical features of the early stage of the Rett syndrome. *Brain Dev.* **12**, 16–19.

Pan, J.W., Lane, J.B., Hetherington, H. & Percy, A.K. (1999): Rett syndrome: ^{1}H spectroscopic imaging at 4.1 Tesla. *J. Child. Neurol.* **14**, 524–528.

Petralia, R.S., Wang, Y.X. & Wenthold, R.J. (2002): NMDA receptors and PSD-95 are found in attachment plaques in cerebellar granular layer glomeruli. *Eur. J. Neurosci.* **15**, 583–587.

Pierce, K. & Courchesne, E. (2001): Evidence for a cerebellar role in reduced exploration and stereotyped behavior in autism. *Biol. Psychiatry* **49**, 655–664.

Pinto, A.D., Lang, A.E. & Chen, R. (2003): The cerebellothalamocortical pathway in essential tremor. *Neurology* **60**, 1985–1987.

Raymond, J.L., Lisberger, S.G. & Mauk, M.D. (1996): The cerebellum: a neuronal learning machine? *Science* **272**, 1126–1131.

Rett, A. (1966): Über ein eigenartiges hirnatrophisches Syndrom bei Hyperammonämie im Kindersalter. [On an unusual brain atrophy syndrome in hyperammonemia in childhood]. *Wien. Med. Wochenschr.* **116**, 723–726.

Riikonen, R. (2003): Neurotrophic factors in the pathogenesis of Rett syndrome. *J. Child Neurol.* **18**, 693–697.

Rossi, F., Saggiorato, C. & Strata, P. (2002): Target-specific innervation of embryonic cerebellar transplants by regenerating olivocerebellar axons in the adult rat. *Exp. Neurol.* **173**, 205–212.

Shahbazian, M.D., Antalffy, B., Armstrong, D.L. & Zoghbi, H.Y. (2002): Insight into Rett syndrome: MeCP2 levels display tissue- and cell-specific differences and correlate with neuronal maturation. *Hum. Mol. Genet.* **11**, 115–124.

Singer, H.S. & Naidu, S. (2001): Rett syndrome: 'We'll keep the genes on for you'. *Neurology* **56**, 582–584.

Sirianni, N., Naidu, S., Pereira, J., Pillotto, R.F. & Hoffman, E.P. (1998): Rett syndrome: confirmation of X-linked dominant inheritance, and localization of the gene to Xq28. *Am. J. Hum. Genet.* **63**, 1552–1558.

Strauss, K.I. & Marini, A.M.: Cyclooxygenase-2 inhibition protects cultured cerebellar granule neurons from glutamate-mediated cell death. *J. Neurotrauma* **19**, 627–638.

Tolbert, D.L. & Heckroth, J. (1998): Purkinje cell transplants in Shaker mutant rats with hereditary Purkinje cell degeneration and ataxia. *Exp. Neurol.* **153**, 255–267.

Townsend, J., Courchesne, E., Covington, J., Westerfield, M., Harris, N.S., Lyden, P., Lowry, T.P. & Press, G.A. (1999): Spatial attention deficits in patients with acquired or developmental cerebellar abnormality. *J. Neurosci.* **19**, 5632–5643.

Townsend, J., Westerfield, M., Leaver, E., Makeig, S., Jung, T., Pierce, K. & Courchesne, E. (2001): Event-related brain response abnormalities in autism: evidence for impaired cerebello-frontal spatial attention networks. *Brain Res. Cogn. Brain Res.* **11**, 127–145.

Trevathan, E. & Naidu, S. (1998): The clinical recognition and differential diagnosis of Rett syndrome. *J. Child Neurol.* **3**, S6-S16.

Villard, L., Levy, N., Xiang, F., Kpebe, A., Labelle, V., Chevillard, C., Zhang, Z., Schwartz, C.E., Tardieu, M., Chelly, J., Anvret, M. & Fontes, M. (2001): Segregation of a totally skewed pattern of X chromosome inactivation in four familial cases of Rett syndrome without MECP2 mutation: implications for the disease. *J. Med. Genet.* **38**, 435–442.

Wan, M., Lee, S.S., Zhang, X., Houwink-Manville, I., Song, H.R., Amir, R.E., Budden, S., Naidu, S., Pereira, J.L., Lo, I.F., Zoghbi, H.Y., Schanen, N.C. & Francke, U. (1999): Rett syndrome and beyond: recurrent spontaneous and familial MECP2 mutations at CpG hotspots. *Am. J. Hum. Genet.* **65**, 1520–1529.

Ward, M.W., Rego, A.C., Frenguelli, B.G. & Nicholls, D.G. (2000): Mitochondrial membrane potential and glutamate excitotoxicity in cultured cerebellar granule cells. *J. Neurosci.* **20**, 7208–7219.

Weimann, J.M., Charlton, C.A., Brazelton, T.R., Hackman, R.C. & Blau, H.M. (2003): Contribution of transplanted bone marrow cells to Purkinje neurons in human adult brains. *Proc. Natl. Acad. Sci. USA* **100**, 2088–2093.

Xiang, F., Zhang, Z., Clarke, A., Joseluiz, P., SakkuBai, N., Sarojini, B., Delozier-Blanchet, C.D., Hansmann, I., Edstrom, L. & Anvret, M. (1998): Chromosome mapping of Rett syndrome: a likely candidate region on the telomere of Xq. *J. Med. Genet.* **35**, 297–300.

Zappella, M., Meloni, I., Longo, I., Canitano, R., Hayek, G., Rosaia, L., Mari, F. & Renieri, A. (2003): Study of MECP2 gene in Rett syndrome variants and autistic girls. *Am. J. Med. Genet.* **119B**, 102–107.

Autistic spectrum disorders, D. Riva and I. Rapin (eds.)
© 2005 John Libbey Eurotext, pp. 35–44.

Chapter 5

Involvement of glutamate receptors in behavioural and neuronal hereditary disorders: genetic analysis, expression studies, and RNA editing

Sergio Barlati and Alessandro Barbon

Division of Biology and Genetics, Department of Biomedical Sciences and Biotechnologies, University of Brescia, viale Europa 11, 25123 Brescia, Italy
barlati@med.unibs.it

Summary

Glutamate mediates its function by binding two classes of receptors: ionotropic and metabotropic. Ionotropic receptors (iGluRs) assemble together forming ion channels. Metabotropic receptors (mGluRs) are coupled to GTP-binding proteins and regulate the production of intracellular messengers. Dysfunction in glutamatergic neurotransmission can cause severe neural damage and might be related to the pathophysiology of several neurological diseases such as Alzheimer's disease, autism, schizophrenia and epilepsy, which may be accompanied by severe cognitive impairment.
No mutations affecting the coding sequences of the glutamate receptor genes have been detected, although GluRs are high ranking candidate genes for many hereditary disorders involving neurological dysfunction. We report the mutation analyses of the ionotropic *GRIK1* gene and of the metabotropic *GRM4* gene, which represent, for position and function, candidate genes for two forms of idiopathic generalized epilepsy (IGE): juvenile absence epilepsy and juvenile myoclonic epilepsy. Our data showed that no mutations affecting the coding sequence and the regulatory elements, such as splicing junctions and promoter regions, are involved in the aetiology of IGE. The findings do not rule out the possibility that mutations in the non-coding sequences regulating post-transcriptional mechanisms may be involved in the disease. By studying the *GRIK2* gene, we showed the importance of post-transcriptional mechanisms, such as alternative splicing and RNA editing, in increasing GRIK2 functions for modulating excitatory neurotransmissions. The identification of cells or tissues, other than in the CNS, expressing the GluRs genes would allow their study in patients with behavioural neuronal disorders.

Introduction

The neurotransmitter L-glutamate is the main mediator of excitatory neurotransmission in the mammalian central nervous system (CNS). Glutamate mediates neurotransmission at central synapses and is significantly involved in the structural and functional plasticity of the synapses, including learning and memory processes.

Alterations in glutamatergic neurotransmission have been involved in the neuronal damage observed after episodes of ischaemia and hypoglycaemia, as well as in the aetiology of a series of neurological conditions including epilepsy, Alzheimer's disease, Huntington's disease, and amyotrophic lateral sclerosis (Dingledine *et al.*, 1999).

Glutamate acts through the activation of ionotropic ligand gate ion channels (iGluRs) and metabotropic G protein coupled receptors (mGluRs). Glutamate receptors are widely expressed throughout the CNS, localized pre-, post-, or extrasynaptically on neurons and non-neuronal glial cells (Hollman & Heinemann, 1994; Dingledine *et al.*, 1999). Glutamate receptors are also expressed outside the CNS in peripheral tissues such as the heart, skin, and bone (Skerry & Genever, 2001).

Molecular studies have identified and cloned 17 cDNA coding ionotropic GluR subunits and eight cDNA coding metabotropic GluRs (Ozawa *et al.*, 1998). Ionotropic GluR subunits are grouped into three families based on their pharmacological properties: N-methyl-D-aspartate (NMDA), α-amino-3-hydroxy-5-methyl-isoxazole-propionate (AMPA), and kainate (KA) receptors. Six cDNAs have been cloned that encode NMDA receptor subunits: NR1, NR2A-D, and NR3A. Four cloned cDNAs encode AMPA receptor subunits (GluR1–4) and five cloned cDNAs encode kainate receptor subunits (GluR5–7, KA1, and KA2). Additionally, two cDNAs have been cloned that encode putative ionotropic GluR subunits: delta-1 and delta-2 (Lomeli *et al.*, 1993).

The topology of ionotropic receptor subunits presents one extracellular domain, four transmembrane domains, and one intracellular carboxyl-terminal domain. The second membrane domain forms a re-entrant membrane pore lining loop with both ends facing the cytoplasm (VanDongen & VanDongen, 1999).

Ionotropic glutamate receptors transduce the glutamate signal by changing their permeability for monovalent (Na^+, K^+) and divalent (Ca^{2+}) ions; these receptors may also transduce the signal by protein-protein interaction. Many functionally diverse proteins either modulate receptor function or transduce a receptor signal (Kennedy, 1997).

Calcium acting as a second messenger plays a central role in the GluR mediated process. Excessive calcium influx through iGluR activation contributes to excitotoxic mechanism, which leads to neurological injury in ischaemia, hypoglycaemia, seizures, physical brain trauma, and chronic neurodegenerative disorders (Huntington's disease and Alzheimer's disease) (Sattler & Tymianski, 2000; Weiss & Sensi, 2000). Interestingly, the calcium permeability of several AMPA and KA receptors is regulated by a post-transcriptional modification called RNA editing (Seeburg *et al.*, 1998).

This post-transcriptional mechanism directs enzymatic deamination of a specific adenosine in the pre-mRNA before splicing and it requires a three dimensional structure composed of the exonic editing sequence and an intronic editing complementary sequence (ECS) (Keegan *et al.*, 2001).

In the case of the AMPA GluR2 subunit and kainate GluR5 and GluR6 subunits, deamination results in the substitution of a codon for glutamine (CAG) with a codon for arginine (CIG) in the membrane domain M2 of the receptor channel, at the so called Q/R site. The presence of arginine confers on the receptor channel reduced Ca^{2+} permeability (Egebjerg & Heinemann, 1993), reduced ion conductance (Swanson *et al.*, 1996; Vissel *et al.*, 2001), and an altered current/voltage relation (Bowie & Mayer, 1995; Kamboj *et al.*, 1995). Furthermore, GluR2, 3, and 4 are edited at the R/G site, where a codon for arginine (AGA) is modified into a codon for a glycine (IGA). This site is located just before the sequences involved in the splicing events forming the so called flip/flop isoforms (Lomeli *et al.*, 1994) and it might influence both the splicing events and the desensitisation properties of the AMPA receptor channels. In addition, the kainate receptor GluR6 can be edited at the I/V and Y/C sites located in the transmembrane 1 domain (TM1), where an isoleucine (ATT) is substituted by a valine (ITT) and a tyrosine (TAC) by a cysteine (TIC), respectively. These editing sites might be involved, in cooperation with Q/R site, in the finer regulation of ion permeability (Kohler *et al.*, 1993).

The eight known metabotropic glutamate receptors (mGluR1–8) have been classified into the superfamily of seven transmembrane G-protein coupled receptors. They are divided into three subgroups based on the downstream effector system and their agonist selectivity. Metabotropic glutamate receptors are widely distributed in the CNS. Their activation modulates synaptic plasticity and is involved in learning and memory, but it also plays a significant role in various CNS disorders (Holmann & Heinemann, 1994; Nakanishi *et al.*, 1998).

Our understanding of the role of glutamate receptor subunits in specific brain circuits is still in the early stages, and made difficult by the enormous diversity of native glutamate receptors generated by subunit assembly, RNA splicing, and RNA editing events. These molecular mechanisms create new receptor isoforms with potentially different functional properties.

It has recently been proposed that an allelic variant of the GRIK1 gene, coding for the GluR5 subunits, might confer susceptibility to a form of epilepsy, juvenile absence epilepsy (JAE) (Sander *et al.*, 1997b); moreover, the level of expression of several kainate receptors is altered in temporal lobe epilepsy (Kortenbruck *et al.*, 2001). Various studies suggest that a GRIK2 genotype variation might be associated with the age of onset of Huntington's disease (Rubinsztein *et al.*, 1997; McDonald *et al.*, 1999). The same polymorphic variation has been analysed to rule out possible involvement of the *GRIK2* gene in idiopathic generalized epilepsy (Sander *et al.*, 1995).

A recent study reported a significant association between *GRIK2* gene and autism (Jamain *et al.*, 2002); in this work a specific amino acid variation in the carboxy-terminal domain was identified, but there were no clues as to possible functional abnormalities. The *GRIK2* gene might also be a good candidate gene for schizophrenia because three independent studies found a positive linkage with the region 6q21 where the gene is localized (Cao *et al.*, 1997; Martinez *et al.*, 1999; Levinson *et al.*, 2000). Another study (Porter *et al.*, 1997), reporting a decrease in the mRNA level of *GRIK2* genes, supports this hypothesis.

Polymorphic variations of the *GRIK3* gene have recently been associated with schizophrenia (Begni *et al.*, 2002) but no mutation analysis has been carried out. The available data indicate a general decrease of kainate receptor expression in schizophrenic patients (Meador-Woodruff *et al.*, 2001).

So far, no mutations affecting the coding sequence of these genes have been found in patients with disorders such as autism, schizophrenia, or epilepsy. These data do not rule out the possibility that mutations might be present in the regulatory non-coding sequences or in intronic sequences involved in the post-transcriptional maturation of RNA, such as alternative splicing or RNA editing.

We recently studied the possible involvement of *GRIK1* and *GRM4* genes, coding for the glutamate receptor GluR5 and mGluR4 subunits, respectively, in the aetiology of IGE. Hereditary factors play a major role in the aetiology of JAE and juvenile myoclonic epilepsy (JME) which are common subtypes of IGE. Sander *et al.* (1997b) reported an allelic association of JAE with the nine copy allele of a tetranucleotide repeat polymorphism in the third intron of the kainate selective GluR5 receptor gene (*GRIK1*) and supportive evidence for linkage of IGE to *GRIK1* in families of JAE probands. These findings suggested that a major genetic determinant of *GRIK1* might confer susceptibility to JAE. Linkage studies in families of JME probands also suggested a susceptibility locus for IGE in the chromosomal region 6p21.3 near the *HLA* region (Sander *et al.*, 1997a, 2000; Janz, 1997; Greenberg *et al.*, 2000). The gene encoding the metabotropic glutamate receptor type 4 *(GRM4)* has been localized within the *EJM1* region and represents a high ranking candidate gene (Barbon *et al.*, 2000).

Moreover, with regard to the *GRIK2* gene coding for GluR6 receptor, we recently reported the importance of RNA splicing and RNA editing in the variation of GRIK2 expression and function. As already mentioned, *GRIK2* is a candidate gene for autism and schizophrenia (Levinson *et al.*, 2000; Jamain *et al.*, 2002) but no mutations have been found in its coding sequence associated with these pathologies.

The level of editing and the pattern of alternative splicing are extremely important in modulating excitatory neurotransmissions and it is an attractive hypothesis that possible alterations involving such mechanisms might be involved in the pathogenesis of neurological disorders.

Material and methods

All the information concerning the material and methods related to the genetic analysis of *GRIK1* and *GRM4* in epilepsy patients have been reported by Izzi *et al.* (2002; 2003).

Details of the *GRIK2* splicing analysis were reported by Barbon *et al.* (2001), while those of the analysis of *GRIK2* editing sites in distinct brain areas were reported by the same investigators in a later paper (Barbon *et al.*, 2003).

Results

GRIK1 and *GRM4* mutational screening

The *GRIK1* and *GRM4* gene structures are shown in *Fig. 1*. An analysis of the coding and regulatory sequences in patients affected by JAE (for *GRIK1* analysis) and by JME (for *GRM4* analysis) did not reveal the presence of mutations.

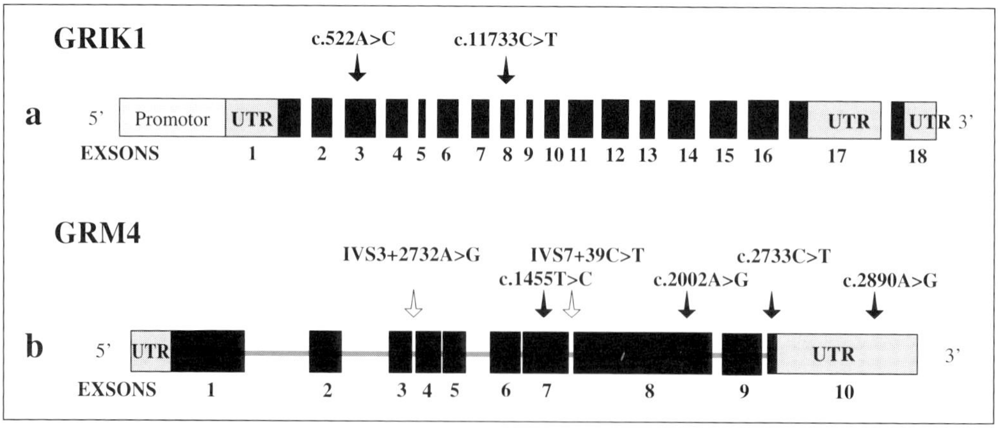

Fig. 1. GRIK1 (a) and GRM4 (b) genomic organizations. Exons and introns are represented by boxes and horizontal lines, respectively. The hatched areas of the first and last exons represent the 5' and 3' untranslated regions (UTR). The polymorphisms analysed are indicated by arrows (black for exonic, white for intronic polymorphisms).

A detailed analysis of the *GRIK2* gene, located in a region of chromosome in linkage with autism and schizophrenia, has also been started in our laboratory and preliminary findings suggest an association of the *GRIK2* with schizophrenia.

Post-transcriptional modification of the *GRIK2* gene

The characterization of the post-transcriptional modification of the *GRIK2* gene has been started by analysing the splicing variants and the editing levels of the GluR6 receptors. This study might identify possible sequences that play a significant role in controlling the expression and function of these complex genes and their possible involvement in predisposing to neurological dysfunction.

The main *GRIK2* mRNA isoforms identified in human brain RNA sample and in neuronal cell in cultures are reported in *Fig. 2*.

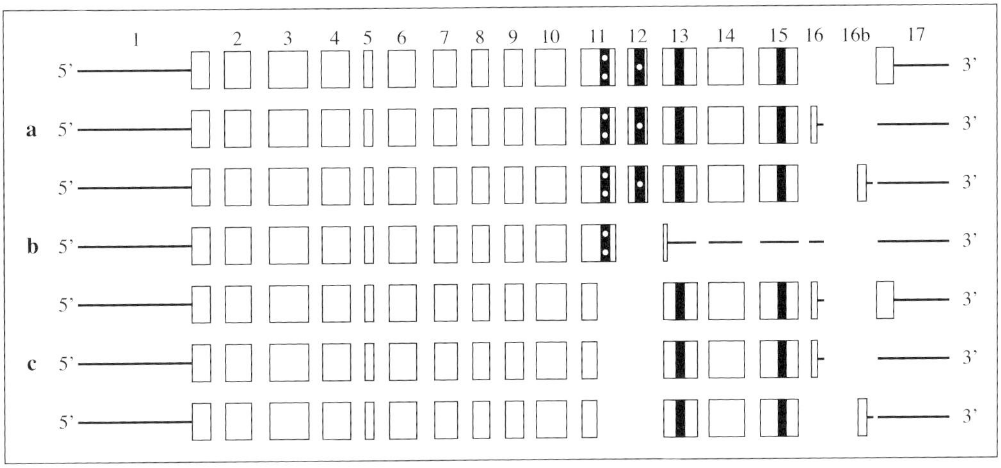

Fig. 2. Schematic representation of the main splicing variants of GRIK2 gene. Coding regions are boxed; the transmembrane domains are represented by black bars in exons 11–13 and 15; the white points inside the black bars represent the editing sites. (a) The first three isoforms differ in the alternative splicing of the carboxyl domain coding sequences: exon 16, 16b, and 17. (b) In the fourth isoform, exon 12 is skipped and an in-frame stop codon truncates the putative protein. (c) In the last three isoforms a cryptic splicing site in exon 11 gives rise to transcripts coding for putative proteins that maintain only the TM3 and TM4 regions and which present the three different carboxyl coding sequences.

Three exons are alternatively spliced in the sequences coding for the carboxyl terminal domains: exon 17 is present in the already cloned human GluR6a isoform, while exon 16, the sequence present in the human homologue to the mouse GluR6–2 (Barbon *et al.*, 2001), and exon 16b are spliced out in the major transcript. In the presence of exon 16 or exon 16b, a premature stop codon leads to different and shorter C-terminal ends *(Fig. 2a)* (Barbon *et al.*, 2001; Jamain *et al.*, 2002).

Multiple splicing events are also present in the sequence coding for the transmembrane domains. A splicing event skips exon 12, and the donor site of exon 11 is directly spliced to exon 13. The new reading frame would generate a stop codon at the beginning of exon 13. This isoform would code for a truncated protein of 584 amino acids (the canonical GluR6 subunit is 908 amino acids long) in which three transmembrane domains (M2, TM3, and TM4) would be missing *(Fig. 2b)*. A cryptic donor splicing site, located within exon 11, is spliced to the normal acceptor site of exon 13. This splicing event would maintain the correct reading frame and the coded protein would lack the whole TM1 and M2 regions, which contain the three editing sites, but would otherwise maintain the TM3 and TM4 regions *(Fig. 2c)*.

In addition to splicing, *GRIK2* mRNA is also subject to RNA editing. The three editing sites of GluR6 subunits shown in *Fig. 3* are modulated in mRNA samples derived from different brain areas. The results of the editing level analysis are shown in *Fig. 3c*.

Figure 4 presents the 26 possible protein variants generated by post-transcriptional modifications (RNA splicing and editing) of *GRIK2* mRNA.

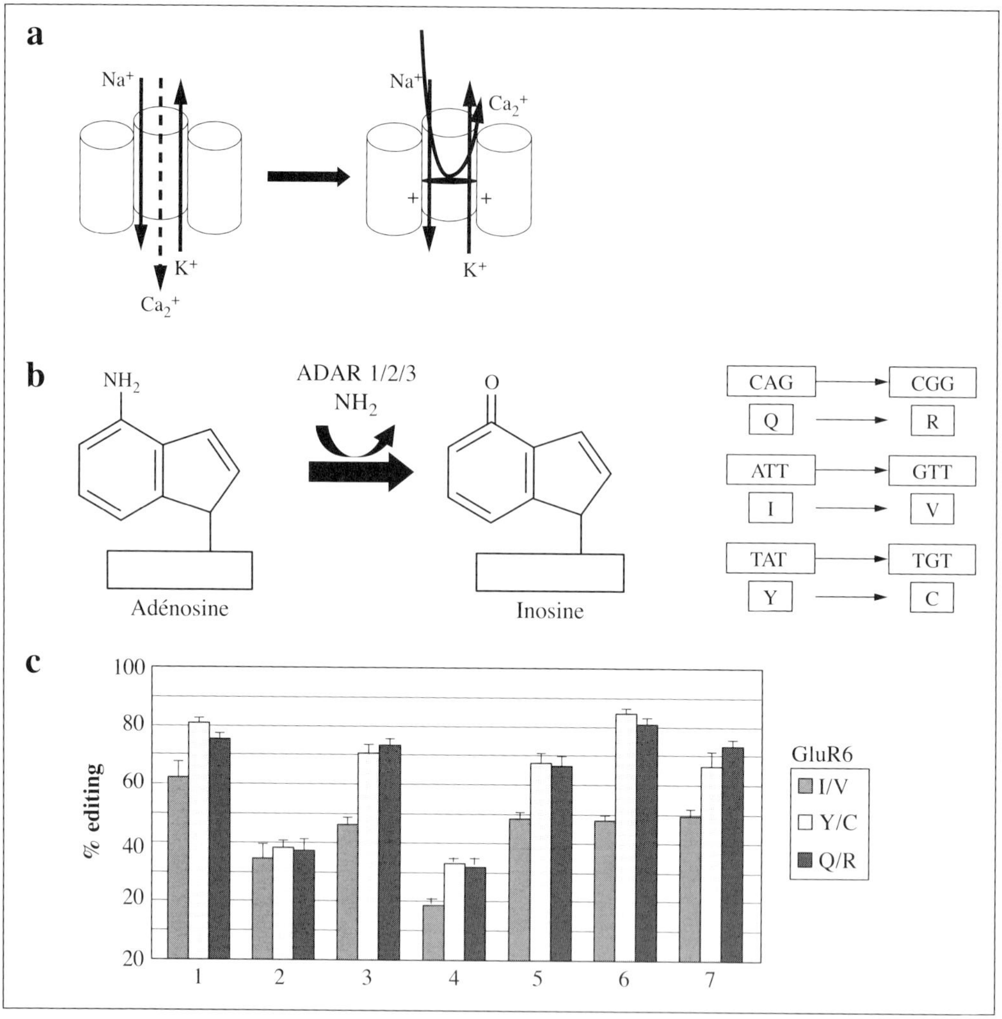

Fig. 3. (a) Effects of Q/R editing on the channel properties of homomeric GluR6 receptor. Introduction of arginine at the Q/R editing site in the second membrane domain (M2) of GluR6 confers a ring of positive charges within the channel pore. This leads to a reduction in single-channel cation conductance (Na^+, K^+ and Ca^{2+}), as indicated by the thickness of the arrows, thus causing a decrease in the unitary conductance of the edited receptors. (b) Scheme of the enzymatic modifications of an adenosine into an inosine, catalysed by ADAR enzymes; the nucleotide and corresponding amino acid variations in the three GluR6 editing sites are reported. (c) GluR6 I/V, Y/C, and Q/R editing levels in different human brain districts. All editing sites underwent direct sequencing analysis. All editing analyses were done in triplicate. 1, Amygdala; 2, corpus callosum; 3, caudate nucleus; 4, spinal cord; 5, thalamus; 6, cerebellum; 7, hippocampus.

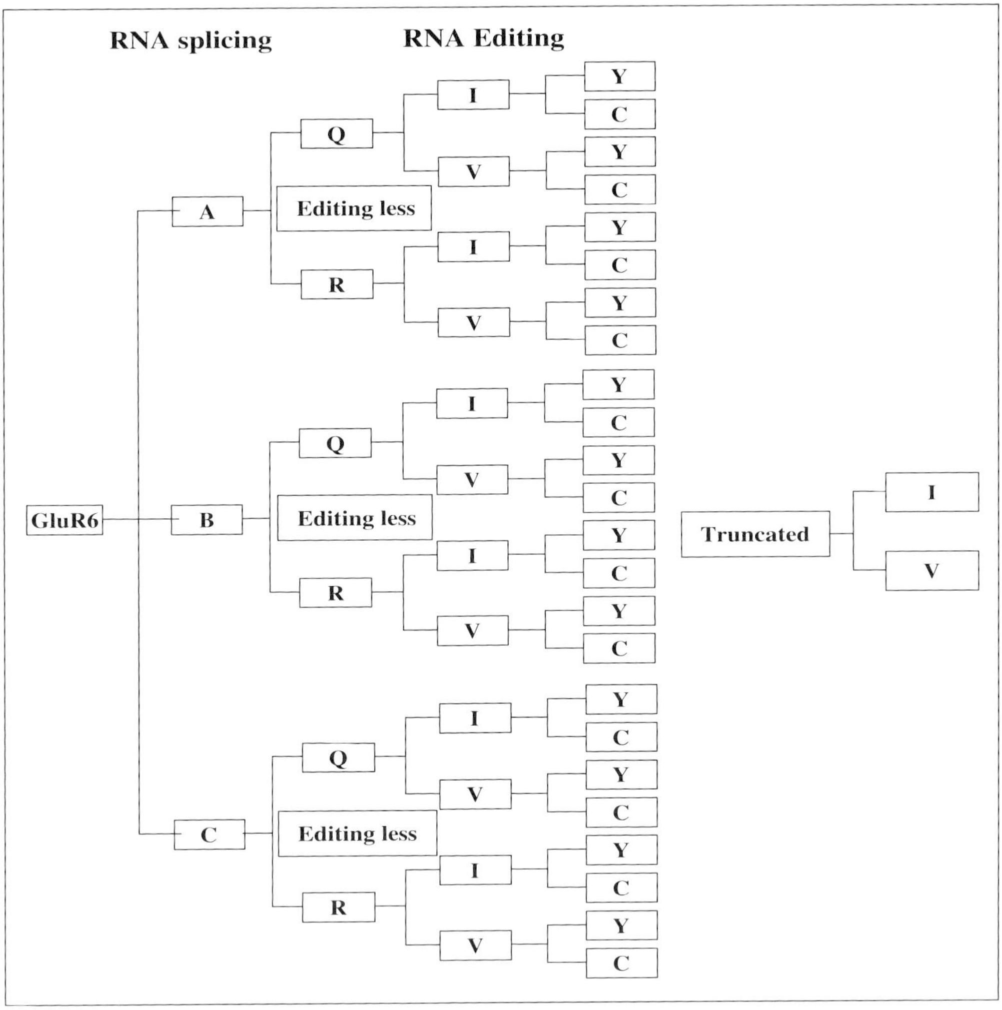

Fig. 4. Protein diversity of the GRIK2 gene, coding for the GluR6 glutamate receptors. Each box represents a distinct protein variant generated by both RNA editing and RNA splicing events. At least 26 proteins might be generated.

Discussion

The fact that no functional mutations have been identified in the genes coding for ionotropic and metabotropic GluRs found in association with epilepsy, autism, or schizophrenia suggests that a negative selection might operate against mutations in these ancient and widespread neurotransmitter receptors.

Studies on glutamate receptor knockout mice have given crucial insights into the functional importance of these subunits in excitatory neurotransmission. In particular, AMPA GluR2 global knockout mice – or mice in which the GluR2 Q/R site has been mutated, creating unedited receptors – are epileptic, hyperexcitable, and short lived, features which mainly reflect higher calcium permeability (Gerlai *et al.*, 1998; Feldmeyer *et al.*, 1999). These data indicate that mutations affecting the protein structures or the main physiological functions of glutamate receptors are probably not compatible with life.

More attention must be paid to the sequences involved in the regulation of the expression and splicing pattern of candidate genes for neurological disorders. Many proteins could be created from a single genomic sequence, with specific and distinct properties, because of post-transcriptional modulations such as RNA alternative splicing and RNA editing, as in the case of *GRIK2* gene and several other GluRs *(Fig. 4)*.

In our studies we have shown that the editing levels of I/V, Y/C, and Q/R GluR6 sites vary in the different brain areas examined. These data indicate that different neural populations require a specific editing level for fine modulation of excitatory neurotransmission. The high level of modulation present in the editing reactions suggests that misregulation could be involved in the genesis of neurological disorders.

Knockout mice deficient in the *ADAR2* gene which codes for the main enzyme catalysing the editing reactions show reduced RNA editing levels, altered AMPA receptor calcium permeability, induction of NMDA receptor-independent long-term potentiation (LTP), and spontaneous lethal seizures; these mice die quickly after birth. These findings show that the editing reaction is critical for survival (Higuchi *et al.*, 2000).

Several studies have focused on the editing level of serotonin or glutamate receptors in the brains of patients affected by several neurological disorders. The editing levels of the serotonin receptor were found to be reduced in patients suffering from schizophrenia (Sodhi *et al.*, 2001) and increased in suicides (Niswender *et al.*, 2001). With regard to glutamate receptors, the editing levels of the GluR2 Q/R site have been found to be altered in the cerebral cortex of patients suffering from schizophrenia, Alzheimer's disease, and Huntington's disease (Akbarian *et al.*, 1996). In addition, the editing level of GluR6 increases in patients with temporal lobe epilepsy (Kortenbruck *et al.*, 2001). These findings, although preliminary, show that the editing reaction might be involved in neurological disorders.

In addition, preliminary unpublished data from our laboratory show misregulation of the editing reactions of specific GluRs in rats treated chronically with phencyclidine (PCP). This drug might mimic in an animal model the cognitive impairments specific to schizophrenic patients, showing the possible involvement of RNA editing reactions in the aetiology of schizophrenia (manuscript in preparation).

The study of the expression of these genes clearly requires the use of animal models or the identification of human tissues, other than from the CNS, in which these neuronal markers are expressed (Skerry & Genever, 2001). Complete knowledge of post-transcriptional processes, which appear to be increasingly interconnected, and their involvement in pathological processes is a requirement and a challenge in this post-genome era.

Acknowledgments: This work was supported by MIUR (Centre of Excellence IDET and Cofin 2001) and by Fondazione Cariplo (OmniExpress).

References

Akbarian, S., Sucher, N.J., Bradley, D., Tafazzoli, A., Trinh, D., Hetrick, W.P., Potkin, S.G., Sandman, C.A., Bunney, W.E. & Jones, E.G. (1996): Selective alterations in gene expression for NMDA receptor subunits in prefrontal cortex of schizophrenics. *J. Neurosci.* **16**, 19–30.

Barbon, A., Ferraboli, S. & Barlati, S. (2000): Assignment of the human metabotropic glutamate receptor gene GRM4 to chromosome 6 band p21 by radiation hybrid mapping. *Cytogenet. Cell Genet.* **88**, 210.

Barbon, A., Vallini, I. & Barlati, S. (2001): Genomic organization of the human GRIK2 gene and evidence for multiple splicing variants. *Gene* **274**, 187–197.

Barbon, A., Vallini, I., La Via, L., Marchina, E. & Barlati, S. (2003): Glutamate receptor RNA editing: a molecular analysis of GluR2, GluR5 and GluR6 in human brain tissues and in NT2 cells following *in vitro* neural differentiation. *Brain Res. Mol. Brain Res.* **117**, 168–178.

Begni, S., Popoli, M., Moraschi, S., Bignotti, S., Tura, G.B. & Gennarelli, M. (2002): Association between the ionotropic glutamate receptor kainate 3 (GRIK3) ser310ala polymorphism and schizophrenia. *Mol. Psychiatry* **7**, 416–418.

Bowie, D. & Mayer, M.L. (1995): Inward rectification of both AMPA and Kainate subtype glutamate receptors generated by polyamine-mediated ion channel block. *Neuron* **15**, 453–462.

Cao, Q., Martinez, M., Zhang, J., Sanders, A.R., Badner, J.A., Cravchik, A., Markey, C.J., Beshah, E., Guroff, J.J., Maxwell, M.E., Kazuba, D.M., Whiten, R., Goldin, L.R., Gershon, E.S. & Gejman, P.V. (1997): Suggestive evidence for a schizophrenia susceptibility locus on chromosome 6q and a confirmation in an independent series of pedigrees. *Genomics* **43**, 1–8.

Dingledine, R., Borges, K., Bowie, D. & Traynelis, S.F. (1999): The glutamate receptor ion channels. *Pharmacol. Rev.* **51**, 1–61.

Egebjerg, J. & Heinemann, S.F. (1993): Ca^{2+} permeability of unedited and edited versions of the kainate selective glutamate receptor GluR6. *Proc. Natl. Acad. Sci. U.S.A.* **90**, 755–759.

Feldmeyer, D., Kask, K., Brusa, R., Kornau, H.C., Kolhekar, R., Rozov, A., Burnashev, N., Jensen, V., Hvalby, O., Sprengel, R. & Seeburg, P.H. (1999): Neurological dysfunctions in mice expressing different levels of the Q/R site-unedited AMAPR subunit GluR-B. *Nature Neurosci* **2**, 57–64.

Gerlai, R., Henderson, J.T., Roder, J.C. & Jia, Z. (1998): Multiple behavioral anomalies in GluR2 mutant mice exhibiting enhanced LTP. *Behav. Brain Res.* **95**, 37–45.

Greenberg, D.A., Durner, M., Keddache, M., Shinnar, S., Resor, S.R., Moshe, S.L., Rosenbaum, D., Cohen, J., Harden, C., Kang, H., Wallace, S., Luciano, D., Ballaban-Gil, K., Tomasini, L., Zhou, G., Klotz, I. & Dicker, E. (2000): Reproducibility and complications in gene searches: linkage on chromosome 6, heterogeneity, association, and maternal inheritance in juvenile myoclonic epilepsy. *Am. J. Hum. Genet.* **66**, 508–516.

Holmann, M. & Heinemann, S. (1994): Cloned glutamate receptors. *Annu. Rev. Neurosci.* **17**, 31–108.

Higuchi, M., Maas, S., Single, F.N., Hartner, J., Rozov, A., Burnashev, N., Feldmeyer, D., Sprengel, R. & Seeburg, P.H. (2000): Point mutation in an AMPA receptor gene rescues lethality in mice deficient in the RNA-editing enzyme ADAR2. *Nature* **406**, 78–81.

Izzi, C., Barbon, A., Kretz, R., Sander, T. & Barlati, S. (2002): Sequencing of the GRIK1 gene in patients with juvenile absence epilepsy does not reveal mutation affecting receptor structure. *Am. J. Med. Genet.* **114**, 354–359.

Izzi, C., Barbon, A., Toliat, M.R., Heils, A., Becker, C., Nurnberg, P., Sander, T. & Barlati, S. (2003): Candidate gene analysis of the human metabotropic glutamate receptor type 4 (GRM4) in patients with juvenile myoclonic epilepsy. *Am. J. Med. Genet.* **123**, 59–63.

Jamain, S., Betancur, C., Quach, H., Philippe, A., Fellous, M., Giros, B., Gillberg, C., Leboyer, M. & Bourgeron, T. (2002): Linkage and association of the glutamate receptor 6 gene with autism. *Mol. Psychiatry* **7**, 302–310.

Janz, D. (1997): The idiopathic generalized epilepsies of adolescence with childhood and juvenile age of onset. *Epilepsia* **38**, 4–11.

Kamboj, S.K., Swanson, G.T. & Cull-Candy, S.G. (1995): Intracellular spermine confers rectification on rat calcium-permeable AMPA and Kainate receptors. *J. Physiol. (Lond.)* **486**, 297–303.

Keegan, P.L., Gallo, A. & O'Connell, M.A. (2001): The many roles of an RNA editor. *Nat. Rev. Genet.* **2**, 869–878.

Kennedy, M.B. (1997). The postsynaptic density at glutamatergic synapses. *Trends Neurosci.* **20** (Suppl. 6), 264–268.

Kohler, M., Burnashev, N., Sakmann, B. & Seeburg, P.H. (1993): Determination of Ca^{2+} permeability in both TM1 and TM2 of high affinity kainate receptor channels; diversity by RNA editing. *Neuron* **10**, 491–500.

Kortenbruck, G., Berger, E., Speckmann, E.J. & Musshoff, U. (2001): RNA editing at the Q/R site for the glutamate receptor subunits GLUR2, GLUR5, and GLUR6 in hippocampus and temporal cortex from epileptic patients. *Neurobiol. Dis.* **8**, 459–468.

Levinson, D.F, Holmans, P., Straub, R.E., Owen, M.J., Wildenauer, D.B., Gejman, P.V., Pulver, A.E., Laurent, C., Kendler, K.S., Walsh, D., Norton, N., Williams, N.M., Schwab, S.G., Lerer, B., Mowry, B.J., Sanders, A.R., Antonarakis, S.E., Blouin, J.L., DeLeuze, J.F. & Mallet, J. (2000): Multicenter linkage study of schizophrenia candidate regions on chromosomes 5q, 6q, 10p, and 13q: schizophrenia linkage collaborative group III. *Am. J. Hum. Genet.* **67**, 652–663.

Lomeli, H., Sprengel, R., Laurie, D.J., Kohr, G., Herb, A., Seeburg, P.H. & Wisden, W. (1993): The rat delta-1 and delta-2 subunits extend the excitatory amino acid receptor family. *FEBS Lett.* **315**, 318–322.

Lomeli, H., Mosbacher, J., Melcher, T., Hoger, T., Geiger, J.R., Kuner, T., Monyer, H., Higuchi, M., Bach, A. & Seeburg, P.H. (1994): Control of kinetic properties of AMPA receptor channels by nuclear RNA editing. *Science* **266**, 1709–1713.

Martinez, M., Goldin, L.R., Cao, Q., Zhang, J., Sanders, A.R., Nancarrow, D.J., Taylor, J.M., Levinson, D.F., Kirby, A., Crowe, R.R., Andreasen, N.C., Black, D.W., Silverman, J.M., Lennon, D.P., Nertney, D.A., Brown, D.M., Mowry, B.J., Gershon, E.S. & Gejman, P.V. (1999): Follow-up study on a susceptibility locus for schizophrenia on chromosome 6q. *Am. J. Med. Genet.* **88**, 337–343.

McDonald, M.E., Vonsattel, J.P., Shrinidhi, J., Couropmitree, N.N., Cupples, L.A., Bird, E.D., Gusella, J.F. & Myers, R.H. (1999): Evidence for the GluR6 gene associated with younger onset age of Huntington's disease. *Neurology* **53**, 1330–1332.

Meador-Woodruff, J.H., Davis, K.L. & Haroutunian, V. (2001): Abnormal kainate receptor expression in prefrontal cortex in schizophrenia. *Neuropsychopharmacology* **24**, 545–552.

Nakanishi, S., Nakajima, Y., Masu, M., Ueda, Y., Nakahara, K. & Watanabe, D. (1998): Glutamate receptors: brain function and signal transduction. *Brain Res. Brain Res. Rev.* **26**, 230–235.

Niswender, C.M., Herrick-Davis, K., Dilley, G.E., Meltzer, H.Y., Overholser, J.C., Stockmeier, C.A., Emeson, R.B. & Sanders-Bush, E. (2001): RNA editing of the human serotonin 5-HT2C receptor. alterations in suicide and implications for serotonergic pharmacotherapy. *Neuropsychopharmacology* **24**, 478–491.

Ozawa, S., Kamiya, H. & Tsuzuki, K. (1998): Glutamate receptors in the mammalian central nervous system. *Prog. Neurobiol.* **54**, 581–618.

Porter, R.H., Eastwood, S.L. & Harrison, P.J. (1997): Distribution of kainate receptor subunit mRNAs in human hippocampus, neocortex and cerebellum, and bilateral reduction of hippocampal GluR6 and KA2 transcripts in schizophrenia. *Brain Res.* **751**, 217–231.

Rubinsztein, D.C., Leggo, J., Chiano, M., Dodge, A., Norbury, G., Rosser, E. & Craufurd, D. (1997): Genotypes at the GluR6 kainate receptor locus are associated with variation in the age of onset of Huntington disease. *Proc. Natl. Acad. Sci. USA* **94**, 3872–3876.

Sander, T., Janz, D., Ramel, C., Ross, C.A., Paschen, W., Hildmann, T., Wienker, T.F., Bianchi, A., Bauer, G. & Sailer, U. (1995): Refinement of map position of the human GluR6 kainate receptor gene (GRIK2) and lack of association and linkage with idiopathic generalized epilepsies. *Neurology* **45**, 1713–1720.

Sander, T., Bockenkamp, B., Hildmann, T., Blasczyk, R., Kretz, R., Wienker, T.F., Volz, A., Schmitz, B., Beck-Mannagetta, G., Riess, O., Epplen, J.T., Janz, D. & Ziegler, A. (1997a): Refined mapping of the epilepsy susceptibility locus EJM1 on chromosome 6. *Neurology* **49**, 842–847.

Sander, T., Hildmann, T., Kretz, R., Furst, R., Sailer, U., Bauer, G., Schmitz, B., Beck-Mannagetta, G., Wienker, T.F. & Janz, D. (1997b): Allelic association of juvenile absence epilepsy with a GluR5 kainate receptor gene (GRIK1) polymorphism. *Am. J. Med. Genet.* **74**, 416–421.

Sander, T., Schulz, H., Saar, K., Gennar, E., Riggio, M.C., Bianchi, A., Zara, F., Luna, D., Bulteau, C., Kaminska, A., Vill, D., Cieuta, C., Picard, F., Prud'homme, J.F., Bate, L., Sundquist, A., Gardiner, R.M., Janssen, G.A., de Haan, G.J., Kasteleijn, N.T.D., Bader, A., Lindhou, D., Riess, O., Wienke, T.F., Janz, D. & Reis, A. (2000): Genome search for susceptibility loci of common idiopathic generalised epilepsies. *Hum. Mol. Genet.* **9**, 1465–1472.

Sattler, R. & Tymianski, M. (2000): Molecular mechanism of calcium-dependent excitotoxicity. *J. Mol. Med.* **78**, 3–13.

Seeburg, P.H., Higuchi, M. & Sprengel, R. (1998): RNA editing of glutamate receptor channels: mechanism and physiology. *Brain Res. Rev.* **26**, 217–229.

Skerry, T.M. & Genever, P.G. (2001): Glutamate signalling in non-neuronal tissues. *Trends Pharmacol. Sci.* **22**, 971–998.

Sodhi, M.S., Burnet, P.W., Makoff, A.J., Kerwin, R.W. & Harrison, P.J. (2001): RNA editing of the 5-HT(2C) receptor is reduced in schizophrenia. *Mol. Psychiatry* **6**, 373–379.

Swanson, G.T., Feldmeyer, D., Kaneda, M. & Cull-Candy, S.G. (1996): Effect of RNA editing and subunit co-assembly single-channel properties of recombinant kainate receptors. *J. Physiol.* (Lond.) **492**, 129–142.

VanDongen, H.M. & VanDongen, A.M. (1999): Determination of membrane topology of glutamate receptors. *Methods Mol. Biol.* **128**, 155–166.

Vissel, B., Royle, G.A., Christie, B.R., Schiffer, H.H., Ghetti, A., Tritto, T., Perez-Otano, I., Radcliffe, R.A., Seamans, J., Sejnowski, T., Wehner, J.M., Collins, A.C., O'Gorman, S. & Heinemann, S.F. (2001): The role of RNA editing of kainate receptors in synaptic plasticity and seizures. *Neuron* **29**, 217–227.

Weiss, J.H. & Sensi, S.L. (2000): Ca^{2+} Zn^{2+} permeable AMPA or kainate receptors: possible key factors in selective neurodegeneration. *Trends Neurosci.* **23**, 365–371.

Autistic spectrum disorders, D. Riva and I. Rapin (eds.)

Chapter 6

Vaccines and autism: no convincing correlation

Isabelle Rapin

The Saul R. Korey Department of Neurology, the Department of Pediatrics, and the Rose F. Kennedy Center for Research in Mental Retardation and Human Development, Albert Einstein College of Medicine, 1300 Morris Park Avenue, Bronx, NY 10461, USA
rapin@aecom.yu.edu

Summary

Despite several lines of evidence that genetics plays the major causative role in autism, and morphometric and pathological evidence for prenatal effects, recent concern has arisen about potential postnatal causation or worsening of autism. These include: (1) reports of a steep increase in identified cases; (2) parents' reports of loss of or regression in language, sociability, and play between ages 18 and 24 months in about one third of children; (3) descriptions of a nodular ileocolitis in some children with autism who have gastrointestinal problems, plus a paper that stated that attenuated measles virus is detectable in their blood, and speculation that the ileocolitis renders their gut permeable to small toxic molecular precursors of neurotransmitters; and (4) the fact that measles and other vaccines contain trace amounts of ethyl mercury (thimerosal) as preservative. Evidence to the contrary is that (1) it is changing diagnostic criteria and increased awareness of the broad spectrum of autism that account for the apparent increase in the prevalence of autism; (2) several large, well conducted epidemiological studies have failed to show an increase in autism after the introduction of measles/mumps/rubella (MMR) vaccine; and (3) there are no inflammatory changes in the brains of the few individuals who have come to necropsy. Thus current evidence casts doubt on both the reality of an autistic 'epidemic', and the viral or toxic role of immunizations as causes of autism. However, until there is an understanding of the pathophysiology of language/autistic regression, doubt will persist over its causes.

Why the concern about vaccines in children with autism?

Until some five years ago, no one was concerned about immunizations as a potential culprit for autism. The pathological evidence from Bauman & Kemper (Bauman & Kemper, 1985; Kemper & Bauman, 1998), starting in 1985, pointed to subtle prenatal cellular maldevelopment in the cerebellar and limbic areas, and more recently in the neocortex (Casanova *et al.*, 2002), with no evidence of infection, inflammation, or destruction. Cross sectional imaging of the brain in children of different ages (Courchesne *et al.*, 2001) revealed atypical growth patterns, and longitudinal evidence (Courchesne *et al.*, 2003) suggested that anatomical changes arise prenatally. Other strong evidence for an innate disorder came from clinical studies of mono- and dizygotic twins, familial cases, and the relatively frequent cytogenetic abnormalities which indicate that genetic factors are a major but not the sole aetiological agent (Bailey *et al.*, 1996; Le Couteur *et al.*, 1996; Spiker *et al.*, 2002, Muhle *et al.*, 2004). The less than 10 per cent recurrence rates within sibships and increasing awareness of a broader phenotype of developmental disorders in families of affected individuals attest to the low frequency of single gene defects and point to predominantly polygenic influences (Folstein *et al.*, 1998). These findings leave no doubt that autism is not a single disorder or disease but is a behaviourally defined syndrome with a very broad range of symptoms and severity.

The term autistic spectrum disorder (ASD) is thus appropriate to encompass the range of childhood disorders that affect the development of sociability and empathy, language, communication and imagination, together with lack of behavioural and cognitive flexibility and a preference for sameness. I use ASD, or autism for short, synonymously with the term pervasive developmental disorder (PDD) adopted in the *Diagnostic and Statistical Manual of Mental Disorders* (DSM-IV) and the *International Classification of Diseases* (ICD-10). ASD is a more transparent label and is less confusing than PDD because it stresses the commonality of the behavioural symptomatology across the behavioural subtypes of PDD and also because it bespeaks biological heterogeneity.

Despite the unassailable evidence just summarized for atypical brain development as the major cause of autism, several recent factors have converged to create heightened concern about potential environmental causes of autism in at least some of the children.

A first factor is a dramatic increase in the number of children identified as having an autistic spectrum disorder (Dales *et al.*, 2001). This steep increase has been interpreted as an epidemic, raising the question of new environmental causes rather than more probable factors like changing diagnostic criteria, better educated professionals, and heightened parental awareness of the more intensive educational services available to children on the autistic spectrum than for those with other diagnoses like delayed language, emotional/behavioural problems, or mental retardation (Fombonne, 2003).

A second powerful factor is the acceptance of reports by hundreds of parents (perhaps as many as one third) that their previously normal, or more normally developing, toddler underwent a regression in language and sociability – in short became autistic or more autistic than before (Tuchman *et al.*, 1991). Analogies with some features of the much rarer but well documented association of loss of previously normal language in the context of clinical or subclinical epilepsy – the so called Landau–Kleffner syndrome or acquired epileptic aphasia – yielded epilepsy as a potential explanation for autistic/language regression (Tuchman & Rapin, 2002). If, despite strong evidence for a genetic influence playing the major aetiological role, autism makes its appearance postnatally in some toddlers or preschool children, might it be that what is inherited is a genetic vulnerability to some generally innocuous environmental influence? This idea has been bolstered by a spate of small, generally unreplicated, reports of various immune humoral and cellular abnormalities in autism (Comi *et al.*, 1999; Korvatska *et al.*, 2002).

A third factor, a thunderclap in the autism community, was Wakefield's report (Wakefield *et al.*, 1998) that he had found ileocolonic lymphonodular hyperplasia, 'a new form of inflammatory bowel disease', significantly more often in children with ASD than in controls. Autistic/language regression is most likely to occur between 18 and 24 months (Shinnar *et al.*, 2001; Sy *et al.*, 2003), by which age the average American child has been immunized against 11 infectious diseases, including live measles, mumps, and rubella (MMR) vaccine, the latter typically given at 17 and 24 months. It took but one step from the paper stating that nodular ileocolitis had been detected more often in children with autism than in those who were not autistic (Wakefield *et al.*, 2000), together with a report that the measles vaccine virus was detectable in peripheral mononuclear cells of children with autism – albeit also in rare children with other bowel diseases – and not in controls, to blaming immunization with attenuated live measles vaccine for 'regressive autism' (Kawashima *et al.*, 2000). The hypothesis was that increased permeability of the gut results in increased resorption of small molecules that may be precursors of neurotransmitters (Kidd, 2002). The potential relevance of the gut to autism was bolstered by statements that children on the autistic spectrum are more likely than controls to have symptoms suggesting abdominal discomfort, to be constipated, or have chronic diarrhoea. These reports of gastrointestinal problems added further impetus to putting children with autism on the severely restricted diets alleged by some parents to improve their behaviour.

A fourth factor is that parents and their advocates discovered that many vaccines, including hepatitis B and polio given in infancy and the infamous MMR vaccine given between 1 and 2 years, contained the preservative and antibacterial ethyl mercury (thimerosal). Although there was concern that the cumulative exposure to this organic mercury compound might exceed 100 μg by 6 months of age, blood levels are in fact very low or undetectable, and excretion in the bowel is rapid (Pichichero *et al.*, 2002). Some professionals and worried parents searched the Internet and drew parallels between their autistic children's symptoms and the symptoms of the victims of a massive industrial epidemic of methyl mercury poisoning (Minimata disease) in Japan (Bernard *et al.*, 2001). The toxicity of chronic industrial exposure to mercury, as in the Mad Hatter of *Alice in Wonderland*, is well documented; it causes cerebellar, visual, and cognitive deficits, and a neuropathy. An archival search for evidence of mercury toxicity in infancy uncovered acrodynia or pink disease (Cheek, 1985), a painful peripheral and autonomic neuropathy that vanished after mercury-containing teething powders, ointments against diaper rash, and calomel purgatives were phased out. Minimata disease resulted from dumping by a vinyl chloride factory of inorganic mercury into Minimata Bay in Japan. The upshot was contamination of fish, which transformed mercuric chloride into the more toxic methyl mercury, which over a decade progressively intoxicated several thousand fish eaters, including pregnant women and their fetuses (Kurland *et al.*, 1960). There is more recent evidence that the 7-year-old children of mothers living in the Faroe Islands, whose diet was very high in fish and whale meat and who were thus exposed to mercury *in utero* and in breast milk, have mild neuropsychologically detectable deficits, without specific mention of an increased risk of autism (Grandjean *et al.*, 2003). Whether these deficits have functional importance is not clear, especially as this effect was not found in the Seychelle Islander children of fish-eating mothers (Palumbo *et al.*, 2000). Publicity about the need to ban amalgam in teeth fillings and elemental mercury in thermometers and in industry, and a decade-long ban in the USA on the sale of bottom scavenger fish, such as sword fish, because of concern about raised levels of mercury in their flesh, probably contributed to parents' anxiety.

The parallels between autism and Minimata or pink diseases are superficial: children with autism do not have neuropathies (a hallmark of mercury poisoning), and the total ethyl mercury burden from vaccines rarely approaches, except transiently, the conservative levels set by environmental protective agencies (Pichichero *et al.*, 2002) which have, nonetheless, recommended phasing out the trace amounts of ethyl mercury (thimerosal) in vaccines, even though it is known to be less toxic than methyl mercury found in fish.

Epidemiological evidence against measles vaccination as a significant cause of autism/autistic regression

The evidence to date is that rigorous epidemiological studies in several countries have failed to yoke a presumed increase in the incidence of autism to the introduction of the MMR vaccine.

In California, Dales *et al.* (2001) reported a 373 per cent relative increase in children identified with an autistic spectrum disorder between 1980 and 1994, during which time MMR vaccine coverage increased by a mere 14 per cent. In the United Kingdom, Taylor *et al.* (1999) found no increase in the prevalence of autism before or after the introduction of MMR vaccination in 1988, no difference in children immunized before or after 18 months of age, and no difference between children who had received the vaccine and those who had not. They identified no clustering of cases of autistic regression 2 to 4 months after immunization and no increase in autistic regression 1 to 2 years or even longer after injection of the vaccine (Farrington *et al.*, 2001). There is no convincing evidence that giving combination vaccines like MMR is more dangerous than giving each agent singly (Halsey, 2001).

The most convincing epidemiological study to examine immunizations as potential contributors to autism was that carried out by Madsen and colleagues in Denmark (Madsen *et al.*, 2002). This country is unique in that it has an essentially complete registry of all medical and immunization data on the entire population, which is quite stable. They investigated all the children born between 1991 and 1998, over half a million in all, and from linked records identified all those in whom a diagnosis of autism (7.6/10,000 immunized children) or an autistic spectrum disorder (9.6/10,000) had been made. The prevalence of an autistic spectrum disorder was no higher among the 18 per cent of children who had been immunized than among those who had not received the MMR vaccine.

Conclusions

The upshot of the public's unsupported but stubborn belief that immunizations, especially the MMR vaccine, increase the risk of autism is worrisome in that many parents have refused immunizations, the consequence of which is a predictable resurgence of measles (Jansen *et al.*, 2003). The already clearly apparent inverse correlation between the proportion of immunized children and an increase in reported cases of measles and the size of measles epidemics is of great concern. Clinical measles is one of the most serious of the childhood diseases which immunization had essentially wiped out in developed countries. As is well known, the acute morbidity of measles is high, and it carries with it a 1/1000 risk of severe neurological complications, especially for immunocompromised individuals. The two most dreaded of these are acute measles encephalitis (Tyler, 2003) which is likely to leave permanent neurological and cognitive sequelae in its wake, and the fortunately much rarer because more often lethal subacute sclerosing panencephalitis (Dyken, 2001). The evidence is unconvincing that MMR vaccine is a factor, either because it contains trace amounts of mercury or because the live attenuated measles virus produces nodular ileocolitis. As stressed by one of the pioneers in the study of autism as a biological disorder, Lorna Wing (Wing & Potter, 2002): 'not one of the possible environmental causes [of autism], including MMR, has been confirmed by independent scientific investigation, whereas there is strong evidence that complex genetic factors play a major role in aetiology'.

The medical profession clearly has the important responsibility of educating the public about evidence-based causes of autism. Physicians and other professionals need to stress that the perceived increase in the prevalence of autism is in doubt, and that not one of the studies implicating immunological deficiency, MMR vaccine, or mercury poisoning sits on solid scientific evidence. Yet it is understandable that, as long as so little is known about the pathophysiology of autism and of autistic regression, parents will continue to look for potentially preventable causes and demand that research into what they consider to be risk factors, including potential inherited enhanced susceptibility to environmental influences, be carried out.

References

Bailey, A., Phillips, W. & Rutter, M. (1996): Autism: towards an integration of clinical, genetic, neuropsychological, and neurobiological perspectives. *J. Child Psychol. Psychiatry* **37**, 89–126.

Bauman, M.L. & Kemper, T.L. (1985): Histoanatomic observations of the brain in early infantile autism. *Neurology* **35**, 866–874.

Bernard, S., Enayati, A., Redwood, L., Roger, H. & Binstock, T. (2001): Autism: a novel form of mercury poisoning. *Med. Hypotheses* **56**, 462–471.

Casanova, M.F., Buxhoeveden, D.P., Switala, A.E. & Roy, E. (2002): Minicolumnar pathology in autism. *Neurology* **58**, 428–432.

Cheek, D.B. (1985): Acrodynia. In: *Practice of pediatrics*, ed. V.C. Kelley, pp. 1–12. Philadelphia: Harper and Row.

Comi, A.M., Zimmerman, A.W., Frye, V.H., Law, P.A. & Peeden, J.N. (1999): Familial clustering of autoimmune disorders and evaluation of medical risk factors in autism. *J. Child Neurol.* **14**, 388–394.

Courchesne, E., Carper, R. & Akshoomoff, N. (2003): Evidence of brain overgrowth in the first year of life in autism. *JAMA* **290**, 337–344.

Courchesne, E., Karns, C.M., Davis, H.R., Ziccardi, R., Carper, R.A., Tigue, Z.D., Chisum, H.J., Moses, P., Pierce, K., Lord, C., Lincoln, A.J., Pizzo, S., Schreibman, L., Haas, R.H., Akshoomoff, N.A. & Courchesne, R.Y. (2001): Unusual brain growth patterns in early life in patients with autistic disorder: an MRI study. *Neurology* **57**, 245–254.

Dales, L., Hammer, S.J. & Smith, N.J. (2001): Time trends in autism and in MMR immunization coverage in California. *JAMA* **285**, 1183–1185.

Dyken, P.R. (2001): Neuroprogressive disease of post-infectious origin: a review of a resurging subacute sclerosing panencephalitis (SSPE). *Ment. Retard. Dev. Disabil. Res. Rev.* **7**, 217–225.

Farrington, C.P., Miller, E. & Taylor, B. (2001): MMR and autism: further evidence against a causal association. *Vaccine* **19**, 3632–3635.

Folstein, S.E., Haines, J. & Santangelo, S.L. (1998): The genetics of autism. *Neurosci. News* **1**, 14–17.

Fombonne, E. (2003): The prevalence of autism. *JAMA* **289**, 87–89.

Grandjean, P., White, R.F., Weihe, P. & Jorgensen, P.J. (2003): Neurotoxic risk caused by stable and variable exposure to methylmercury from seafood. *Ambul. Pediatr.* **3**, 18–23.

Halsey, N.A. (2001): Combination vaccines: defining and addressing current safety concerns. *Clin. Infect. Dis.* **33** (Suppl. 4), S312-S318.

Jansen, V.A.A., Stollenwerk, N., Jensen, H.J., Ramsay, M.E., Edmunds, W.J. & Rhodes, C.J. (2003): Measles outbreaks in a population with declining vaccine uptake. *Science* **301**, 804.

Kawashima, H., Mori, T., Kashiwagi, Y., Takekuma, K., Hoshika, A. & Wakefield, A. (2000): Detection and sequencing of measles virus from peripheral mononuclear cells from patients with inflammatory bowel disease and autism. *Dig. Dis. Sci.* **45**, 723–729.

Kemper, T.L. & Bauman, M. (1998): Neuropathology of infantile autism. *J. Neuropathol. Exp. Neurol.* **57**, 645–652.

Kidd, P.M. (2002): Autism, an extreme challenge to integrative medicine. Part 1. The knowledge base. *Altern. Med. Rev.* **7**, 292–316.

Korvatska, E., Van de, W.J., Anders, T.F. & Gershwin, M.E. (2002): Genetic and immunologic considerations in autism. *Neurobiol. Dis.* **9**, 107–125.

Kurland, L.T., Faro, S.N. & Siedler, H. (1960): Minimata disease. *World Neurol.* **1**, 370–390.

Le Couteur, A., Bailey, A., Goode, S., Pickles, A., Robertson, S., Gottesman, I. & Rutter, M. (1996): A broader phenotype of autism: the clinical spectrum in twins. *J. Child Psychol. Psychiatry* **37**, 785–801.

Madsen, K.M., Hviid, A., Vestergaard, M., Schendel, D., Wohlfahrt, J., Thorsen, P., Olsen, J. & Melbye, M. (2002): A population-based study of measles, mumps, and rubella vaccination and autism. *N. Engl. J. Med.* **347**, 1477–1482.

Muhle, R., Trentacoste, S.V. & Rapin, I. (2004): The genetics of autism. *Pediatrics* **113**, e472-e486.

Palumbo, D.R., Cox, C., Davidson, P.W., Myers, G.J., Choi, A., Shamlaye, C., Sloane-Reeves, J., Cernichiari, E. & Clarkson, T.W. (2000): Association between prenatal exposure to methylmercury and cognitive functioning in Seychellois children: a reanalysis of the McCarthy Scales of Children's Ability from the main cohort study. *Environ. Res.* **84**, 81–88.

Pichichero, M.E., Cernichiari, E., Lopreiato, J. & Treanor, J. (2002): Mercury concentrations and metabolism in infants receiving vaccines containing thimerosal: a descriptive study. *Lancet* **360**, 1737–1741.

Shinnar, S., Rapin, I., Arnold, S., Tuchman, R.F., Shulman, L., Ballaban-Gil, K., Maw, M., Deuel, R.K. & Volkmar, F.R. (2001): Language regression in childhood. *Pediatr. Neurol.* **24**, 185–191.

Spiker, D., Lotspeich, L.J., Dimiceli, S., Myers, R.M. & Risch, N. (2002): Behavioral phenotypic variation in autism multiplex families: evidence for a continuous severity gradient. *Am. J. Med. Genet.* **114**, 129–136.

Sy, W., Djukic, A., Shinnar, S., Dharmani, C. & Rapin, I. (2003): Clinical characteristics of language regression in children. *Dev. Med. Child Neurol.* **45**, 508–514.

Taylor, B., Miller, E., Farrington, C.P., Petropoulos, M.C., Favot-Mayaud, I., Li, J. & Waight, P.A. (1999): Autism and measles, mumps, and rubella vaccine: no epidemiological evidence for a causal association. *Lancet* **353**, 2026–2029.

Tuchman, R.F. & Rapin, I. (2002): Epilepsy in autism. *Lancet Neurol.* **1**, 352–358.

Tuchman, R.F., Rapin, I. & Shinnar, S. (1991): Autistic and dysphasic children. I. Clinical characteristics. *Pediatrics* **88**, 1211–1218.

Tyler, H.R. (2003): Neurological complications of rubeola (measles). *Medicine* **36**, 147–167.

Wakefield, A.J., Anthony, A., Murch, S.H., Thomson, M., Montgomery, S.M., Davies, S., O'Leary, J.J., Berelowitz, M. & Walker-Smith, J.A. (2000): Enterocolitis in children with developmental disorders. *Am. J. Gastroenterol.* **95**, 2285–2295.

Wakefield, A.J., Murch, S.H., Anthony, A., Linnell, J., Casson, D.M., Malik, M., Berelowitz, M., Dhillon, A.P., Thomson, M.A., Harvey, P., Valentine, A., Davies, S.E. & Walker-Smith, J.A. (1998): Ileal-lymphoid-nodular hyperplasia, non-specific colitis, and pervasive developmental disorder in children. *Lancet* **351**, 637–641.

Wakefield, A.J., Anthony, A., Murch, S.H, Thomson, M., Montgomery, S.M., Davies, S., O'Leary, J.J., Berelowitz, M. & Walker-Smith, J.A. (2000): Enterocolitis in children with developmental disorders. *Am. J. Gastroenterol.* **95**, 2285–2295.

Wing, L. & Potter, D. (2002): The epidemiology of autistic spectrum disorders: is the prevalence rising? *Ment. Retard. Dev. Disabil. Res. Rev.* **8**, 151–161.

Autistic spectrum disorders, D. Riva and I. Rapin (eds.)

Chapter 7

Asperger syndrome: clinical picture of deficits focused on language

Charles Njiokiktjien[1], Leo de Sonneville[2] and Catharina Anna Verschoor[2]

[1] *Developmental Dysphasia Foundation, WG-Plein 316, NL-1054 SG Amsterdam, The Netherlands;*
[2] *Department of Child Neuropsychology, Pediatric outpatients clinic, Free University Medical Centre, PO Box 7057, NL-1007 MB Amsterdam, The Netherlands*
cn@suyi.nl

Summary

Asperger's syndrome (AS) is a subtype of autism in high-functioning people. The clinical symptoms of AS include abnormal social relatedness and a restricted range of behaviours and interests, and exclude marked formal spoken language disorders (developmental dysphasia). Underlying deficits are present in the following neuropsychological domains: 1. Body language (facial identity recognition; emotion recognition of face as well as whole body; expressive flatness in face, body and voice), 2. Executive functions (difficult mental set and intermodal attention shifting, including obsessional activities) 3. Motor functions (constructive dyspraxia) as well as minor handmotor signs and axial clumsiness, 4. Sensory functions (hypo- and hypersensitivities). 5. Learning (more non-verbal than verbal problems). 6. Language (receptive and expressive semantic-pragmatic deficits and affective prosody included). Each of these domains may also be (partially) dysfunctional beyond AS. In that case the disorder is not accompanied by a severe lack of understanding of other people's intentions and feelings and insufficient reciprocity. We will discuss the clinical picture and its pathogenesis and focus on the differential diagnosis of the spoken language disorders.

What is Asperger syndrome? Introduction

The syndrome is named after the Viennese physician Hans Asperger (1944) who was the first to publish the clinical picture under the name 'autistic psychopaths'.

As 'autos' (αυτός) is the Greek word for 'self' and autism means 'being by yourself', it seems to us that a brief, acceptable clinical definition of autistic behaviour could be 'deficient or absent social relatedness'. This definition places the developmental disorder Asperger syndrome (AS) on the autism spectrum. The syndrome is not only accepted as a mild subtype of autism (Green, 1990; Tantam, 1988; Tsatmari *et al.*, 1989; Wing, 1981), but it has also been argued that the name should be retained and Asperger syndrome should continue to be seen as a clinical entity with specific characteristics, which include genetic traits, a better prognosis and a higher prevalence rate than autism with more severe verbal components (Ehlers & Gillberg, 1993; Ozonoff *et al.*, 1991).

AS is not only a 'stand alone' genetic disorder, it may be seen in mild or covert forms in so called right hemisphere deficit syndrome, equivalent to the non-verbal learning disability (NLD) profile, which is a behavioral phenotypic trait of some known syndromes. NLD will be discussed farther along.

Language dysfunction in AS is under debate. Most children have a semantic-pragmatic language disorder (SPLD). We will discuss ways to consider the nature of this disorder and how to look at it in apparently non-autistic children. Our ideas on this issue have been guided by the literature and our own studies.

As is known today, AS is based on several neuropsychological deficits, for the majority of which the pathophysiologic mechanisms are approximately known. How these deficits interrelate and how they come into being, *e.g.* by genetic mechanisms, is less well understood and will be discussed elsewhere in this volume. The neuropsychological deficits of AS symptoms will be briefly mentioned.

The clinical picture of Asperger syndrome

The clinical picture of AS, summarized in the abstract, includes abnormal social relatedness and a restricted range of behaviours and highly specialized interests, and excludes marked formal spoken language disorders and other significant cognitive deficits and neuropsychiatric disorders. Throughout the literature there are small differences depending on whether one looks at the work of individual authors (Ehlers & Gilberg, 1993; Tantam, 1988; Tsatmari *et al.*, 1989), or at diagnostic criteria in DSM-IV (American Psychiatric Association, 1994) or ICD-10 (World Health Organization, 1992). Many authors today refine their diagnoses by the use of formalized parent interviews such as the ADI-R (Lord *et al.*, 1994). In this chapter we will review in brief what is today considered as the clinical picture, supplemented by our own study, and will focus on the SPLD.

Body language (facial identity recognition; expressive and receptive emotion processing, face as well as whole body language)

We wondered whether children with AS have agnosias pertaining to various aspects of the non-verbal or body language. In a previous study (Njiokiktjien *et al.*, 2001) anamnestic data and observation of three boys, diagnosed as AS autists, suggested a severe lack of comprehension of emotions in other people. With a set of computerized tests developed to evaluate speed and accuracy of processing facial emotion information (De Sonneville *et al.*, 2002), we were able to show that our patients do have problems in perceiving basic facial emotions, especially the negative ones (anger, fear and sadness), in the absence of other visuospatial processing deficits. Identification is sometimes performed by reasoning after detection of a detail. Some children have only covert perception problems, reflected by very slow reaction times for all or for some emotions. This study corroborated other research (Langdell, 1978; Tantam *et al.*, 1989). Hobson's studies showed that autistic children are impaired in the ability to appropriately link drawn or photographed faces with videotaped emotional gestures and voices (Hobson, 1986a), or to link drawn gestures with faces on video (Hobson, 1986b) and also faces with voices (Hobson *et al.*, 1988). This means a lack of coherent processing of emotional signals, called lack of central coherence (Frith, 1989). Weeks & Hobson (1987) clearly stated that autistic children tend to be insensitive to other people's facial expression of emotions. Macdonald *et al.* (1989) also stressed the disturbed expression of emotions in autists. Some children even have prosopagnosia (Kracke, 1994; Njiokiktjien *et al.*, 2001), which seems rare. Developmental prosopagnosia may occur without clinical autism. Most authors feel that the difficulty in processing emotions in body language is not restricted to AS, but occurs in other autists as well.

Lack of empathy has been considered a central characteristic of AS. The lack of emotion perception may also lead to a lack of affective empathy, because one cannot feel what other people feel when one ignores overt signs of these feelings. The adoption of the point of view of others has been called cognitive empathy or having a 'theory of mind'. Impaired empathy in individuals with AS may be due to impaired integration of the cognitive and affective facets of the other person's mental state (Shamay-Tsoori *et al.*, 2002), another aspect of lacking central coherence.

Difficult mental set shifting and lack of quick intermodality attention shifting

The mental set is rigid in children with AS. This is an executive dysfunction that hinders the child in daily life, making it difficult to switch easily from one situation to another or from one thought to another, especially on command of the environment. This probably also means that a person with AS is unable to switch from his own to another people's viewpoint (cognitive empathy). Kinsbourne (1991) has put forward the concept of overfocused attention disorder (OFAD, acronym of author CN), the description of which resembles mental set rigidity. Mental set rigidity/OFAD may also occur in non-autistic children with developmental disorders and has to be differentiated from stubbornness in toddlers. In children with AS, the difficulty of set shifting might also be explained as secondary to anxiety about encountering new people or situations, whereas mental set rigidity as an executive dysfunction pertains probably more to disengagement problems.

Quick intermodality attention shifting has been tested on a simple level with auditory and visual stimuli. This has been proven to be slow in cerebellar non-autistic patients, in non-AS autists, in children with AS and in non-autistic children with Williams syndrome (Lincoln, 2002). This is a different level of mental shifting with another neural substrate – possible Purkinje cell abnormalities in the cerebellar vermis –, but again this dysfunction can occur in AS as well as in non-autistic people.

Repetitive patterns, interests, rituals and other special activities such as collecting strange things possibly belong to difficult mental set shifting, but these activities also enable the child to focus on details and to avoid social contacts.

Complex motor function (constructive dyspraxia)

In the motor domain one may see many children with AS having tics. In fact, there is a considerable overlap between AS and Tourette syndrome (TS). In our study we also saw tics in other autists. Children with TS often also have an NLD profile of right hemisphere (RH) dysfunction and children with TS often have traits of ADHD (Nass & Gutman, 1997). Whereas ADHD points to RH dysfunction (Njiokiktjien & Verschoor, 1998), NLD, AS, TS, and ADHD overlap on account of certain RH dysfunctions.

Motor function in the proper sense is also abnormal. There are reports of stiff and awkward gait with uncoordinated posture.

Clumsiness, usually mentioned without specification, may be interpreted in several ways. Nass & Gutman (1997) found numerous soft signs such as overflow movements and dysrhythmicity in five boys with AS. Children with NLD and AS often have leftsided handmotor clumsiness, but also poor visuospatial perception and as a result constructive dyspraxia. Finally, lack of visual imagination in AS leads to impoverished ideomotor praxis and play.

There is still debate on whether the definition of AS should include clumsiness. For example, clumsiness is included in ICD-10, but not in DSM-IV. According to Ghaziuddin *et al.* (1994) clumsiness is not specific for AS, because it also occurs in other autists. We have the same experience.

Sensory function (hypo- and hypersensitivities)

There are many hyper and hyposensitivities for taste, and for tactile and auditory stimuli in children with AS, *e.g.* they are afraid of loud noises. Certain children with AS are totally indifferent to tastes or they have special preferences, whereas some even have an agnosia for tastes and/or smells (Njiokiktjien *et al.*, 2001b).

Learning (more non-verbal than verbal problems)

Learning may be variable and depend on IQ. Children with NLD, and as a consequence children with AS, are often easily distracted and have attention deficits for complex stimuli. They have a tendency to focus overly on details. They have problems with arithmetic, more than with verbal tasks, when memory plays a role. Reading comprehension might be difficult, when complex thoughts are included in the text. Some of the children with AS are, on the contrary, highly gifted in physics, chess and mathematics.

Spoken language (semantic-pragmatic deficits, receptive and expressive pragmatic and affective prosody included)

Lorna Wing (1981) was the first to make AS better known to the clinical world. She found that about one half of her 34 patients with AS had slow speech acquisition. She also found that language was grammatically correct, but often rote and unoriginal. Thereafter, many reports point to the fact that children with AS, although they may speak correctly in the linguistic sense, show signs of SPLD.

Pilot study with 26 schoolchildren referred with autistic-like symptoms

Methods

We did a study with 26 high-functioning autistic children (aged 9 to 14). There was one girl with PDD, and one girl with autism. The clinical diagnosis, made by the first author, was verified by DSM-IV criteria. Separate ADI-R interviews by a third person, uninformed of the clinical diagnosis, were performed. Children were assessed with neuropsychological tests, computerized tasks for facial emotion and identity recognition (De Sonneville *et al.*, 2001) and underwent speech and language tests. All the methods are described in a previous publication (Njiokiktjien, 2001b). We focused on the speech-language domain *(Table 1)*.

Table 1. Three subgroups of HFA children and their language deficit profiles

Subgroups	Early language delay	Expressive & receptive deficit	Developmental dysphasia	Semantic-pragmatic disorder
PDD-NOS	2	0	2	6
Autism	5	5	8	7
Asperger S.	3	0	0	8

Results

The results are shown in *Table 1*. The 26 patients could be divided in three HFA subgroups. Using the ADI-R, 16 children were diagnosed as autistic, which leaves nine children with PDD. The language criterium has placed eight of the autistic children in the AS group because they had no formal linguistic deficits. Whereas the definition already selects for language characteristics, there were no AS children with developmental dysphasia or expressive/receptive deficits (as defined in the section on developmental dysphasia below). All children with AS had SPLD, and of these only two children had an early and transient speech language delay. SPLD could be recognized in 13 of the remaining 18 children as well. All 26 children had overt or covert problems with facial emotion recognition. Interestingly, in each of the subgroups, three children had tics.

What is semantic-pragmatic language disorder (SPLD)?

Semantic-pragmatic deficits were recognized by Rapin & Allen (1982) as a separate category of developmental language disorders, named 'semantic-pragmatic syndrome'. Bishop & Rosenbloom (1987) called the same language deficits 'semantic-pragmatic disorders'.

Both Rapin & Allen (1982) and Bishop (1989) describe the clinical picture of the SPLD. Children are delayed in speech acquisition but after this they are fluent and articulate clearly, although children with AS (Shriberg *et al.*, 2001) and children with NLD (Rourke, 1986) make residual speech sound distortion errors. Usually children with SPLD have a good rote memory, so that they can learn by heart what they essentially do not understand, and sometime they are hyperlexic. Rapin & Allen (1982) found echolalia in young children. In these young children, receptive difficulties may dominate the clinical picture, but this will improve considerably. Comprehension problems are still present in these children when language becomes complex, especially when a metalinguistic language content and language with implied meaning is offered to them, *e.g.* in humour or metaphors. Children, as is heard in their answers, understand this kind of language in an over-literal way. Questions are often not understood and get answered in a strange way. Usually children with NLD as well as children with SPLD speak a lot, and they are verbose without taking the listener into account. They do not match the listener's messages.

There is only scarce literature about the development of pragmatics. A review of Bara *et al.* (1999) concludes that two factors play a role in the emergence of pragmatic competence: the ability to attribute mental states to others and the ability to construct and manipulate representations of communicative interaction. According to Perkins (1998) pragmatics is seen as the consequence of interactions between a set of linguistic and non-linguistic cognitive subsystems. Pragmatic aspects like turn-taking, initiating and sustaining a conversation, but also prosodic understanding and expression are a problem for children with AS. Their expressive speech is pedantic, monotonous and has peculiar voice characteristics.

Why literal understanding prevails over other, more complex or abstract interpretations, when children with AS interpret metaphors, is neurologically mysterious. Possibly there is a deficit in connecting several verbal signals in the story heard and a failure to connect these in turn to body language. This seems to involve a lack of central coherence and makes these children rely on their first, infantile, literal meaning.

As yet, there are no tests for diagnosing SPLD. Rapin and Allen (1982) pointed to marked problems in continuous discourse. Observation and analysis of conversational behaviour is the best method used as yet.

Clinical occurrence and differential diagnosis of SPLD

SPLD is usually associated with autism. However, Rapin & Allen (1982) found that this syndrome could occur in children without autism, such as in hydrocephalus as well as in rare isolated familial cases. In her article 'Asperger's syndrome and semantic pragmatic disorder: Where are the boundaries' Bishop (1989) posits an implicit difference with questionable boundaries between three clinical pictures: autism, AS and semantic-pragmatic disorder. The last disorder, however, is more a symptom that, nosologically, is not equivalent to a syndrome like AS. This symptom can occur in non-autistic children or be part of AS.

SPLD occurs in AS, that always has, according to some authors, a profile of NLD/RH deficit (discussed below). The profile of NLD can be found, interestingly, in AS, but also in classified syndromes and hydrocephalus. These conditions are also the ones associated with semantic-pragmatic deficits without marked autism.

Children with AS have SPLD. One is inclined to think that this way of using language is caused in part by the autistic key condition of absent social reciprocity and empathy. The poor pragmatic use of language is intertwined with poor eye contact and understanding of emotional facial and body language. Thus deficient semantic-pragmatic language and deficient non-verbal language reinforce each other (see Perkins, 1998 in the previous section).

It might be that a lack of understanding of emotional facial and body language as well as lacking empathy are also the case in hydrocephalus (Swisher & Pinsker, 1971) or Williams syndrome (Udwin, Yule & Martin, 1987, Volterra *et al.*, 1996). This has to our knowledge never been assessed. However, children with Williams syndrome have outstanding musical hearing and rhythmic abilities (Levitin & Bellugi, 1998) and possibly a normal prosody; they rely on hearing in communication. This makes these children less autistic than AS, because they are able to compensate for other body language deficits.

Finally we have to differentiate SPLD from other developmental language disorders (next section).

The pathogenetic brain mechanism of SPLD is unknown as yet, let alone a comprehensive theory of what this language disorder is. Some hypotheses and causal explanations of pragmatic difficulties can be found in a recent review by Martin & McDonald (2003).

Developmental dysphasia

In the literature people have used the term developmental dysphasia (DD), now replaced by specific language impairment (SLI), defined as receptive and/or expressive language deficits without any other non-verbal problem. This definition is too wide.

DD is defined by us in a narrower sense and the term is essentially used for a developmental expressive speech-language disorder, most resembling the phonologic-syntactic syndrome (Rapin & Allen, 1982) and the DSM subtype expressive language disorder 315.31. Thus, by definition, receptive language is higher in DD. Expression shows clinically deviant features, not present in younger children (Njiokiktjien, 1988). There is often also a discrepancy between language comprehension and the rest of the person's cognitive development. The clinical core symptom of DD is a disturbance in the transition from the observed object, the memory, the feeling, the thought, or the idea to the spoken word, to story-telling and to overt speech in general, but also to inner speech. Word-finding and fluency problems are core symptoms and so striking that one tends to view the entire clinical picture of DD as a verbal memory retrieval disorder.

Story-telling often takes place chaotically; we call this a disordered 'liaison des idées' (lack of discourse cohesion). This is accompanied by recurrent hesitation and word-finding problems, which occur more frequently when children are urged to speak in dialogue than when speaking spontaneously. Children have typical verbalization problems in the 'on command' situation. The quality of speech also depends on the general cognitive level. Although they nearly always occur together in young children (in these children language = speech), all these expressive linguistic characteristics have to be distinguished from the clearness and the speed of speech (oral motor praxis).

Articulation, sentence construction (morphosyntax), verbal short-term memory, auditory perception and language comprehension skills can exhibit great variation and can influence the entire clinical picture. The combination of these symptoms along with the core symptoms is what determines the linguistic sub-typing of DD. In this view DD is not a unitary condition.

Although DD is essentially an expressive complex of deficits, receptive problems may occur. Even in so-called mixed receptive-expressive DLD (developmental language disorders), many children have traits of developmental dysphasia in the sense described above. The lower the non-verbal IQ, and the more retarded the child is, the lower is the receptive level. It must be stressed, however, that many children with severe receptive deficits are not autistic.

So-called mute-autistic children (Rapin & Allen, 1982) without speech and without any understanding may have only basic eye contact, body language and cuddling behaviour. They are essentially not autists, but grow into autism because of the absence of semantic function and deficits in other non-verbal functions such as praxis.

DD is the most frequently occurring DLD; children with DD are not autistic. On the contrary, children with DD try harder to make contact, by looking at the face and lips and by excessive gesturing. However, DD does not exclude autism. Many lower-functioning autistic children indeed have DD or mixed receptive expressive DLD with DD traits. Moreover, there are autistic children who show a regression of speech at around the age of two and become mute. Conversely, children with severe expressive problems may withdraw from social contact and begin to show autistic features or a worsening of autistic features that are already present. After treatment of DD, social contact may improve.

The concept of non-verbal learning disabilities (NLD)

Since the 1980s, neurologists (Voeller, 1986; Weintraub & Mesulam, 1983) have recognized what is called right hemisphere (RH) deficit syndrome, in which the patients have left-sided motor and sensory signs as well as certain cognitive and behavioural deficits. At the same time, psychologists (Myklebust, 1975; Rourke, 1995) became aware of a specific psychological test profile in schoolchildren, described as non-verbal learning disability (NLD). They found motor and sensory deficits on the left side, as well. In fact both RH deficit syndrome and NLD converge; the RH seems to be an important common deviant neural substrate for the majority of the symptoms.

NLD entails much better verbal functions, especially rote verbal memory. There are dyscalculia, visuospatial and haptic dysfunction, gestalt agnosia, constructive dyspraxia, and handmotor soft neurological signs, as well as problems in behaviour and contact. Learning is slow, especially when concept formation is required; this pertains to spoken language, to praxis and to learning at school. Often there are comorbid symptoms such as being frightened by novelty, or showing mental inflexibility, and autistic contact avoidance.

Rourke points to a typical ontogenetic course in NLD children. As babies and toddlers they acquire motor and speech milestones somewhat late and they do not explore much. Thereafter there is catch-up in speech and locomotion, but complex new motor learning is slow and there are attention deficits. At school age, beginning reading progresses slowly, reading comprehension is below standard and mathematical concepts are acquired slowly. In the years that follow, spoken language and reading become significantly better. After kindergarten, children with NLD speak fluently and are talkative, but the content of what they say does not always make sense and their use of language resembles that found in SPLD. Mathematics (dyscalculia) as well as general concept acquisition and social contact become worse.

NLD occurs as a behavioural phenotype in certain syndromes such as Turner syndrome, velo-cardiofacial (VCF or Shprintzen) syndrome, Williams syndrome and hydrocephalus. Children with hydrocephalus often have a relatively low performance IQ (Dennis *et al.*, 1981) and they are socially isolated (Kokkonen *et al.*, 1994). Interestingly, the NLD profile occurs in AS, and authors (*e.g.* Rourke, 1995; Gunter *et al.*, 2002) state that all children with AS have an NLD profile, which implies RH dysfunction.

In some NLD children there is a regression of function at school age: the performance IQ can go down 20 to 50 points in the course of a few years. NLD occurs more often in girls than in boys. Neither of these characteristics, however, was seen by us in our studies of AS.

Rourke (1995) proposed on several grounds, *e.g.* Goldberg and Costa's (1981) concept of the dominant role of the RH for learning, that NLD is caused by RH dysfunction, notably a 'white matter' disorder in the RH. In our view, pathology of the 'white matter' should be interpreted as abnormal 'connectivity', not primarily as abnormal myelin. Whether the developmental dysfunctions in NLD are associated with interhemispheric and/or intrahemispheric variations in cortical connectivity, may be elucidated by EEG coherence functions. We have confirmed the hypothesis of RH hypoconnection in NLD (Njiokiktjien *et al.*, 2001a), demonstrating that children with NLD have lower intrahemispheric coherences in the RH in the gamma band (28–50 Hz) and that a control clinical group with verbal learning disability (developmental dysphasia without non-verbal comorbidity or autism) does not show this.

Many clinical features of AS converge with the profile of NLD, including abnormal interpretation and expression of affect. The RH seems to be an important common deviant neural substrate for the majority of the symptoms. This common location does not sufficiently answer the question why, in a person with AS, known to occur in both males and females, several domains are all simultaneously dysfunctional. Deficient 'central coherence', proposed by Frith (1989), i.e. poor gestalt processing and concept formation, might explain several clinical symptoms and, consequently, is a candidate for psychophysiological and genetic enquiry.

Conclusion

SPLD is a disorder of language use, reflecting a deficit in understanding of metalinguistic and metaphoric language. It has pragmatic aspects such as absent lack of turn-taking, poor taking into account other peoples' viewpoints, and dysprosody, receptive and/or expressive. Although formal language is fluent and correct, the SPLD may give rise to communicative misunderstanding and hinders social relatedness. If the disorder is mild and 'stands alone' ('specific', Bishop, 1989) there might not be clinical autism. When deficits in social contact, such as mental rigidity and poor body language interaction, co-occur, social relatedness becomes so poor that the clinical threshold for the autism spectrum will be reached.

SPLD seems to be the core language deficit in autists and, if not confounded by other expressive or receptive DLD, is most clear in AS. By definition, in other autists, especially the lower-functioning ones, the majority also have other DLDs. So, SPLD is not located on a continuum with developmental dysphasia but seems, rather, comorbid to it.

References

American Psychiatric Association (1994): *DSM IV-Diagnostic and statistical manual of mental disorders*. 4th ed. Washington DC: American Psychiatric Association.

Asperger, H. (1944): Die 'Autistischen Psychopathen' im Kindesalter. *Arch. Psychiatr. Nervenkrankh.* **117**, 76–136.

Bara, B.G., Bosco, R.M. & Bucciarelli, M. (1999): Developmental pragmatics in normal and abnormal children [Review]. *Brain Lang.* **68**, 507–528.

Bishop, D.V.M. (1989): Autism, Asperger's syndrome and semantic-pragmatic disorder: where are the boundaries? *Br. J. Dis. Commun.* **24**, 107–121.

Bishop, D.V.M. & Rosenbloom, L. (1987): Classification of childhood language disorders In: *Language development and disorders*, eds. W. Yule & M. Rutter. Clinics in Developmental Medicine. No. 101/102, pp. 16–41. London: McKeith Press.

Dennis, M., Fitz, Ch. R., Netley, Ch.T., Sugar, J., Harwood-Nash, D.C.F., Hendrick, E.B., Hoffman, H.J. & Humphreys, R.P. (1981): The intelligence of hydrocephalic children. *Arch. Neurol.* **38**, 607–615.

De Sonneville, L.M.J., Verschoor, C.A., Njiokiktjien, C., Op het Veld, V. & Toorenaar, N. (2002): Facial identity and facial emotions: speed, accuracy and processing strategies in children and adults. *J. Clin. Exp. Neuropsychol.* **24**, 200–213.

Ehlers, S. & Gillberg, C. (1993): The epidemiology of Asperger syndrome. A total population study. *J. Child Psychol. Psychiat.* **34**, 1327–1350.

Ghaziuddin, M., Butler, E., Tsai, L. & Ghazziuddin, L. (1994): Is clumsiness a marker for Asperger syndrome? *J. Intell. Disab. Res.* **38**, 519–27.

Goldberg, E. & Costa, L.D. (1981): Hemisphere differences in the acquisition and use of descriptive systems. *Brain Lang.* **14**, 144–73.

Green, J. (1990): Is Asperger's a syndrome? *Dev. Med. Child Neurol.* **32**, 743–747.

Gunter, H.L., Ghaziuddin, M. & Ellis, H.D. (2002): Asperger syndrome: tests of right hemisphere functioning and interhemispheric communication. *J. Autism Dev. Dis.* **32**, 263–281.

Hobson, R.P. (1986a): The autistic child's appraisal of expressions of emotion. *J. Child Psychol. Psychiat.* **27**, 321–342.

Hobson, R.P. (1986b): The autistic child's appraisal of expressions of emotion: a further study. *J. Child Psychol. Psychiat.* **27**, 671–680.

Hobson, R.P., Ouston, J. & Lee, A. (1988): Emotion recognition in autism: coordinating faces and voices. *Psychological Medicine* **18**, 911–923.

Kinsbourne, M. (1990): Overfocusing: an apparent subtype of attention deficit-hyperactivity disorder. In: *Pediatric neurology: behavior and cognition of the child with brain dysfunction*, eds. N. Amir, I. Rapin and D. Branski, pp. 18–35. Basel: Karger.

Kokkonen, J., Serio, W., Saukkonen, A-L. & Juolasmaa, A. (1994): Long-term prognosis for children with shunted hydrocephalus. *Child's Nerv. Syst.* **10**, 384–387.

Kracke, I. (1994): Developmental prosopagnosia in Asperger syndrome: presentation and discussion of an individual case. *Med. Child Neurol.* **36**, 873–86.

Langdell, T. (1978): Recognition of faces: an approach to the study of autism. *J. Child Psychol. Psychiat.* **19**, 255–268.

Levitin, D.J. & Bellugi, U. (1998): Musical abilities in individuals with Williams syndrome [Review]. *Music Perception* **15**, 357–89.

Lincoln, A., Lai, Z. & Jones, W. (2002): Shifting attention and joint attention dissociation in Williams syndrome: implications for the cerebellum and social deficits in autism. *Neurocase* **8**, 226–32.

Lord, C., Rutter, M. & Le Couteur, A. (1994): Autism diagnostic interview–revised: a revised version of a diagnostic interview for caregivers of individuals with possible pervasive developmental disorder. *J. Autism Dev. Disord.* **24**, 659–75.

McDonald, H., Rutter, M., Howlin, P., Rios, P., Le Conteur, A., Evered, C. & Folstein, S. (1989): Recognition and expression of emotional cues by autistic and normal adults. *J. Child Psychol. Psychiat.* **30**, 865–877.

Martin, I. & McDonald, S. (2003): Weak coherence, no theory of mind, or executive dysfunction? Solving the puzzle of pragmatic language disorders. *Brain Lang.* **85**, 451–466.

Myklebust, H.R. (1975): Non-verbal learning disabilities: assessment and intervention. In: *Progress in learning disabilities.* Vol. III, ed. HR Myklebust, pp. 85–121. New York: Grune and Stratton.

Nass, R. & Gutman, R. (1997): Boys with Asperger's disorder, exceptional verbal intelligence, tics and clumsiness. *Dev. Med. Child Neurol.* **39**, 691–695.

Njiokiktjien, C. & Verschoor, C.A. (1998): Attention and the right hemisphere. *J. Human Physiol.* **24**, 145–151.

Njiokiktjien, C., de Rijke, W. & Jonkman, E.J. (2001a): Children with non-verbal learning disabilities (NLD): coherence values in the resting state may reflect hypofunctional long distance connections in the right hemisphere. *Hum. Physiol.* **27**, 17–22.

Njiokiktjien, C., Verschoor, C.A., de Sonneville, L., Huyser, C., Op het Vekld, V. & Toorenaar, N. (2001b): Disordered recognition of facial identity and emotions in three Asperger type autists. *Eur. J. Child Adol. Psych.* **10**, 79–90.

Ozonoff, S., Pennington, B.F. & Rogers, S.J. (1991): Asperger's syndrome: evidence of an empirical distinction from high-functioning autism. *J. Child Psychol. Psychiat.* **32**, 1107–1122.

Perkins, M.R. (1998): Is pragmatics epiphenomenal evidence from communication disorders? *J. Pragm.* **29**, 291–311.

Rapin, I. & Allen, D.A. (1982): Developmental language disorders: nosologic considerations. In: *Neuropsychology of language, reading and spelling*, eds. I. Rapin & D.A. Allen, pp. 157–86. New York: Academic Press.

Rourke, B.P. (1995): *Syndrome of non-verbal learning disabilities: neurodevelopmental manifestations.* New York: Guilford Press.

Frith, U. (1989): *Autism: explaining the enigma.* Oxford: Basil Blackwell.

Shamay-Tsoori, S.O., Tomer, R., Yaniv, S. *et al.* (2002): Empathy deficits in Asperger syndrome: a cognitive profile. *Neurocase* **8**, 245–252.

Shriberg, L.D., Paul, R., McSweeny, J.L., Klin, A., Cohen, D.J. & Volkmar, F.R. (2001): Speech and prosody characteristics of adolescents and adults with high-functioning autism and Asperger syndrome. *J. Speech Lang. Hearing Res.* **44**, 1097–1115.

Swisher, L.P. & Pinsker, E.J. (1971): The language characteristics of hyperverbal hydrocephalic children. *Dev. Med. Child Neurol.* **13**, 746–755.

Szatmari, P., Bremner, R. & Nagi, L. (1989): Asperger's syndrome: a review of clinical features. *Can. J. Psychiat.* **34**, 554–560.

Tantam, D. (1988): Asperger's syndrome. Annotation. *J. Child Psychol. Psychiat.* **29**, 245–255.

Voeller, K.K.S. (1986): Right-hemisphere deficit syndrome in children. *Am. J. Psychiat.* Vol. 143, pp. 1004–1009.

Volterra, V., Capirci, O., Pezzini, O. *et al.* (1996): Linguistic abilities in Italian children with Williams syndrome. *Cortex* **32**, 663–77.

Weeks, S.J. & Hobson, P. (1987): The salience of facial expression far autistic children. *J. Child Psychol. Psychiat.* **28**, 137–152.

Weintraub, S. & Mesulam, M.M. (1983): Developmental learning disabilities of the right hemisphere: emotional, interpersonal, and cognitive components. *Arch. Neurol.* **40**, 463–468.

Wing, L. (1981): Asperger's syndrome: a clinical account. *Psychol. Med.* **11**, 115–129.

World Health Organization (1992): *International classification of diseases. 10th revision.* (May 1990 draft for field trials) Geneva: WHO.

Autistic spectrum disorders, D. Riva and I. Rapin (eds.)
© 2005 John Libbey Eurotext, pp. 61–67.

Chapter 8

Clinical and genetic observations on early-onset Tourette syndrome with reversible autistic behaviour (dysmaturational syndrome)

Michele Zappella

Section of Child Neuropsychiatry, Siena General Hospital, viale Bracci, 53100 Siena, Italy
m.zappella@ao-siena.toscana.it

Summary

Early-onset Tourette syndrome with reversible autistic behaviour is described in a group of 14 children, including a pair of concordant monozygotic twins and a girl belonging to a heterozygotic twin couple, discordant for the disorder. Tics were present in six parents, confirming the genetic component of the disorder. Its clinical features and course were identical to previous studies, while the autistic regression was slightly less severe and the outcome at follow-up more favourable. In the monozygotic twins the disorder was similar in the two children, with only minor differences. Compared with previous studies, these data suggest a spectrum of severity both in the regression and in the outcome of this disorder. Regression could be related to fluctuating dysfunction in the brain area responsible for tics but also for impaired social interaction and communication.

Introduction

Early-onset Tourette syndrome with reversible autistic behaviour (or dysmaturational syndrome) has been the subject of a series of articles over the past 10 years involving 71 subjects in all (Zappella, 1994; 1996; 1999; 2002). Available data suggest that this syndrome almost always occurs in males, is often accompanied by familial tics, and is characterized by initially normal development, followed by regression with autistic features and the appearance of multiple motor and vocal tics between 1 and 2 years of age. As a consequence of treatment, principally carried out by the parents, the child loses the autistic features and recovers normal mental abilities, but usually remains affected by Tourette syndrome, accompanied in most cases by attention deficit-hyperactivity disorder (ADHD). More data have accrued over the past 4 years, including a pair of concordant monozygotic twins, adding further information about this disorder, in which a persistent form of Tourette syndrome with ADHD is apparently co-morbid with potentially reversible autistic behaviour. These observations are described in this chapter.

Patient evaluation and methods

Among the children attending the Section of Child Neuropsychiatry in Siena, those described in this article were selected as follows: they had been examined from January 2000 to December 2003; their ages were below 5½ years; they had an initial diagnosis of autism or pervasive developmental disorder (PDD); they showed the presence of tics; and the autistic features subsequently disappeared. None of these children have been reported before. A minimum follow-up of 1 year and a final outcome with normal abilities, evaluated either through formal testing or by clinical observation, were additional prerequisites for inclusion in this series. The majority (n = 10) were seen as outpatients, the minority (n = 4) were repeatedly admitted to the ward. Within the latter subgroup there were a pair of monozygotic twins and a girl who had a heterozygotic twin; only in these three cases were retrospective criteria for autistic behaviour accepted for reporting in this article, but they were not included in the main series. The children's ages at the first visit ranged from 2 years 1 month to 4 years 1 month (average 2 years 10 months). The follow-up lasted from 1 to 4 years (average 2 years 3 months). Their physical, neurological, and psychiatric examination was conducted by me as well as by another child neuropsychiatrist in the four cases seen as inpatients, and the results were concordant. DSM-IV assessment for autistic behaviour and the autism behaviour checklist (ABC) were carried out at the initial and final visits. At the first visit the child's general abilities were evaluated with the help of the Portage checklist; at the final visit IQ measurement was obtained through the Wechsler Intelligence Scale for Children-Revised (WISC-R) in five cases. In the other cases the evaluation relied on the Portage checklist for those under 6 years and on clinical and anamnestic information for social and scholastic attainments. The personal history of the child was obtained from both parents, who were also interviewed for mental disorders and, in particular, for tics, ADHD, obsessive-compulsive disorder, and mood disorders, using DSM-IV criteria. These criteria were also employed for the final evaluation of the child in relation to the presence of ADHD or obsessive-compulsive disorder.

Results of family studies

In the family history, multiple motor tics were present in six parents (five fathers and one mother; 50 per cent). ADHD was present in two fathers (16 per cent). Only one mother had postpartum depression. There were two pairs of twins: two monozygotic twins, who are described in detail below, and a girl who had a normal dizygotic twin.

Cases A and B were monochorionic, identical, monozygotic twins (confirmed through multiplex polymerase chain reaction testing of 14 loci). The father, a policeman aged 30 years when the children were born, has multiple motor tics that had been present since childhood; in adolescence he had an obsessive-compulsive disorder and describes himself as having ADHD. A paternal brother had tics in early adolescence. The parents appeared to be a united couple and the mother, a part time teacher who worked only a few hours a week, was present at home for most of the time. Both parents were emotionally adequate and affectionate with their sons.

Case A

There was a normal pregnancy lasting 38 weeks and a normal delivery, with birth weight 3150 g. The first year of life was reported as normal. He walked at 13 months. At 1 year his behaviour became odd: he would insistently align various objects, including pieces of furniture, would turn objects such as dishes obsessively, and would run around looking persistently at a railing and turned his head with peculiar movements of the eyes and face. These movements subsequently changed: his head was turned upwards, he opened both hands, passing them over his eyes, or clenching one of them like a telescope; these movements varied in intensity over time. At 2 years vocal tics became apparent. During his second and third year he was described as being profoundly isolated and hyperactive. At 3 years a diagnosis of autism was made by doctors in his home town. He was sent to a nursery and some improvement in his behaviour was observed, including increased linguistic comprehension, the appearance of a few words, and the ability to repeat nursery songs.

He was seen in our department at the age of 3 years 6 months. He had multiple complex motor tics – in particular his head was arched backwards and at the same time his arms were bent – and he displayed simple vocal tics. His behaviour was markedly avoidant; his ABC was 64 and a DSM-IV evaluation for autistic disorder was concordant, (1) a+, b+, c+, d+; (2) a+, d+ (3)a+, b+, falling within the autistic range. He was able to point but did not have joint attention. Symbolic play was absent. His general abilities, evaluated with the Portage checklist (Sherer & Sherer, 1972), were around 2 years in the cognitive and autonomy areas, and between 1 and 2 years in social and linguistic abilities. He could only scribble, said a few words, and carried out few verbal requests.

Treatment was started along the lines described below and speech therapy and motor sensory stimulation (psychomotricity) were also begun. Three months later his progress was remarkable: ABC fell to 31 and he gained 51 items in four of the Portage checklist scales (more than double what one would expect for a child with his mental abilities) (Sherer & Sherer, 1972).

On a subsequent admission 6 months later he had gained 45 items and his abilities were in the range of 3 to 4 years, while the ABC remained stable at previous values. His symbolic play was rich and varied, he had attained joint attention and his reciprocal behaviour with his parents appeared more adequate. His linguistic abilities had greatly expanded, with long phrases and a greater mastery of grammatical details, including the use of articles; his verbal comprehension was to a large extent adequate.

He was seen again at age 4 years 11 months and at 5 years 8 months. During this last admission he appeared adequate from the point of view of language, social interactions and symbolic play and had gained in all the items present in the Portage checklist for a child of his age. No items of the autistic spectrum were present at a DSM-IV evaluation, and the ABC was 5. He maintained occasional complex motor tics of his face (grimacing) and arms (clenched fists). No vocal tics were noticed. His behaviour fulfilled the criteria for ADHD. His IQ was 78 on the WPSI.

At the age of 6 years 3 months he was reading and writing adequately for his age, engaging in satisfactory social activity with his peers, and had an IQ of 105 on WISC-R. He had multiple complex motor tics and simple vocal tics and a full ADHD.

Case B

Case B's early development was similar to that of his brother; birth weight was 3650 g and the first year was normal. He walked alone by 14 months. However, at around 1 year of age he appeared isolated, avoided interaction with others, was apparently alarmed by the presence even of close relatives, and would cry if his grandparents visited him. He passed most of his time turning over every object he touched. At around 18 months multiple motor tics appeared: simple ocular tics and more complex movements, turning his head and raising a shoulder. One year later a notable improvement was evident: he started speaking his first words and began to relate increasingly adequately. When seen with his brother at 3 years 6 months his abilities were adequate on the scales of the Portage checklist with the exception of language, which was moderately delayed. ABC rated 4. He no longer had tics and he behaved as the leader of the twin couple. At 4 years 5 months a WPPSI gave an IQ of 101 (V 82; P 122). At 6 years 3 months he could read and write adequately for his age and socialize adequately with his peers; he had an IQ of 107 on the WISC-R, and had multiple complex motor tics and ADHD.

Case C

Case C has a normal heterozygotic twin sister. Her initial development was reported as normal, and she was able to walk alone and to say some words by 14 months. At 18 months she developed regression with autistic features, diagnosed as autism by a doctor in her home town, and by 2 years multiple motor tics and simple vocal tics became evident. From 3 years her behaviour improved and over the months she began to acquire new abilities, develop better interaction, and speak some words appropriately. At 3 years 10 months she was seen in our ward. At this time multiple motor tics and vocal tics were still present but her ABC was 23 (much below the values usually found with this test in subjects with autism) and her overall behaviour could not be classified as autistic. Speech therapy and the treatment described below were initiated. She has been seen repeatedly over the following years. At 6 years 7 onths she had no signs of autistic behaviour (ABC = 5), her IQ was 76 (WISC-R), but motor and vocal tics were still present.

Treatment protocol

Treatment is based on coaching the parents to develop affectionate interactions and physical play with their children, including reciprocal caresses and exploration of the face, tossing the child, piggyback riding, bouncing them on their knee, chasing and tickling, and running together: these activities often increased the child's motivation for subsequent cooperation with the parents on various items included in the Portage method (Sherer & Sherer, 1972), which was also suggested to the parents. This method provides the parents with a list of activities to be done with a child who has experienced a lengthy period of inadequate development and is therefore in need of an active programme of stimulation. The gradual approach to items on the Portage list that is suggested by the method was often useful, because some of these children show elements of dyspraxia and in these cases splitting an item into simpler tasks and making use of manual prompts and other supports was an advantage. Speech therapy was given to six of these children.

Results of clinical observations

In all cases parents reported a regression with autistic features accompanied by the appearance of tics occurring in the second year of life. On first examination the 12 children in the present series fulfilled DSM-IV criteria for autistic spectrum disorders and ABC values ranged from 39 to 64 (mean value 49.2). Their abilities were in all cases notably below the norm, scoring no more than 70 per cent of the items expected for their age; four children were below these values (below 50 per cent). The latter were not able to utter a word and had inadequate oral and manual motor coordination (for example, they could not blow out a candle and were unable to point out specific objects). Signs of high sensitivity, specific to a particular noise or to some type of touch, were common. In the first year of treatment recovery was rapid: in some children a few months were sufficient to attain adequate abilities, in others it took more time – a year or two or even longer. The outcome included the following features:

- Measured IQs were, respectively, 100, 105, and 114 in three cases (outside of the series, twin B had an IQ of 107 and twin C 76). In the remaining children clinical observation coupled with data obtained from the Portage checklist or from their school results suggested abilities within the normal range.
- DSM-IV items for ASD were absent and ABC values ranged from 1 to 9 (average 3.7).
- Tourette syndrome was still present in seven children (all with co-morbid ADHD and six with fathers with motor tics) and multiple motor tics in two (one co-morbid with ADHD).
- ADHD was present in 10. No obsessive-compulsive disorder, dyslexia, or mood abnormalities were noted in these children. One child was entirely normal, had no tics or ADHD, and his IQ was 114. The only girl of the series appeared entirely adequate from a social and school point of view, with only mild motor tics (see Table 1). None of these children had features of Asperger syndrome or multiple complex developmental disorder (MCDD).

The incidence of this disorder in my outpatient clinic should also be noted. Between 2000 and 2004, and excluding children with Asperger syndrome, Rett syndrome, and MCDD, 108 children with an ASD diagnosis have been examined: 10 of these were diagnosed with the present disorder – that is, 9.2 per cent of the total, similar to previous evaluations (Zapella, 2002).

Table 1. Data concerning 11 children with Dysmaturational Syndrome

Cases	**n = 11**
Parents with tics	6/11
Fathers with ADHD	2/11
Normal 1st year	10/11
Regression 2nd yr	11/11
TS in 2nd yr	11/11
1st visit (2–4 yrs)	2 yrs 10 m (m.r.)
DSM-IV (A&PDD)	11/11
ABC	49 (m.r.)
Outcome at follow-up (1–4 yrs)	
DSM-IV (A&PDD)	0/11
ABC	3.7 (m.r.)
IQ	76–114 or n
TS	7/11
Multiple motor tics	2/11
ADHD	10/11
No TS or ADHD	2/11

ABC, autism behaviour checklist; ADHD, attention deficit-hyperactivity disorder; DSM-IV, *Diagnostic and Statistical Manual of Mental Disorders*, fourth edition; IQ, intelligence quotient; TS, Tourette syndrome; DSM-IV (A&PDD): DSM-IV for Autism and Pervasive Developmental Disorders.

Discussion

Compared with the results obtained in a previous study conducted using the same criteria (Zappella, 2002), the present series shows basic similarities and some differences. The occurrence in parents of multiple motor tics is lower (50 *versus* 75 per cent) and the same applies to ADHD (16 *versus* 45 per cent). Initial ABC values were less severe than in the previous series (49 *versus* 63) while final ABC results were about the same (3.7 *versus* 4.3). Three of 12 children lost their tics, as was observed in the previous study, while ADHD was present at follow-up in almost the same percentage (83.3 *versus* 91.6 per cent). These data, together with the interesting pair of monozygotic twins in whom some early differences in development ended up with similar results at an assessment at 2 years 9 months, suggest that the phenotypic expression of this disorder may vary. Within a continuum of severity including both the degree of regression and the outcome, some subjects may evolve in adolescence towards a rather severe type of Tourette syndrome with ADHD, while others lose their tics and become adequate and at times even brilliant children, with no sequelae. Regression was reported by all the parents. This disorder should be suspected in children with the features described above who improve rapidly during the early observation period if physical play and interactions promoting socialization are provided, but a definite diagnosis may require time and can only be achieved if autistic features diminish and general abilities improve to a substantial degree: there are in fact children with autism and Tourette syndrome, familial or otherwise, who must be included in the differential diagnosis. The presence of tics in the parents, the observation of one monozygotic twin pair with a similar disorder and of another heterozygotic pair of twins where a girl was affected while her sister was normal, contrasting with the usually normal family environment, supports the hypothesis of a genetic basis for this disorder. Two girls are reported in this article; considering another, described in a previous publication (Zappella, 1996), only three of 85 cases have been girls, giving a male to female ratio of 28:1.

Pronounced difficulties in forming relationships have been noted in a high proportion of adolescents with Tourette syndrome (Kadesjo & Gillberg, 2000) and symptoms of ASD in children with ADHD (Clarke *et al.*, 1999). These partial overlaps among different developmental disorders (ASD, Tourette syndrome, ADHD) suggest that early-onset Tourette syndrome can be co-morbid with autistic behaviour, probably because of interference of the brain dysfunction underlying tics with the brain areas devoted to communication and social interaction in a specific period of brain development. For example, when seen at 3 years 6 months, twin A had the full picture of Tourette syndrome, accompanied by autistic behaviour; at the same time twin B had no tics nor any of the symptoms of autistic behaviour that had previously been present. This suggests that in these cases persistence of tics in a particular period of brain development was related to a parallel dysfunction in areas related to communication and social interaction (still present at 3 years 6 months in twin A but not in twin B). In fact, when seen at 6 years 3 months both children had a similar IQ and social and communicative competence; both had multiple tics, but at this age a possible interference with developing areas concerned with interaction and communication was apparently no longer influencing their behaviour. These data can explain the 'spontaneous' recovery of twin B and the need for more intensive therapeutic effort in twin A, which possibly counteracted the operant dysfunction present in his case by directly stimulating brain areas concerned with communication.

In this respect the efficacy of parental interactions in promoting attachment, affection, exploration, and physical play must be considered. These children come from an experience of more or less severe autistic withdrawal affecting the innate biological basis of reciprocal interactions. A powerful and pleasant emotional stimulation involving communication, interaction, and related cerebral areas is an appropriate way of supporting their development, thus achieving strong motivation to relate to others and to cooperate. These interactions belong to the broad category of approach behaviour; among them, physical play has the advantage of being elicited very early and possibly continued for several years (MacDonald & Parke, 1986). The tactile component of this type of interaction is important, and this basic level of stimulation explains the intensity of the emotional response. However, visual and vocal interactions are also an integral part of this dual approach. This type of interaction plays a role in the development of social abilities and sex roles, subsequently developed with peers (MacDonald & Parke, 1984; 1986). In their dual parent/child interactions as well as in the subsequent collective interaction with peers, they have the immediate reward of supporting social interaction and cooperation: as it is fun, it is worth continuing to expand the interaction; every new proposal may carry promise of further fun! This extensive sensorimotor stimulation may be of help in appropriately modulating a dysfunctional 'mirror neurons' system, a possible relevant factor in autistic behaviour.

The efficacy of these interactions is enriched by the use of other interactional modes that are part of the normal way in which children are brought up, including attachment, reciprocal exploration and so on, and may in some cases require other pedagogic tools and eventually speech therapy.

Other examples of reversible autistic behaviour, such as those cases of early-onset epilepsy described by Deonna (1999), have also been explained in a similar manner – that is, through the hypothesis that areas concerned with communication and social interaction are rendered intermittently unavailable by seizure activity at times that are especially relevant for their programmed development. In contrast, children with autism usually need both an adaptation of their environment and support in their relational abilities, with limited results because of aberrant neurodevelopment, possibly starting in the first two trimesters of prenatal life (Casanova *et al.*, 2002). This is not the case in the dysmaturational syndrome, active only in the postnatal period, where a rigidly prescribed environment could be an inappropriate limitation to the child's natural curiosity and initiative.

It may well be that a number of those cases of children reported as 'recovered from autism', often through intense behavioural therapies, in fact belong to the syndrome described here, where a positive result was obtained through an accurate neurological diagnosis and a simple and inexpensive therapeutic approach.

References

Casanova, M.F., Buxhoeveden, D.P. & Brown, C. (2002): Clinical and macroscopic correlates of minicolumnar pathology in autism. *J. Child Neurol.* **17**, 692–695.

Clark, T., Feehan, C., Tinline, C. & Vostanis, P. (1999): Autistic symptoms in children with attention deficit-hyperactivity disorder. *Eur. Child dolesc. Psychiatry* **8**, 50–55.

Deonna, T. (1999): Developmental consequences of epilepsies in infancy. In: *Childhood epilepsies and brain development*, eds. A. Nehlig, J. Motte, L.M. Solomon & P. Plouin, pp. 113–122. London: John Libbey & Co.

Kadesjo, B. & Gillberg, C. (2000): Tourette's disorder: epidemiology and comorbidity in primary school children. *J. Am. Acad. Child Adolesc. Psychiatry* **39**, 548–555.

MacDonald, K.B. & Parke, R.D. (1984): Bridging the gap: parent-child play interactions and peer interactive competence. *Child Dev.* **55**, 1265–1277.

MacDonald, K.B. & Parke, R.D. (1986): Parent-child physical play: the effects of sex and age of children and parents. *Sex Roles* **7/8**, 367–378.

Sherer, E.M. & Sherer, D.E. (1972): The Portage project: a model for easing childhood education. *Exceptional Children* **39**, 210–217.

Zappella, M. (1994): Bambini autistici che guariscono: l'esempio dei tic complessi familiari. *Terapia Familiare* **46**, 51–62.

Zappella, M. (1996): Autismo Infantile: studi sulla affettività e le emozioni. Roma: Carocci.

Zappella, M. (1999): Familial complex tics and autistic behaviour with favourable outcome in young children. *Inf. Rev. Neuropsiquiatr. Inf. Adolesc.* **7**, 61–66.

Zappella, M. (2002): Early-onset Tourette syndrome with reversible autistic behaviour: a dysmaturational disorder. *Eur. Child Adolesc. Psychiatry* **11**, 18–23.

Autistic spectrum disorders, D. Riva and I. Rapin (eds.)

Chapter 9

Seizure disorder in autism spectrum disorders: an overview

Mohammad Ghaziuddin

Division of Child Psychiatry, University of Michigan, 1500 East Medical Center Drive, Ann Arbor 48109–0390, Michigan, USA
mghaziud@med.umich.edu

Summary

Autism is a neurodevelopmental disorder characterized by a distinct pattern of reciprocal social deficits, communication impairment, and rigid ritualistic interests. It is classified as a pervasive developmental disorder along with other conditions such as Asperger syndrome and Rett's syndrome. One of the main lines of evidence that establishes its biological origins is its close association with seizure disorder. Over the decades, several studies have found that seizures are common in children with autism, occurring in at least 30 per cent. They are of all types, particularly of the complex partial type, and show a bimodal pattern of age of onset. While the majority of seizures occur around puberty, a substantial number have their onset in the preschool years. The prevalence is higher in those with severe mental retardation, and tends to be lower in those with high-functioning autism. The diagnosis of seizure disorder is of critical importance to the outcome of autism. This chapter will focus on recent studies of seizure disorder in autism. The impact of seizures on the outcome of autism is discussed. The distinction of autism from Landau–Kleffner syndrome and the overlap between some forms of autism and temporal lobe epilepsy is also discussed. Treatment aspects, including the use of drugs, are outlined.

Introduction

Autism is a severe handicapping disorder of early childhood characterized by a distinct pattern of social impairment, communication deficits, and rigid ritualistic interests. It forms the main category in a group of disorders labelled as pervasive developmental disorders (PDD) (American Psychiatric Association, 1994). Other categories included within PDD include Asperger syndrome, disintegrative disorder, and Rett's syndrome. Patients who do not belong to any of these categories are said to have 'Pervasive Developmental Disorder-Not Otherwise Specified' (PDD-NOS). In the years immediately following the initial description of autism by Leo Kanner in 1943 (Kanner, 1943), it was widely believed that autism was a psychogenic disorder caused by, among other factors, bad parenting. However, later research proved convincingly that the disorder was caused by biological factors.

Two main findings that were instrumental in pointing out the organic basis of this condition were the association of autism with mental retardation, and the later emergence of seizures in this population. Thus, in an early long-term study of autism, Rutter and colleagues showed that of 64 children, 18 (about 30 per cent of those not epileptic in early childhood) developed epilepsy during adolescence, and the prevalence of epilepsy was higher in those with severe mental retardation (Rutter & Bartak, 1971). Of the 27 children who had an IQ of 50 or below, 15 developed seizures in adolescence and another two had fits since early childhood (Rutter & Bartak, 1971). Later studies replicated these findings. For example, Deykin & MacMahon (1979) examined 183 children with autism. Age-specific incidence rates of autism were found to be three times higher than that of the general population. In addition, the study found that fully autistic children were at increased risk from childhood to adolescence but especially after puberty, whereas partially autistic children (that is, those who would probably be diagnosed as PDDNOS today) were at increased risk up to the age of 10 years (Deykin & MacMahon, 1979).

More recently, Volkmar & Nelson (1990) re-examined the association of autism with epilepsy. After assessing 192 subjects with autism, these investigators concluded that the age-specific incidence of epilepsy was three to 22 times that of the general population. In addition, the study also found that the risk was highest in early childhood followed by adolescence. Thus it is now generally accepted that the risk of epilepsy in autism persists throughout the early years, and tends to be exacerbated around puberty and in the preschool years. On the whole, at least 30 per cent of patients with autism show superimposed seizures, which tend to occur more commonly in those patients who suffer from additional mental retardation. Most studies have investigated the association of seizure disorder with traditional autism. However, few reports have also commented on the occurrence of seizures in persons with Asperger syndrome and PDD-NOS. While it is possible that seizures are less common in Asperger syndrome than in traditional autism, it is unclear if the same also applies to patients with PDD-NOS.

Types of seizure

Several studies have attempted to investigate the pattern of seizures that occur in persons with autism spectrum disorders. The results vary depending on the type and origin of the sample and the thoroughness of medical investigations performed. While all types of seizures can occur, complex partial seizures are particularly common and pose special problems in diagnosis, because quite often they are mistaken for behavioural outbursts and temper tantrums seen in some autistic children. In a population-based study, Gillberg (1991) found the following pattern of occurrence of seizures: complex partial (82 per cent); generalized tonic-clonic (30 per cent); juvenile myoclonic (24 per cent); and infantile spasms (11 per cent). Many patients had a mixed pattern.

Epileptic syndromes of autism

Some epilepsy syndromes are particularly related to autism. Autism may result from infantile spasms with a hypsarrhythmic EEG or from the Lennox–Gastaut syndrome, an age specific epileptic syndrome in infants and young children that is likely to be the cause when autism is associated with tuberous sclerosis; it is characterized by drop attacks and absence seizures in preschool children associated with diffuse slow spike–wave complexes on the EEG. The typical seizure, described as a jack-knife seizure in which the child suddenly bends forward at the waist, should alert the clinician to the presence of tuberous sclerosis. When present, infantile spasms may directly contribute to the emergence of autistic symptoms (Taft & Cohen, 1971). However, autism is not the only disorder that occurs in children with infantile spasms, also called West syndrome. For example, in a long-term follow-up study of 192 children in Finland (Riikonen, 2001), psychiatric disorders were found in 53 of the children, 24 had infantile autism, and further 14 had 'transient' symptoms of autism. Sixteen of these children were also hyperactive. In the entire group, 29 cases were hyperactive. Children identified as autistic in this sample often had psychomotor epilepsy and temporal lobe abnormalities; this suggests that organic lesions that selectively occur in these areas of the brain are associated with an increased risk of autism. Studies have implicated mutations of the AXR gene on the X chromosome in the aetiology of infantile spasms. Mutations of this gene may cause a range of abnormalities in individuals with infantile spasms, including mental retardation and autism (Stromme *et al.*, 2002).

Autism is also strongly associated with the Landau–Kleffner syndrome. In this condition, the child loses speech with the onset of seizures. This typically occurs around 2 years of age, and is sometimes referred to as acquired epileptiform aphasia. There is evidence that the language disorder is directly caused by epileptic discharges in the critical language areas. As about a quarter of autistic children also show signs of language regression around 2 years of age, it is important to rule out whether this is because of Landau–Kleffner syndrome.

Common mechanisms

The association of seizures with autism is not fully understood, although several possible mechanisms have been proposed.

First, both autism and the seizure disorder may result from a common underlying cause. Epilepsy may also disrupt brain functions necessary for language development by an associated intellectual disability or directly as a consequence of the seizures. The relation between epilepsy and language function is complicated by the fact that neuroanatomical circuits are common to both. Impairment of language function has long-term consequences for social and academic functions, including causing deficits in memory and learning.

Second, one condition may lead to the other and *vice versa*. As both autism and epilepsy are multifactorial in nature and are influenced by genetic factors, it is reasonable to assume that they may have overlapping genetic mechanisms. In this context, it is important to note that while epilepsy is commonly associated with autism, the same does not seem to be the case with the broader phenotype of the disorder. Thus first degree relatives of autistic probands do not have an excess prevalence of seizure disorder even if they do show some of the milder deficits of the condition.

The mechanisms that determine the exact onset of seizures in autism are also not fully understood. The fact that a great number of patients with autism have their first seizures around the age of puberty suggests the possible role of stress and maturational factors. This also points to the possibility that the putative pathological process may lie dormant until adolescence and then be triggered by precipitants the nature of which is not fully understood at present.

Assessment

Every patient with autism spectrum disorders should be routinely evaluated for the presence of seizure disorder. While an EEG is helpful, by itself it does not clinch the diagnosis. This is because the EEG has to be taken during a seizure to be diagnostic. A 24-hour EEG may provide more useful data. Studies have shown that about 30–50 per cent of children with autism have EEG abnormalities, the incidence of which rises with the level of mental retardation. Certain types of patient with autism spectrum disorders should be suspected of having seizure disorder, such as those who are in their preschool years or in their adolescence, those who have a history of staring spells especially in their school years; those with a history of aggressive outbursts and temper tantrums; those who have concomitant mental retardation and other genetic syndromes; and those with a history of altered mood or behaviour resembling psychosis.

A detailed physical examination should be carried out to exclude any underlying causes of seizure disorder such as tuberous sclerosis. Likewise, a complete psychiatric assessment should also be done because the risk of all psychiatric disorders, including depression and psychotic disorders, is increased independently in individuals with seizure disorder.

Treatment

The treatment of epilepsy in autism incorporates a multimodal approach including the use of drugs, environmental manipulation, and counselling.

Anticonvulsants

Anticonvulsants are used in autism spectrum disorders not only for the control of seizures but also for the treatment of associated psychiatric symptoms such as aggressive outbursts, temper tantrums, mood instability, and depression. At times, they are administered 'routinely' when abnormalities are detected on an EEG even in the absence of clinical seizures. They belong to two groups: traditional anticonvulsants and newer anticonvulsants.

Traditional anticonvulsants

Traditional anticonvulsants include drugs such as depakote and carbamazepine (Tegretol). Depakote is increasingly used to control mood instability and aggressive outbursts. It is also used as an antimanic agent in patients with bipolar disorder. Some open-label studies have suggested its potential for use in patients with autism spectrum disorders (Hollander *et al.*, 2001). However, reports have suggested that ingestion of depakote during pregnancy increases the risk of having a child with autism (Williams *et al.*, 2001). Carbamazepine is also used in patients with autism as a mood stabilizer and an anticonvulsant. Both drugs have side effects – such as effects on the liver, excessive sedation, problems with coordination, and so on – that need to be monitored closely.

Newer anticonvulsants

Several newer anticonvulsants have been introduced recently. While few systematic data are available, many of them are used to treat children with autism spectrum disorders, not only for the control of seizures, but also for the treatment of mood and behaviour symptoms. Anticonvulsants that are used for this purpose are as follows.

Gabapentin

Gabapentin is sometimes used in the treatment of children and adolescents with autism, although there are few published reports. The drug acts through its effect on the GABA neurotransmitter system. Reports in intellectually disabled children and adults have yielded mixed results. For example, in a study of 26 mentally retarded children with refractory partial seizures, at least a 50 per cent reduction in seizure frequency was noted in nine children (Mikati *et al.*, 1998). Unfortunately, studies that have described the use of this drug in people with mental retardation have not provided enough data about whether they suffered from autism as well. Although it is generally well tolerated, the drug can sometimes aggravate certain types of seizure, such as absence and myoclonic seizures. Anger outbursts and temper tantrums have also been reported.

Felbamate

This drug has a broad spectrum of action against a variety of seizures. It inhibits NMDA receptor activity and is useful in the treatment of partial seizures and the Lennox-Gastaut syndrome. However, it has serious side effects, the most dangerous being liver failure and aplastic anaemia. For these reasons it is only tried as a second line of treatment. The drug should be started in small doses and be closely monitored.

Lamotrigine

Many reports have described the safety and efficacy of lamotrigine in people with mental retardation, many of whom also have autism. Improvement in seizure control has been shown, along with improvement in behavioural symptoms (Uvebrant & Bauziene, 1994). Some studies have suggested combined treatment with lamotrigine and valproate (Maganti *et al.*, 2002). Side effects include paradoxical aggression and irritability and severe rashes.

ACTH

Adrenocorticotrophic hormone (ACTH) has been the mainstay for the therapeutic management of infantile spasms and other developmental epilepsies. Clinical benefits of ACTH in infantile spasms could partially be related to its stimulatory effects on the release of adrenocorticosteroids and steroids. Glucocorticoids, pyridoxine, and ketogenic diet therapy have all been used for the treatment of refractory infantile spasms. Steroids have also been used in the treatment of Landau–Kleffner syndrome.

Counselling and psychotherapy

In addition to anticonvulsants and other drugs, treatment should also include counselling and psychotherapy. This should ideally consist of supportive psychotherapy and interventions aimed at decreasing exposure and response to stressful situations that are known to exacerbate the seizures. A detailed history of such environmental stressors and precipitants should be obtained in every case.

Outcome

Seizures have a negative impact on the outcome of autism. The severity and the frequency of seizures, along with the presence of additional factors such as mental retardation, contribute to the prognosis. Traditionally, two factors that have generally been accepted to play a critical role in the outcome of autism are the level of intelligence and the presence of verbal skills. It is now becoming increasingly clear that the presence of accompanying conditions such as seizure disorder also affects the long-term outcome. A few cases of improvement of autistic symptoms have been reported in some individuals after surgical treatment of intractable epilepsy.

References

American Psychiatric Association (1994): *Diagnostic and statistical manual for mental disorders*, 4th ed. Washington, DC: APA.

Deykin, E.Y. & MacMahon, B. (1979): The incidence of seizures among children with autistic symptoms. *Am. J. Psychiatry* **136**, 1310–1312.

Gillberg, C. (1991): Treatment of epilepsy in autism. *J. Autism Dev. Disord.* **21**, 61–77.

Hollander, E., Dolgoff-Kaspar, R., Cartwright, C., Rawitt, R. & Novotny, S. (2001): An open trial of divalproex sodium in autism spectrum disorders. *J. Clin. Psychiatry* **62**, 530–534.

Kanner, L. (1943): Autistic disturbances of affective contact. *Nervous Child* **2**, 217–250.

Maganti, R., Gidal, B.E., Shaw, R. & Rutecki, P. (2002): Concomitant use of divalproex sodium and lamotrigine in developmentally disabled patients with epilepsy: a retrospective evaluation of efficacy and tolerability. *Epilepsy Behavior* **3**, 275–279.

Mikati, M.A., Choueri, R., Khurana, D.S., Riviello, S., Helmers, S. & Holmes, G. (1998): Gabapentin in the treatment of partial epilepsy in children with intellectual disability. *J. Intellect. Disabil. Res.* **42** (Suppl. 1), 57–62.

Riikonen, R. (2001): Long-term outcome of patients with West syndrome. *Brain Dev.* **23**, 683–687.

Rutter, M. & Bartak, L. (1971): Causes of infantile autism: some considerations from recent research. *J. Autism Child. Schizophrenia* **1**, 20–32.

Stromme, P., Mangelsdorf, M.E, Shaw, M.A., Lower, K.M., Lewis, S.M., Bruyere, H, Lutcherath, V., Gedeon, A.K., Wallace, R.H., Scheffer, I.E., Turner, G., Partington, M., Frints, S.G., Fryns, J.P., Sutherland, G.R., Mulley, J.C. & Gecz, J. (2002): Mutations in the human ortholog of Aristaless cause X-linked mental retardation and epilepsy. *Nat. Genet.* **30**, 441–445.

Taft, L.T. & Cohen, H.J. (1971): Hypsarrhythmia and infantile autism. *J. Autism Child. Schizophrenia* **1**, 327–36.

Uvebrant, P. & Bauziene, R. (1994): Intractable epilepsy in children: the efficacy of lamotrigine treatment, including non-seizure-related benefits. *Neuropediatrics* **25**, 284–289.

Volkmar, F.R. & Nelson, D.S. (1990): Seizure disorders in autism. *J. Am. Acad. Child Adolsc. Psychiatry* **29**, 127–129.

Williams, G., King, J., Cunningham, M., Stephan, M., Kerr, B. & Hersh, J.H. (2001): Fetal valproate syndrome and autism: additional evidence of an association. *Dev. Med. Child Neurol.* **4**, 202–206.

Autistic spectrum disorders, D. Riva and I. Rapin (eds.)

Chapter 10

The cognitive/behavioural phenotype and neurological basis of autism

Daria Riva, Francesca Nichelli, Chiara Vago, Elena Andreucci, Nicoletta Paruta and Sara Bulgheroni

Developmental Neurology Division, National Neurological Institute 'C. Besta', via Celoria 11, 20133 Milan, Italy
driva@istituto-besta.it

Summary

The neuropsychological-cognitive phenotype of childhood autism (generally used in this chapter to refer to classic autism or DSM/ICD autistic disorder) is characterized by abilities/disabilities in a variety of mental domains and unique behavioural syndrome. This syndrome correlates with demonstrable malfunction in a complex cerebral network that links the prefrontal regions, limbic system, and cerebellum. It may be that in some cases only one or another of these structures, or their interconnections (that is, the white matter) is malfunctioning. It is likely, of course, that other brain regions are also part of the network. Responsibility for this disorder in its extraordinary complexity thus is unlikely to be pathology in a single affected area but in the disruption of a network connecting these different brain regions which are strongly related with each other in the timing of their maturation. The prefrontal cortex and cerebellum develop in parallel and any lesion affecting one of them will also strongly influence the maturation of the other. The behavioural deficits of individuals with autism have much in common with those of patients with frontal lesions or lesions affecting brain regions connected to the frontal lobes such as the basal ganglia, temporo-medial structures, and thalamus. Along with the frontal lobes, other regions involved in this network include the limbic system and the cerebellum. A number of studies of autism disclosed structural abnormalities in the limbic system, the amygdala and hippocampus in particular, which help explain some of autism's clinical features. Several research studies described cerebellar abnormalities, particularly those affecting the posterior vermis (lobules VI and VII), but others have not.

The complex ability to gauge the mental state of others (theory of mind) is a fundamental deficiency in autism. It is supported by a widespread neural network that involves brain regions activated by language processing, the frontal lobes, the right parietal cortex, and the amygdalar system. In short, while numerous deficits can be correlated quite precisely with anomalous processing in defined brain areas or circuits, it is impossible to attribute the extraordinarily complex behavioural features of autism to malfunction of a single part of the brain, but rather to a complex maldevelopment of interconnected brain structures.

Introduction

The behavioural complexity of autism (autistic disorder) and of its characteristic mental symptoms reflects the complexity of the underlying neuropsychological mechanisms and consequent difficulty in evaluating them – hence the paucity of studies on this topic up to the 1980s. In the last 20 years there has been a burst of new research in this field and some of the most interesting contributions unquestionably include those of neuropsychologic and cognitive type which have had a crucial influence on approaches to the rehabilitation of individuals with autism. (The term *cognitive*, as used here, also encompasses emotions and interactive behaviour. It refers to all human behaviours processed by neuropsychologically based brain activity.)

Besides the complexity of the behavioural phenotype, the cognitive/neuropsychological phenotype of autism is extremely variable. Phenotypic complexity stems from the fact that the impairment pervades many but not all mental domains and – along with the claim that autistic subjects generally have a global functional impairment – there is evidence of areas of strength and weakness, with dissociations between functions and subcomponents of the same function. Exceptional talents are rare (Howe *et al.*, 1998). Such talents (such as the one magnificently interpreted by Dustin Hoffman in the Barry Levinson film 'Rain Man') are implicit – that is, the subject is unaware of them, they are natural, not learnt, and they do not improve with experience. Examples are individuals with an exceptional memory for the names of the Saints on the calendar or the numbers in the telephone directory, or who are capable of instantly calculating a person's age almost before they finish hearing his date of birth, but who are unable to do straightforward arithmetic.

A major characteristic of autistic disorder is that the majority of affected individuals are mentally retarded (with an IQ of less than 70, the percentage varying in different studies between 65 and 85 per cent). They generally have a stable WISC pattern characterized by a discrepancy in their IQ, with a dissociation between their verbal and performance IQ in favour of performance. Among the performance subtests, they tend to do better with the Block Design cubes and Object Assembly items, giving rise to the uneven profile typical of the disorder (Shah & Frith, 1993). This pattern seems to persist at different ages and in subjects with different intellectual levels. It consists not just of the verbal/performance discrepancy just mentioned, but also of an internal specificity that – although not a feature of all autistic subjects – is not typical of other neurodevelopmental disorders. Autistic subjects have many additional neuropsychological impairments in various skills, again with dissociations within ostensibly closely related functions such as different aspects of memory: they may have excellent recall for detail but not for the global view; or they may have an adequate short-term memory but significant deficits in categorical and episodic recall abilities (Baron *et al.*, 1995).

Paradoxically, attention invariably presents two diametrically opposed deficits. Subjects are easily distracted, often with hyperactivity and short-lived interests, yet the same individual may be hyperfocused, but only on rigid and unchangeable objects or rituals, making it very difficult or impossible to divert his or her attention elsewhere (Baron *et al.*, 1995).

Asperger syndrome requires special mention (Gillberg & Coleman, 2000a). Affected individuals have normal intelligence and language development (the latter is not always the case), and somewhat limited interests. Consequently these individuals are often nitpicking and methodical, excelling in occupations where precision and excessive control are important. They also show a variable degree of reticence in social interactions so that, although they can cohabit with other people, they have a strong preference for solitude. Persons with Asperger syndrome have variably severe impairments in several domains (for example, using and understanding body language and the pragmatics of communication); they lack flexibility in their thinking, together with obsessive and overly precise behaviour patterns. In addition, some but not all of them have difficulty with complex motor skills and sensory functions, tending to be either hyposensitive or hypersensitive (Gillberg & Coleman, 2000a).

Impairment of language and communication

Language

Rapin & Dunn (2003) describe language impairment as the first obvious symptom that may prompt a physician (even a general practitioner) to suspect autism. Expressive language is totally lacking in one third of children with classic autism, while the other two thirds develop language to a variable degree. Many of those who speak produce only a few, albeit grammatically complete, clichés (referred to as formulaic speech or delayed echolalia). Autistic language impairment varies a great deal in both quantitative and qualitative terms (Rutter & Bailey, 1993).

The most obvious impairment in individuals with autism is non-verbal communication, which is almost universally severely impaired. Salient features are the absence of pointing in infants and toddlers and a profound deficit in shared attention (Tomasello, 1992), an extraordinary indifference to the context of the interactive situation, and an inability to decode the feelings or interests of the person interacting with them (Ozonoff & Miller, 1996).

Like other skills in autism, some aspects of *language* are deficient while others are preserved. Some children with autism have a genuine specific developmental language disorder, which suggests left temporofrontal dysfunction. Those with a classic language disorder deserve a diagnosis of dysphasia. In our opinion, dysphasia of this type cannot be considered an inclusion criterion for autism and should be considered separately under the heading of developmental language disorder. It is likely that there may be a link between language disorders and autism, particularly as there is evidence that genes on chromosome 7q are abnormal in both autism and certain language disorders. Rutter (1968) considered it unlikely that the language disorder in itself is responsible for the communication dysfunction of autism and thus he argued that it is not at the 'core' of autism. Language is absent among the more severely autistic patients, but such subjects should not generally be considered as 'dumb', that is without language – they are non-communicative as they are equally unable to use other channels such as the facial expressions or gestures generally used by children with a genuine language disorder or deafness to make themselves understood.

According to Ricks & Wing 1976, when autistic children produce vocalizations, these are only recognized by their parents, not by the parents of other autistic or normal children, whereas normal children have a great variety of vocalizations which translate very different emotional situations and states, but are universally decoded by all types of listeners. Therefore, it is lack of the drive to communicate, rather than an intrinsic language disorder, that seems to be the core problem. The presence of *echolalia*, enabling the repetition (even after some time) of sentences or even whole conversations, means that the processing of *phonology* and development of *syntax* are unaffected in these children.

In some severely affected children delayed language development may be the consequence of mental retardation, but there is no doubt that in general it is related with the child's indifference to communication. Normal children learn to name an object on the strength of indicative and communicative gestures, direction of gaze, and shared attention (Tomasello, 1992), a behaviour which is more or less severely deficient in autism. Pronoun reversal (confusing 'you' and 'I', or using the third person instead of 'I') may be explained in some cases in terms of echolalia, but it is perhaps more likely that it reflects inability to comply automatically with the rules of normal conversation (Baron *et al.*, 1995). The autistic child's *semantics* have scarcely been investigated, given the obvious difficulties involved, but there is often evidence of an erudite vocabulary with a poor use of semantics (Baron *et al.*, 1995). *Pragmatics*, on the other hand, being more readily observable have been studied in depth: the prosody and intonation normally used to express and address emotions or important information are deviant in autism, as is the use of mimicry and gaze (Baron *et al.*, 1995). *Figurative language*, for example 'I am burning' or 'I am bursting', is lacking – both in production and in comprehension (Baron *et al.*, 1995). *Academic learning* often represents an 'islet of ability': in fact, some autistic children learn to read before they know how to use significant spoken language (Baron *et al.*, 1995).

Social interaction

Social interaction can be characterized by two extremes: on the one hand, indifference may be evident from a very early age, with severely impaired communication skills and very little demand for attention; on the other, a state of irreducible irritability, the child proving very hard or impossible to console, having severe eating difficulties, and irregular sleeping rhythms to the point of malignant insomnia. Social relationships can vary considerably, from intense solitude and social detachment, with complete indifference to other people's feelings, to an exaggerated attachment to one person (who may not necessarily be a family member), often with a pathological dependence on one of the parents.

As the children grow older, solitude becomes more evident, along with the inability to make friends and engage in games with other people or learn social rules. Although the basic rules of behaviour may be acquired automatically, they are used only rarely and then with rigidity (American Psychiatric Association, 2000).

Stereotypy

Another pathognomonic behavioural trait of autism is a limited repertoire of interests, with related iterative activities. These include repetitive rituals and excitable behaviour (in both negative and positive situations), such as hand flapping. These individuals are often strongly attracted to certain objects, sounds, TV or radio programmes and so on, and they very often react badly, even to the point of extreme behaviour, to any outside attempt to introduce change (Folstein, 1999).

Several theories have been formulated to explain this complexity, which has advanced our understanding of the mental functioning of autistic children. These theories, based on extensive observation or batteries of tests, have also enabled us to hypothesize the mechanisms of the children's mental functioning. They are discussed in the next section.

Cognitive theories of autism

The merit for focusing on the importance of cognition to explain the mental functioning of autistic children goes to Hermelin & O'Connor (1970), who were the first to compare autism with other forms of mental deficiency of diverse aetiology, and to claim that neither mental retardation nor peripheral sensory deficits explained the peculiarities of autism adequately. They applied an 'information processing' model in a highly original way to studies of neurodevelopmental disorders, making a distinction between central and peripheral information and suggesting that central information processing is deficient in autism. This model prompted subsequent studies of subjects with mental deficiencies or other types of neurodevelopmental disorders, with a view to identifying those neuropsychological and behavioural features of autistic functioning that may be typical of autistic subjects but are not specific to autism.

There are four main theories: social cognition deficit (which combines three lines of evidence), theory of mind, executive function impairment, and weak central coherence.

Deficient social cognition theory

The idea that autism is the consequence of a social-relational disorder has met with the most widespread acceptance. Three convergent lines of evidence that underlie this theory differ only as to the sequence of events thought to give rise to autism. The three deficiencies in the early stages of social development considered responsible for the disorder include: early interpersonal relationships, shared attention, and the capacity for imitation.

Interpersonal relationships

According to Hobson *et al.* (1988), autistic children display deficient interpersonal relationships from the earliest stages of their lives. They lack the affective skills that depend on observation and the mirroring of mimicry and body expressions (of the mother in particular), fundamental deficits of the disorder. Unfortunately, Hobson's observations were not supported by systematic studies. He personally studied older autistic children's inadequate ability to recognize emotional expressions, and showed that they lacked the ability of normal children to associate distinct human emotional signals with each other; for instance, autistic children could not associate the emotional expression of a face with the tone of voice corresponding to the emotion expressed on the face, although they were able to cope with non-emotional stimuli, for example associating a dog's bark with a dog.

Shared attention

The second line of evidence concerns lack of shared attention – that is, autistic children's failure to share their focus of attention. An example is the autistic child who sees an expression of fear on the mother's face when she looks at an object, does not realize the object is dangerous, and therefore does not keep away from it. This lack of shared attention is not characteristic of other mental disorders. Its cause is still uncertain, and no one knows whether this deficit is the cause or simply an early sign of the more typically autistic behaviour that will become apparent later on.

Imitation deficit

The third line of evidence is failure to imitate. Meltzoff (1988) showed that normal infants innately imitate certain simple expressions – for example, opening their mouth or sticking out their tongue – even when they are very small. The capacity to imitate is essential to the development of reciprocal social relations. Meltzoff & Gopnik (1993) suggested that autistic children lack the capacity for emotional mimicry, which is part of a more complex impairment that jeopardizes other imitative abilities as well. Indeed, Rogers & Pennington (1991) found that older autistic children were unable to imitate complex sequences of gestures.

Theory of mind

In the 1980s neuropsychologists attempted to explain how Wing's triad (impairments of communication, imagination, and social interaction) might derive from a single cause. The most important of the theories advanced (in part because of its influence on subsequent research) was the *theory of mind*, according to which autistic individuals are incapable of representing to themselves their own and other people's mental states. A strength of this theory is its ability to predict the behaviour of autistic children. Baron-Cohen *et al.* (1985) provided support for this theory by showing that an autistic subject was unable to predict where another child would look for a toy which had been moved in his absence from where he had left it. Instead of answering on the basis of what the child would think, the autistic child answers according to where the toy is currently hidden. This inability to attribute mental states differing from factual reality has been recorded in numerous studies, including in adults.

This 'mentalizing' deficit helps to explain main symptoms of autism: for instance, why it is that children with autism can play with their parents but cannot join in shared attention (behaviour requiring an understanding of another person's mental state); or why they can repeat a message verbatim, but are unable to discriminate who already knows the message and who doesn't by decoding a series of metamessages (Perner *et al.*, 1989).

Lack of imagination was documented by Wing & Gould's (1979) observation that autistic children do not play symbolic games. Leslie (1987) pointed out that 'pretence' provides striking evidence of the ability to mentalize and that it depends on the ability to distinguish between a real state and an imaginary, simulated one. Many autistic children are able to play some even quite difficult mechanical games because these do not require this capacity to symbolize.

In short, theory of mind succeeds because it explains numerous features of autism, and also helps to understand why there may be islets of normality in certain activities involved in social interaction, communication, and object handling. This success explains the theory's considerable influence and how it has inspired so much research. It has also prompted the fine adjustment of very early screening tools and the choice of suitable rehabilitation methods.

The theory, nonetheless, has several limitations. The first and most important is that 15 to 55 per cent of autistic children pass first order ('I think that he thinks') theory of mind experiments, although so far no autistic child has been able to attribute mental states at a level corresponding to his or her actual age. The second shortcoming of the theory is that it fails to explain autistic children's early social impairments, because their inadequate mentalization stems from mechanisms that mature later. The third major criticism is that, although the theory more than adequately explains Wing's triad, it cannot explain the stereotypic words and actions, limited repertoire of interests, and cognitive ability/disability patterns of autism.

Theory of impaired executive function

Along with Wing's triad (1993), which is considered fundamental to the diagnosis of autism, another distinctive characteristic of the condition is a narrow range of interests and rigid repetition of numerous actions and behaviour patterns. The stereotypic behaviour of autism is much the same as that seen in patients with frontal lesions. This theory, based on the outcome of numerous neuropsychological studies, interprets autistic behaviour as typical of subjects with frontal lobe lesions (Ridley, 1994). It is supported by the fact that autistic children fail in numerous frontal tests such as the Wisconsin Card Sorting Test, the Tower of Hanoi, and others. Executive functions include a large set of skills that together govern numerous higher order cognitive processes such as inhibiting inadequate responses, planning sequences, focusing on a topic, monitoring performance, etc., and the ability to shift attention rapidly instead of restricting it to a single aspect of what a person is doing (Duncan, 1995). As of yet, not all executive functions have been studied adequately, but research has clearly demonstrated that autistic children are deficient in planning (Hughes *et al.*, 1994), generating categorical words, and drawing (Turner, 1996). Inefficient frontal performance is also seen in cases of Asperger syndrome, thus suggesting that this type of deficit is characteristic of the wide spectrum of autistic disorders. Frontal deficits are found in a variety of brain pathologies because the frontal associative areas are linked with numerous brain regions. On the other hand, this theory fails to explain the uneven WISC profile, and especially the good performance with the Block Design cubes, considered a convincing test of 'fluid' intelligence dependent on frontal lobe activity. It is important to note that malfunction of the frontal system is not generalized. Because the frontal lobes are organized into discrete circuits presumably dedicated to processing separate and diverse functions, it may be that only some of these are impaired in autism whereas others function relatively efficiently (Rogers & Pennington, 1991).

Theory of weak central coherence

This theory differs from the others in that, instead of attempting to explain the disorder, it attempts to identify a certain mental approach typical of autism. Frith (1989) reviewed and reinterpreted the published data relating to language, memory, and perception in autistic children, showing that they seem to gain little from information being highly structured and meaningful. For instance, whereas most children, be they normal or mentally retarded, are better at repeating meaningful sentences than strings of words that make no sense, the autistic children do not profit from the meaning (Hermelin & O'Connor, 1967). For similar reasons, autistic children are better than normal or mentally retarded children at repeating the formal aspects of a story rather than its content.

The fact that autistic children pay scarce attention to context and more to detail would explain why they do so well with the Block Design cubes. In fact, if this task is broken down by deconstructing the figure into its components by separating the cubes that form them, thus enhancing the details, the performance of both the normal and mentally retarded children improves considerably (Shah & Frith, 1993) This cognitive style, *i.e.*, attention to detail rather than to the bigger picture, is not part of the theory of mind, but is an additional and independent factor typical of autism. The inadequate central coherence view is supported by the finding that even autistic children who pass the theory of mind tests continue to have cognitive characteristics consistent with it.

The conclusion of this review is that no single theory accounts for all the deficits of autism. Moreover, the consequences of executive function impairment and weak central coherence may overlap and each of these may interact with and contribute to the specific social deficiencies at the core of autism.

Neuropsychology of autism

Neuropathological studies of autism provide a basis for attempts to correlate autistic deficits with the brain areas where pathology has been found. As early as 1978, Damasio & Maurer pointed out that the prominent characteristics of autistic behaviour resemble those of patients with lesions in the frontal regions and the regions linked with them (the basal ganglia, medial temporal lobe, and thalamus). It is quite unlikely that all these brain regions are involved in autism; more probably, the malfunction affects a circuit that links them. This would account for the observation that autism mimics some focal lesions of these areas. The salient spared abilities of autistic children, the lack of macroscopically detectable lesions by clinical imaging, and the small number of available necropsy suggest that autism is most likely caused by the malfunction in a complex network rather than by anatomically discrete lesions. The regions involved include the frontal lobes, limbic system (hippocampus/amygdala), cerebellum, white matter, corpus callosum, and parietal lobes.

It has been amply demonstrated by studies on children with very early, even foetal, focal lesions that the child's brain becomes specialized in functionally efficient areas very early in life (Riva & Cazzaniga, 1986), and that the complexity of higher order social and cognitive behaviours derive from networks involving a number of different brain regions. The complexity of autism is compounded by the fact that the brain regions involved – for example, the cerebellum and prefrontal regions – develop in parallel (Dow, 1942), thus influencing each other's maturation. As a result, it is most unlikely that any localized lesion or dysfunction is universal or pathognomonic of autism, hence the failure to identify hypoplasia of the vermis, cerebellar hemispheres, or other areas universally in autistic subjects.

Another important factor is the timing of any damage or maldevelopment. Available anatomical evidence (Bailey *et al.*, 1996, Kemper and Bauman, 1998) indicates that the neuropathology of autism dates to prenatal or perinatal brain development and triggers pathological alterations that extend into adult life. A prenatal or very early error prevents the expected progressive functional link between all the areas involved, and is thus responsible for permanent malfunction and jeopardizes from the start the acquisition of complex neuropsychological and social cognitive abilities. Moreover, because the frontal system and cerebellum evolve in parallel during neurogenesis, damage to one system is bound to affect the other severely as well (Dow, 1942). Rather than supporting the hypothesis of localized pathology, the studies point to malfunction in a network of different but interconnected brain regions, any one (or several) of which may have suffered the consequences of atypical development, pathology, or miswiring (Kemper & Bauman, 1998).

Brain/behaviour correlations

As the cognitive-behavioural phenotype of the autistic spectrum is so complex and diverse that it forms a continuum of clinical conditions, it is not feasible to correlate these behaviourally defined conditions with specific anomalies in brain function. The strategy adopted by neuropsychology is to extract the 'core' symptoms of autism – that is, those essential to a diagnosis of pervasive developmental disorders shared by each condition on the spectrum – and then to correlate them with the deficits resulting from well documented lesions in patients with defined brain lesions. The core symptoms are impairment of verbal and non-verbal communication and reciprocal social interaction, and restricted mental interests.

Even after they have been purged of differences responsible for particular clinical pictures distinct from the core deficits, the complexity of the symptoms of autism illustrates that the complexity of the underlying neural networks. Moreover, autism has no one aetiology and there is an array of paediatric neurological pathologies, most of them rare or very rare, which, in the aggregate, account at most for a small minority of cases. Only mental retardation, and epilepsy which is related to the severity of the underlying brain dysfunction and may occasionally result in fluctuations of language and behaviour (Tuchman & Rapin 2002), are frequent, neither of which of course is a single disorder. Encephalitis, various types of metabolic and degenerative brain diseases, certain major brain malformations, and occasionally trauma and other acquired damage to the immature brain are some of the causes of autism which, in the majority of cases, is polygenetically influenced (Gillberg & Coleman, 2000b).

Studies have focused on brain areas or circuits responsible for processing of the core functions deficient in autism in normal and brain-damaged subjects (mainly adults). As already stated, the regions involved in the network include the frontal lobes, limbic system (hippocampus/amygdala), cerebellum, white matter, corpus callosum, and parietal lobes. We consider in this chapter only the frontal lobes, the limbic system, and the cerebellum. It may well be that other brain regions are also involved, although empirical evidence is currently lacking. The reciprocal links connecting the cerebellum to these other structures have been demonstrated in many studies. Reciprocal connections between the cerebellum and supratentorial areas (here we will consider only the frontal and prefrontal neocortex and the limbic regions) include a very large descending pathway from the frontal cortex to the cerebellum through the pons and *vice versa* from the cerebellum through the thalamus to the frontal cortex. Reciprocal anatomical connections between the parahippocampal structures, the cingulate gyrus, and the hypothalamus to the cerebellum are also well documented (Schmahmann & Pandya, 1990; 1997).

Frontal lobes

The frontal lobes form a complex, ontogenetically recent associative system that undergoes a particularly lengthy maturation process which continues to evolve right up to adolescence. They are responsible for processing complex functions, mainly those related to the more sophisticated human cognitive behaviours (Smith *et al.*, 1992). Within the frontal system, specific areas process different functions: the dorso-lateral region is responsible for controlling activities critical to the integration of the cognitive functions, self-control, and self-regulation. The orbito-medial regions process the integration of affective and social behaviours, and motivation. The orbito-basal regions oversee the controlling of impulses and maintenance and programming of highly elaborated behaviours. Generally speaking, the complex mental functions processed by frontal circuits can be said to include inventiveness and creativity, executive functions, strategic programming, fluent and flexible thinking, shared attention and rapid attentional shifts, the capacity to deduce rules, and, lastly, the capacity to 'mentalize' – that is, to attribute mental states to oneself and others known as 'theory of mind' (Stone *et al.*, 1998).

In varying combinations and with differing levels of severity, impairments of these complex behaviours occur in adults with frontal lesions of various kinds and intra-frontal locations. Rarely (but more for want of looking than for their actual absence), they can also be seen in children with brain tumours, congenital malformations, dysplastic lesions, tuberous sclerosis, and other lesions in frontal locations. These symptoms occur in variable combinations, particularly in association with clinical and subclinical frontal epileptic foci. In our personal experience (unpublished data) of a series of 120 children with frontal lesions of various kinds, 15 per cent had an autistic or autistic-like picture, 80 per cent of whom had an active frontal epileptogenic focus. Our findings have been confirmed by a study by Hashimoto *et al.* (2001) in a sample of 101 autistic children, 47 of whom had an active focus, 76 per cent of which affected the frontal site. Functional magnetic resonance imaging (fMRI) studies in autistic subjects showed lower activation of Brodman areas 9 and 46 (prefrontal and dorso-lateral areas) and area 23 (the posterior cingulum) (Luna *et al.*, 2002). fMRI studies in autistic subjects undergoing theory of mind tests showed lower activation of the prefrontal cortex and posterior gyrus cinguli (Luna *et al.*, 2002). These findings are consonant with the observations that subjects with orbito-frontal lesions fail theory of mind tests (Rowe *et al.*, 2001).

Although MRI spectroscopy in Asperger syndrome (Murphy *et al.*, 2002) has identified higher levels of N-acetyl aspartic acid and choline in the prefrontal lobe, these indicators identify neuronal abnormalities with the peaks correlating with the severity of obsessive and social symptoms. These studies consequently confirm that, in tests evaluating frontal abilities, the activation of these circuits is lower in autistic subjects, and that subjects with brain lesions in these areas fail in the same tests.

To further pinpoint the level at which the processing error occurs, we pass from the areas to the circuits. Casanova *et al.* (2002) analysed the brains of autistic subjects at necropsy and found that the mini-columns of the neocortex (Brodman areas 9, frontal, and 21-22, posterior temporal), involved in the processing of visual and auditory stimuli, are smaller, more compact, and more numerous in autism than control brains. Casanova speculates that if the number of thalamo-cortical terminals is unchanged and the cortical minicolumns are smaller but more numerous in autism, the consequence will be more minicolumns innervated per thalamic afferent, in comparison to their number in control brains. The corollary is an exorbitant flow of sensory stimuli to the cortex that might result in an incessant background noise interfering with processing.

Limbic system

The limbic system is composed of a number of brain structures whose function remains incompletely understood (we refer here to the description provided by Kandel (Kandel & Schwartz, 1985). According to Kandel, the limbic system comprises a number of interconnected structures. While it is generally agreed that these include the gyrus cinguli, parahippocampal gyrus, hippocampus, and amygdala, there is no consensus on the septal area, hypothalamus, reticular substance, olfactory areas, and their connections with the thalamus and neocortex. In the present context, we consider only the hippocampus and amygdala. The functions of the limbic system are complex and, in macro-categories, they refer to the processing of memory components, social functions, and affective functions.

Hippocampus

The hippocampus is an ontogenetically very ancient structure located medially in the temporal lobes. It is responsible for processing complex functions such as the acquisition and consolidation of new memories, capacity to learn, the ability to recognize personal space, and episodic or autobiographic memory (that is, the capacity to place and contextualize personal memories in a spatial-temporal frame) (Riva *et al.*, 2001).

The hippocampus is an extraordinary structure which is required for metacognitive activities which depend on the ability to make conscious combinations of fragments of memories and reassemble them to make new memories. This capacity does not apply only to personal memories, but also to learned recall such as language, where the great demand for different combinations is self-evident and where the role of the hippocampus is most obvious.

Necropsy examinations in autistic subjects have revealed greater 'neuronal packing' (Bauman & Kemper, 1985) and a reduction of neurons in the dentate gyrus of the hippocampus, considered the processor of declarative memory (Preston *et al.*, 2004). This is confirmed by the fact that children with early bilateral medial temporal sclerosis present with clinical pictures typical of autism of varying severity (DeLong, 1992, 1997; Chugani *et al.*, 1996). Episodic memory tends to be deficient in autistic children (returning to the realms of psychoanalysis, this is translated into the observation that autistic subjects are incapable of reconstructing interior experiences) who have little or no capacity to make the just mentioned combinations in memory. This prevents some of those with severe bilateral pathology from constructing a language (for which this capacity is fundamental).

Amygdala

The amygdala is strongly connected to the neocortex and hypothalamus, and is responsible for 'drive-related behavioural patterns' – that is, for associating a given type of stimulus with a subjective affective experience (fear, interest, joy, pain, and so on) and reacting with behaviours typical of the human species (for example, a frightening stimulus prompts an aggressive or escapist reaction which is not only behavioural but associated with biological reactions), and behaviours appropriate to the stimulus. Consequently, the amygdala is responsible for emotional learning, for participating in recognizing faces and feelings and for associating stimuli with the corresponding behaviour patterns (Sweeten *et al.*, 2002).

Clearly, impaired processing in this sphere interferes with the person's behaviour and with the interpretation of facial expressions and the feelings related to them, as is typical of autistic behaviour. Encephalitic lesions, brain tumours, and tuberous sclerosis may be associated with disordered emotional conduct, observations confirmed by the fact that experimentally induced lesions of the amygdala in animal models induce the animal to associate the wrong behaviour with a given stimulus. Necropsy studies revealed alterations and neuroimaging has confirmed signal changes in the amygdala of autistic subjects.

Cerebellum

The cerebellum was the first brain structure to be identified as abnormal in autistic subjects (Bauman & Kemper, 1985: Courchesne *et al.*, 1988). To understand the real contribution of the cerebellum to the processing of complex behaviour, we need to bear in mind that numerous studies over the last 20 years have extended the role of the cerebellum not only to the ordinary and extraordinary modulation of complex motor tasks and sequences, but also to the modulation of patterns of thought and language, as well as of social and communicative behaviour. The cerebellum is primarily an associative brain structure, entrusted with the harmonization of complex cognitive and social actions by controlling their speed and correct sequencing (Schmahmann & Sherman, 1997; Schmahmann & Sherman, 1998; Riva & Giorgi, 2000).

Alongside a medio-lateral topographic organization for processing motor actions, Schmahmann & Sherman (1997, 1998) propose a similar organization for processing cognitive and emotional actions. They identified the medial cerebellum (vermis and fastigii and globosus nuclei) as the cerebellar limbic system, and the cerebellar hemispheres (neocortex) as the modulators of language planning.

By comparing the brains of autistic and normal subjects at necropsy, Bauman & Kemper (1985) found cerebellar alterations consisting of fewer and smaller Purkinje cells and fewer granular cells in the inferior regions of the paleo- and neocerebellum. Later, Courchesne (1988, 1991, 1997) reported that autistic subjects had smaller lobules VI and VII of the posterior vermis. (Although these data have been confirmed in other studies, they are still questioned by some.)

To confirm involvement of the cerebellum in the processing of complex behaviours, we described a sample of children with brain tumours whose emotional behaviour was disrupted after the surgical removal of lesions in the vermis (Riva & Giorgi, 2000). Their behaviour was characterized by a preference for solitude, irritability, and other features which proved to be transient and reversible. One case was particularly dramatic, however: a 9-year-old girl with medulloblastoma infiltrating the posterior part of the vermis underwent surgery that involved destruction of the surrounding area, including lobules VI and VII. The result was a clinical picture very similar to classic autism (solitude seeking, dislike of physical contact, gaze aversion, complex gestural and verbal stereotypies). This initially dense behavioural abnormality subsequently improved to become a picture of disturbed social interaction and empathy. She later developed signs of frontal lobe malfunction with an agrammatical aphasia and impaired executive function (Riva & Giorgi, 2000). The observations in this girl (and the other children) confirm the critical role of the cerebellum in coordinating these complex behaviours, not directly but through the mechanism of diaschisis of the cerebellum's connections with supratentorial structures – the prefrontal regions in this case (Schmahmann & Sherman, 1997; Riva & Giorgi, 2000).

Mirror neurons

From an evolutionary standpoint, 'theory of mind' – the complex ability to understand one's own and another person's mental states is an ability that emerges around 3 years of age, and is dependent on the maturation of particularly complex brain circuits and networks. Because idiopathic autism is a congenital condition originating in prenatal development, as demonstrated by available anatomical evidence (Bailey *et al.*, 1996; Kemper & Bauman, 1998), failure of the theory of mind to evolve must stem from a developmental deficit of processes and mechanisms maturing earlier in development. This previous developmental stage is called 'inter-subjectivity'; it comprises a complex pre-reflexive behaviour that makes it possible for us to grasp the wealth of experiences we share with others, and to perceive others as similar to ourselves in terms of their actions, sensations, and emotions. It is this shared ability that enables communication between subjects and the attribution of intentionality and subsequently triggers the development of theory of mind. In order for this ability to develop, mental mechanisms for matching the actions, sensations, and emotions of others depend on the maturation, very early in life, of the circuits whose function underlies them. These mechanisms reside in the mirror neurons discovered and described in the context of more specific action domains. They represent a fundamental aspect of the brain's structure and function which enables us to enjoy a rich and diversified inter-subjective experience (Willimas *et al.*, 2001). The system of mirror neurons (which also exists in other primates) is located in the premotor frontal cortex and appears to be responsible for our understanding the actions of others, in the sense that humans can understand other people's actions by mapping the visual representation of observed actions onto a mental representation of their own actions (Rizzolatti *et al.*, 2001).

Conclusions

The cognitive-behavioural phenotype of autism depends on two sets of variables: the variability/severity dimension that underlies the different phenotypes included in a continuum appropriately defined as a 'spectrum of autistic disorders'; and its 'core' symptoms without which a diagnosis of autism cannot be made.

Genotype-phenotype correlation (not discussed in detail here) remains impossible because of the uncertainties surrounding the many autistic genotypes which are currently the subject of intensive investigations. The current hypothesis is that the great variability of autistic phenotypes is most consistent with a polygenic model.

Finally, if we consider the core symptoms of autism, we can correlate quite accurately behavioural/functional impairments with the malfunctions of specific brain areas or circuits. Consequently, the autistic behavioural phenotype can be related to the more or less adequate functioning of a network connecting defined parts of the brain with distinct specializations (in this chapter we have discussed the frontal lobes, hippocampus, amygdala, and cerebellum). This network view can explain, for instance, why not all autistic children have cerebellar abnormalities, although they may have abnormalities elsewhere in the network, or even in areas or systems not considered here.

From the neuro-evolutionary standpoint, we emphasized that inability to understand one's own and other people's actions, and the coexisting incapacity to imitate and share attention, can be attributed to malfunction in a group of neurons located in the frontal cortex called 'mirror neurons', which are activated both by specific self-generated actions and by actions observed in others. We hypothesize that early malfunction of the mirror neuron system may instigate a cascade of deficient developmental events that eventuate in inadequate development of theory of mind and the consequent picture of frank autism.

References

American Psychiatric Association (2000): DSM-IV-TR. Manuale diagnostico e statistico dei disturbi mentali. Milan: Masson.

Bailey, A., Philips, W. & Rutter, M. (1996): Autism: toward an integration of clinical, genetic, neuropsychological, and neurobiological perspectives. *J. Child Psychol. Psychiatry* **37**, 89–126.

Baron-Cohen, S., Leslie, A.M. & Frith, U. (1985): Does the autistic child have a 'theory of mind'? *Cognition* **21**, 37–46.

Baron, I.S., Fennell, E.B. & Voeller, K.K.S. (1995): Neuropsychiatric disorders. In: *Pediatric neuropsychology in the medical setting*, eds. I.S. Baron, E.B. Fennell & K.K.S. Voeller, pp. 384–427. New York: Oxford University Press.

Bauman, M. & Kemper, T.L. (1985): Histoanatomic observation of the brain in early infantile autism. *Neurology* **35**, 866–874.

Casanova, M.F., Buxhoeveden, D.P., Switala, A.E. & Roy, E. (2002): Minicolumnar pathology in autism. *Neurology* **58**, 428–432.

Chugani, T.H., Silva, E.D. & Chugani, D.C. (1996): Infantile spasm: III. Prognostic implication of bitemporal hypometabolism on positron emission tomography. *Ann. Neurol.* **39**, 643–649.

Courchesne, E., Yeung-Courchesne, R., Press, G.A., Hesselink, J.R. & Jernigan, T.L (1988): Hypoplasia of cerebellar vermal lobules VI and VII in autism. *New Engl. J. Med.* **18**, 1349–1354.

Courchesne, E. (1991): Neuroanatomic imaging in autism. *Pediatrics* **87**, 781–790.

Courchesne, E. (1997): Brainstem, cerebellum and limbic neuroanatomical abnormalities in autism. *Curr. Opin. Neurobiol.* **7**, 269–278.

Damasio, A.R. & Maurer, R.G. (1978): A neurological model for childhood autism. *Arch. Neurol.* **35**, 777–786.

DeLong, G.R. (1992): Autism, amnesia, hippocampus and learning. *Neurosci. Biobehav. Rev.* **16**, 63–70.

Dow, R.S. (1942): The evolution and anatomy of the cerebellum. *Biol. Rev.* **17**, 179–220.

Duncan, J. (1995): Attention, intelligence and the frontal lobes. In: *The cognitive neuroscience*, ed. M.S. Gazzaniga, 2nd ed., pp. 721–733. London: MIT Press.

Folstein, S.E. (1999): Autism. *Int. Rev. Psychiatry* **11**, 269–277.

Frith, U. (1989): Autism: explaining the enigma. Oxford: Blackwell.

Gillberg, C. & Coleman, M. (2000a): Asperger syndrome. In: *The biology of the autistic syndromes*, ed. C. Gillberg & M. Coleman, 3rd ed., pp. 39–52. Cambridge: Cambridge University Press.

Gillberg, C. & Coleman, M. (2000b): Epilepsy and electrophysiology. In: *The biology of the autistic syndromes*, ed. C. Gillberg & M. Coleman, 3rd ed., pp. 185–216. Cambridge: Cambridge University Press.

Hashimoto, T., Sasaki, M., Sugai, K., Hanaoka, S., Fukumizu, M. & Kata, T. (2001): Paroxysmal discharges on EEG in young autistic patients are frequent in frontal regions. *J. Med. Invest.* **48**, 175–180.

Hermelin, B. & O'Connor N. (1967): Remembering of words by psychotic and subnormal children. *Br. J. Psychol.* **58**, 213–218.

Hermelin, B. & O'Connor, N. (1970): Psychological experiments with autistic children. Oxford: Pergamon.

Hobson, R.P., Ouston, J. & Lee. A. (1988): What's in a face? The case of autism. *Br. J. Psychol.* **79**, 441–453.

Howe, M.J., Davidson, J.W. & Sloboda, J.A. (1998): Innate talents: reality or myth? *Behav. Brain Sci.* **21**, 399–407.

Hughes, C., Russell, J. & Robbins, T.W. (1994): Evidence for executive dysfunction in autism. *Neuropsychologia* **32**, 477–492.

Kandel, E.R. & Schwartz, J.H. (1985): Hypothalamus, limbic system and cerebral cortex. In: *Principles of neural science*, ed. E.R. Kandel & J.H. Schwartz, 2nd ed., pp. 609–619. New York: Elsevier Science.

Kemper, T.L. & Bauman, M. (1998): Neuropathology of infantile autism. *J. Neuropathol. Exp. Neurol.* **57**, 645–652.

Leslie, A.M. (1987): Pretence and representation: the origins of 'theory of mind'. *Psychol. Rev.* **94**, 412–426.

Luna, B., Minshew, N.J., Garver, K.E., Lazar, N.A., Thulborn, K.R., Eddy, W.F. & Sweeney, J.A. (2002): Neocortical system abnormalities in autism: an fMRI study of spatial working memory. *Neurology* **59,** 834–840.

Meltzoff, A.N. & Gopnik, A. (1993): The role of imitation in understanding persons and developing a theory of mind. In: *Understanding other minds: perspectives from autism*, ed. S. Baron-Cohen, H. Tager-Flusberg, D.J. Cohen, pp. 335–366. Oxford: Oxford University Press.

Meltzoff, A.N. (1988): Infant imitation and memory: nine month-olds in immediate and deferred tests. *Child Dev.* **59**, 217–225.

Murphy, D.G., Critchley, H.D., Schmitz, N., McAlonan, G., Van Amelsvoort, T., Robertson, D., Daly, E., Rowe, A., Russell, A., Simmons, A., Murphy, K.C. & Howlin, P. (2002): Aperger syndrome: a proton magnetic resonance spectroscopy study of brain. *Arch. Gen. Psychiatry* **59**, 885–891.

Ozonoff, S. & Miller, J.N. (1996): An exploration of right hemisphere contributions to the pragmatic impairments of autism. *Brain Lang.* **52**, 411–434.

Perner, J., Frith, U., Leslie, A.M., & Leekam, S.R. (1989): Exploration of the autistic theory of mind: knowledge, belief and communication. *Child Dev.* **60**, 689–700.

Preston, A.R., Shrager, Y., Dudukovic, N.M. & Gabrieli, J.D. (2004): Hippocampal contribution to the novel use of relational information in declarative memory. *Hippocampus* **14**, 148–152.

Rapin, I. & Dunn, M. (2003): Update on the language disorders of individuals on the autistic spectrum. *Brain Dev.* **25**, 166–172.

Ricks, D.M. & Wing, L. (1976): Language, communication and the use of symbols in normal and autistic children. *J. Autism Child Schizophr.* **5**, 191–221.

Ridley, R.M. (1994): The psychology of perseverative and stereotyped behaviour. *Prog. Neurobiol.* **44**, 221–231.

Riva, D. & Cazzaniga, L. (1986): Late effects of unilateral brain lesions sustained before and after age one. *Neuropsychologia* **24**, 423–428.

Riva, D. & Giorgi, C. (2000): The cerebellum contributes to higher functions during development. Evidence from a series of children surgically treated for posterior fossa tumours. *Brain* **123**, 1051–1061.

Riva, D., Saletti, V. & Bulgheroni, S. (2001): Memory disturbances in early hippocampal pathology. In: *Limbic seizures in children*, ed. G. Avanzini, A. Beaumanoir & L. Mira, pp. 167–174. London: John Libbey.

Rizzolatti, G., Fogassi, L. & Gallese, V. (2001): Neurophysiological mechanism underlying the understanding and imitation of action. *Nat. Rev. Neurosci.* **2**, 661–670.

Rogers, S.J. & Pennington, B.F. (1991): A theoretical approach to the deficits in infantile autism. *Dev. Psychopathol.* **3**, 137–162.

Rowe, A.D., Bullock, P.R., Polkey, C.E. & Morris, R.G. (2001): 'Theory of mind' impairments and their relationship to executive functioning following frontal lobe excisions. *Brain* **124**, 600–616.

Rutter, M. (1968): Concepts of autism: a review of research. *J. Child Psychol. Psychiatry* **9**, 1–25.

Rutter, M. & Bailey, A. (1993): Thinking and relationships: mind and brain – some reflection on theory of mind and autism. In: *Understanding other minds: perspective from autism*, ed. S. Baron-Cohen, H. Tager-Flusberg & D.J. Cohen, pp. 481–504. Oxford: Oxford University Press.

Schmahmann, J.D. & Pandya, D.N. (1990): Anatomical investigation of projection from the thalamus to the posterior parietal cortices in the rhesus monkey: a WGA-HRP and fluorescent tracer study. *J. Comp. Neurol.* **295**, 299–326.

Schmahmann, J.D. & Pandya, D.N. (1997): The cerebro-cerebellar system. In: *The cerebellum and cognition. International Review of Neurobiology*, ed. J.D. Schmahmann, vol. 41, pp. 31–60. San Diego: Academic Press.

Schmahmann, J.D. & Sherman, J.C. (1997): Cerebellar cognitive syndrome. *Rev. Neurobiol.* **41**, 433–440.

Schmahmann, J.D. & Sherman, J.C. (1998): Cerebellar cognitive syndrome. *Brain* **121**, 561–579.

Shah., A. & Frith, U. (1993). Why do autistic individuals show superior performance on the block design task? *J. Child Psychol. Psychiatry* **34**, 1351–1364.

Smith, M.L., Kates, M.H. & Vriezen, E.R (1992): The developmental of frontal-lobe functions. In: *Handbook of neuropsychology*, ed. S.J. Segalowitz, I. Rapin, vol. 7, pp. 309–330, Amsterdam: Elsevier.

Stone, V.E., Baron-Cohen, S. & Knight, R.T.J. (1998): Frontal lobe contributions to theory of mind. *J. Cogn. Neurosci.* **10**, 640–656.

Sweeten, T.L., Posey, D.J., Shekhar, A. & McDougle, C.J. (2002): The amygdala and related structures in the pathophysiology of autism. *Pharmacol. Biochem. Behav.* **71**, 449–455.

Tomasello, M. (1992): The social bases of language acquisition. *Soc. Devel.* **1**, 67–87.

Tuchman, R. & Rapin, I. (2002): Epilepsy in autism. *The Lancet Neurol.* **1**, 352–358.

Turner, M. (1996): Repetitive behaviour and cognitive functioning in autism. Cambridge: University of Cambridge. [PhD thesis.]

Wing, L. & Gould, J. (1979): Severe impairments of social interaction and associated abnormalities in children: epidemiology and classification. *J. Autism Dev. Disord.* **9**, 11–29.

Wing, L. (1993): The definition and prevalence of autism: a review. *Eur. Child Adolesc. Psychiatry* **2**, 61–74.

Willimas, J.H.G., Whiten, A., Suddendorf, T. & Perrett, D.I. (2001): Imitation, mirror neurons and autism. *Neurosci. Biobehav. Rev.* **25**, 287–295.

Autistic spectrum disorders, D. Riva and I. Rapin (eds.)

Chapter 11

The cerebellum and control of attention in autism

Natacha Akshoomoff

Department of Psychiatry, School of Medicine, University of California, 9500 Gilman Drive, San Diego, CA 92093–0603, USA
natacha@ucsd.edu

Summary

The development of the brain is affected in a variety of complex ways in autism. Abnormalities in the cerebellum have been a consistent finding across published reports. Postmortem and brain imaging studies of very young children suggest that cerebellar abnormalities are present early in development. While the cerebellum is typically associated with motor control, cognitive neuroscience investigations over the past 15 years have shown that it also plays an important role in a variety of cognitive functions, including attention. Anticipatory functions are important when humans perform a variety of cognitive tasks, particularly those involving the regulation of attention. Based on evidence that the cerebellum plays an important role in anticipatory functions, a neuropsychological model of attention in autism has been proposed. Early abnormalities in the development of the cerebellum in autism are hypothesized as contributing to a cascade of neurodevelopmental events, which in turn affect early social, language, and cognitive development.

Introduction

Various studies have focused on determining the brain abnormalities in patients with autism and related disorders. Consistent with the complex and varied behavioural features of the autistic spectrum of disorders, neurobiological investigations have shown that the neural abnormalities are also complex and variable (for review, see Akshoomoff *et al.*, 2002). In this chapter I will focus on one area of interest, the cerebellum.

Cerebellar abnormalities in autism

Postmortem studies of individuals with autism offer the potential of more detailed neuroanatomical information than is available from *in vivo* studies, although there are advantages to both methods. The most apparent and consistent abnormalities across postmortem cases have been confined to the cerebellum and the related inferior olive. Specifically, the most consistently reported pathological observation in the postmortem brain in autism is a reduced number of Purkinje cells (Ritvo *et al.*, 1986; Bailey *et al.*, 1998; Bauman & Kemper, 2003). Purkinje neurons are the main output cells in the cerebellum. The nature of the neuronal abnormalities is suggestive of earlier rather than later developmental age at the time of loss or maldevelopment.

Quantitative magnetic resonance imaging (MRI) studies have identified abnormally reduced size of cerebellar hemispheres and subregions within the cerebellar vermis in children, adolescents, and adults with autism (for example, Murakami *et al.*, 1989; Courchesne *et al.*, 1994a; Hashimoto *et al.*, 1995; Levitt *et al.*, 1999).

Paediatric head circumference measurements are typically well correlated with total brain volume (Bartholomeusz *et al.*, 2002). Based on paediatric head circumference records, it appears that total brain volume is normal at birth in children later diagnosed with autism but shows an abnormal increase in size by 14 months of age (Courchesne *et al.*, 2003). Measurements of brain volume from MRI data indicated that by 2 to 4 years of age, 90 per cent of children with autism have a brain volume significantly larger than average, and 37 per cent have brain volumes consistent with developmental macrencephaly (Courchesne *et al.*, 2001). A similar increase in whole brain volume has also been reported in another study of preschool children with autistic spectrum disorders (Sparks *et al.*, 2002).

To determine the details of abnormal growth, anatomical parcellation and segmentation was carried out on the MRI data collected in our laboratory (Courchesne *et al.*, 2001). Cerebral white and grey matter volumes were abnormally large in the preschool children with autism, whereas older children and adolescents with autism did not have such enlarged grey and white matter volumes compared with a control group. Cerebellar grey matter volume from the youngest children with autism was more similar to age-matched control subjects, while among the older subjects with autism cerebellar grey matter volume was significantly smaller than normal. It thus appears that while cerebellar volume typically increases with age, the rate of increase is smaller in children with autism, so the difference in cerebellar grey matter volume between autism and typical groups increases in magnitude with age. Cerebellar white matter volume showed an unexpected and striking abnormality. In the youngest subjects with autism, the matter volumes were about 38 per cent larger than in the control group. However, in the control group there were robust age-related increases in volume, which eventually reached the volume seen in the youngest autistic children, while in the autism group the volume increased little with age. Cerebellar vermis lobules VI and VII were reduced in size across the entire autism group (ages 2 to 16) compared with the control group, and unlike the control group there were no age-related size increases in the area of the cerebellar vermis.

It is noteworthy that cerebellar white matter volume during the preschool period was abnormally increased in both low-functioning and high-functioning children with autism, as well as in children diagnosed with PDD-NOS (Pervasive Developmental Disorders–Not Otherwise Specified) after the age of 5 (Akshoomoff *et al.*, 2004). Using a discriminant function analysis, differences in cerebellar white matter volume most significantly separated the lower-functioning autism group from the control group, while differences in the area of the anterior and posterior cerebellar vermis and cerebral white matter volume most significantly separated the higher-functioning autism group from the control group. It thus appears that neuroanatomical variability during the preschool period is related to diagnostic and functional outcome. It is also interesting to note that in a study of 22 relatively high-functioning male individuals with autism (12 to 50 years of age), the total volumes of the cerebellum and of the cerebellar hemispheres were significantly larger in the autism group (Hardan *et al.*, 2001).

The cerebellum and attention

While it is clear that the cerebellum is important for motor coordination, autism is a disorder that is not typically associated with motor control abnormalities. Various studies have shown that the cerebellum is active during non-motor tasks and appears to play an important support role in computations carried out by other parts of the brain (for review, see Courchesne & Allen, 1997).

At the time that cognitive neuroscientists were beginning to examine this idea, I decided to investigate the possibility that damage to the cerebellum may affect the control of attention. Deficits in attention are very common in children with autism (see Lovaas *et al.*, 1979; Dawson & Lewy, 1989; Casey *et al.*, 1993; Courchesne *et al.*, 1995; Bryson *et al.*, 1997; Allen & Courchesne, 2001). Studying patients with circumscribed damage to the cerebellum in a controlled experiment provided a potential neuropsychological model of damage to the cerebellum in autism. I conducted a series of experiments with children who had suffered localized damage to the cerebellum owing to surgical removal of a cerebellar astrocytoma. In each experiment, there were two conditions: a 'shift attention' condition and a 'focus attention' condition. In the shift attention condition, the subjects wait for a target and after responding to that target, must now shift their attention to the other class of stimuli and wait for that target. The first experiment included visual and auditory stimuli (Akshoomoff & Courchesne, 1992) and the second experiment included two types of visual stimuli (Akshoomoff & Courchesne, 1994). In the focus attention condition, the subject responds to the target every time it occurs and ignores the stimuli in the other modality or class. The results indicated that children with acquired damage to the cerebellum, but who were otherwise developmentally normal and who had reaction times similar to the control group, were impaired in rapidly shifting their attention. In another experiment, we found that individuals with autism also showed a similar deficit in rapidly shifting attention (Courchesne *et al.*, 1994b). These results suggested that perhaps the behavioural similarities between the two patient groups reflected damage to the same brain structure, the cerebellum.

Townsend and her colleagues have also conducted several studies to investigate speed of attention orienting in autism, and the brain systems that underlie these operations (Townsend & Courchesne, 1994; Townsend *et al.*, 1996a; Townsend *et al.*, 1996b; Akshoomoff *et al.*, 1997; Townsend *et al.*, 1999; Townsend *et al.*, 2001). These studies have shown that damage to the cerebellum leads to extremely slowed attention orienting. Patients with acquired cerebellar damage as well as those with autism are abnormally slow in their ability to detect a target presented shortly after an attentional cue, but normal in performance when given more time to orient their attention following a cue. A similar pattern of deficits was also observed in children with a diagnosis of autism or PDD-NOS (Harris *et al.*, 1999), and the degree of slowed orientation to visual cues was significantly correlated with the degree of cerebellar abnormality but not with frontal lobe volume.

This pattern of performance was also observed in a task in which performance depends upon speed of perceptual processing (target discrimination) rather than on the speed of motor response (target detection) (Townsend *et al.*, 1996b; Townsend *et al.*, 1999). There was also a significant correlation between the area of lobules VI-VII in the vermis divided by total brain volume (to control for overall brain size) and the degree of orienting deficit. Attentional dysfunction in more naturalistic settings in young children with autism has also been linked to cerebellar abnormalities (Pierce & Courchesne, 2001).

Functional brain imaging techniques have allowed researchers to investigate brain activation patterns as a function of different task demands. Allen and his colleagues conducted an fMRI experiment (based on the focus attention task from Akshoomoff & Courchesne, 1994) to determine how the cerebellum may be involved in the non-motor aspects of attention (Allen *et al.*, 1997). In order to differentiate brain activation associated with the motor response, a simple motor task was administered. A sensory task was also administered to differentiate brain activation caused by visual stimulation in the absence of attentional demands. Allen and colleagues found that motor activation was localized to the ipsilateral anterior posterior cerebellar hemisphere, while activation during the non-spatial selective attention task was localized to the superior posterior cerebellar hemispheres (bilaterally). Several other studies have also reported similar patterns of cerebellar activation that is independent of motor demands during different types of attention tasks (Rees *et al.*, 1997; Corbetta *et al.*, 1998; Coull & Nobre, 1998; Le *et al.*, 1998; Casey *et al.*, 2000).

In another study, Allen and Courchesne administered three different attention tasks to healthy adults and adults with autism during fMRI (Allen & Courchesne, 2003). These tasks varied as a function of the speed of stimulus presentation: the 'slow task' had interstimulus intervals ranging from 350 to 850 ms; the 'medium task' had interstimulus intervals ranging from 300 to 550 ms; and the 'fast task' (also used in the Allen *et al.*, 1997 study) had interstimulus intervals ranging from 200 to 450 ms. The control subjects showed bilateral superior posterior cerebellar hemisphere activation during the attention task. Even when matched for task difficulty, the individuals with autism showed minimal cerebellar activation during the attention task. During the motor task, individuals with autism showed a pattern of activation that was more diffuse than normal.

A network of brain regions regulates attention. Several studies have shown that even when individuals with autism are normal in their behavioural performance in attention tasks, they achieve this normality using abnormal physiological means. For example, in a sustained covert attention task that normally activates a network of superior parietal, middle temporal, dorsolateral prefrontal, premotor, and medial frontal cortices, the ventral occipital and striate regions of cortex were activated in individuals with autism (Belmonte & Yurgelun-Todd, 2003). Studies using electrophysiological techniques suggest abnormal frontal and parietal responses (Townsend & Courchesne, 1994; Townsend *et al.*, 1996a; Townsend *et al.*, 2001). Future studies that examine cortical and cerebellar activation during attention tasks will provide information on how these systems work together and how they are affected in autism.

Attention and autism

My colleagues and I have proposed that the fundamental function of the cerebellum is to learn predictive relations among sequences of events (Akshoomoff *et al.*, 1997; Courchesne & Allen, 1997). When an analogous sequence occurs, the cerebellum can generate predictions about upcoming events and prepare the necessary neural systems. In the attention experiments described above, the stimulus sequence is random and yet the cerebellum is active. It may be that the cerebellum is active in an attempt to learn and predict the sequence but until the sequence becomes predictable, the cerebellum does not provide much useful preparatory output to other neural systems. The cerebellum is needed for rapid sensory tracking (Crispino & Bullock, 1984; Gao *et al.*, 1996; Parsons *et al.*, 1997), which may also help to explain the robust finding of cerebellar activation during attention tasks.

If the cerebellum is not active when individuals with autism are undertaking these attention tasks, then how are they able to perform as well as control subjects under most circumstances? Their performance was worse than expected when the presentation rate was faster (Allen & Courchesne, 2003). Similarly, the behavioural performance of individuals with autism or patients with acquired cerebellar damage was worse than expected under faster presentation rates or when the attentional demands were increased by presenting the target detection sequences rapidly. This leaves open the possibility that when performance is adequate in individuals with autism, it requires them to expend a great deal more effort than normal. Adequate performance thus reflects the compensatory strategies they have developed over time to achieve normal performance, which include the use of lower level or less efficient neural networks to regulate attention.

It is also possible that damage outside the cerebellum in autism has an impact on performance and activation patterns, including the activation of cerebellar circuits. Finally, developmental abnormalities in cerebellar circuitry formation may have effects on the functional development of other neural regions, perhaps helping to explain the observed differences in ability level associated with autism. Further study with protocols that allow detailed analysis of cerebellar activation as well as cerebral activation patterns are needed.

These results suggest that in autism, early damage to the cerebellum affects the ability to rapidly orient, focus, and shift attention – skills that are important for the development of joint social attention. Joint social attention is critical for the development of language skills (Bakeman & Adamson, 1984; Bates *et al.*, 1988). Children with autism are known to have difficulty with joint social attention, and deficits in social attention are typically correlated with language skill levels (Loveland & Landry, 1986; Kasari *et al.*, 1990; Mundy *et al.*, 1990; Leekam *et al.*, 2000). Thus the cerebellar abnormalities in autism may affect early development of attention necessary for the development of social and linguistic functions (Courchesne *et al.*, 1994b; Akshoomoff, 2000). On a similar note, anticipation is critical for social interactions. If the ability to anticipate is aided by the cerebellum, then abnormal development of the cerebellum may make anticipatory functions suboptimal in autism. The characteristic 'maintenance of sameness' feature of autism may reflect the difficulty these children have in dealing with uncertainty.

A key step in working with young children with an autistic spectrum disorder is to help them respond more readily when others try to attract their attention (such as responding when someone calls their name). As children become more responsive, it then becomes possible to help them develop the skills necessary to obtain the attention of others in a communicative fashion. Despite the widespread abnormalities that are present in the brain, environmental influences can have a lasting impact on the developing brain, leading to the possibility of improved outcome in the lives of these children.

Acknowledgments: I am grateful to the Mariani Foundation for promoting the Conference in Assisi. Support for this work was provided by the National Institute of Neurological Disorders and Stroke (R01 NS-19855) and the National Institute of Mental Health (R01 MH-36840).

References

Akshoomoff, N. (2000): Neurological underpinnings of autism. In: *Autism spectrum disorders: a transactional developmental perspective*, eds. A.M. Wetherby & B.M. Prizant, pp. 167–190. Baltimore: Paul H. Brookes Publishing Co.

Akshoomoff, N.A. & Courchesne, E. (1992): A new role for the cerebellum in cognitive operations. *Behav. Neurosci.* **106**, 731–738.

Akshoomoff, N.A. & Courchesne, E. (1994): ERP evidence for a shifting attention deficit in patients with damage to the cerebellum. *J. Cogn. Neurosci.* **6**, 388–399.

Akshoomoff, N.A., Courchesne, E. & Townsend, J. (1997): Attention coordination and anticipatory control. *Int. Rev. Neurobiol.* **41**, 575–598.

Akshoomoff, N., Pierce, K. & Courchesne, E. (2002): The neurobiological basis of autism from a developmental perspective. *Dev. Psychopathol.* **14**, 613–634.

Akshoomoff, N., Lord, C., Lincoln, A.J., Courchesne, R.Y., Carper, R.A., Townsend, J. & Courchesne, E. (2004): Outcome classification of preschool children with autism spectrum disorders using MRI brain measures. *J. Am. Acad. Child Adolesc. Psychiatry* **43**, 349–357.

Allen, G. & Courchesne, E. (2001): Attention function and dysfunction in autism. *Front. Biosci.* **6**, D105-D119.

Allen, G. & Courchesne, E. (2003): Differential effects of developmental cerebellar abnormality on cognitive and motor functions in the cerebellum: an fMRI study of autism. *Am. J. Psychiatry* **160**, 262–273.

Allen, G., Buxton, R.B., Wong, E.C. & Courchesne, E. (1997): Attentional activation of the cerebellum independent of motor involvement. *Science* **275**, 1940–1943.

Bailey, A., Luthert, P., Dean, A., Harding, B., Janota, I., Montgomery, M., Rutter, M. & Lantos, P. (1998): A clinicopathological study of autism. *Brain* **121**, 889–905.

Bakeman, R. & Adamson, L.B. (1984): Coordinating attention to people and objects in mother-infant and peer-infant interaction. *Child Dev.* **55**, 1278–1289.

Bartholomeusz, H.H., Courchesne, E. & Karns, C. (2002): Relationship between head circumference and brain volume in healthy normal toddlers, children, and adults. *Neuropediatrics* **33**, 239–241.

Bates, E., Bretherton, I. & Snyder, L.S. (1988): *From first words to grammar: individual differences and dissociable mechanisms.* New York: Cambridge University Press.

Bauman, M.L. & Kemper, T.L. (2003): The neuropathology of the autism spectrum disorders: what have we learned? In: Novartis Foundation Symposium. *Autism: neural basis and treatment possibilities*, vol. 251, eds. G. Bock & J. Goode, pp. 112–122. Chichester: John Wiley & Sons, discussion 122-128, 281–297.

Belmonte, M.K. & Yurgelun-Todd, D.A. (2003): Functional anatomy of impaired selective attention and compensatory processing in autism. *Cogn. Brain Res.* **17**, 651–664.

Bryson, S.E., Landry, R. & Wainwright, J.A. (1997): A componential view of executive dysfunction in autism. In: *Attention, development, and psychopathology*, eds. J.A. Burack & J.T. Enns, pp. 232–259. New York: Guilford Press.

Casey, B.J., Gordon, C.T., Mannheim, G.B. & Rumsey, J.M. (1993): Dysfunctional attention in autistic savants. *J. Clin. Exp. Neuropsychol.* **15**, 933–946.

Casey, B.J., Thomas, K.T., Welsh, T.F., Badgaiyan, R.D., Eccard, C.H., Jennings, J.R. & Crone, E.A. (2000): Dissociation of response conflict, attentional selection, and expectancy with functional magnetic resonance imaging. *Proc. Natl. Acad. Sci. USA* **97**, 8728–8733.

Corbetta, M., Akbudak, E., Conturo, T.E., Snyder, A.Z., Ollinger, J.M., Drury, H.A., Linenweber, M.R., Petersen, S.E., Raichle, M.E., Van Essen, D.C. & Shulman, G.L. (1998): A common network of functional areas for attention and eye movements. *Neuron* **21**, 761–773.

Coull, J.T. & Nobre, A.C. (1998): Where and when to pay attention: the neural systems for directing attention to spatial locations and to time intervals as revealed by both PET and fMRI. *J. Neurosci.* **18**, 7426–7435.

Courchesne, E. & Allen, G. (1997): Prediction and preparation, fundamental functions of the cerebellum. *Learn. Mem.* **4**, 1–35.

Courchesne, E., Townsend, J. & Saitoh, O. (1994a): The brain in infantile autism: posterior fossa structures are abnormal [see comments]. *Neurology* **44**, 214–223.

Courchesne, E., Townsend, J., Akshoomoff, N.A., Saitoh, O., Yeung-Courchesne, R., Lincoln, A.J., James, H.E., Haas, R.H., Schreibman, L. & Lau, L. (1994b): Impairment in shifting attention in autistic and cerebellar patients. *Behav. Neurosci.* **108**, 848–865.

Courchesne, E., Akshoomoff, N.A., Townsend, J. & Saitoh, O. (1995): A model system for the study of attention and the cerebellum: infantile autism. *Electroencephalogr. Clin. Neurophysiol. Suppl.* **44**, 315–325.

Courchesne, E., Karns, C., Davis, H.R., Ziccardi, R., Carper, R., Tigue, Z., Chisum, H.J., Moses, P., Pierce, K., Lord, C., Lincoln, A.J., Pizzo, S., Schreibman, L., Haas, R.H., Akshoomoff, N. & Courchesne, R.Y. (2001): Unusual brain growth patterns in early life in patients with autistic disorder: an MRI study. *Neurology* **57**, 245–254.

Courchesne, E., Carper, R. & Akshoomoff, N. (2003): Evidence of brain overgrowth in the first year of life in autism. *JAMA* **290**, 337–344.

Crispino, L. & Bullock, T.H. (1984): Cerebellum mediates modality-specific modulation of sensory responses of midbrain and forebrain in rat. *Proc. Natl. Acad. Sci. U.S.A.* **81**, 2917–2920.

Dawson, G. & Lewy, A. (1989): Arousal, attention, and the socioemotional impairments of individuals with autism. In: *Autism: nature, diagnosis, and treatment*, ed. G. Dawson, pp. 49–74. New York: Guilford Press.

Gao, J.H., Parsons, L.M., Bower, J.M., Xiong, J., Li, J. & Fox, P.T. (1996): Cerebellum implicated in sensory acquisition and discrimination rather than motor control [see comments]. *Science* **272**, 545–547.

Hardan, A.Y., Minshew, N.J., Harenski, K. & Keshavan, M.S. (2001): Posterior fossa magnetic resonance imaging in autism. *J. Am. Acad. Child Adolesc. Psychiatry* **40**, 666–672.

Harris, N.S., Courchesne, E., Townsend, J., Carper, R.A. & Lord, C. (1999): Neuroanatomic contributions to slowed orienting of attention in children with autism. *Cogn. Brain Res.* **8**, 61–71.

Hashimoto, T., Tayama, M., Murakawa, K., Yoshimoto, T., Miyazaki, M., Harada, M. & Kuroda, Y. (1995): Development of the brainstem and cerebellum in autistic patients. *J. Autism Dev. Disord.* **25**, 1–18.

Kasari, C., Sigman, M., Mundy, P. & Yirmiya, N. (1990): Affective sharing in the context of joint attention interactions of normal, autistic, and mentally retarded children. *J. Autism Dev. Disord.* **20**, 87–100.

Le, T.H., Pardo, J.V. & Hu, X. (1998): 4 T-fMRI study of nonspatial shifting of selective attention: cerebellar and parietal contributions. *J. Neurophysiol.* **79**, 1535–1548.

Leekam, S.R., López, B. & Moore, C. (2000): Attention and joint attention in preschool children with autism. *Dev. Psychol.* **36**, 261–273.

Levitt, J., Blanton, R., Capetillo-Cunliffe, L., Guthrie, D., Toga, A. & McCracken, J. (1999): Cerebellar vermis lobules VIII-X in autism. *Prog. Neuropsychopharmacol. Biol. Psychiatry* **23**, 625–633.

Lovaas, O.I., Koegel, R.L. & Schreibman, L. (1979): Stimulus overselectivity in autism: a review of research. *Psychol. Bull.* **86**, 1236–1254.

Loveland, K.A. & Landry, S.H. (1986): Joint attention and language in autism and developmental language delay. *J. Autism Dev. Disord.* **16**, 335–349.

Mundy, P., Sigman, M. & Kasari, C. (1990): A longitudinal study of joint attention and language development in autistic children. *J. Autism Dev. Disord.* **20**, 115–128.

Murakami, J.W., Courchesne, E., Press, G.A., Yeung-Courchesne, R. & Hesselink, J.R. (1989): Reduced cerebellar hemisphere size and its relationship to vermal hypoplasia in autism. *Arch. Neurol.* **46**, 689–694.

Parsons, L.M., Bower, J.M., Gao, J.H., Xiong, J., Li, J. & Fox, P.T. (1997): Lateral cerebellar hemispheres actively support sensory acquisition and discrimination rather than motor control. *Learn. Mem.* **4**, 49–62.

Pierce, K. & Courchesne, E. (2001): Restricted interests and stereotyped behaviors in autism: the role of the cerebellum. *Biol. Psychiatry* **49**, 655–664.

Rees, G., Frackowiak, R. & Frith, C. (1997): Two modulatory effects of attention that mediate object categorization in human cortex. *Science* **275**, 835–838.

Ritvo, E.R., Freeman, B.J., Scheibel, A.B., Duong, T., Robinson, H., Guthrie, D. & Ritvo, A. (1986): Lower Purkinje cell counts in the cerebella of four autistic subjects: initial findings of the UCLA-NSAC Autopsy Research Report. *Am. J. Psychiatry* **143**, 862–866.

Sparks, B.F., Friedman, S.D., Shaw, D.W., Aylward, E.H., Echelard, D., Artru, A.A., Maravilla, K.R., Giedd, J.N., Munson, J., Dawson, G. & Dager, S.R. (2002): Brain structural abnormalities in young children with autism spectrum disorder. *Neurology* **59**, 184–192.

Townsend, J. & Courchesne, E. (1994): Parietal damage and narrow 'spotlight' spatial attention. *J. Cogn. Neurosci.* **6**, 220–232.

Townsend, J., Courchesne, E. & Egaas, B. (1996a): Slowed orienting of covert visual-spatial attention in autism: Specific deficits associated with cerebellar and parietal abnormality. *Dev. Psychopathol.* **8**, 563–584.

Townsend, J., Harris, N.S. & Courchesne, E. (1996b): Visual attention abnormalities in autism: delayed orienting to location. *J. Int. Neuropsychol. Soc.* **2**, 541–550.

Townsend, J., Courchesne, E., Singer-Harris, N., Covington, J., Westerfield, M., Lyden, P., Lowry, T.P. & Press, G.A. (1999): Spatial attention deficits in patients with acquired or developmental cerebellar abnormality. *J. Neurosci.* **19**, 5632–5642.

Townsend, J., Westerfield, M., Leaver, E., Makeig, S., Jung, T.-P., Pierce, K. & Courchesne, E. (2001): Event-related brain response abnormalities in autism: evidence for impaired cerebello-frontal spatial attention networks. *Cogn. Brain Res.* **11**, 127–145.

Autistic spectrum disorders, D. Riva and I. Rapin (eds.)
© 2005 John Libbey Eurotext, pp. 99–114.

Chapter 12

PDD-associated behavioural disorders: neurobiology and therapeutic strategies

Alessandro Zuddas*, Maria Grazia Iacolina*, Laura Anchisi*, Alessandra Fois*, GianLuigi Melis* and Adriana DiMartino*°

* *Child Neuropsychiatry, Department of Neuroscience, University of Cagliari, via Ospedale 119, 09124 Cagliari, Italy;*
° *Institute for Pediatric Neuroscience, NYU Child Study Center, New York, NY, USA*
azuddas@unica.it

Summary

Pervasive developmental disorders (PDD), and autism in particular, are neurodevelopmental disorders involving an extensive network of brain regions that modulate social cognition from the early steps of postnatal development. Brain regions involved in social cognition (amygdala, hippocampus, prefrontal cortex and other specific parieto-temporal regions) are also impaired in other neuropsychiatric disorders such as anxiety and depression; impairment of frontal regions modulating the amygdala and hippocampus has also been observed in schizophrenia, obsessive-compulsive disorder, and attention deficit-hyperactivity disorder. Several neurotransmitters modulate the brain regions involved in the physiopathology of PDD; manipulation of serotonin and dopamine neurotransmission appears to be the most promising strategy for pharmacological amelioration of both core and associated symptoms. As no specific pharmacological treatments have been developed for autism or other PDD, current pharmacological strategies are based on drugs previously shown to be effective in co-morbid disorders or on symptoms often associated with the core triad of PDD.

Introduction

Autism and the pervasive developmental disorders (PDD) are chronic neurodevelopmental disorders characterized by impairment in the ability of social interaction, verbal and non-verbal communication, and by restricted interest and stereotypic patterns of behaviour. Qualitative impairments in reciprocal social interaction include inadequate appreciation of emotional and social cues (shown by a lack of responses to others' emotions), poor use of social signals, and lack of emotional and social reciprocity. Restricted patterns of interest, unusual responses to the environment, striking linguistic deviance (when language is present), and unusual motor behaviour (stereotyped, purposeless, repetitive activities) are common. The impairment of social interaction and communicative skills may improve over time but persists throughout life; it is often worsened by hyperactivity, irritability, temper tantrums, and aggressiveness against others or self; in many autistic/PDD children and adolescents, the impact of these behaviours may be so severe as to lead to institutionalization.

There are no biological markers for autism. Several lines of evidence indicate discrete changes in activity and morphology in specific brain areas of patients suffering from this group of disorders. Classical neuropathological observations are consistent with increased cell packing and smaller neuronal size in the limbic system, a decreased number of Purkinje cells in the cerebellum, and cortical dysgenetic lesions in a significant number of patients. Current evidence suggests that the deficit in social cognition and communication in autism may be related to dysfunction in the amygdala, hippocampus, and related limbic and cortical areas, with the cerebellum being a part of a distributed neuronal network responsible for social cognition and communication. At the neurochemical level, several neurotransmitters modulate the brain regions involved in these disorders; manipulation of serotonin and dopamine neurotransmission appear the most promising strategies for pharmacological amelioration of both core and associated symptoms.

Theory of mind, face recognition, and social cognition

The impairment in social competence is one of the most disabling features of the autistic disorder: the child shows deficits in specific aspects of joint attention such as declarative gestures, dyadic eye contact, or triadic gaze switching. Spontaneous appreciation of social emotional cues can be deficient, as well as the recognition of others' emotions, feelings, and interests. Affected individuals may be unable to anticipate others' behaviours and they have difficulty in understanding that their peers or classmates may have thoughts and emotions. They may be indifferent when parents embrace them, appearing self centred, eccentric, or uncaring to adults and to normal children. These specific impairments have been defined as a deficit of *'theory of mind'*.

The term of 'theory of mind', or mentalizing, describes the ability to understand the mental states (beliefs, desires, knowledge, and intentions) of others and to appreciate how they differ from one's own. The mentalizing system of the brain becomes active at about 18 months of age, allowing implicit attribution of intentions and other mental states. Between the ages of 4 and 6 years explicit mentalizing becomes possible, and from this age children are able to explain the misleading reasons that have given rise to a false belief (Frith & Frith, 2003). A discrete region of the temporo-parietal junction has recently been described as being specifically involved in reasoning about the contents of another person's mind (that is, the content of the mental state). A paper of Abu-Akel (2003a) proposes a single neurobiological model for the theory of mind, composed of a representational component centred in the posterior brain regions (temporal and parietal) and an application/execution component subserved by the prefrontal regions. The brain regions presented in this distributed network can be divided in terms of their involvement in the mentalizing process as follows:

(1) Representation of one's own mental states is subserved by the inferior parietal lobule region.

(2) Representation of others' mental states is subserved by the superior temporal sulcus region.

(3) Mental states represented in these regions are fed forward to the limbic-paralimbic system for socio-emotional regulation and interpretation.

(4) Processed information is then projected to the medial prefrontal cortex and inferolateral frontal cortex regions for application processing.

It has been also suggested that the theory of mind abilities are contingent on the integrity of the serotonergic and dopaminergic systems (Abu-Akel, 2003b).

An elegant series of functional imaging studies measured activation of specific brain areas during watching an animated sequence: an animation depicting two triangles moving randomly, in a goal-directed fashion (chasing, fighting) or interactively with implied intentions (coaxing, tricking) and eliciting description by the viewer in terms of mental state. Normal subjects showed increased activation of medial prefrontal cortex, superior temporal sulcus at the temporo-parietal junction, and the temporal pole (amygdala and hippocampus). Subjects with autism or Asperger syndrome showed lower activation in all these areas. Activation of the extrastriate cortex, on the other hand, was similar in both autistic and control groups, suggesting a reduced functional connectivity of the occipital visual regions with the superior temporal sulcus at the parietal-temporal junction, an area associated with processing of mentalizing, and with the temporal pole (Castelli *et al.*, 2002).

Processing the human face is an integral part of both interpersonal interactions and successful functioning within a social group; it is considered to be related the development of the theory of mind. A bilaterally distributed neural system supports face processing in the brain. A core system, consisting of the occipito-temporal regions in the extrastriate visual cortex, mediates the visual analysis of faces. The functional organization of this system embodies a distinction between the representation of invariant aspects of faces, which is the basis for recognizing individuals, and the representation of changeable aspects – such as eye gaze, expression, and lip movement – which underlies the perception of information that facilitates social communication. Features common to all faces – in contrast to no-face objects – engage a set of circuits centred on the ventral temporal lobe (fusiform gyrus or fusiform facial area). Other brain regions appear particularly sensitive to the innate emotionally evocative aspects of the face. Faces with a fearful expression specifically engage the amygdala, whereas faces evoking angry expressions specifically engage the ventral frontal lobe (Whalen *et al.*, 1998; Glascher *et al.*, 2004; Adolphs *et al.*, 2005). Functional brain imaging studies have also shown that expressions of fear and anger selectively activate the amygdala and prefrontal cortex, even when the faces conveying the emotion are presented briefly and masked to prevent conscious perception (Morris *et al.*, 1998; Whalen *et al.*, 1998). It has been postulated that the facial emotions may signal a potential threat: they can be rapidly extracted from the human visual system and automatically processed in the absence of conscious face perception (Williams & Mattingley, 2004).

When fearful, happy, or neutral faces are presented rapidly, the amygdala is preferentially activated in response to fearful and sad *versus* neutral faces (Adolphs & Tranel, 2004) but a rapid habituation process is prominent for fearful and sad faces (Breiter *et al.*, 1996). Several findings generated in non-human primate by selective lesions suggest a crucial role for the amygdala in detecting potential threats and mobilizing an appropriate behavioural response (part of which is fear), (Birbaumer *et al.*, 1998; Prather *et al.*, 2001; Amaral & Corbett, 2003). Amygdala lesions may blunt the monkey's response to normally fear-inducing stimuli, such as snakes. In humans, bilateral lesions of the amygdala impair recognition of fear in some but not all patients (Adolphs *et al.*, 1995).

Taken together, these studies indicate that the human amygdala responds preferentially to emotional stimuli (that is, faces) and rapidly habituates to them. They also suggest that effective strategies of exposure-based desensitization of the amygdala could be considered as one of the basic biological mechanism of cognitive-behavioural therapy: repeated exposure to fear/anxiety inducing stimuli 'desensitizes' the patient to those stimuli, inducing symptom amelioration and allowing the development of alternative cognitive compensatory strategies.

Morphological and functional abnormalities in the brain of autistic patients

The modular arrangement of the neocortex is based on the cell minicolumn, a self-contained ecosystem of neurons and their afferent, efferent, and interneuronal connections. Studies by Casanova *et al.* (2002) indicate that minicolumns in the brains of autistic patients are narrower, with an altered internal organization. More specifically, their minicolumns reveal less peripheral neuropil space and increased spacing among their constituent cells. The peripheral neuropil space of the minicolumn is the conduit, among other things, for inhibitory local circuit projections. The increased cell packing density in subcortical structures and a defect in the GABAergic fibres may be correlated with the anomalous signal processing (for example, filtering capacity of the neocortex) which is followed by an amplification of impulse and an increased prevalence of seizures among autistic patients (Casanova *et al.*, 2003). Abnormal modular arrangement of the neocortex could be considered as the neural basis of the abnormal discrimination of sensory stimuli such as hypersensitivity or hyposensitivity to noise, light, touch, or pain, and the anomalous posture observed in several autistic children; it could also be related to impaired modulation by the prefrontal cortex on the limbic areas involved in social cognition.

In normal young adults, functional imaging studies have shown that the fusiform gyrus, the amygdala, the temporal pole, the medial prefrontal cortex, and the infero-lateral frontal and superior temporal cortices are engaged in a social attribution task involving the perception of human-like interaction among three simple geometric shapes. Although the fusiform gyrus is typically activated in the perception of faces, its activation in a task without faces indicates that this region may also encode semantic information associated with faces that could be retrieved for social computation (Schultz *et al.*, 2003). In individuals with autism spectrum disorders, imaging studies have also shown the lack (or significant decrease) of activation in the response of the fusiform gyrus to emotionally neutral faces (Critchley *et al.*, 2000; Schultz *et al.*, 2000). During face processing a higher signal was measured in the more object-related medial occipital gyrus as well as in the visual search brain regions such as the superior parietal lobule and the medial frontal gyrus, where the frontal eye fields are located (Hubl *et al.*, 2003). It is important to note, however, that in children and adolescents with autistic spectrum disorders, only a minimal decrease in activation of the fusiform gyrus by facial affect processing has been shown by others (Hadjikhani & de Gelder, 2003; Wang *et al.*, 2004). During the experimental paradigm of one of these studies, amygdala activity was moderated by task demands in the typically developing children and adolescents but not in the group with autistic spectrum disorder.

Although several studies have shown anatomical and functional alterations of the amygdala in PDD (Kemper & Bauman, 1993; Bachevalier, 1994; Baron-Cohen *et al.*, 2000), the interpretation of these results is still puzzling; for example, amygdala volumes have been shown to be diminished (Aylward *et al.*, 1999; Haznedar *et al.*, 2000) or bilaterally enlarged (Howard *et al.*, 2000), suggesting abnormal neuronal pruning in early development. In fact, although several lines of evidence indicate that abnormalities in the amygdala could be considered the biological correlate of impairment of social interaction, the possibility that in autistic subjects this region may contribute to their abnormal fears and increased anxiety rather than to their abnormal social behaviours should be considered (Baron-Cohen *et al.*, 2000; Adolphs *et al.*, 2002).

Recent studies have indicated a bilateral significant decrease in grey matter concentration in the superior temporal sulcus, in the right temporal pole and in the cerebellum of autistic children (Boddaert *et al.*, 2004); others have shown that the amygdala is enlarged in children but not in adolescents, whereas the hippocampus is enlarged at all ages (Schumann *et al.*, 2004) and that a larger hippocampus is present in the healthy parents of autistic children as well (Rojas *et al.*, 2004). Dementieva and co-workers (2005) have observed an abnormal acceleration in head growth during the first and second months of life in a subgroup of autistic individuals.

Taken together, these results further support the view that PDD, and autism in particular, are neurodevelopmental disorders involving an extensive network of brain regions modulating social cognition from the early stages of postnatal development. Both morphological and functional abnormalities of specific brain regions, as well as the degree of functional impairment, may vary with age: specific abilities lacking at specific ages can be acquired later on, but a persistent impairment of social cognition remains present in adult life (Frith, 2001).

Social cognition: modulation by serotonin

Brain regions involved in social cognition (amygdala, hippocampus, and other specific parieto-temporal regions) are also impaired in other neuropsychiatric disorders such as anxiety and depression. Impairment of the frontal regions modulating the amygdala and hippocampus has also been observed in schizophrenia, obsessive-compulsive disorder, and attention deficit-hyperactivity disorder (ADHD). As no specific pharmacological treatments have been developed for autism or other PDD, current pharmacological strategies are based on drugs previously shown to be effective in co-morbid disorders or on symptoms often associated to the core triad of PDD.

The brain regions involved in social cognition are modulated by a dense serotoninergic innervation from the raphé nuclei of the brain stem. Raphé nuclei contain almost all the cell bodies of the serotoninergic neurons which project rostrally to the brain and caudally to the spinal cord, leading to a rich innervation of the basal ganglia, amygdala, hippocampus, hypothalamus, septum, thalamus, and several cortical regions.

In adult animals, serotonin plays important roles in mediating sleep, arousal, aggression, sensory gating, impulsivity, and attachment. In humans, reduced serotoninergic function has been associated with worsened sleep, depressed mood, altered arousal, increased aggression, greater impulsivity, and reduced social behaviours. The actions of serotonin (5-HT) are complex and depend greatly upon the specific location and class of receptor stimulated; depending on brain regions, a marked increase in extracellular 5-HT release can reduce appetite and aggression but also lead to a syndrome of distinctive repetitive behaviours (Anderson, 2002). A large body of evidence indicates that serotonin plays an important role in pre- and postnatal brain development. Serotonin and its associated transporters and receptors are found very early in development (by 4 months of gestation in humans) (Anderson, 2002). Serotonin regulates several aspect of the brain development, including cell division, differentiation, neurite outgrowth, and synaptogenesis. During childhood serotonin levels are significantly higher than in adult life, declining before puberty (Chugani *et al.*, 1997; Chugani *et al.*, 1999; Chugani, 2002). In autistic children, serotonin-synthesizing capacity increases gradually between the ages of 2 and 15 years to values 1.5 times the adult normal values in both males and females. Significant differences have been detected between the autistic and epileptic groups and between the autistic and sibling groups in age-related serotonin synthesizing capacity. These data suggest that humans undergo a period of high brain serotonin synthesizing capacity during childhood, and that this developmental process is disrupted in autistic children (Chugani *et al.*, 1999).

The role of the serotonin transporter (5-HTT) in the development of neuropsychiatric disorders has also been widely investigated. The highly evolutionarily conserved serotonin transporter regulates the entire serotoninergic system and its receptors by modulation of extracellular serotonin concentrations. Differences in serotonin transporter expression and function have been observed in several human disorders. Screens of DNA from patients with autism, ADHD, bipolar disorder, and Tourette's syndrome have detected signals in the chromosome 17q region where the serotonin transporter is located (Murphy *et al.*, 2004). Although association with a specific haplotype of the promoter for the 5-HTT transcription and autism is still controversial (Cook *et al.*, 1997; Maestrini *et al.*, 1999; Persico *et al.*, 2000; Conroy *et al.*, 2004; McCauley *et al.*, 2004; Mulder *et al.*, 2005), replicated studies have shown that the polymorphisms in the serotonin transporter gene influence SSRI response and the appearance of side effects (Mancama & Kerwin, 2003; Murphy *et al.*, 2004; Smits *et al.*, 2004). The polymorphisms have been found associated with an increased risk for hyperserotonaemia in a group of autistic patients who possibly represent a separate aetiological group (Coutinho *et al.*, 2004; Mulder *et al.*, 2004), but these findings have been not replicated by others (Persico *et al.*, 2000, Betancur *et al.*, 2002).

Executive dysfunction in autism: a role for dopamine

The associated behavioural symptoms with autism may be correlated with a specific deficit of executive functions (Dawson *et al.*, 2002; Sergeant *et al.*, 2002; Martin & McDonald, 2003; Hill & Frith, 2003; Hill, 2004). 'Executive function' (EF) is an umbrella term for functions such as planning, working memory, impulse control, inhibition, and mental flexibility, as well as for the initiation and monitoring of action. The executive control system coordinates multiple specific neural processes in order to direct behaviour, detecting the presence of a target, initiating mental operations, and ordering multiple responses. Future planning and behavioural modification are thought to require experience-dependent plasticity in neuronal circuits involving the prefrontal cortex, nucleus accumbens, and amygdala. A relation between deficits in executive function and the everyday behavioural difficulties and deficits in communication, play, and social relationships has been shown (Gilotty *et al.*, 2002). Autism has been labelled as an executive disorder because it is associated with various deficits of executive function. Cognitive flexibility, planning, and working memory have been reported significantly impaired in autism (Bishop, 1993; Hughes *et al.*, 1994; Ozonoff & Strayer, 1997; Ozonoff *et al.*, 2004).

While working memory and inhibitory control have been considered relatively spared in individuals with autism (Hughes *et al.*, 1999; Ozonoff & Strayer, 1997; Ozonoff & Strayer, 2001), recent studies showed that children with high-functioning autism exhibit a generalized and more profound impairment with EF tasks including inhibitory control than that observed in ADHD (Geurts *et al.*, 2004; Bishop & Norbury, 2005).

In autism, deficits in all executive function domains were observed, with a significant impairment in planning and cognitive flexibility, probably related to the stereotyped repetitive patterns of behaviour that are characteristic of the disorder (Happé & Frith, 1996).

The *executive control* system is centred on the prefrontal cortex and the anterior cingulate gyrus and includes the basal ganglia (Posner & Peterson, 1990); all these regions are functionally modulated by dopamine and other monoaminergic neurotransmitters. Dopamine suppresses the spontaneous activity of prefrontal cortex neurons, enhancing their response to specific input (Thierry *et al.*, 1992). Decreased dopamine function at prefrontal synapses (the mesocortical dopamine system) leads to deficits in inhibitory control and working memory (Goldman-Rakic, 1992). In this circuit, increasing postsynaptic dopaminergic function promotes the integration of relevant inputs from other cortical regions and enhances executive functions. Dopamine also interacts with other systems, such as the 5-HT system, which are components of the multiple attentional networks. In fact, fluoxetine, a selective blocker of the serotonin transporter, has been shown to reduce the hyperactivity trait in the dopamine transporter knockout mouse (Gainetdinov *et al.*, 1999).

Dopamine also plays a role as a trophic factor during maturation, influencing the later cortical specification, particularly of the prefrontal cortical areas. Moreover, the characteristic extension of the dopaminergic cortical innervations in the rostro-caudal direction during the last stages of evolution in mammals can also be related to the appearance of progressively more developed cognitive capacities. Such an extension of cortical dopamine innervation could be related to increased processing of cortical information through basal ganglia, during the course of either evolution or development (see Nieoullon, 2002 for review). Dopamine could therefore be considered a key neuroregulator that contributes to behavioural adaptation and to the anticipatory processes necessary for preparing voluntary action consequent upon intention. Impairment of dopaminergic transmission could contribute to cognitive impairment: normalizing dopamine transmission improves cognitive deficits in several neurological and psychiatric disorders.

Pharmacotherapy

There is no specific treatment designed to cure autism. The goals of intervention are currently to improve functioning and adaptability, and to reduce interfering behavior. Currently the best treatment is considered to be a combination of psychosocial and educational intervention combined with pharmacological therapies, when necessary, to target specific interfering symptoms.

Treatment methods for PDD involve special education, speech, language therapy, and family support. There are no drugs specifically designed for the treatment of autism and no pharmacological treatments have been shown to decrease the core symptoms of social and communication impairment typical of PDD. Several controlled studies have, however, demonstrated the efficacy of various different drugs in the treatment of the associated symptoms of autism. In PDD children with severe behaviour or emotional disorders, or with other co-morbid psychiatric disorders, pharmacotherapy can enhance the response to other non-pharmacological interventions. As part of an integrated treatment programme, different drugs with effects on the dopaminergic and serotonergic systems have been used in patients with pervasive developmental disorders.

Modulation of serotonin function by SSRI

Repetitive behaviours observed in autism mimic those of obsessive-compulsive disorder (OCD): serotonin reuptake inhibitors – including both the non-selective inhibitors such as clomipramine and the selective serotonin reuptake inhibitors (SSRIs) fluoxetine, sertraline, fluvoxamine, and paroxetine (an effective treatment for OCD) – have been used to ameliorate interfering repetitive behaviours, aggression and social relatedness in some children, adolescents, and adults with PDD.

A double-blind, placebo-controlled crossover study of fluoxetine in low doses, in two acute 8-week phases, showed that it is more effective than placebo in the treatment of repetitive behaviours in childhood autism (Hollander *et al.*, 2005). Beneficial effects of treatment with fluoxetine were described by Delong *et al.* (1998) in a subgroup of children with autistic spectrum disorder, treated for a mean of 21 months. Fluoxetine treatment resulted in improvement in temperament, social interaction, language production and language ability, awareness, and attention; and sometimes improvement in motor skills, self-care, and practical problem solving. Fluoxetine efficacy has been related to a family history of major affective disorder (especially bipolar), unusual achievement, and hyperlexia in the children (Delong *et al.*, 2002). Bipolar disorder, unusual intellectual achievement, and autistic spectrum disorders appear to cluster in specific families, suggesting they may share genetic determinants. Delong (2004) advanced the hypothesis that this subgroup of autism represents an early life phenotype of major mood disorder. If confirmed, this hypothesis would suggest that the basic biological defects determining major mood disorders might have prominent neurodevelopmental and cognitive dimensions. A positron emission tomographic study of the metabolic regional effects of fluoxetine in the brain of a patient with PDD confirm results observed in depression, with higher cingulate gyrus metabolic rates at baseline predicting an SSRI response (Buchsbaum *et al.*, 2001).

A double-blind, placebo-controlled study of the SSRI fluvoxamine has been published. In adult patients, fluvoxamine was significantly more effective than placebo at reducing repetitive thoughts and behaviour, maladaptive behaviour, and aggression. Fluvoxamine reduced inappropriate repetitive language use. Adverse effects included nausea and sedation, which were transient and of minor severity (McDougle *et al.*, 1996). Contrasting results have been reported in similar studies on children and adolescents (McDougle *et al.*, 2000). In children, several adverse effects such as sleep disturbance, climbing to high places, gastrointestinal symptoms, hyperactivity, and excitement have been reported during fluvoxamine treatment.

In a retrospective study citalopram has been shown to be effective in ameliorating anxiety symptoms associated with PDD in 66 per cent of patients, and mood symptoms improved significantly in 47 per cent. Mild side effects were reported (Namerow *et al.*, 2003). Posey *et al.* (1999) reported that paroxetine was effective in controlling a broad range of symptoms – including irritability, temper tantrums, and interfering preoccupations – in a 7-year-old boy with autism.

Current evidence does not support selection of one SSRI over another for any impairment associated with autism (Moore *et al.*, 2004). Clomipramine may also be effective at reducing repetitive thoughts and actions and aggressive behaviour, and for improving some elements of social behaviour such as eye contact and verbal responsivity in adults with PDD (Brodkin *et al*, 1997). Careful monitoring of adverse effects, particularly seizures, is warranted. Clomipramine, haloperidol, and placebo were compared with baseline in a study by Remington and coworkers (2001), and overall outcome, specific symptoms, and side effects were examined. Clomipramine proved comparable to haloperidol in terms of improvement compared with baseline, but only haloperidol proved superior to baseline on a global measure of autistic symptom severity, as well as specific measures for irritability and hyperactivity. Clomipramine did not seem to be more effective on a measure of stereotypy, nor was it better tolerated (compared with haloperidol, significantly more individuals receiving clomipramine interrupted the trial because of side effects, lack of efficacy, or behaviour problems).

Modulation of dopamine function by antipsychotic agents

Conventional antipsychotic drugs are commonly prescribed for patients with autistic spectrum disorder. However, a high incidence of severe adverse reactions such as sedation, acute dystonia, dyskinesia, and cognitive blunting made these drugs obsolete (Campbell *et al.*, 1997). Over the past 15 years, considerable interest has been generated by the introduction of the so-called 'atypical' or second generation antipsychotic agents. Atypical antipsychotic drugs have combined serotonin 5-HT_2 and dopamine D2 receptor antagonist properties: they have been reported effective in ameliorating some autistic symptoms, with a lower incidence of adverse reactions because they have combined serotonin 5-HT_2 and dopamine D2 receptor antagonist properties. The affinity of these agents for serotonin receptors may also provide protection against extrapyramidal symptoms. In contrast to the multireceptor hypotheses, Kapur & Seeman (2001) predict that the atypical antipsychotic effect can be produced by appropriate modulation of the D2-type dopamine receptor alone. Given the lower frequency of extrapyramidal symptoms with atypical antipsychotic agents and their reported efficacy for treating both positive and negative symptoms in adults with schizophrenia, these agents are often given to children with developmental disorders.

Several small, open label studies have suggested the clinical efficacy of clozapine (Zuddas *et al.*, 1996) and olanzapine (Potenza *et al.*, 1999; Malone *et al.*, 2001; Kemner *et al.*, 2002) in reducing irritability, impulsivity, hyperactivity, self injury, aggression, and interfering repetitive behaviours in autistic children and adolescents. Quetiapine appears to have moderate efficacy in the treatment of adolescent patients with autism (Findling *et al.*, 2004), while significant side effects have been reported by others (Martin *et al.*, 1999a). In individuals with autism, ziprasidone appears to have a beneficial effect on behaviour, as does a switch to ziprasidone from other atypical antipsychotic agents, while it has been shown to improve major health indices including weight and lipid levels (McDougle *et al.*, 2002; Cohen *et al.*, 2004).

Several open label studies with risperidone (Simeon *et al.*, 1995; Fisman *et al.*, 1996; McDougle *et al.*, 1997; Findling *et al.*, 1997; Horrigan & Barnhill, 1997; Perry *et al.*, 1997; Zuddas *et al.*, 2000; Vercellino *et al.*, 2001; Malone *et al.*, 2002; Masi *et al.*, 2003; Mukkades *et al.*, 2004) and double-blind placebo-controlled studies (Aman *et al.*, 2002; McCracken *et al.*, 2002; Shea *et al.*, 2004) have confirmed the clinical efficacy of risperidone in autistic and PDD patients. The multisite, randomized, double-blind placebo-controlled study conducted by the Research Units on Pediatric Psychopharmacology Autism Network appears to be the most important. In all, 101 children were studied for 8 weeks and the result was a reduction in irritability, tantrums, aggression, or self injurious behaviours. In two thirds of the children with a positive response to risperidone at 8 weeks, the benefit was maintained at 6 months (McCracken *et al.*, 2002). Other studies confirmed the clinical efficacy of risperidone after 6 months without a significant increase in side effects (Zuddas *et al.*, 2000; Malone *et al.*, 2002; Di Martino & Zuddas, 2003; Masi *et al.*, 2003).

Risperidone and the other second generation antipsychotic agents have shown relatively consistent positive effects on working memory, executive functioning, and attention in schizophrenic patients; these effects appear to be mediated by modulation of 5-HT_2 receptors (Green *et al.*, 1997; Meltzer & McGurk, 1999). An alternative line of evidence indicates that risperidone and other antipsychotic drugs, but not haloperidol or other typical neuroleptics, increase dopamine and noradrenaline release in the prefrontal cortex. Both noradrenergic and dopaminergic systems are considered intimately associated with the modulation of higher cortical functions including attention, alertness, and vigilance because they are active on prefrontal cortical neurons. Dysregulation of the noradrenergic neurons causes functional disruption to both posterior and frontal attention systems. Decreased dopamine function at prefrontal synapses leads to deficits in inhibitory control and working memory. On the other hand, very high levels of catecholamines released during severe stress seem to disrupt cognitive functions in the prefrontal cortex, suggesting an inverse U-shaped response where too little or too much noradrenaline or dopamine receptor stimulation impairs neuronal and subsequent cognitive function (Arnsten, 2000).

Weight gain is a common side effect of atypical antipsychotic drugs. Moreover, risperidone therapy is associated with increased appetite, fatigue, drowsiness, dizziness, and drooling (McCracken *et al.*, 2002). Changes in liver function, glucose metabolism, or EEG and increase in night time sleep have been reported in children and adolescents taking risperidone, and less frequently, olanzapine and clozapine. An increase in serum prolactin and possible amenorrhoea have been also reported (Hellings *et al.*, 2001; Gagliano *et al.*, 2004; Martin *et al.*, 2004). Despite these limitations (Findling *et al.*, 1997; Horrigan & Barnhill, 1997; McDougle *et al.*, 1997; Perry *et al.*, 1997; Nicolson *et al.*, 1998), these drugs, and risperidone, can be considered as first line therapy in managing behavioural disruption in autistic children and adolescents.

Hyperactivity and impulsivity in autism: a role for the psychostimulants?

In a recent survey of over 3,000 families that are members of the Autism Society of North Carolina, the most frequently prescribed psychotropic drugs were antidepressants, followed by antipsychotics and stimulants (Langworthy-Lam *et al.*, 2002). In a similar study, about 20 per cent of patients with higher-functioning PDD received methylphenidate or dextroamphetamine at some time in their life (Martin *et al.*, 1999b), prescribed mainly to target symptoms of hyperactivity and inattention/distractibility. Despite the burgeoning literature on the efficacy of methylphenidate in children with ADHD (MTA Cooperative Group, 1999; Santosh & Taylor, 2000), and the substantial rates of prescribing of methylphenidate for children and adolescents with PDD combined with hyperactivity, inattention, and impulsivity, the use of this drug for PDD has been based mainly on anecdotal data, research in this area being limited and the results conflicting.

In the 1970s, Campbell and colleagues reported that amphetamine treatment for children with PDD was associated with an increased rate of stereotypy and irritability (Campbell *et al.*, 1972; Campbell *et al.*, 1976). Subsequent open-label studies also reported exacerbations of stereotypy, irritability, tics, and aggression, which discouraged the use of stimulants in this population (Aman *et al.*, 1997). By contrast, two controlled studies (Quintana *et al.*, 1995; Handen *et al.*, 2000) suggested that methylphenidate is effective for ADHD related symptoms in autistic children and adolescents, with minimal adverse effects, particularly at doses of less than 0.6 mg/kg/day (Handen *et al.*, 2000).

In a recent study, medical records of 195 patients (174 male; age 7.3 ± 3.4 years) with PDD treated with a stimulant were reviewed retrospectively. Only 24.6 per cent, 23.2 per cent, and 11.1 per cent of patients with a history of one, two, or three stimulant trials, respectively (Stigler *et al.*, 2004), responded to their first stimulant trial. Patients with Asperger's disorder, in contrast to those with autistic disorder or PDD-Not Otherwise Specified (PPD-NOS), were significantly more likely to respond to a stimulant trial; the use of concomitant medication positively affected the response, whereas no association was found between stimulant type, IQ and response. Adverse effects, including agitation, dysphoria, and irritability, often occurred. The investigators concluded that, overall, stimulants appeared ineffective and poorly tolerated for the majority of patients with PDD, although the response may differ according to PDD subtype.

Another recent pilot open study investigated the effects of ongoing methylphenidate treatment on ADHD-related and autistic symptoms in PDD children who did not have any adverse effects with an initial single dose. The results of the study indicated that, in a subgroup of children with PDD, methylphenidate can be tolerated and can be clinically useful, with persisting improvement in hyperactivity, impulsivity, and inattention. There was considerable agreement between the clinical assessments and both parent and teacher ratings. In contrast to the striking benefits observed for ADHD-related symptoms, no significant changes were measured for any of the autistic symptoms. Nevertheless, an improvement in global functioning was measured after 1 month, which persisted at the 3-month assessment. Parents reported that improvements in interfering behaviours allowed these children to attend longer activities with peers, and made them more amenable to other social activities with their parents. Children suffering from Asperger's disorder or from PDD-NOS tolerate methylphenidate better than those suffering from autistic disorder. The combination of language development, cognitive maturation, and the number of impaired clinical domains (rather than a single factor by itself) appeared to modulate the clinical effects of methylphenidate (Di Martino *et al.*, 2004).

Overall, current evidence suggests that treatment with methylphenidate in PDD, when effective, is exclusively symptomatic, affecting hyperactivity and impulsivity primarily, in addition to other related disruptive behaviours (for example, temper tantrums, oppositional behaviours). The administration of a single dose of methylphenidate can be used to minimize the risks of an adverse response and to improve the likelihood of recognizing PDD subjects who can benefit from ongoing methylphenidate treatment.

As reducing interfering behaviours appeared to allow some children with PDD to have better access to educational and psychosocial interventions, a large controlled study is currently being conducted by the Research Units for Pediatric Psychopharmacology of Autism Network to determine whether age, diagnosis, cognitive functions, or other factors are related to psychostimulant response in PDD patients (McDougle & Posey, 2002).

References

Abu-Akel, A. (2003a): A neurobiological mapping of theory of mind. *Brain Res. Brain Res. Rev.* **43**, 29–40.

Abu-Akel, A. (2003b): The neurochemical hypothesis of 'theory of mind'. *Med. Hypotheses* **60**, 382–386.

Adolphs, R. & Tranel, D. (2004): Impaired judgments of sadness but not happiness following bilateral amygdala damage. *J. Cogn. Neurosci.* **16**, 453–462.

Adolphs, R., Tranel, D., Damasio, H. & Damasio, A.R. (1995): Fear and the human amygdala. *J. Neurosci.* **15**, 5879–5891.

Adolphs, R., Baron-Cohen, S. & Tranel, D. (2002): Impaired recognition of social emotions following amygdala damage. *J. Cogn. Neurosci.* **14**, 1264–1274.

Adolphs, R., Gosselin, F., Buchanan, T.W., Tranel, D., Schyns, P. & Damasio, A.R. (2005): A mechanism for impaired fear recognition after amygdala damage. *Nature* **433**, 68–72.

Aman, M.G., Van Bourgondien, M.E., Osborne, P.W. & Sarphare, G. (1997): Side effects associated with psychoactive medication in individuals with autism. *J. Autism Dev. Disord.* **27**, 342–344.

Aman, M., De Smedt, G., Derivan, A., Lyons, B. & Findling, R.L. (2002): Double-blind, placebo-controlled study of risperidone for the treatment of disruptive behaviors in children wirh subaverage intelligence. *Am. J. Psychiatry* **159**, 1337–1346.

Amaral, D.G. & Corbett, B.A. (2003): The amygdala, autism and anxiety *Novartis Found. Symp.* **251**, 177–187.

Anderson, G.M. (2002): Genetics of childhood disorders. XLV. Autism, part 4. Serotonin in autism. *J. Am. Acad. Child Adolesc. Psychiatry* **41**, 1513–1516.

Arnsten, A.F. (2000): Genetics of childhood disorders: XVIII. ADHD, part 2. Norepinephrine has a critical modulatory influence on prefrontal cortical function. *J. Am. Acad. Child Adolesc. Psychiatry* **39**, 1201–1203.

Aylward, E.H., Minshew, N.J., Goldstein, G., Honeycutt, N.A., Augustine, A.M., Yates, K.O., Barta, P.E. & Pearlson, G.D. (1999): MRI volumes of amygdala and hippocampus in non-mentally retarded autistic adolescents and adults. *Neurology* **53**, 2145–2150.

Bachevalier, J. (1994): Medial temporal lobe structures and autism: a review of clinical and experimental findings. *Neuropsychologia* **32**, 627–648.

Baron-Cohen, S., Ring, H.A., Bullmore, E.T., Wheelwright, S., Ashwin, C. & Williams, S.C. (2000): The amygdala theory of autism. *Neurosci. Biobehav. Rev.* **24**, 355–364.

Betancur, C., Corbex, M., Spielewoy, C., Philippe, A., Laplanche, J.L., Launay, J.M., Gillberg, C., Mouren-Simeoni, M.C., Hamon, M., Giros, B., Nosten-Bertrand, M. & Leboyer, M. (2002): Serotonin transporter gene polymorphisms and hyperserotonemia in autistic disorder. *Mol. Psychiatry* **7**, 67–71.

Birbaumer, N., Grodd, W., Diedrich, O., Klose, U., Erb, M., Lotze, M., Schneider, F., Weiss, U. & Flor, H. (1998): fMRI reveals amygdala activation to human faces in social phobics. *Neuroreport* **9**, 1223–1226.

Bishop, D.V. (1993): Annotation: autism, executive functions and theory of mind: a neuropsychological perspective. *J. Child Psychol. Psychiatry* **34**, 279–293.

Bishop, D.V. & Norbury, C.F. (2005): Executive functions in children with communication impairments, in relation to autistic symptomatology. 2: Response inhibition. *Autism* **9**, 29–43.

Bishop, D.V. & Norbury, C.F. (2005): Executive functions in children with communication impairments, in relation to autistic symptomatology. 1: Generativity. *Autism* **9**, 9–27.

Boddaert, N., Chabane, N., Gervais, H., Good, C.D., Bourgeois, M., Plumet, M.H., Barthelemy, C., Mouren, M.C., Artiges, E., Samson, Y., Brunelle, F., Frackowiak, R.S. & Zilbovicius, M. (2004): Superior temporal sulcus anatomical abnormalities in childhood autism: a voxel-based morphometry MRI study. *Neuroimage* **23**, 364–369.

Breiter, H.C., Etcoff, N.L., Whalen, P.J., Kennedy, W.A., Rauch, S.L., Buckner, R.L., Strauss, M.M., Hyman, S.E. & Rosen, B.R. (1996): Response and habituation of the human amygdala during visual processing of facial expression. *Neuron* **17**, 875–887.

Brodkin, E.S., McDougle, C.J., Naylor, S.T., Cohen, D.J. & Price, L.H. (1997): Clomipramine in adults with pervasive developmental disorders: a prospective open-label investigation. *J. Child Adolesc. Psychopharmacol.* **7**, 109–121.

Buchsbaum, M.S., Hollander, E., Haznedar, M.M., Tang, C., Spiegel-Cohen, J., Wei, T.C., Solimando, A., Buchsbaum, B.R., Robins, D., Bienstock, C., Cartwright, C. & Mosovich, S. (2001): Effect of fluoxetine on regional cerebral metabolism in autistic spectrum disorders: a pilot study. *Int. J. Neuropsychopharmacol.* **4**, 119–125.

Campbell, M., Fish, B., David, R., Shapiro, T., Collins, P. & Koh, C. (1972): Response to triiodothyronine and dextroamphetamine: a study of preschool schizophrenic children. *J. Autism Child Schizophr.* **2**, 343–358.

Campbell, M., Small, A.M., Collins, P.J., Friedman, E., David, R. & Genieser, N. (1976): Levodopa and levoamphetamine: a crossover study in young schizophrenic children. *Curr. Ther. Res. Clin. Exp.* **19**, 70–86.

Campbell, M., Armenteros, J.L., Malone, R.P., Adams, P.B., Eisenberg, Z.W. & Overall, J.E. (1997): Neuroleptic-related dyskinesias in autistic children: a prospective, longitudinal study. *J. Am. Acad. Child Adolesc. Psychiatry.* **36**, 835–843.

Casanova, M.F., Buxhoeveden, D.P., Switala, A.A.E. & Roy, E. (2002): Microcolumnar pathology in autism. *Neurology* **12**, 428–42

Casanova, M.F., Buxhoeveden, D. & Gomez, J. (2003): Disruption in the inhibitory architecture of the cell minicolumn: implications for autism. *Neuroscientist* **9**, 496–507.

Castelli, F., Frith, C., Happe, F. & Frith, U. (2002): Autism, Asperger syndrome and brain mechanisms for the attribution of mental states to animated shapes. *Brain* **125**, 1839–1849.

Chugani, D.C. (2002): Role of altered brain serotonin mechanisms in autism. *Mol. Psychiatry* **7** (Suppl. 2), S16-S17.

Chugani, D.C., Muzik, O., Rothermel, R., Behen, M., Chakraborty, P., Mangner, T., da Silva, E.A. & Chugani, H.T. (1997): Altered serotonin synthesis in the dentatothalamocortical pathway in autistic boys. *Ann. Neurol.* **42**, 666–669.

Chugani, D.C., Muzik, O., Behen, M., Rothermel, R., Janisse, J.J., Lee, J. & Chugani, H.T. (1999): Developmental changes in brain serotonin synthesis capacity in autistic and nonautistic children. *Ann. Neurol.* **45**, 287–295.

Cohen, S.A., Fitzgerald, B.J., Khan, S.R. & Khan, A. (2004): The effect of a switch to ziprasidone in an adult population with autistic disorder: chart review of naturalistic, open-label treatment. *J. Clin. Psychiatry* **65**, 110–113.

Conroy, J., Meally, E., Kearney, G., Fitzgerald, M., Gill, M. & Gallagher, L. (2004): Serotonin transporter gene and autism: a haplotype analysis in an Irish autistic population. *Mol. Psychiatry* **9**, 587–593.

Cook, E.H., Courchesne, R., Lord, C., Cox, N.J., Yan, S., Lincoln, A., Haas, R., Courchesne, E. & Leventhal, B.L. (1997): Evidence of linkage between the serotonin transporter and autistic disorder. *Mol. Psychiatry* **2**, 247–250.

Coutinho, A.M., Oliveira, G., Morgadinho, T., Fesel, C., Macedo, T.R., Bento, C., Marques, C., Ataide, A., Miguel, T., Borges, L. & Vicente, A.M (2004): Variants of the serotonin transporter gene (SLC6A4) significantly contribute to hyperserotonemia in autism. *Mol. Psychiatry* **9**, 264–271.

Critchley, H.D., Daly, E.M., Bullmore, ET., Williams, S.C., Van Amelsvoort, T., Robertson, D.M., Rowe, A., Phillips, M., McAlonan, G., Howlin, P. & Murphy, D.G. (2000): The functional neuroanatomy of social behaviour: changes in cerebral blood flow when people with autistic disorder process facial expressions. *Brain* **123**, 2203–2212.

Dawson, G., Webb, S., Schellemberg, G.D., Dager, S., Friedman, S., Aylward, E. & Richards, T. (2002): Defining the broader phenotype of autism: genetic, brain, and behavioral perspectives. *Dev. Psychopathol.* **14**, 581–611.

DeLong, R. (2004): Autism and familial major mood disorder: are they related? *J. Neuropsychiatry Clin. Neurosci.* **16**, 199–213.

DeLong, G.R., Teague, L.A. & McSwain Kamran, M. (1998): Effects of fluoxetine treatment in young children with idiopathic autism. *Dev. Med. Child Neurol.* **40**, 551–562.

DeLong, G.R., Ritch, C.R. & Burch, S. (2002): Fluoxetine response in children with autistic spectrum disorders: correlation with familial major affective disorder and intellectual achievement. *Dev. Med. Child Neurol.* **44**, 652–659.

Dementieva, Y.A., Vance, D.D., Donnelly, S.L., Elston, L.A., Wolpert, C.M., Ravan, S.A., Delong, G.R., Abramson, R.K., Wright, H.H. & Cuccaro, M.L. (2005): Accelerated head growth in early development of individuals with autism. *Pediatr. Neurol.* **32**, 102–108.

Di Martino, A. & Zuddas, A. (2003): Long-term risperidone treatment in pervasive developmental disorders: efficacy, safety, and putative mechanism of action. *Consens. Child Neurol.* 82–86.

Di Martino, A., Melis, G., Cianchetti, C. & Zuddas, A. (2004): Methylphenidate for pervasive developmental disorders: safety and efficacy of acute single dose test and ongoing therapy: an open-pilot study. *J. Child Adolesc. Psychopharmacol.* **14**, 207–218.

Findling, R.L., Maxwell, K. & Wiznitzer, M. (1997): An open clinical trial of risperidone monotherapy in young children with autistic disorder. *Psychopharmacol. Bull.* **33**, 155–159.

Findling, R.L., McNamara, N.K., Gracious, B.L., O'Riordan, M.A., Reed, M.D., Demeter, C. & Blumer, J.L. (2004): Quetiapine in nine youths with autistic disorder. *J. Child Adolesc. Psychopharmacol.* **14**, 287–294.

Fisman, S., Steele, M., Short, J., Byrne, T. & Lavallee, C. (1996): Case study: anorexia nervosa and autistic disorder in an adolescent girl. *J. Am. Acad. Child Adolesc. Psychiatry* **35**, 937–940.

Frith, U. (2001): Mind blindness and the brain in autism. *Neuron* **32**, 969–979.

Frith, U. & Frith, C.D. (2003): Development and neurophysiology of mentalizing. *Philos. Trans. R. Soc. Lond. B Biol. Sci.* **358**, 459–473.

Gagliano, A., Germano, E., Pustorino, G., Impallomeni, C., D'Arrigo, C., Calamoneri, F. & Spina, E. (2004): Risperidone treatment of children with autistic disorder: effectiveness, tolerability, and pharmacokinetic implications. *J. Child Adolesc. Psychopharmacol.* **14**, 39–47.

Gainetdinov, R.R., Wetsel, W.C., Jones, S.R., Levin, E.D., Jaber, M. & Caron, M.G. (1999): Role of serotonin in the paradoxical calming effect of psychostimulants on hyperactivity. *Science* **283**, 397–401.

Geurts, H.M., Verte, S., Oosterlaan, J., Roeyers, H. & Sergeant, J.A. (2004): How specific are executive functioning deficits in attention deficit-hyperactivity disorder and autism? *J. Child Psychol. Psychiatry* **45**, 836–854.

Gilotty, L., Kenworthy, L., Sirian, L., Black, D.O. & Wagner, A.E. (2002): Adaptive skills and executive function in autism spectrum disorders. *Neuropsychol. Dev. Cogn. C Child Neuropsychol.* **8**, 241–248.

Glascher, J., Tuscher, O., Weiller, C. & Buchel, C. (2004): Elevated responses to constant facial emotions in different faces in the human amygdala: an fMRI study of facial identity and expression. *BMC Neurosci.* **5**, 45.

Goldman-Rakic, P.S. (1992): Dopamine mediated mechanism of prefrontal cortex. *Semin. Neurosci.* **4**, 149–159.

Green, M.F., Marshall, B.D., Wirshing, W.C., Ames, D., Marder, S.R., McGurk, S., Kern, R.S. & Mintz, J. (1997): Does risperidone improve verbal working memory in treatment-resistant schizophrenia? *Am. J. Psychiatry* **154**, 799–804.

Hadjikhani, N. & de Gelder, B. (2003): Seeing fearful body expressions activates the fusiform cortex and amygdala. *Curr. Biol.* **13**, 2201–2205.

Handen, B.L., Johnson, C.R. & Lubetsky, M. (2000): Efficacy of methylphenidate among children with autism and symptoms of attention-deficit hyperactivity disorder. *J. Autism Dev. Disord.* **30**, 245–255.

Happe, F. & Frith, U. (1996): The neuropsychology of autism. *Brain* **119**, 1377–1400.

Haznedar, M.M., Buchsbaum, M.S., Wei, T.C., Hof, P.R., Cartwright, C., Bienstock, C.A. & Hollander, E. (2000): Limbic circuitry in patients with autism spectrum disorders studied with positron emission tomography and magnetic resonance imaging. *Am. J. Psychiatry* **157**, 1994–2001.

Hellings, J.A., Zarcone, J.R., Crandall, K., Wallace, D. & Schroeder, S.R. (2001): Weight gain in a controlled study of risperidone in children, adolescents and adults with mental retardation and autism. *J. Child Adolesc. Psychopharmacol.* **11**, 229–238.

Hill, E.L. (2004): Executive dysfunction in autism. *Trends Cogn. Sci.* **8**, 26–32.

Hill, E.L. & Frith, U. (2003): Understanding autism: insights from mind and brain. *Philos. Trans. R. Soc. Lond. B Biol. Sci.* **358**, 281–289.

Hollander, E., Phillips, A., Chaplin, W., Zagursky, K., Novotny, S., Wasserman, S. & Iyengar, R. (2005): A placebo controlled crossover trial of liquid fluoxetine on repetitive behaviors in childhood and adolescent autism. *Neuropsychopharmacology* **30**, 582–589.

Horrigan, J.P. & Barnhill, L.J. (1997): Risperidone and explosive aggressive autism. *J. Autism Dev. Disord.* **27**, 313–323.

Howard, M.A., Cowell, P.E., Boucher, J., Broks, P., Mayes, A., Farrant, A. & Roberts, N. (2000): Convergent neuroanatomical and behavioural evidence of an amygdala hypothesis of autism. *Neuroreport* **11**, 2931–2935.

Hubl, D., Bolte, S., Feineis-Matthews, S., Lanfermann, H., Federspiel, A., Strik, W., Poustka, F. & Dierks, T. (2003): Functional imbalance of visual pathways indicates alternative face processing strategies in autism. *Neurology* **61**, 1232–1237.

Hughes, C., Russell, J. & Robbins, T.W. (1994): Evidence for executive dysfunction in autism. *Neuropsychologia* **32**, 477–492.

Hughes, C., Plumet, M.H. & Leboyer, M. (1999): Towards a cognitive phenotype for autism: increased prevalence of executive dysfunction and superior spatial span amongst siblings of children with autism. *J. Child Psychol. Psychiatry* **40**, 705–718.

Kapur, S. & Seeman, P. (2001): Does fast dissociation from the dopamine d(2) receptor explain the action of atypical antipsychotics? A new hypothesis. *Am. J. Psychiatry* **158**, 360–369.

Kemner, C., Willemsen-Swinkels, S.H., de Jonge, M., Tuynman-Qua, H. & van Engeland, H. (2002): Open-label study of olanzapine in children with pervasive developmental disorder. *J. Clin. Psychopharmacol.* **22**, 455–460.

Kemper, T.L. & Bauman, M.L. (1993): The contribution of neuropathologic studies to the understanding of autism. *Neurol. Clin.* **11**, 175–187.

Langworthy-Lam, K.S., Aman, M.G. & Van Bourgondien, M.E. (2002): Prevalence and patterns of use of psychoactive medicines in individuals with autism in the Autism Society of North Carolina. *J. Child Adolesc. Psychopharmacol.* **12**, 311–321.

Maestrini, E., Lai, C., Marlow, A., Matthews, N., Wallace, S., Bailey, A., Cook, E.H., Weeks, D.E. & Monaco, A.P. (1999): Serotonin transporter (5-HTT) and gamma-aminobutyric acid receptor subunit beta3 (GABRB3) gene polymorphisms are not associated with autism in the IMGSA families. The International Molecular Genetic Study of Autism Consortium. *Am. J. Med. Genet.* **88**, 492–496.

Malone, R.P., Cater, J., Sheikh, R.M., Choudhury, M.S. & Delaney, M.A. (2001): Olanzapine *versus* haloperidol in children with autistic disorder: an open pilot study. *J. Am. Acad. Child Adolesc. Psychiatry* **40**, 887–894.

Malone, R.P., Maislin, G., Choudhury, M.S., Gifford, C. & Delaney, M.A. (2002): Risperidone treatment in children and adolescents with autism: short- and long-term safety and effectiveness. *J. Am. Acad. Child Adolesc. Psychiatry* **41**, 140–147.

Mancama, D. & Kerwin, R.W. (2003): Role of pharmacogenomics in individualising treatment with SSRIs. *CNS Drugs* **17**, 143–151.

Martin, I. & McDonald, S. (2003): Weak coherence, no theory of mind, or executive dysfunction? Solving the puzzle of pragmatic language disorders. *Brain Lang.* **85**, 451–466.

Martin, A., Koenig, K., Scahill, L. & Bregman, J. (1999a): Open-label quetiapine in the treatment of children and adolescents with autistic disorder. *J. Child Adolesc. Psychopharmacol.* **9**, 99–107.

Martin, A., Scahill, L., Klin, A. & Volkmar, F.R. (1999b): Higher-functioning pervasive developmental disorders: rates and patterns of psychotropic drug use. *J. Am. Acad. Child Adolesc. Psychiatry* **38**, 923–931.

Martin, A., Scahill, L., Anderson, G.M., Aman, M., Arnold, L.E., McCracken, J., McDougle, C.J., Tierney, E., Chuang, S. & Vitiello, B. (2004): Weight and leptin changes among risperidone-treated youths with autism: 6-month prospective data. *Am. J. Psychiatry* **161**, 1125–1127.

Masi, G., Cosenza, A., Mucci, M. & Brovedani, P. (2003): A 3-year naturalistic study of 53 preschool children with pervasive developmental disorders treated with risperidone. *J. Clin. Psychiatry* **64**, 1039–1047.

McCauley, J.L., Olson, L.M., Dowd, M., Amin, T., Steele, A., Blakely, R.D., Folstein, S.E., Haines, J.L. & Sutcliffe, J.S. (2004): Linkage and association analysis at the serotonin transporter (SLC6A4) locus in a rigid-compulsive subset of autism. *Am. J. Med. Genet. B Neuropsychiatr. Genet.* **127**, 104–112.

McCracken, J.T., McGough, J., Shah, B., Cronin, P., Hong, D., Aman, M.G., Arnold, L.E., Lindsay, R., Nash, P., Hollway, J., McDougle, C.J., Posey, D., Swiezy, N., Kohn, A., Scahill, L., Martin, A., Koenig, K., Volkmar, F., Carroll, D., Lancor, A., Tierney, E., Ghuman, J., Gonzalez, N.M., Grados, M., Vitiello, B., Ritz, L., Davies, M., Robinson, J. & McMahon, D., Research Units on Pediatric Psychopharmacology Autism Network (2002): Risperidone in children with autism and serious behavioral problems. *N. Engl. J. Med.* **347**, 314–321.

McDougle, C.J. & Posey, D. (2002): Genetics of childhood disorders. XLIV. Autism, part 3. Psychopharmacology of autism. *J. Am. Acad. Child Adolesc. Psychiatry* **41**, 1380–1383.

McDougle, C.J., Naylor, S.T., Cohen, D.J., Volkmar, F.R., Heninger, G.R. & Price, L.H. (1996): A double-blind, placebo-controlled study of fluvoxamine in adults with autistic disorder. *Arch. Gen. Psychiatry* **53**, 1001–1008.

McDougle, C., Holmes, J., Bronson, M., Anderson, G., Volkmar, F., Price, L. & Cohen, D. (1997): Risperidone treatment of children and adolescents with pervasive developmental disorders: a prospective, open-label study. *J. Am. Acad. Child Adolesc. Psychiatry* **36**, 685–693.

McDougle, C.J., Kresch, L.E. & Posey, D.J. (2000): Repetitive thoughts and behavior in pervasive developmental disorders: treatment with serotonin reuptake inhibitors. *J. Autism Dev. Disord.* **30**, 427–435.

McDougle, C.J., Kem, D.L. & Posey, D.J. (2002): Case series: use of ziprasidone for maladaptive symptoms in youths with autism. *J. Am. Acad. Child Adolesc. Psychiatry* **41**, 921–927.

Meltzer, H.Y. & McGurk, S.R. (1999): The effects of clozapine, risperidone, and olanzapine on cognitive function in schizophrenia. *Schizophr. Bull.* **25**, 233–255.

Moore, M.L., Eichner, S.F. & Jones, J.R. (2004): Treating functional impairment of autism with selective serotonin-reuptake inhibitors. *Ann. Pharmacother.* **38**, 1515–1519.

Morris, JS., Friston, KJ., Buchel, C., Frith, CD., Young, AW., Calder, AJ. & Dolan, RJ. (1998): A neuromodulatory role for the human amygdala in processing emotional facial expressions. *Brain* **121**, 47–57.

M.T.A. Cooperative Group (1999): A 14-month randomized clinical trial of treatment strategies for attention-deficit/hyperactivity disorder. The MTA Cooperative Group. Multimodal treatment study of children with ADHD. *Arch. Gen. Psychiatry* **56**, 1073–1086.

Mukaddes, N.M., Abali, O. & Gurkan, K. (2004): Short-term efficacy and safety of risperidone in young children with autistic disorder (AD). *World J. Biol. Psychiatry* **5**, 211–214.

Mulder, E.J., Anderson, G.M., Kema, I.P., de Bildt, A., van Lang, N.D., den Boer, J.A. & Minderaa, R.B. (2004): Platelet serotonin levels in pervasive developmental disorders and mental retardation: diagnostic group differences, within-group distribution, and behavioral correlates. *J. Am. Acad. Child Adolesc. Psychiatry* **43**, 491–499.

Mulder, E.J., Anderson, G.M., Kema,. IP., Brugman, A.M., Ketelaars, C.E., de Bildt, A., van Lang, N.D. den Boer, J.A. & Minderaa, R.B. (2005): Serotonin transporter intron 2 polymorphism associated with rigid-compulsive behaviors in Dutch individuals with pervasive developmental disorder. *Am. J. Med. Genet. B Neuropsychiatr. Genet.* **133B**, 93–96.

Murphy, D.L., Lerner, A., Rudnick, G. & Lesch, K.P. (2004): Serotonin transporter: gene, genetic disorders, and pharmacogenetics. *Mol. Interv.* **4**, 109–123.

Namerow, L.B., Thomas, P., Bostic, J.Q., Prince, J. & Monuteaux, M.C. (2003): Use of citalopram in pervasive developmental disorders. *J. Dev. Behav. Pediatr.* **24**, 104–108.

Nicolson, R., Awad, G. & Sloman, L. (1998): An open trial of risperidone in young autistic children. *J. Am. Acad. Child Adolesc. Psychiatry* **37**, 372–376.

Nieoullon, A. (2002): Dopamine and the regulation of cognition and attention. *Prog. Neurobiol.* **67**, 53–83.

Ozonoff, S. & Strayer, D.L. (1997): Inhibitory function in nonretarded children with autism. *J. Autism Dev. Disord.* **27**, 59–77.

Ozonoff, S. & Strayer, D.L. (2001): Further evidence of intact working memory in autism. *J. Autism Dev. Disord.* **31**, 257–263.

Ozonoff, S., Cook, I., Coon, H., Dawson, G., Joseph, RM., Klin, A., McMahon, W.M., Minshew, N., Munson, J.A., Pennington, B.F., Rogers, S.J., Spence, M.A., Tager-Flusberg, H., Volkmar, F.R. & Wrathall, D. (2004): Performance on Cambridge Neuropsychological Test Automated Battery subtests sensitive to frontal lobe function in people with autistic disorder: evidence from the Collaborative Programs of Excellence in Autism network. *J. Autism Dev. Disord.* **34**, 139–150.

Perry, R., Pataki, C., Mounoz-Silva, D., Armenteros, J. & Silva, R. (1997): Risperidone in children and adolescents with pervasive developmental disorder: pilot trial and follow-up. *J. Child Adolesc. Psychopharmacol.* **7**, 167–179.

Persico, A M., Militerni, R., Bravaccio, C., Schneider, C., Melmed, R., Conciatori, M., Damiani, V., Baldi, A. & Keller, F. (2000): Lack of association between serotonin transporter gene promoter variants and autistic disorder in two ethnically distinct samples. *Am. J. Med. Genet.* **96**, 123–127.

Posey, D.I., Litwiller, M., Koburn, A. & McDougle, C.J. (1999): Paroxetine in autism. *J. Am. Acad. Child Adolesc. Psychiatry* **38**, 111–112.

Posner, M.I. & Peterson S.E. (1990): The attention system of the human brain. *Annu. Rev. Neurosci.* **13**, 25–42.

Potenza, M.N., Holmes, J.P., Kanes, S.J. & McDougle, C. (1999): Olanzapine treatment of children, adolescents, and adults with pervasive developmental disorders: an open-label pilot study. *Clin. Psychopharmacol.* **19**, 37–44.

Prather, M.D., Lavenex, P., Mauldin-Jourdain, M.L., Mason, W.A., Capitanio, J.P., Mendoza, S.P. & Amaral, D.G. (2001): Increased social fear and decreased fear of objects in monkeys with neonatal amygdala lesions. *Neuroscience* **106**, 653–658.

Quintana, H., Birmaher, B., Stedge, D., Lennon, S., Freed, J., Bridge, J. & Greenhill, L. (1995): Use of methylphenidate in the treatment of children with autistic disorder. *J. Autism Dev. Disord.* **25**, 283–294.

Remington, G., Sloman, L., Konstantareas, M., Parker, K. & Gow, R. (2001): Clomipramine *versus* haloperidol in the treatment of autistic disorder: a double-blind, placebo-controlled, crossover study. *J. Clin. Psychopharmacol.* **21**, 440–444.

Rojas, D.C., Smith, J.A., Benkers, T.L., Camou, S.L., Reite, M.L. & Rogers, S.J. (2004): Hippocampus and amygdala volumes in parents of children with autistic disorder. *Am. J. Psychiatry* **161**, 2038–2044.

Santosh, P.J. & Taylor, E. (2000): Stimulant drugs. *Eur. Child Adolesc. Psychiatry* **9** (Suppl. 1), I27-I43.

Schultz, R.T., Gauthier, I., Klin, A., Fulbright, R.K., Anderson, A.W., Volkmar, F., Skudlarski, P., Lacadie, C., Cohen, D.J. & Gore, J.C. (2000): Abnormal ventral temporal cortical activity during face discrimination among individuals with autism and Asperger syndrome. *Arch. Gen. Psychiatry* **57**, 331–340.

Schultz, R.T., Grelotti, D.J., Klin, A., Kleinman, J., Van der Gaag, C., Marois, R. & Skudlarski, P. (2003): The role of the fusiform face area in social cognition: implications for the pathobiology of autism. *Philos. Trans. R. Soc. Lond. B Biol. Sci.* **358**, 415–427.

Schumann, C.M., Hamstra, J., Goodlin-Jones, B.L., Lotspeich, L.J., Kwon, H., Buonocore, M.H., Lammers, C.R., Reiss, A.L. & Amaral, D.G. (2004): The amygdala is enlarged in children but not adolescents with autism; the hippocampus is enlarged at all ages. *J. Neurosci.* **24**, 6392–6401.

Sergeant, J., Geurts, H. & Oosterlaan, J. (2002): How specific is a deficit of executive functioning for attention-deficit/hyperactivity disorder? *Behav. Brain Res.* **130**, 3–28.

Shea, S., Turgay, A., Carroll, A., Schulz, M., Orlik, H., Smith, I. & Dunbar, F. (2004): Risperidone in the treatment of disruptive behavioral symptoms in children with autistic and other pervasive developmental disorders. *Pediatrics* **114**, 634–641.

Simeon, J., Carrey, N., Wiggins, D., Milin & Hosendocus, S. (1995): Risperidone effects in treatment-resistant adolescents: preliminary case reports. *J. Child Adolesc. Psychopharmacol.* **15**, 69–79.

Smits, K.M., Smits, L.J., Schouten, J.S., Stelma, F.F., Nelemans, P. & Prins, M.H. (2004): Influence of SERTPR and STin2 in the serotonin transporter gene on the effect of selective serotonin reuptake inhibitors in depression: a systematic review. *Mol. Psychiatry* **9**, 433–441.

Stigler, K.A., Desmond, L.A,. Posey, D.J., Wiegand, R.E. & McDougle, C.J. (2004): A naturalistic retrospective analysis of psychostimulants in pervasive developmental disorders. *J. Child Adolesc. Psychopharmacol.* **14**, 49–56.

Thierry, A.M., Mantz, J. & Glowinski, J. (1992): Influence of dopaminergic and noradrenergic afferents on their target cells in the rat medial prefrontal cortex. *Adv. Neurol.* **57,** 545–554.

Vercellino, F., Zanotto, E., Ravera, G. & Veneselli, E. (2001): Open-label risperidone treatment of six children and adolescents with autism. *Can. J. Psychiatry* **46**, 559–560.

Wang, A.T., Dapretto, M., Hariri, A.R., Sigman, M. & Bookheimer, S.Y. (2004): Neural correlates of facial affect processing in children and adolescents with autism spectrum disorder. *J. Am. Acad. Child Adolesc. Psychiatry* **43**, 481–490.

Whalen, P.J., Rauch, S.L., Etcoff, N.L., McInerney, S.C., Lee, M.B. & Jenike, M.A. (1998): Masked presentations of emotional facial expressions modulate amygdala activity without explicit knowledge. *J. Neurosci.* **18**, 411–418.

Williams, M.A. & Mattingley, J.B. (2004): Unconscious perception of non-threatening facial emotion in parietal extinction. *Exp. Brain Res.* **154**, 403–406.

Zuddas, A., Ledda, G., Fratta, A., Muglia, P. & Cianchetti, C. (1996): Clinical effects of clozapine on autistic disorder. *Am. J. Psychiatry* **153**, 738.

Zuddas, A., Di Martino, A., Muglia, P. & Cianchetti, C. (2000): Long-term risperidone for pervasive developmental disorder: efficacy, tolerability, and discontinuation. *J. Child Psychopharmacol.* **10**, 79–90.

Autistic spectrum disorders, D. Riva and I. Rapin (eds.)

Chapter 13

Pharmacotherapy of pervasive developmental disorders in children and adolescents

Gabriele Masi

IRCCS Stella Maris, Institute of Child Neurology and Psychiatry, via dei Giacinti 2, 56018 Calambrone, Pisa, Italy
gabriele.masi@inpe.unipi.it

Summary

In the broader context of a multimodal approach, including educational and behavioural interventions, the appropriate use of pharmacotherapy can improve some symptoms and behaviours of pervasive developmental disorders (PDDs) and increase the response to non-pharmacological interventions. Pharmacotherapy aims at stabilizing the dysregulated systems which are thought to underlie the abnormal behaviour, namely the serotonergic and dopaminergic systems. This chapter is a critical review of the published reports on the pharmacotherapy of PDDs in children and adolescents. Drugs acting on 5-hydroxytryptamine (5-HT) (serotonergic agents such as clomipramine, fluoxetine, paroxetine, sertraline, and fluvoxamine), on dopamine (dopamine blocking agents such as the neuroleptics haloperidol and pimozide), and on both 5-HT and dopamine (such as the atypical antipsychotic drugs clozapine, risperidone, olanzapine, quetiapine, and ziprasidone) are presented, along with efficacy and safety data. The chapter concludes with a brief discussion of other psychotropic drugs such as opioid antagonists, clonidine and guanfacine, psychostimulants, mood stabilizers, glutamatergic compounds (lamotrigine, amantadine), buspirone, and secretin.

Introduction

The appropriate use of drugs can improve some maladaptive behaviours in pervasive developmental disorders (PDDs) and increase the affected person's ability to benefit from non-pharmacological interventions. Primary behavioural targets of pharmacotherapy in autism include severe behavioural disorders, aggression toward self and others, irritability, hyperactivity, stereotypies, repetitive phenomena, and to a lesser degree impaired social behaviour.

Several neurochemical systems are believed to be of particular relevance to the pathophysiology and drug treatment of the syndrome. Because most biological research in the pathophysiology of autism to date has implicated serotonin (5-HT) and, to some extent, dopamine neuronal dysfunction, drugs acting on these systems will be the principal focus of this review. I will also briefly discuss other drugs that have been studied in PDD populations. I have addressed all the currently available literature on children and adolescents with PDDs.

Drugs acting on the serotonin system

Preliminary evidence suggests that 5-HT serotonin reuptake inhibitors (SRIs), including the non-selective SRI tricyclic clomipramine and the selective SRIs (SSRIs), may be useful for reducing interfering repetitive behaviour and aggression, and possibly for improving aspects of social relatedness, in some children and adolescents with autism and other PDDs. However, definite conclusions cannot be drawn from these studies because the great majority were uncontrolled, and the similarity of repetitive thoughts and behaviours in PDDs and obsessive-compulsive disorder is questionable.

Clomipramine

Gordon and colleagues (1993) found clomipramine (mean dose 152 mg daily) superior to placebo and the noradrenergic tricyclic agent desipramine in reducing some core symptoms of autism, obsessive-compulsive behaviours, and anger/uncooperativeness, assessed using the Child Psychiatric Rating Scale (CPRS) and the Clinical Global Impression (CGI) scale in a 10-week double-blind, crossover study of 24 children and adolescents with autistic disorder. Adverse effects were a prolongation of the QT interval on the electrocardiogram, tachycardia, and grand mal seizures. Some studies suggest that children may tolerate clomipramine less well than adults, being more prone to cardiac side effects. Furthermore, PDD children may be less responsive to clomipramine than adults, and show an increased risk of seizure and exacerbation of agitation and aggressiveness (Sanchez *et al.*, 1996). For this side effect and efficacy profile, clomipramine is not currently a first-line drug in paediatric population with PDDs.

Fluoxetine

DeLong and coworkers (1998) have treated 37 autistic children (aged 2.25 to 7.75 years) with fluoxetine (0.2 to 1.4 mg/kg/day), with excellent response in 11 subjects and a good response in the other 11, mainly in behavioural, cognitive, and affective areas. Hyperactivity, aggression and agitation were the most frequent reasons for discontinuation. Interestingly, the main predictor of a good response was a family history of affective disorders. These findings have been confirmed by the same research group in an extension of the previous study involving 129 autistic children (aged 2 to 8 years) (DeLong *et al.*, 2002). Fluoxetine (0.15 to 0.5 mg/kg) was given for 5 to 76 months (mean 32 to 36 months), with excellent response in 22 subjects (17 per cent), good response in 67 (52 per cent), and fair/poor response in 40 (31 per cent). The treatment response was highly correlated with familial major affective disorder (mainly bipolar disorder) and with unusual intellectual achievement (exceptional abilities and achievements requiring systematic organization of emotionally neutral information) and, in the children, with hyperlexia. A bipolar disorder occurred in five children during treatment.

Sertraline

A decrease in anxiety symptoms, irritability, and the need for sameness has been reported in a case series of nine autistic children treated for 2 to 8 weeks with low dose sertraline (25 to 50 mg daily) (Steingard *et al.*, 1997). However, three of the eight responders had a recurrence of symptoms after 3 to 7 months. Two patients showed behavioural activation when dosage was increased to 75 mg/day.

Fluvoxamine

Promising results from a placebo-controlled study in autistic adults treated with fluvoxamine (276.7 mg daily) (McDougle *et al.*, 1996) were not confirmed in a 12-week, double-blind placebo-controlled study in 34 PDD children and adolescents from the same research group; the drug had poor efficacy (only one of the 18 treated patients showed significant improvement) and many subjects had side effects (insomnia, hyperactivity, agitation, aggression). Developmental differences in the 5-HT system across the lifespan, as well as specific features of serotonergic function in autistic patients, may affect efficacy and tolerability of SSRIs in younger patients.

Citalopram

Couturier & Nicolson (2002) retrospectively assessed the efficacy of treatment with citalopram (5 to 40 mg, mean dose 19.7 ± 7 mg) in 17 patients (aged 4 to 15 years, mean age 9.4 ± 2.9 years). Ten patients (59 per cent) were considered responders according to CGI-I (Clinical Global Impressions-Improvement) for behavioural and anxiety symptoms, even though social relatedness did not improve significantly. Namerow and colleagues (2003) reviewed the medical records of 15 subjects (aged 6 to 16 years) with PDDs treated with citalopram (16.9 ± 12.1 mg) for 218 ± 167 days. Eleven were improved at their most recent visit, with the greatest improvement being in anxiety and mood symptoms. Tolerability was good.

Newer antidepressants with dual serotonergic-noradrenergic action

More recently, newer antidepressants with a selective dual action on both serotonin and norepinephrine have been marketed. The noradrenergic action may improve hyperactive and inattentive symptoms, which are often associated with the core PDD symptomatology. Hollander and colleagues (2000) treated 10 consecutive PDD patients (age range 3 to 21 years, mean age 10.46 years) with venlafaxine, starting at a dose of 12.5 mg/day, with flexible increases. Six subjects were considered responders at low dosages (mean 24.37 mg/day, range 6.25 to 50 mg), based on the CGI-I. Besides a decrease in repetitive behaviours and interests, social and communication deficits, hyperactivity and inattention also improved. Side effects included mild behavioural activation.

Posey and colleagues (2001a) explored efficacy and tolerability of mirtazapine (mean dose 30.3 mg/day, range 7.5 to 45 mg) in 26 subjects with PDDs (age range 3.8 to 23.5 years, mean age 10.1 years). Nine subjects (34.6 per cent) showed a good clinical response, assessed with the CGI-I, with a significant improvement as to aggression, self-injury, irritability, hyperactivity, anxiety, and depression. Core symptoms of social and communication impairment were not affected by the treatment. Increased appetite, transient sedation, and irritability were the most frequent side effects.

Conventional antipsychotic agents

The high potency antipsychotic haloperidol, which has dopamine (D_2) receptor antagonist properties, has been extensively studied in controlled trials in children with autism, and remains the most studied drug used in the treatment of autism. A seminal placebo-controlled, randomized study by Campbell *et al.* (1978) showed efficacy of haloperidol to a maximum dose of 4 mg/day (mean optimal dose 1.65 mg/day) in a 12-week study in 40 autistic children (hospital inpatients), aged from 2.6 to 7.2 years (mean 4.5 years). Haloperidol treatment was associated with an improvement in stereotypies and withdrawal, but 12 children experienced dose-dependent sedation and two had acute dystonic reactions. Other similar studies from the same research group confirmed an improvement in withdrawal, stereotypies, hyperactivity, abnormal object relations, negativism, angry affect, and lability of mood. A prospective longitudinal study (Campbell *et al.*, 1997) specifically addressed the occurrence of drug-related dyskinesias in 118 PDD patients during treatment with haloperidol (mean daily dose 1.75 mg). The mean duration of treatment was 708.4 days (range 25 to 3610 days). Forty children (33.9 per cent) developed withdrawal dyskinesias, and nine (7.6 per cent) developed tardive dyskinesia.

In summary, available data show that haloperidol can improve maladaptive behaviours in children and adolescents with autism. However, given the frequency of acute and withdrawal-related dyskinesias, as well as of cognitive toxicity, safer agents such as the new atypical antipsychotics have been studied in individuals with autism and other PDDs.

Atypical antipsychotic agents

A common feature of the atypical antipsychotic agents is their ability to produce an antipsychotic effect with a reduced incidence of acute or subacute extrapyramidal side effects. Other clinical features include a low incidence of tardive dyskinesias with prolonged treatment, little effect on prolactin levels, superior efficacy on the negative symptoms of schizophrenia, and reduced cognitive toxicity. It is still matter of debate whether these features are better accounted for by a relatively high ratio of 5-HT2A/D2 receptor antagonism, or by looser binding with the D2 receptor, with a transient occupation and rapid dissociation, or by both mechanisms.

Clozapine

Only a few reports on the use of clozapine in children and adolescents with autism are available. Zuddas *et al.* (1996) described three children (8 to 12 years of age) with marked hyperactivity, fidgetiness, or aggression who did not benefit from typical antipsychotic agents. CPRS scores improved by 19 per cent, 35 per cent, and 39 per cent, respectively, after 3 months' treatment at dosages of up to 200 mg/day, but one patient returned to pretreatment values after 5 months with higher dosages (450 mg/day).

Risperidone

Risperidone is currently the atypical antipsychotic agent most commonly used in PDD patients. Two controlled studies of risperidone have been published in individuals with autism and related PDDs, one in adult patients (McDougle *et al.*, 1998) and the other in children and adolescents (RUPP, 2002). In the latter multi-site, double-blind placebo-controlled study, 101 children and adolescents (age range 5 to 17 years, mean age 8.8 years) were randomized to receive risperidone (dose range 0.5 to 3.5 mg/daily) or placebo for 8 weeks. Based on the CGI-I and the Aberrant Behaviour Checklist (ABC) irritability score, 69 per cent of the patients in the risperidone group and 12 per cent in the placebo group were assessed as responders at the 8th week. At the 6th month, the rate of response decreased to 47 per cent. Irritability, hyperactivity, and stereotypies were more sensitive to treatment than social withdrawal and inappropriate speech. Increased appetite and weight gain (2.7 ± 2.9 kg), fatigue, and drowsiness were the most commonly reported side effects.

Multiple open label reports of risperidone in PDD children and adolescents are available (McDougle *et al.*, 1997; Nicolson *et al.*, 1998; Zuddas *et al.*, 2000; Malone *et al.*, 2002). Although PDDs begin in the first 3 years of life, and a timely effective treatment (both psychosocial and pharmacological) may help improving prognosis, only sparse data are available on pharmacological treatments in preschool children. Masi *et al.* (2001a) described efficacy and tolerability of risperidone treatment in children aged 3.6 to 6.6 years (mean 4.6 years) in a 16-week open-label trial. Maximum risperidone dosage was 0.04 mg/kg/day. According to both a 25 per cent improvement at the CPRS and a CGI-I score of 1 or 2, eight subjects (36.4 per cent) were assessed as responders. Hyperactivity and lability of affect were more sensitive to treatment than social interaction. Risperidone was well tolerated; 13 subjects (54.1 per cent) did not show any side effect, and only three had a weight gain of more than 10 per cent. Masi and colleagues (2003) have recently reported an expansion of the previous study, describing systematic data from a 3-year naturalistic study on 53 PDD preschool children (age range 3.5 to 6.6 years, mean 4.6 years). They received risperidone (maximum dose 1 mg/day) for a period ranging from 1 to 32 months (mean 7.9 ± 6.8 months). At the time of writing, 25 patients (47.1 per cent) were still receiving risperidone, while 28 (52.9 per cent) had discontinued it because of side effects (22.6 per cent), parental choice (18.8 per cent), lack of efficacy (5.6 per cent), or the decision of the treating psychiatrist (5.6 per cent). Based on both an improvement of 25 per cent in CPRS and a score of 1 or 2 on CGI-I, 46.8 per cent of the subjects were considered to be responders. Behavioural disorders and dysregulation of affect were more sensitive to treatment than interpersonal functioning. Responders received higher doses and for a longer period, and had a greater weight gain than non-responders. Increased prolactin levels without clinical signs, and increased appetite were the most frequent side effects.

Olanzapine

Three open-label studies and several anecdotal case reports have described clinical effects of the atypical antipsychotic drug olanzapine in patients with PDDs. A pilot study examined the efficacy and safety of olanzapine treatment in eight patients (age range 5 to 42 years) with autism and other PDDs (Potenza *et al.*, 1999). Seven patients completed a 12-week open-label study, and six were responders based upon the CGI-I, with a mean dose of 7.8 ± 4.7 mg/day (range 5 to 20 mg/day). Malone and colleagues (2001) compared olanzapine and haloperidol, openly randomizing 12 autistic children (mean age 7.8 ± 2.1 years) for 6 weeks in two treatment groups (final dosage of olanzapine 7.9 ± 2.5 mg/day, final dosage of haloperidol 1.4 ± 0.7 mg/day). Patients from both groups improved in their symptomatology; five of six in the olanzapine group and three of six in the haloperidol group were responders according to their CGI-I score. Weight gain was significantly greater in the olanzapine group. Finally, Kemner *et al.* (2002) openly explored the efficacy and tolerability of olanzapine (final mean dose 10.7 mg/day) in 25 children and adolescents (age range 6 to 16 years). Twenty-three subjects completed the study and showed significant improvements as to irritability, hyperactivity, excessive speech, and some autistic symptoms, assessed using the ABC. However, only three subjects were responders according to CGI-I scores. Increased appetite and weight gain were the most frequent side effects.

Quetiapine

Only one report of quetiapine in the treatment of children with PDDs is available (Martin *et al.*, 1999). Six subjects with autism and mental retardation (mean age 10.9 ± 3.3 years) participated in a 16-week, open-label study of quetiapine (mean daily dose 225 ± 108 mg, range 100 to

350 mg/day), but only two subjects completed the trial and were considered responders, based on the CGI-I, and only one continued to benefit from long-term treatment. There was no statistically significant improvement during the study for the group on various rating scales. Sedation, behavioural activation, increased appetite, and weight gain (range 0.9 to 8.2 kg) were reported.

Ziprasidone

McDougle and coworkers (2002) reported a preliminary evaluation of the efficacy of ziprasidone in 12 patients with PDDs (age range 8 to 20 years, mean age 11.6 ± 4.4 years). The mean duration of treatment was 14.2 weeks (range 6 to 30 weeks) and the final dose was 59.2 mg/day (range 20 to 120 mg). Six patients (50 per cent) were classed as responders according to CGI-I. Mild sedation was the most frequent side effect. No significant weight gain or cardiovascular effects were reported.

Atypical antipsychotic agents: data on safety

Weight gain

Weight gain was the most significant side effect in all the studies on risperidone, olanzapine, and clozapine, in PDDs as well as in other psychiatric disorders. Increased appetite and weight gain are often reported in the subjects treated with risperidone, with a mean increase in weight ranging from 2.7 ± 2.9 kg in the double-blind study on risperidone in children and adolescents (RUPP, 2002) to 7.2 kg (mean) in the long-term study (McDougle *et al.*, 1997). Increased appetite and weight gain occurred during treatment with olanzapine in the studies by Potenza *et al.* (about 8 kg), Malone *et al.* (mean 9 lb = 4.1 kg), and Kemner *et al.*, (mean 4.7 kg). This side effect cannot be disregarded, given the increased morbidity in subjects with obesity. Furthermore, the difficult management of food craving in patients with PDDs adds further conflict in the families. Dietary recommendations and psychoeducational counselling are needed at the start of the treatment. Careful monitoring of weight gain, liver function, and glycaemia is recommended in these patients. At present there is no standardized pharmacological treatment for antipsychotic-induced weight gain. Trials with amantadine, orlistat, metformin, nizatidine, and topiramate have been reported in adult patients, but only topiramate has been tested anecdotally in children.

Hyperprolactinaemia

Although hyperprolactinaemia is a common side effect of antipsychotic agents in adult patients, there is sparse information in children and adolescents. The clinical implications of asymptomatic antipsychotic-induced hyperprolactinaemia in young children are not clear. A study specifically addressed prolactin levels during treatment with risperidone (dosage range 0.25 to 0.75 mg/day, mean dose 0.50 mg/day) in 25 young autistic children (mean age 4.1 years) (Masi *et al.*, 2001b). Serum prolactin was 9.77 ± 3.94 ng/ml at baseline, and 25.92 ± 13.9 ng/ml at the 10th week of treatment ($P < 0.001$). Eight children (28 per cent) had a prolactin level of more than twice the upper limit of normal (30 ng/ml). Levels of prolactin did not show significant correlations with age, weight, risperidone dosage, or clinical outcome. None of the children had clinical signs of hyperprolactinaemia. In a more recent 3-year study from the same research group (Masi *et al.*, 2003), data were available on 37 subjects. Mean prolactin level at baseline was 13.3 ± 7.8 ng/ml, while the mean value at the last observation was 28.38 ±

22.45 ng/ml ($P < 0.0001$). Thirteen patients (35 per cent) had normal levels of prolactin (below 15 ng/ml), five (14 per cent) had increased prolactin between 30 and 50 ng/ml, and six (16 per cent) had values over 50 ng/ml. Subjects with the highest and the lowest prolactin values did not differ in age, drug dosage, severity scores at baseline, or weight gain. In some patients, when risperidone was reintroduced after discontinuation because of high levels of prolactin, the prolactin concentration rose to a lesser degree.

Extrapyramidal side effects

Data from the above-mentioned studies suggest that risperidone is associated with significantly milder and more transient extrapyramidal effects than typical antipsychotic agents such as haloperidol. For example, acute dystonic reactions did not occur in the 49 patients taking risperidone in the placebo-controlled study (RUPP, 2002), and only one of the 53 children in the 3-year naturalistic study showed dystonic movements during the first month of treatment, requiring discontinuation of the drug, while another had only mild and transient tremors (Masi *et al.*, 2003). However, monitoring of abnormal motor movements is warranted.

Seizures

Though atypical antipsychotic agents produce EEG abnormalities, the greatest risk of dose-dependent epileptic seizures is associated with clozapine treatment, while the risk is milder with risperidone and quetiapine (Centorrino *et al.*, 2002). This risk is particularly significant in autistic patients, who are particularly predisposed to developing seizures.

Agranulocytosis

The greatest risk of agranulocytosis is associated with clozapine treatment, and mandatory monitoring of white blood cells is a feature of the drug guidelines. However, granulocytopenia is seldom reported during treatment with olanzapine and quetiapine. A blood cell count is warranted when clinical features suggest the possibility of leucopenia (for example, recurrent infections).

Hyperglycaemia and hyperlipidaemia

Atypical antipsychotic agents, particularly clozapine and olanzapine, are associated with raised plasma levels of glucose and lipids, while for risperidone the risk is lower (Wirshing *et al.*, 2002). Specific data on children and adolescents are sparse. Bloch and colleagues reported on five adolescents who developed overt diabetes (two subjects) or glucose dysregulation (three subjects) during olanzapine treatment (Bloch *et al.*, 2003). A regular metabolic follow-up including fasting blood glucose is recommended in healthy adolescents receiving olanzapine or clozapine treatment.

Other types of drug treatment

Opioid antagonists

Exogenous opioids have been found to induce socioemotional blindness and absence of separation distress in animal models, and these phenomena were reversed by opioid receptor blockage. The opioid antagonist naltrexone has been investigated as a potential treatment for self injurious behaviour, social deficits, and aggressiveness. Controlled studies have either failed to confirm efficacy, or have reported transient and moderate results on hyperactivity; in some subjects there was a worsening of behavioural symptoms and stereotypies (Kolmen *et al.*, 1995).

Clonidine and guanfacine

The α-adrenergic agent clonidine, generally used in subjects with hyperactivity and impulsivity, was employed in a small double-blind placebo-controlled crossover study in eight autistic children, with mixed results (Jaselskis *et al.*, 1992). The efficacy of guanfacine in 80 PDD subjects (age range 3 to 18 years, mean 7.7 years) was retrospectively assessed by Posey and coworkers (2001b). At a mean dose of 2.6 mg/day (range 0.25 to 9 mg), 19 subjects (23.8 per cent) were responders according to the CGI score, with significant improvement in hyperactivity, inattention, insomnia, and tics.

Psychostimulants

Symptoms of attention deficit-hyperactivity disorder (ADHD) are frequently reported in children with PDDs. Recently 13 children with autism and symptoms of ADHD participated in a double-blind placebo-controlled crossover study of methylphenidate (0.3 and 0.6 mg/kg/dose) (Handen *et al.*, 2000). Eight patients were considered responders, based on a reduction of at least 50 per cent in the Conners hyperactivity index. However, scores on the Child Autism Rating Scale (CARS), which assesses the severity of global autistic symptoms, did not change. Furthermore, significant side effects occurred during the treatment, mainly at 0.6 mg/kg/dose, including irritability and social withdrawal.

Mood stabilizers

An emerging literature documents the co-occurrence of mania in children with PDDs, suggesting that up to 21 per cent of PDD children may also meet criteria for mania. Hollander and colleagues (2001) assessed the efficacy of divalproex sodium (mean dose 768 mg/day, range 125 to 2500 mg, mean blood level 75.8 g/ml) in an open trial in 14 PDD patients (age range 5 to 40 years, mean age 17.9 years). Ten patients (71 per cent) were classed as responders according to their CGI-I score. Core symptoms of autism, as well as impulsivity and aggression, improved during treatment.

Uvebrant & Bauziene (1994) treated 13 young patients with autism and treatment-refractory epilepsy with the anticonvulsivant lamotrigine. In eight of these patients the autistic symptoms improved significantly. This finding was not confirmed in a more recent double-blind study with lamotrigine (Belsito *et al.*, 2001). Fourteen autistic children (age range 3 to 11 years, mean 5.8 years) received lamotrigine (5 mg/kg/day) for 4 weeks, without any significant difference from a placebo group according to the ABC and Vineland scales, and CARS.

Glutamatergic compounds

Based on the hypothesis of a glutamatergic component in the pathophysiology of autism, interest in the efficacy of glutamatergic compounds such as lamotrigine and amantadine in the treatment of autism has led to specific studies. The data on lamotrigine were discussed in the section on mood stabilizers (see above). The efficacy of amantadine was assessed in a double-blind placebo-controlled study in 39 autistic children and adolescents (age range 5 to 19 years, mean age 7 years) (King *et al.*, 2001). Patients were randomized to placebo or amantadine (2.5 mg/kg/day) in one daily dose for one week, then placebo or amantadine (5 mg/kg/daily) in two daily doses for 3 weeks. A significant improvement as to hyperactivity and inappropriate speech was found, even though the parent rated measure failed to show any clinical effect. Amantadine was well tolerated.

Secretin

Secretin is a polypeptide hormone secreted by endocrine cells in the upper small intestine, and is involved in the control of pancreatic exocrine function. After anecdotal reports of the efficacy of secretin in the social functioning of some autistic children treated for gastrointestinal problems, two controlled studies have attempted to confirm these early findings (Sandler *et al.*, 1999; Owley *et al.*, 2001). To date, though research on the psychotropic effects of gastrointestinal hormones shows promise, the findings do not support the use of secretin in the treatment of autistic symptoms.

Conclusions

Pharmacological treatment can be considered for the relief of symptoms in children and adolescents with behavioural disorders associated with the autistic core symptomatology. Hyperactivity, aggression, lability of mood, and repetitive phenomena are the most sensitive target symptoms, while the social impairment aspect is more resistant to pharmacological interventions.

Serotonergic agents may be effective in some children with PDDs, especially when repetitive phenomena or affective symptoms are prominent, even though their effectiveness seems to be less than in adolescent and adults, probably because of developmental factors. The efficacy of newer antidepressants with both serotonergic and noradrenergic action (venlafaxine, mirtazapine) on anxiety, depression, and hyperactivity-inattention needs further research. Behavioural activation (irritability, agitation, hyperactivity, aggressiveness) is often reported during treatment with clomipramine, fluvoxamine, sertraline and fluoxetine.

Atypical antipsychotic agents (mainly risperidone and olanzapine) are drugs with actions on a broad range of symptoms, and they are particularly indicated when more serious behavioural symptoms are prominent – such as aggression, self-injurious behaviours, hyperactivity, and tantrums. However, atypical antipsychotics may be beneficial in repetitive behaviours and, in some cases, in social relatedness. When hyperactivity and inattention are prominent features, α_2-adrenergic agents, such as clonidine or guanfacine, or stimulants can be indicated, even if some children show worsening of behaviour after treatment with a stimulant drug.

Further research is warranted, mainly on the efficacy and safety of drugs for specific subtypes of patients, according to their age and clinical profile. Long-term data are needed, given the paucity of information about the pharmacodynamic effects on the developing brain of drugs given for extended periods during the first years of life, when dramatic developmental changes in neurotransmitters and receptors occur. Naturalistic prospective studies might represent an important source of information about the effectiveness of a treatment over extended periods under routine clinical conditions.

References

Belsito, K.M., Law, P.A., Kirk, K.S., Landa, R.J. & Zimmerman, A.W. (2001): Lamotrigine therapy for autistic disorder: a randomized, double-blind, placebo-controlled trial. *J. Autism Dev. Disord.* **31**, 175–181.

Bloch, Y., Vardi, O., Mendlovic, S., Levkovitz, Y., Gothelf, D. & Ratzoni, G. (2003): Hyperglycemia from olanzapine treatment in adolescents. *J. Child Adolesc. Psychopharmacol.* **13**, 97–102.

Campbell, M., Anderson, L., Meier, M., Cohen, I.L., Small, A.M., Samit, C. & Sachar, E.J. (1978): A comparison of haloperidol and behavior therapy and their interaction in autistic children. *J. Am. Acad. Child Psychiatry* **7**, 640–655.

Campbell, M., Armenteros, J.L., Malone, R.P., Adams, P.B., Eisenberg, Z.W. & Overall, J.E. (1997): Neuroleptic-related dyskinesias in autistic children: a prospective, longitudinal study. *J. Am. Acad. Child Adolesc. Psychiatry* **36**, 835–843.

Centorrino, F., Price, B.H., Tuttle, M., Bahk, W.M., Hennen, J., Albert, M.J. & Baldessarini, R.J. (2002): EEG abnormalities during treatment with typical and atypical antipsychotics. *Am. J. Psychiatry* **159**, 109–115.

Couturier, J.L. & Nicolson, R. (2002): A retrospective assessment of citalopram in children and adolescents with pervasive developmental disorders. *J. Child Adolesc. Psychopharmacol.* **12**, 243–248.

DeLong, G.R., Ritch, C.R. & Burch, S. (2002): Fluoxetine response in children with autistic spectrum disorder: correlation with familial major affective disorder and intellectual achievement. *Dev. Med. Child Neurol.* **44**, 652–659.

DeLong, G.R., Teague, L.A. & Kamran, M.M. (1998): Effects of fluoxetine treatment in young children with idiopathic autism. *Dev. Med. Child Neurol.* **40**, 551–562.

Gordon, C.T., State, R.C., Nelson, J.E., Hamburger, S.D. & Rapoport, J.L. (1993): A double-blind comparison of clomipramine, desipramine, and placebo in the treatment of autistic disorder. *Arch. Gen. Psychiatry* **50**, 441–447.

Handen, B.L., Johnson, C.R. & Lubetsky, M. (2000): Efficacy of methylphenidate among children with autism and symptoms of attention-deficit hyperactivity disorder. *J. Autism Dev. Disord.* **30**, 245–255.

Hollander, E., Dolgoff-Kaspar, R., Cartwright C., Rawitt, R. & Novotny, S. (2001): An open-trial of divalproex sodium in autism spectrum disorders. *J. Clin. Psychiatry* **62**, 530–534.

Hollander, E., Kaplan A., Cartwright, C. & Reichman, D. (2000): Venlafaxine in children, adolescents and adults with autism spectrum disorder: an open retrospective clinical report. *J. Child Neurol.* **15**, 132–135.

Jaselskis, C.A., Cook, E.H., Fletcher, K.E. & Leventhal, B.L. (1992): Clonidine treatment of hyperactive and impulsive children with autistic disorder. *J. Clin. Psychopharmacol.* **12**, 322–327.

Kemner, C., Willemsen-Swinkels, S.H., DeJonge, M., Tuynman-Qua, H. & van Engeland, H. (2002): Open-label study of olanzapine in children with pervasive developmental disorders. *J. Clin. Psychopharmacol.* **22**, 455–460.

King, B.H., Wright, D.M., Habden, J., Sikich, L., Zimmerman, A.W., McMahon, W., Cantwell, E., Davanzo, P.A., Dourish, C.T., Dykens, E.M., Hooper, S.R., Jaselskis, C.A., Leventhal, B.L., Levitt, J., Lord, C., Lubetsky, M.J., Myers, S.M., Ozonoff, S., Shah, B.G., Snape, M., Shernoff, E.W., Williamson, K. & Cook, E.H. (2001): Double-blind, placebo-controlled study of amantadine hydrochloride in the treatment of children with autistic disorder. *J. Am. Acad. Child Adolesc. Psychiatry* **40**, 658–665.

Kolmen, B.K., Feldman, H.M., Handen, B.L. & Janosky, J.E. (1995): Naltrexone in young autistic children: a double-blind placebo-controlled, cross-over study. *J. Am. Acad. Child Adolesc. Psychiatry* **34**, 223–231.

Malone, R.P., Cater, J., Sheikh, R.M., Choudhury, M.S. & Delaney, M.A. (2001): Olanzapine *versus* haloperidol in children with autistic disorder: an open pilot study. *J. Am. Acad. Child Adolesc. Psychiatry* **40**, 887–894.

Malone, R.P., Maislin, G., Choudhury, M.S., Gifford, C. & Delaney, M.A. (2002): Risperidone treatment in children and adolescents with autism: short- and long-term safety and effectiveness. *J. Am. Acad. Child Adolesc. Psychiatry* **41**, 140–147.

Martin, A., Koenig, K., Scahill, L. & Bregman, J. (1999): Open-label quetiapine in children and adolescents with autistic disorder. *J. Child Adolesc. Psychopharmacol.* **9**, 99–107.

Masi, G., Cosenza, A. & Mucci, M. (2001a): Open trial of risperidone in 24 young children with pervasive developmental disorders. *J. Am. Acad. Child Adolesc. Psychiatry* **40**, 1206–1214.

Masi, G., Cosenza, A. & Mucci, M. (2001b): Prolactin levels in preschool autistic children during risperidone treatment. *J. Child Adolesc. Psychopharmacol.* **11**, 389–394.

Masi, G., Cosenza, A., Mucci, M. & Brovedani, P. (2003): A three-year naturalistic study of 53 preschool children with pervasive developmental disorder treated with risperidone. *J. Clin. Psychiatry* **64**, 1039–1047.

McDougle, C.J., Holmes, J.P., Bronson, M.R., Anderson, G.M., Volkmar, F.R., Price, L.H. & Cohen, D.J. (1997): Risperidone treatment of children and adolescents with pervasive developmental disorders: a prospective open-label study. *J. Am. Acad. Child Adolesc. Psychiatry* **36**, 685–693.

McDougle,C.J., Holmes, J.P., Carlson, D.C., Pelton, G.H., Cohen, D.J. & Price, L.H. (1998): A double-blind, placebo-controlled study of risperidone in adults with autistic disorder and other pervasive developmental disorders. *Arch. Gen. Psychiatry* **55**, 633–641.

McDougle, C.J., Kem, D.L. & Posey, D.J. (2002): Case series: use of ziprasidone for maladaptive symptoms in youths with autism. *J. Am. Acad. Child Adolesc. Psychiatry* **41**, 921–927.

McDougle, C.J., Naylor, S.T., Cohen, D.J., Volkmar, F.R., Heninger, G.R. & Price, L.H. (1996): A double-blind, placebo-controlled study of fluvoxamine in adults with autistic disorder. *Arch. Gen. Psychiatry* **53**, 1001–1008.

Namerow, L.B., Thomas, P., Bostic, J.Q., Prince, J. & Monuteaux, M.C. (2003): Use of citalopram in pervasive developmental disorders. *J. Dev. Behav. Pediatr.* **24**,104–108.

Nicolson, R., Awad, G. & Sloman, L. (1998): An open trial of risperidone in young autistic children. *J. Am. Acad. Child Adolesc. Psychiatry* **37**, 372–376.

Owley, T., McMahon, W., Cook, E.H., Laulhere, T., South, M., Mays, L.Z., Shernoff, E.S., Lainhart, J., Modahl, C.B., Corsello, C., Ozonoff, S., Risi, S., Lord, C., Leventhal, B.L. & Filipek, P.A. (2001): Multisite, double-blind, placebo-controlled trial of porcine secretin in autism. *J. Am. Acad. Child Adolesc. Psychiatry* **40**, 1293–1299.

Posey, D.J., Guenin, K.D., Kohn, A.E., Swiezy, N.B. & McDougle, C.J. (2001a): A naturalistic open-label study of mirtazapine in autistic and other pervasive developmental disorders. *J. Child Adolesc. Psychopharmacol.* **11**, 267–277.

Posey, D.J., Decker, J., Sasher, T.M., *et al.* (2001b): A retrospective analysis of guanfacine in the treatment of autism. *Proc. Am. Psychiatric Assoc.*, New Research Abstract No. 816.

Potenza, M.N., Holmes, J.P., Kanes, S.J. & McDougle, C.J. (1999): Olanzapine treatment of children, adolescents, and adults with pervasive developmental disorders: an open-label pilot study. *J. Clin. Psychopharmacol.* **19**, 37–44.

Research Units on Pediatric Psychopharmachology (RUPP) Autism Network (2002): Risperidone in children with autism and serious behavioral problems. *N. Engl. J. Med.* **347**, 314–321.

Sanchez, L.E., Campbell, M., Small, A.M., Cueva, J.E., Armenteros, J.L. & Adams, P.B. (1996): A pilot study of clomipramine in young autistic children. *J. Am. Acad. Child Adolesc. Psychiatry* **35**, 537–544.

Sandler, A.D., Sutton, K.A., DeWeese, J., Girardi, M.A., Sheppard, V. & Bodfish, J.W. (1999): Lack of benefit of a single dose of synthetic human secretin in the treatment of autism and pervasive developmental disorders. *N. Engl. J. Med.* **341**, 1801–1806.

Steingard, R.J., Zimnitzky, B., DeMaso, D.R., Bauman, M.L. & Bucci, J.P. (1997): Sertraline treatment of transition-associated anxiety and agitation in children with autistic disorder. *J. Child Adolesc. Psychopharmacol.* **7**, 9–15.

Uvebrant, P. & Bauziene, R. (1994): Intractable epilepsy in children: the efficacy of lamotrigine treatment, included non-seizure-related benefits. *Neuropediatrics* **25**, 284–289.

Wirshing, D.A., Boyd, J.A., Meng, L.R., Ballon, J.S., Marder, S.R. & Wirshing, W.C. (2002): The effects of novel antipsychotics on glucose and lipid levels. *J. Clin. Psychiatry* **63**, 856–865.

Zuddas, A., Di Martino, A., Muglia, P. & Cianchetti C. (2000): Long-term risperidone for pervasive developmental disorder: efficacy, tolerability, and discontinuation. *J. Child Adolesc. Psychopharmacol.* **10**, 79–90.

Zuddas, A., Ledda, M.G., Fratta, A., Muglia, P. & Cianchetti, C. (1996): Clinical effects of clozapine on autistic disorder. *Am. J. Psychiatry* **153**, 738.

Autistic spectrum disorders, D. Riva and I. Rapin (eds.)
© 2005 John Libbey Eurotext, pp. 127–139.

Chapter 14

Screening and diagnostic tools

Sara Bulgheroni, Francesca Nichelli, Chiara Vago and Daria Riva

Developmental Neurology Division, National Neurological Institute 'C. Besta', via Celoria 11, 20133 Milan, Italy
neuropsicologia@istituto-besta.it

Summary

The diagnosis of autism in early infancy poses multiple problems to the clinician for several reasons, such as comorbidity of mental retardation, differential diagnosis of other pervasive developmental disorders and correct nosographical delimitation. In this paper, we will present the most popular instruments for screening and early diagnosis that recent literature had shown to be helpful to direct timely plans of adequate assistance to children and their families. As recently suggested from guidelines of the American Academies of Neurology, Pediatrics, and Child and Adolescent Psychiatry, an evaluation that considers different sources of information and settings for infant observation is necessary, and a multiprofessional approach is fundamental in order to obtain a reliable functional diagnosis.

Introduction

The American Academies of Neurology, Pediatrics, and Child and Adolescent Psychiatry have recently proposed practice parameters for the screening and diagnosis of autistic spectrum disorders (ASD). These represent the work of a multidisciplinary consensus panel comprising health care professionals, clinical research workers, and parents' organizations. As outlined by Filipek *et al.* (1999; 2000), the appropriate diagnosis of autism requires a dual-level approach: 1) routine developmental surveillance, and 2) diagnosis and evaluation of autism.

Level One is routine developmental surveillance by a primary care physician, carried out on all children at all well-child visits, to identify those at risk of any type of atypical development. In Level One screening, the professional should ask about specific developmental milestones and evaluate parental concerns, as well as observing the child directly. The consensus panel identified the following red flags, or critical developmental milestones, to be monitored specifically at Level One assessment: absence of babbling or gestures by 12 months of age; absence of single words by 16 months; absence of spontaneous two-word phrases by 24 months; and loss of any language or social skills at any age *(Table 1)*. Although it is not specifically mentioned in this list of red flags, research using retrospective home video analysis suggests that it would also be important to assess failure to orient, to name, lack of eye contact, and problems with joint attention, such as pointing and showing, by the end of the first year (Osterling & Dawson, 1994; Werner *et al.*, 2000; Osterling *et al.*, 2002).

Table 1. Parental concerns that are red flags for autism (adapted from Filipek *et al.*, 1999)

Communication concerns	**Behavioural concerns**
Does not respond to his or her name	Has tantrums
Cannot tell what he or she wants	Is hyperactive/uncooperative or oppositional
Language is delayed	Does not know how to play with toys
Does not follow directions	Toe walks
Appears deaf at times	Has unusual attachments to toys (*e.g.* always holding a certain object)
Seems to hear sometimes but not always	Lines things up
Does not point or wave bye-bye	Is oversensitive to certain textures or sounds
Social concerns	Has odd movements
Does not smile socially	
Seems to prefer to play alone	**Absolute indications for immediate further evaluation**
Gets things for himself or herself	No babbling by 12 months
Is very independent	No gesturing (pointing, waving bye-bye, etc.) by 12 months
Does things 'early'	No single words by 16 months
Has poor eye contact	No spontaneous words or phrases (not just echolalic) by 24 months
Is in his or her own world	Any loss of any language or social skills at any age
Tunes us out	
Is not interested in other children	

Failure to meet any of these milestones indicates a greater likelihood of a developmental disability, so the children involved should have additional Level One screening procedures. These include a laboratory assessment, with formal audiological evaluation and screening for lead poisoning, as well as autism-specific screening.

Only children who fail this autism-specific screening should move on to Level Two. Level Two entails a more in-depth evaluation of children identified as being at risk, and helps to provide a differential diagnosis between autistic spectrum conditions and other developmental disorders. An official diagnosis of autism should be made by an experienced clinician in accordance with DSM-IV-TR (American Psychiatric Association, 2000) or ICD-10 criteria (World Health Organization, 1993), using standardized diagnostic instruments that include both parent interview and observation. A comprehensive cross-disciplinary evaluation should be conducted for a better understanding of the child's individual profile and to formulate appropriate treatment recommendations.

Growing familiarity with these guidelines among paediatricians and the increasing availability of appropriate and reliable assessment tools have continued to improve the chances of paediatricians and other health professionals in being able to detect and diagnose autism early on in a child's development. Extant assessment tools are providing hope for the consistent and accurate screening of children as young as 18 months of age. Significant challenges remain, however, in terms of increasing the sensitivity and specificity of these methods and developing techniques for assessing children at even younger ages. As diagnosticians continue to lower the age at which a diagnosis is reached, it will become more difficult to differentiate accurately between disorders with features in common, such as autism, developmental delay, and specific language impairment.

Screening tools

A screening test is one that determines whether a child's performance is sufficiently different from that of other children of the same age to warrant further evaluation (Bricker & Losardo, 2000). The tools reviewed here are for screening purposes, as they are neither extensive enough nor deep enough to diagnose autism or any other social communication disorder. They are considered merely a quick and economical method of identifying children who need further evaluation.

The Checklist for Autism in Toddlers (CHAT)

The original version of CHAT was a simple screening tool for identifying autistic children at 18 months of age in the United Kingdom (Baron-Cohen *et al.*, 1992).

Section A of the CHAT is a self-administered questionnaire for parents. It consists of nine yes/no questions addressing the following areas of child development: rough-and-tumble play, social interest, motor development, social play, pretend play, protoimperative pointing (pointing to ask for something), protodeclarative pointing (pointing in order to share an interest), functional play, and showing. Section B of the CHAT consists of five items recorded through observation of the child by a general practitioner or health visitor. These items address the child's eye contact and ability to follow a point (gaze monitoring), pretend (pretend play), produce a point (protodeclarative pointing), and make a tower of blocks *(Table 2)*.

Table 2. Checklist for Autism in Toddlers (CHAT)

Section A – Ask parent:
Yes or No?
1) Does your child enjoy being swung, bounced on your knee, etc.?
2) Does your child take an interest in other children?
3) Does your child like climbing on things, such as up stairs?
4) Does your child enjoy playing peek-a-boo/hide-and-seek?
5) Does your child ever pretend, for example, to make a cup of tea using a toy cup and teapot, or pretend other things?
6) Does your child ever use his/her index finger to point, to ask for something?
7) Does your child ever use his/her index finger to point, to indicate interest in something?
8) Can your child play properly with small toys (*e.g.*, cars or bricks) without just mouthing, fiddling, or dropping them?
9) Does your child ever bring objects over to you, to show you something?
Section B – GP's observation
i) During the appointment, has the child made eye contact with you?
ii) Get child's attention, then point across the room at an interesting object and say 'Oh look! There's a (name a toy)!' Watch child's face. Does the child look across to see what you are pointing at? NOTE – to record yes on this item, ensure the child has not simply looked at your hand, but has actually looked at the object you are pointing at.
iii) Get the child's attention, then give child a miniature toy cup and teapot and say 'Can you make a cup of tea?' Does the child pretend to pour out the tea, drink it etc.? NOTE – if you can elicit an example of pretending in some other game, score a yes on this item.
iv) Say to the child 'Where's the light?' or 'Show me the light'. Does the child point with his/her index finger at the light? NOTE – Repeat this with 'Where's the teddy?' or some other unreachable object, if child does not understand the word 'light'. To record yes on this item, the child must have looked up at your face around the time of pointing.
v) Can the child build a tower of bricks? (If so, how many?) (Number of bricks...)

Baron-Cohen *et al.* (1996; 2000) hypothesized that children lacking joint attention (including protodeclarative pointing and gaze monitoring) and pretend play at 18 months were at high risk of autism.

Three key behaviours are:

(1) *Protodeclarative pointing* (A 7 and B iv): indicating an object for the exclusive purpose of inducing another person to look at it.

(2) *Gaze monitoring* (B ii): the child turns to look in the direction in which an adult is gazing. Both protodeclarative pointing and gaze monitoring are signs of joint attention, which has to do with the ability to focus attention on something shared with another person by pointing, showing, or monitoring the other's gaze (such as when the child's gaze shifts backwards and

forwards from an adult's face to the object or event he/she is looking at). Joint attention enables children to learn from others, *i.e.* not only what a word refers to (that is, the referential value of words and gestures), but also what to pay attention to in their surroundings (social references). Joint attention is the earliest expression of a child's capacity for mind reading, which reveals their sensitivity to what the other person is interested in. Pointing in order to share an interest (or protodeclarative pointing) can be distinguished from the more straightforward action of pointing to ask for something.

(3) *Pretend play* (A 5 and B iii): playing that implicates substituting objects and/or attributes imaginary features/properties to people, things, or events. In this kind of play the object is treated as if it represented something else, and the mind reading skill is involved since the child should understand that whoever is pretending (whether it be the child or someone else) is imagining something. Pretend play is distinct from more straightforward forms, such as functional play (using toys according to their conventional purpose) and sensory-motor play (exploring the physical features of objects, but disregarding their function, for example hitting, sucking, shaking, or throwing things).

As concerns the psychometric results, a six-year follow-up study in the United Kingdom on more than 16,000 children screened with the CHAT at 18 months of age showed a sensitivity of only 0.40 and a specificity of 0.98, with a positive predictive value of 0.26 (Baird *et al.*, 2000). Its specificity was good in that, of the 12 children identified by the CHAT as being at risk for autism, 10 were later diagnosed as autistic and the other two had developmental delays. The sensitivity was not so favourable, however. Although only 12 children were identified as being possibly autistic at 18 months, by 7 years of age 50 of the originally screened children had been diagnosed with autism and 44 with other autistic spectrum disorders (ASDs) (Baird *et al.*, 2000). Although the number of false positives was low, the large number of false negatives, especially when ASDs were also considered, is reason for concern. Rescreening the potentially autistic children with the same tool at 19 months led to a higher positive predictive value of 0.75, so the investigators suggested that children were likely to have autism if they failed the CHAT at 18 months and failed it again a month later (Baird *et al.*, 2001).

The CHAT's most outstanding strengths lie in the fact that it is short and has shown good specificity. It has two main drawbacks: its sensitivity is low, though it is better for autism than for other disorders in the autistic spectrum (Baron-Cohen *et al.*, 1992; Charman *et al.*, 1998); and the epidemiological study conducted to validate it as a screening tool disregarded subjects with mental retardation, thus failing to allow for the fact that, for clinical purposes, the differential diagnosis between ASDs and severe mental delay without autism is one of the most crucial aspects, especially in early infancy.

Modified Checklist for Autism in Toddlers (M-CHAT)

Given its poor sensitivity for autism, Robins *et al.* (2001) attempted to modify the original CHAT to a format that was only questionnaire based – that is, the M-CHAT. Although Robins *et al.*, describe the M-CHAT as an extension of the CHAT, there are major changes in its format and content.

The M-CHAT is composed of 23 yes/no questions for parents concerning their child's current skills and behaviours. The first nine items were drawn from the CHAT and the other 14 are original questions largely directed towards social communication abilities. The M-CHAT is administered when a child is 24 months old (the CHAT at 18). Shifting the screening further into the developmental process identifies some children who show no signs of autism at

18 months but may regress by 24 months. (It is estimated that regression has occurred in approximately one-third of children diagnosed with autism.) Analysing the 23 questions used in the M-CHAT indicated that six of them had a stronger discriminating power: three were drawn from the original CHAT and three were new. These new questions ask whether the child imitates the parents (social relatedness), responds when his/her name is called (communication), and follows a protodeclarative pointing to an object across the room (joint attention). As children with autism often experience sensory problems, such as overreaction to sound or touch, and may be seen to engage in repetitive behaviour, items relating to these abilities are also included in the M-CHAT. A telephone interview was instituted for children who had failed the initial M-CHAT screening. It served to confirm previous responses on the M-CHAT, and was found to improve the test's overall statistical power.

Psychometric data from the M-CHAT are still preliminary, with only 1,293 children screened so far, but both its sensitivity (0.87) and its specificity (0.99) seem promising. These statistics are based on M-CHAT responses that were confirmed by a follow-up telephone interview and when children initially flagged by health care providers were included in the group to be referred for evaluation.

Positive aspects of the M-CHAT are that, like the CHAT, it is short and easy to administer. It eliminates the need to obtain responses from children while in the physician's office, where they may show atypical behaviour. It does not need to be readministered, as the CHAT does, although a telephone interview increases its statistical power.

Checklist for Autism in Toddlers-23 (CHAT-23)

Wong *et al.* (2004) recently examined whether a new screening tool could be devised by combining the observational part of the original CHAT (section B) and the M-CHAT (parental questionnaire) to distinguish Chinese children with autism at 18–24 months of age. The seven key questions identified related to the following areas of normal child development: *social relatedness* (that is, imitation and interest in other children); *pretend play*; *joint attention* (that is, protodeclarative pointing, bringing objects to show parents and following a point); and *social referencing* (that is, checking the other's reaction). The seven key discriminating questions were the same as in the original CHAT and the M-CHAT, except for the question about social referencing ('Does your child look at your face to check your reaction when faced with something unfamiliar?'). This question was not in the original CHAT or the M-CHAT because not all of the subjects answered it. Social referencing belongs to the constellation of social-communicative behaviours called joint attention behaviours, together with following another's gaze, protodeclarative pointing, and showing. Social referencing entails noticing another's affective state or facial expression and using it as a cue to guide one's own behaviour, so it is a more complex example of joint attention in that it involves orienting, attending, and recognising expressions.

The authors found that a two-stage screening programme for autism could be a good cost-effective method for the early detection of autism at 18 to 24 months of age. For CHAT-23, using both parental questionnaires and direct observation and adopting the criterion of failing any two of seven key questions yielded the highest sensitivity (0.93), but a relatively low specificity (0.77), whereas using part B yielded the highest specificity (0.91) but a lower sensitivity (0.74). Wong *et al.* (2004) therefore recommend identifying possible positive cases using part A (parental questionnaire) and then proceeding to part B (observation) with trained assessors.

Questionario sullo Sviluppo Comunicativo e Linguistico nel secondo anno di vita (QSCL)
[or questionnaire on communication and language development in the second year of life]

QSCL (Camaioni *et al.*, 1992) provides a quantitative and qualitative assessment of the communication strategies children use spontaneously, even at a very early age. Unlike the CHAT or M-CHAT, this is a method for screening social and communication abilities that should be administered several times during the second year of life, so that an impression of a given child's behaviour can be gained very early on, and then tested at subsequent visits.

This structured questionnaire is available in two versions: Form I has been validated in a population of normal children aged 12 and 16 months, while Form II has been validated in a normal population aged 20 months. The Italian Questionnaire has been validated on 50 children evaluated at 12, 18 and 20 months in accordance to longitudinal approach.

The questionnaire covers six different settings involving both daily routine and play, and for each setting there is a set of categories or measures relating to communication and other types of behaviour that the child may exhibit:

1. What does the child do when hungry?
2. What does the child do when he/she wants to go out?
3. How does the child behave when he/she wants a toy?
4. When the person the child prefers is absent, what does the child do to call them back?
5. What does the child do when you read or look at a book together?
6. What does the child do when you play 'peek-a-boo' together?

The following communication modes are assessed on a three level scale (0, never; 1, sometimes, *i.e.*, two to three times during the observation period; 2, often, *i.e.*, more than three times): (1) crying; (2) instrumental use of the adult (bringing the adult towards what the child wants); (3) solitary behaviour; (4) protoimperative pointing; (5) using referential gestures (for example, cupping a hand over one ear to pretend to make a phone call); (6) vocalizations (for example, using a particular vocalization in relation to food); (7) using words or phrases; and (8) pointing associated with verbal output.

The QSCL confirms the autistic child's limited use of language to exchange information, together with a preverbal communication pattern characterized by joint attention deficit and sparse use of complex combinations of non-verbal behaviour (the child has a strong tendency to use single gestures, unaccompanied by any vocalizations). This communication pattern reflects the autistic child's difficulty in understanding that the others possess mental states and that language is the key to unravel people's thoughts, beliefs, and emotions. Being unable, or finding it very difficult, to mind-read has a profound impact on communicational capabilities, because the fundamental motivation to communicate relies on the desire to share emotions, thoughts, and intentions with others, and the chance to conduct a conversation depends on the ability to identify adequate strategies for interpreting and assessing communicational intentions (Surian,1997).

A recent study by Bernabei *et al.* (2001) emphasizes that specific communication profiles, differentiating autistic children from those with developmental delay, can be identified through the QSCL by the age of 2 years. Subjects with developmental delay are seen to gradually acquire communicational competence, which increases when they pass from the second to the third year of life, whereas autistic children seem to stop using the more mature communication modes (pointing, a more varied repertoire of communication gestures, words, and the beginnings of phrases). The two groups do not differ in their use of crying, vocalizations, solitary behaviour, and recourse to the adult, and their use of these somewhat primitive signalling methods and communication tools remains much the same as they grow older (persisting even at 2 years old). It is worth noting that autistic children have a particular, atypical way of using the adult as a tool, that is generally mediated by close contact rather than by distal gestures (such as pointing), and it is almost never accompanied by eye contact.

Diagnostic tools

The diagnostic process proposed by Filipek *et al.* (1999; 2000) involves a more in-depth assessment of the child suspected of having a developmental delay or atypia, which helps in the differential diagnosis between autistic spectrum disorders and other developmental disorders, as well as in defining the child's cognitive and behavioural profile.

By incorporating the diagnostic process in a continuum with the therapeutic process, the goal is to arrive at a functional and multiprofessional assessment that considers each child's needs and potential in order to develop a treatment plan tailored to each case.

To obtain a picture that is as faithful as possible to a child's real capabilities, it is not only necessary to combine information from different sources (parents, teachers, operators), but it is also advisable to conduct an assessment in different settings (in the relationship with parents or other adult members of the family, with strangers and with the educator, in situations of spontaneous play and in structured activities). To establish the performance profile, we need to be able to use formal diagnostic procedures that provide for a more in-depth analysis of specific abilities. Most widely used tools at international level are as follows:

- clinical diagnosis: DSM-IV-TR, ICD-10;
- interviews and checklists: ADI-R, ABC;
- observational tools: CARS, PEP-R, ADOS-G;
- cognitive (Leiter-R, Wechsler scales) and developmental scales (Mental Developmental Griffiths Scales);
- adaptive behaviour assessment (Vineland scales);
- verbal tasks according to language comprehension and production;
- neuropsychological and school tests (particularly for executive and metacognitive abilities, and for reading, writing and arithmetic skills);
- behaviour checklists (CBCL, DBC).

Here the aim is to review the observational tools, interviews and checklists used for the purpose of differential diagnosis in our institute.

The Childhood Autism Rating Scale (CARS; Schopler *et al.*, 1988) is a semistructured observational diagnostic tool designed to identify children with autism from the age of 2 years, and to distinguish them from children with other developmental deficits, also providing an assessment of the severity of the disorder. It takes from 30 to 45 minutes to administer and requires the recording of information from various sources (parents, educators, teachers, therapists), accompanied by direct observation of the child in situations suggested by the tool itself.

The following 15 categories of behaviour are investigated and evaluated on a Likert seven-point scale (from 1 = behaviour adequate for age to 4 = severely abnormal behaviour): relating to people; imitation; emotional response; body use; object use; adaptation to change; visual response; listening response; taste, smell, touch response and use; fear or nervousness; verbal communication; non-verbal communication; activity level; level and consistency of intellectual response; and the general impression. An example item with scoring is shown in *Table 3*.

Table 3. Example item of the Childhood Autism Rating Scale

Item I: RELATING TO PEOPLE
1 *No evidence of difficulty or abnormality in relating to people*: The child's behaviour is appropriate for his or her age. Some shyness, fussiness, or annoyance at being told what to do may observed, but not to an atypical degree.
1.5
2 *Mildly abnormal relationships*: The child may avoid looking the adult in the eyes, avoid the adult or become fussy if interaction is forced, be excessively shy, not be as responsive to the adult as is typical, or cling to parents somewhat more than most children of the same age.
2.5
3 *Moderately abnormal relationships*: The child shows aloofness (seems unaware of adult) at times. Persistent and forceful attempts are necessary to get the child's attention at times. Minimal contact is initiated by the child.
3.5
4 *Severely abnormal relationships*: The child is consistently aloof or unaware of what the adult is doing. He or she almost never responds or initiates contact with the adult. Only the most persistent attempts to get the child's attention have any effect.

Designed as a diagnostic tool for distinguishing autism from other paediatric developmental disorders, this test suggests a cut-off of 30 for the diagnosis of autism (27 for adolescents and 32 for children under 3 years old); it also enables the distinction between mild to moderate (scores of 30 to 37) and severe autism (> 37). Although it can be used to diagnose autism in adolescents and adults, it is not adequate to recognize atypical autism or Asperger's syndrome.

The CARS has been tested on more than 1,500 cases over a period of 15 years and it offers numerous advantages: it is easy to use, even for operators with little experience of autism; it enables a direct and easy follow-up of the child's disability; and it gives the clinician considerable freedom in collecting information by reading the child's clinical history, watching a videotape of the child in his home environment, and observing him during the administration of other structured tests.

The weaknesses of this tool lie in the fact that it does not take into account the anamnestic data, the onset of symptoms, and any evolution of the behavioural patterns investigated; moreover, all the items examined are taken into account for the final score, including those relating to characteristics that are often present but are not specific for autism (activity level, sensory modalities, anxiety/fear, cognitive functioning).

Published reports nonetheless suggest good reliability and general validity of this tool, though it tends to produce false negatives at preschool age (Eaves & Milner, 1993; DiLalla & Rogers, 1994). It shows a strong correlation with the DSM criteria and a good diagnostic consistency with the more recently standardized Autism Diagnostic Interview-Revised (87.5 per cent) (ADI-R, Rutter *et al.*, 2003), while there is no such consistency when it comes to ruling out a diagnosis of autism. The disagreement between various diagnostic procedures may be attributable to the different sources of information used by the two tools (parents' reports *vs* clinicians' observations) and their different limits of time and space (the child's developmental history *vs* observation of his current behaviour during a limited period of time) (Pilowsky *et al.*, 1998).

The second tool presented here is the Autism Behavior Checklist (ABC), a checklist designed to measure the degree of autistic behaviour in subjects with severe mental retardation at school (it is part of the Autism Screening Instrument for Educational Planning) (Krug *et al.*, 1980). Because of its not very powerful psychometric properties, it proves more useful in monitoring treatment-related changes than for purely diagnostic purposes. It can be administered from 18 months to 35 years of age and it comprises 57 items, drawn from other diagnostic tools, grouped into five symptom areas: (1) sensory; (2) socialization; (3) body and object use; (4)

language; and (5) daily living skills. The items are attributed scores from 1 to 4, weighted according to their autism-predictive power (4 indicates the items that are most autism-specific). A score of 67 or more is indicative of a high likelihood of autism, < 53 of a low likelihood of autism. According to a study by Eaves & Milner (1993), correlations between ABC and CARS vary from 0.16 to 0.73.

Investigations have revealed that those tools are scarcely sensitive to highly functional autistic and Asperger disorder subjects. The CARS is rather more sensitive, but needs to be supported by other sources. The two tools should be used in combination.

Turning now to consider another extremely useful observational tool, the Psychoeducational Profile-Revised (PEP-R; Schopler *et al.*, 1990) evaluates the abilities and behaviour of children with autism and communication disorders. It is suitable for preschool children and in subjects with a chronological age between 6 months and 7 years.

The examiner observes, assesses, and records the child's reactions during the test, which includes 43 behavioural items and 131 developmental items. Depending on the child's developmental level and behavioural control problems, the total time to administer the test can vary from 45 to 90 minutes.

This assessment tool enables us to obtain information on the developmental level of seven functions (imitation, perception, fine motor control, gross motor control, eye-hand integration, cognitive level, and verbal performance) and identifies the degree of behavioural abnormality in four areas (relations and affections; play and interests; sensory responses; language). The assessment is conducted while children play at structured activities involving minimal use of the verbal channel, both for their understanding of the instructions and for the required response modality.

The levels of assessment are: unsuccessful; successful; and emerging abilities – that is, activities in which the child is seen to possess some knowledge of what is needed to perform the required activity, but fails to arrive at a full comprehension and is unable to complete the task (Schopler *et al.*, 1990). The items on the behavioural scale are based on those used in the CARS. The sum of the dysfunctional or unusual behaviours is quantified and qualified and indicates the severity of the child's behavioural difficulties: behaviour is judged to be adequate, mildly anomalous, or more severely anomalous.

The profile emerging from the administration of the test shows the child's strengths and weaknesses in the various aspects of development and areas of behaviour, proving extremely useful and practical for evaluating their emerging abilities with a view to creating rehabilitation programmes, as the profile enables to provide precise recommendations on the areas where the child has the best chance of success.

To base educational programmes on these emerging capacities means to focus such programmes on skills that have yet to be entirely acquired, but choosing tasks that are not too difficult for the child and are thus more likely to enable a pleasant relationship to be established between educator, child, and parents, thereby reducing the frustration and stressful situations to a minimum.

There is also a version of the PEP for adolescents and adults (Adolescent and Adult Psychoeducational Profile; Mesibov *et al.*, 1988), which evaluates the subjects' aptitudes, level of independence, capacity to organize their free time, communication, and social abilities at home and at school.

The last tool that we consider here is the Vineland Adaptive Behavior Scale (Sparrow *et al.*, 1984): this is a semistructured interview administered to the subject's caregiver. The original includes three versions, an interview–short form (261 items), which takes between 20 and 30 minutes to administer; an interview–full form (540 items), which takes 60 to 90 minutes to administer; and a version for use at school. In the Italian standardization, data are only available for the full form.

The Vineland Scale enables a valid assessment of adaptive behaviour – that is, interaction between individuals and their environment and the activities of daily living that subjects must be able to handle in order to be sufficiently independent and cope with the tasks connected to their role in society, so as to comply with what their environment expects of an individual of corresponding age and cultural context.

The scale is useful for an ecological assessment of a subject with mental retardation and other developmental disorders, and it offers guidelines for planning and assessing educational and rehabilitative measures designed to increase the subject's appropriate responses to the environment.

The Italian version can be administered from age 2 to 18 years and enables an assessment of adaptive behaviour in four different interrelated scales:

1. socialization (ability in interpersonal relations, in playing and recreational activities, and knowledge of and adaptation to social rules);
2. daily living skills (personal, domestic, and community skills);
3. communication (receptive, expressive and written);
4. motor skills (fine and gross motor control) – only for children less than 6 years old or with severe motor deficits.

Evaluating motor skills can prove particularly important in cases with problems of delay, dysfunction, or regression of such skills. Occult neurological deficits may have an impact on the individual's functional skills or activities of daily living.

The full version of the scale is the most useful for autistic children, whose adaptive functions are usually lower than their cognitive level (Volkmar *et al.*, 1993). Additional standards have recently been published for autistic individuals (Carter *et al.*, 1998).

In the early seventies, the American Association on Mental Retardation formally introduced the adaptive behaviour construct in the definition of mental delay and, because mental retardation is often (in 75 per cent of cases) associated with autistic disorder, administering the scale has proved particularly useful in documenting this feature. Assessing adaptive behaviour also helps us to identify the subject's strengths and weaknesses so as to plan a tailored rehabilitation treatment. Finally, it can be used to monitor the subject's progress in time and in different settings.

Unlike intellectual functioning, adaptive behaviour is liable to change and may consequently be the area in which rehabilitation treatment has the greatest effect. The scores attributed are coded as follows:

- 2: the activity is usually completed successfully;
- 1: it is only sometimes or only partially successful;
- 0: it is never completed because the subject is too young or immature, the activity is beyond their capabilities, or physical or sensory deficit prevent its completion;
- N or 'lack of opportunity': the activity is not performed because of an external contingent impediment;
- NS: skill in which the interviewee does not know how the subject would perform.

The starting-point usually coincides with the chronological age rounded down, while for subjects with disabilities the starting-point is the subject's estimated mental or social age. The limitations of the Italian version lie in the lack of deviation quotient from the mean of normal population for comparison with IQ, and in the fact that the normal levels for disabled subjects are calculated on the sample as a whole, disregarding the intellectual level.

The Vineland scales can nonetheless discriminate adequately between autistic subjects and cases of developmental delay or Pervasive Developmental Disorder-Not Otherwise Specified (PDD-NOS), recording significantly lower scores than might be expected at the same mental age on the scale for socialization (low scores are achieved in the items that assess interpersonal relations and interactive play).

The instruments ADOS and ADI are discussed in the following chapter by Tancredi & Parrini.

Conclusions

This review emphasizes the need to use sensitive and specific tools for early screening, and the importance of a functional and multiprofessional assessment that takes the needs and potential of each child into account.

It is essential to formulate a diagnosis based on the use of standardized assessment tools, first to quantify the disorder and facilitate communication between experts, and subsequently to monitor the progress of the subject's symptoms, design suitable rehabilitation treatment, as well as evaluate its outcome in the long term.

Moreover, using standardized tools can help clinicians in the difficult task of establishing an early diagnosis for neurodevelopmental disorders that have no biological marker and must be identified on the strength of behavioural indices with varying ages of onset, making them scarcely specific in early infancy. On the other hand, the importance of an early diagnosis has now been amply documented by various studies and it is an issue of fundamental interest on the epidemiological level as well. In fact, while initial estimates suggested a prevalence of autism of 4–5 per 10,000 (Lotter, 1966), recent research has revealed considerably higher figures of around 1–2 per 1,000 (Fombonne, 1999; Gillberg & Wing, 1999).

In addition, an early diagnosis of autism not only helps the family to cope (containing the generalized stress felt by the family system as a whole, owing to the parents' disorientation when they cannot understand their child's atypical behaviour), but it also enables the prompt implementation of early and intensive educational planning and rehabilitation treatment, which can improve the outcome of a lifelong disorder. Several studies have shown that if we can adequately organize the child's times, spaces, and activities between the ages of 2 and 4 years, we may be able to influence the child's immediate potential and the long-term quality of their adaptive behaviour, on which the quality of life of the entire family system depends (Dawson & Osterling, 1997; American Academy of Pediatrics, 2001; Muratori *et al.*, 2003).

References

American Academy of Pediatrics, Committee on Children with Disabilities (2001): The pediatrician's role in the diagnosis and management of autistic spectrum disorder in children. *Pediatrics* **107**, 1221–1226.

American Psychiatric Association (2000): *Diagnostic and statistical manual of mental disorders, 4th edition, text revision (DSM-IV-TR)*. Italian edition (2002). Milan: Masson.

Baird, G., Charman, T., Baron-Cohen, S., Cox, A., Swettenham, J., Wheelwright, S. & Drew, A. (2000): A screening instrument for autism at 18 months of age: a six year follow-up study. *J. Am. Acad. Child Adolesc. Psychiatry* **39**, 694–702.

Baird, G., Charman, T., Cox, A., Baron-Cohen, S., Swettenham, J., Wheelwright, S. & Drew, A. (2001): Current topic: screening and surveillance for autism and pervasive developmental disorders. *Arch. Dis. Child.* **84**, 468–475.

Baron-Cohen, S., Allen, J. & Gillberg, C. (1992): Can autism be detected at 18 months? The needle, the haystack, and the CHAT. *Br. J. Psychiatry* **161**, 839–843.

Baron-Cohen, S., Cox, A., Baird, G., Swettenham, J., Nightingale, N., Morgan, K., Drew, A. & Charman, T. (1996): Psychological markers in the detection of autism in infancy in a large population. *Br. J. Psychiatry* **168**, 158–163.

Baron-Cohen, S., Wheelwright, S., Cox, A., Baird, G., Charman, T., Swettenham, J., Drew, A. & Doehring, P. (2000): Early identification of autism by the Checklist for Autism in Toddlers (CHAT). *J. R. Soc. Med.* **93**, 521–525.

Bernabei, P., Camaioni, L., Paolesse, C. & Longobardi, E. (2001): Lo sviluppo comunicativo-linguistico in soggetti con autismo e con ritardo mentale: una ricerca condotta tramite il QSCL. *Psicologia clinica dello sviluppo* **2**, 169–188.

Bricker, D. & Losardo, A. (2000): A model for linking assessment and intervention for children with developmental disorders. In: *Handbook of early language impairment in children: assessment and treatment*, eds. L. Watson, E. Crais & T. Layton, pp. 111–119. Albany, NY: Delmar/Thompson Learning.

Camaioni, L., Caselli, M.C., Volterra, V. & Lucenti, S. (1992): *Questionario sullo Sviluppo Comunicativo e Linguistico nel secondo anno di vita.* Firenze: Organizzazioni Speciali.

Carter, A.S., Volkmar, F.R., Sparrow, S.S., Wang, J.J., Lord, C., Dawson, G., Fombonne, E., Loveland, K., Mesibov, G. & Schopler, E. (1998): The Vineland Adaptive Behavior Scales: supplementary norms for individuals with autism. *J. Autism Dev. Disord.* **28**, 287–302.

Charman, T., Swettenham, J., Baron-Cohen, S., Cox, A., Baird, G. & Drew, A. (1998): An experimental investigation of social-cognitive abilities in infants with autism: clinical implications. *Inf. Ment. Health J.* **19**, 260–275.

Dawson, G. & Osterling, J. (1997): Early intervention in autism. In: *The effectiveness of early intervention*, ed. M. Guralnick, pp. 307–326. Baltimore: Paul H. Brookes Publishing.

DiLalla, D.L. & Rogers, S. (1994): Domains of the Childhood Autism Rating Scale: relevance for diagnosis and treatment. *J. Autism Dev. Disord.* **24**, 115–128.

Eaves, R.C. & Milner, B. (1993): The criterion-rated validity of the Childhood Autism Rating Scale and the Autism Behavior Checklist. *J. Abnorm. Child Psychol.* **5**, 481–491.

Filipek, P., Accardo, P.J., Ashwal, S., Baranek, G.T., Cook, E.H., Dawson, G., Gordon, B., Gravel, J.S., Johnson, C.P., Kallen, R.J., Levy, S.E., Minshew, N.J., Ozonoff, S., Prizant, B.M., Rapin, I., Rogers, S.J., Stone, W.L., Teplin, S.W., Tuchman, R.F. & Volkmar, F.R. (1999): The screening and diagnosis of autistic spectrum disorders. *J. Autism Dev. Disord.* **29**, 439–484.

Filipek, P.A., Accardo, P.J., Ashwal, S., Baranek, G.T., Cook, E.H., Dawson, G., Gordon, B., Gravel, J.S., Johnson, C.P., Kallen, R.J., Levy, S.E., Minshew, N.J., Ozonoff, S., Prizant, B.M., Rapin, I., Rogers, S.J., Stone, W.L., Teplin, S.W., Tuchman, R.F. & Volkmar, F.R. (2000): Practice parameter: screening and diagnosis of autism: report of the Quality Standards Subcommittee of the American Academy of Neurology and the Child Neurology Society. *Neurology* **55**, 468–479.

Fombonne, E. (1999): The epidemiology of autism: a review. *Psychol. Med.* **29**, 769–786.

Gillberg, C. & Wing, L. (1999): Autism: not an extremely rare disorder. *Act. Psychiatr. Scand.* **99**, 399–406.

Krug, D.A., Arick, J. & Almond, P. (1980): *Autism screening instrument for educational planning*. Portland, OR: ASIEP Educational Co.

Lotter, V. (1966): Epidemiology of autistic conditions in young children. I. Prevalence. *Soc. Psychiatry* **1**, 124–137.

Mesibov, G.B., Schopler, E., Schaffer, B. & Landrus, R. (1988): *Individualized assessment for autistic and developmentally disabled children: Adolescent and Adult Psychoeducational Profile (AAPEP)*, vol. 4. Austin, TX: PRO-ED Inc.

Muratori, F., Tancredi, R., Parrini, B. & Floriani, C. (2003): Interventi precoci nei disturbi pervasivi dello sviluppo: una review. *Giorn. Neuropsic. Età Evol.* **23**, 72–88.

Osterling, J. & Dawson, G. (1994): Early recognition of children with autism: a study of first birthday home videotapes. *J. Autism Dev. Disord.* **24**, 247–257.

Osterling, J., Dawson, G. & Munson, J. (2002): Early recognition of 1-year-old infants with autism spectrum disorder *versus* mental retardation. *Dev. Psychopathol.* **14**, 239–251.

Pilowsky, T., Yirmiya, N., Shulman, C. & Dover, R. (1998): The Autism Diagnostic Interview–Revised and the Childhood Autism Rating Scale: differences between diagnostic systems and comparison between genders. *J. Autsim Dev. Disord.* **28**, 143–151.

Robins, D., Fein, D., Baron, M. & Green, J. (2001): The modified checklist for autism in toddlers: an initial study investigating the early detection of autism and pervasive developmental disorders. *J. Autism Dev. Disord.* **31**, 131–144.

Rutter, M., Le Couter, A. & Lord, C. (2003): *ADI.-R: Autism Diagnostic Interview–Revised*. Los Angeles: WPS Edition.

Schopler, E., Reichler, R.J. & Rochen-Renner, B. (1988): *The Childhood Autism Rating Scale (CARS)*. Los Angeles, CA: Western Psychological Services.

Schopler, E., Reichler, R.J., Bashford, A., Lansing, M.D. & Marcus, L.M. (1990). Psycho-educational profile–revised (PEP-R), Italian translation (1995). Lucerna: Edizione SZH/SPC.

Sparrow, S.S, Balla, D.A. & Cicchetti, D.V. (1984): *Vineland Adaptive Behavior Scales*. Italian version adapted by Balboni, G. & Pedrabissi, L. (2003). Firenze: Organizzazioni Speciali.

Surian, L. (1997): Metarappresentazione e comunicazione nei bambini con autismo. *Psicologia clinica dello sviluppo* **2**, 275–290.

Volkmar, F.R., Carter, A., Sparrow, S.S. & Cicchetti, D.V. (1993): Quantifying social development in autism. *J. Am. Acad. Child Adolesc. Psychiatry* **32**, 627–632.

Werner, E., Dawson, G., Osterling, J. & Dinno, N. (2000): Brief report: recognition of autism spectrum disorder before one year of age: a retrospective study based on home videotapes. *J. Autism Dev. Disord.* **30**, 157–62.

Wong V., Hui, L.H., Lee, W.C., Leung, L.S., Ho, P.K., Lau, W.L., Fung, C.W. & Chung, B. (2004): A modified screening tool for autism [Checklist for Autism in Toddlers (CHAT-23)] for Chinese children. *Pediatrics* **114**, e166-e176.

World Health Organization (1993): *The ICD-10 classification of mental and behavioural disorders*, Italian translation (1995). Milan: Masson.

Autistic spectrum disorders, D. Riva and I. Rapin (eds.)

Chapter 15

Tools for a standardized diagnosis

Raffaella Tancredi and Barbara Parrini

IRCCS Stella Maris, viale del Tirreno 331, 56018 Pisa, Italy
raffaella.tancredi@inpe.unipi.it;
barbara.parrini@inpe.unipi.it

Summary

An important aid for all mental health personnel working with pervasive developmental disorder is the use of standardised instruments that can facilitate communication, foster a comparable viewpoint in the diagnostic process, and generate more homogeneous groups for research. Such instruments are the Autism Diagnostic Interview–Revised (ADI-R) (Lord *et al.*, 1994) and the Autism Diagnostic Observation Schedule–Generic (ADOS-G) (Lord *et al.*, 1996). These complementary instruments are currently considered the gold standard among diagnostic instruments.
In Italy, ADI-R and ADOS-G are not yet in widespread use, but our clinical experience with these instruments shows that they provide a great deal of information about the children and a clearer idea of the nature of their problems.

Introduction

Research in the past 10 years has provided much useful information on the nature of autism-specific deficits in social and communication skills. However, at present there is no objective procedure for the diagnosis of autism. Clinicians must accordingly rely on their clinical judgement, aided by such guides to diagnosis as DSM-IV (American Psychiatric Association, 1994) and ICD-10 (World Health Organization, 1993), as well as the results of various assessment instruments (checklists, interviews, rating scales, and observation schedules).

An important aid for all mental health personnel working with this disorder is the use of standardised instruments that can facilitate communication, foster a comparable viewpoint in the diagnostic process, and generate more homogeneous groups for research. Such instruments are the Autism Diagnostic Interview–Revised (ADI-R) (Lord *et al.*, 1994) and the Autism Diagnostic Observation Schedule–Generic (ADOS-G) (Lord *et al.*, 1996). These complementary instruments are currently considered the gold standard among diagnostic instruments.

ADI-R

ADI-R is a standardized, semistructured, investigator-based interview for caregivers of autistic individuals which provides a diagnostic algorithm for the ICD-10 and DSM-IV definition of autism. It has undergone progressive changes, beginning in 1980. Over the years, improvements have produced a shorter interview which is more specific for autistic disorders, and more useful and suitable for preschool age children.

The interview focuses primarily on the diagnostic criteria specified in ICD-10 and DSM-IV – namely those features concerned with developmental delay, or impairment in some function, and deviance, or qualitative abnormality, in that function; however, the focus throughout is upon deviance rather than delay.

The standardization of the structure of this interview lies in the detail of the predetermining open ended questions and the coding of each behavioural item. The 'investigator-based' approach reflects the fact that it is up to the interviewer to continue cross-questioning until it is clear that the requisite information has been obtained for each coding. The focus is upon obtaining detailed descriptions of actual behaviours and then establishing whether they are sufficiently typical and pervasive for a diagnosis of autism.

The interview is composed of six sections.

• The first section (family history; schools attended; current picture of the child) provides background information about the subject and their family that can help the interviewer to better formulate later questions.

• The second section (parental concerns; first concerns; motor and toileting milestones) covers the early development history with questions, for example, on when the parents first became aware that something might be wrong with their child (and what it was that caused concern at that time), and on various developmental milestones.

• The next three sections are about specific areas related to the diagnosis of autism: *communication and language* (with different questions about verbal and non-verbal aspects of communication); *social development and play* (in which the interviewer asks about the presence, for example, of sharing behaviours, emotional reciprocity and so on); and *repetitive and stereotyped behaviours and unusual interests.*

• The sixth and final section concerns non-specific behavioural difficulties and special abilities.

For each section of the interview there is an initial obligatory question followed by other optional supplementary questions that the interviewers can ask until they have obtained sufficient examples of behaviour; 'yes' or 'no' answers are never coded as such; rather, behavioural descriptions are recorded.

The interview is designed to be applicable across a wide age range but there are specific age periods to which ratings apply: behaviours that are deviant at any age (for example delayed echolalia) are coded as 'current/ever'; behaviours that are strongly conditioned by maturational level (for example communication and social behaviours) are coded as 'most abnormal during the 4 to 5 year age period/current'.

For each item we obtain a coding: '0' means that the behaviour specified in the coding was not present; '1' means that the behaviour investigated by the question is present but not severe, frequent, or marked; '2' or '3' means that the abnormal behaviour is clearly present and of an important degree of severity.

The most discriminant items from three behavioural domains (social reciprocal interaction; communication; restricted, repetitive and stereotyped behaviours and interests) are presented in a diagnostic algorithm that enables the presence of autistic disorder to be established.

In a study by Lord *et al.* (1993) the results showed that ADI-R had a low specificity in children with a chronological and mental age of less than 20 months. In particular, some items related to verbal and non-verbal communication were very specific. In addition, items such as 'difficulty in seeking comfort', 'declarative pointing', or greeting behaviours did not discriminate between autistic disorder and other forms of developmental delay.

At 3 years of age many items can discriminate between autistic and not-autistic children, probably because in autism some regression has occurred by this time, while children with developmental delay continue to show some improvement in skills. Also, while the child is growing up the parents are more able to identify developmental difficulties.

Here is an example of questioning about a boy (item 11: use of other's body to communicate), which refers to the communication section:

Question: 'How does... usually let you know he wants something?' (if subject is now using speech, ask: 'How did he let you know before he was able to use words?') Did/does he ever show you what he wants by taking your hand or wrist or some other part of your body? What exactly does he do? What does he do if he is brought the object wanted? Does he ever use your hand as if it were a tool or an extension of their own arm (such as pointing with your hand or getting your hand to turn a door knob)? Does he look at you when doing this? Does he combine taking your hand with trying to communicate with sounds or words? When does he do this? Does he try to communicate with sounds or words? When does he do this? Does he try to communicate first by sounds or gesture?

Coding: □ CURRENT □ EVER
0 = no use of other's body to communicate, except in situations where other strategies have not worked (for example, when the parent is conversing with someone and the subject cannot get their attention).
1 = occasional placement of hands on objects or use of hand as a tool or to point, but some combination with other modes of communication (merely taking someone's hand to lead them places should be coded '0').
2 = occasional placement of hands on objects or use of hand as a tool or to demonstrate 'for' the subject without integration with other modes of communication.
3 = regular use of other's hand as a tool or to gesture 'for' the subject.
(...)
8 = little or no spontaneous communication.
9 – not known or not asked.

ADOS-G

This instrument is a combination of two earlier instruments: the 1989 version of the Autism Diagnostic Observation Schedule (Lord *et al.*, 1989), which was for adults and children who had language skills at the 3-year-old level at minimum; and the Pre-Linguistic Autism Diagnostic Observation Scale (PL-ADOS; DiLavore *et al.*, 1995), which was intended for use with children who had limited or no language skills.

ADOS-G (G = Generic) is an instrument that collects standard information about a child's behaviour in response to a predeterminated schedule of activities. Activities and behaviours were taken from empirical research in autism and child development, and refer to social and communicative features. During ADOS-G the examiners deliberately vary their behaviour to maintain interaction and demonstrate the limits of the child's abilities. In this way the interactive assessment generates a social occasion, through play and verbal interchange, using the examiner as a tool. The information provided is minimally affected by the child's language level.

Four different modules are available in the ADOS; the examiner selects the one that best matches the expressive language level of the child: *module 1* is for children who are preverbal or present single words; *module 2* is for children with phrase speech; *module 3* is for children/younger adolescents with fluent speech; *and module 4* is for older adolescents/adults with fluent speech.

Modules 1 and 2 focus on joint attention skills and non-verbal social behaviours such as sharing, giving, showing, and requesting. The examiner is most physically interactive with the child and tests a set of behavioural hypotheses through different play in semistructured situations.

Modules 3 and 4 place less emphasis on physical tasks and focus on conversational skills; the examiner tests a set of behavioural hypotheses through different verbal semistructured situations *(Table 1)*.

Table 1. Characteristics of the modules of ADOS-G

	Module 1	Module 2	Module 3	Module 4
Minimum expressive language level	No speech	Flexible three-word phrases	Verbally fluent	Verbally fluent
Maximum expressive language level	Simple phrases	Verbally fluent	–	–
Examiner's difficulties	Administering	Administering	Coding	Coding
Behaviours observed	Sharing, giving, showing, requesting	Sharing, giving, showing, requesting	Conversation	Conversation

For each item/behaviour we obtain a coding similar to ADI: '0' means that the behaviour specified in the coding was not present; '1' means that behaviour is present but not severe, frequent, or marked; '2' or '3' means that abnormal behaviour is clearly present and of an important degree of severity.

The most discriminating social and communicative behaviours (stereotyped behaviours are not included in the algorithm) for each module are present in a diagnostic algorithm that enables the presence of autistic disorder to be established.

Conclusions

In our experience of the use of these instruments we can identify various advantages. During the diagnostic process clinicians probably normally use internal criteria that define 'clinical judgment'; this is an important tool, but it does not permit clear sharing and communication between operators. Standardised instruments can be a great help in providing a common approach to diagnostic criteria and in leaving behind the outdated stereotypical picture of 'the autistic child' (for example, a very isolated child who does not speak!).

In addition, research workers can use these instruments to select a more homogeneous sample; in this way we can attain better communication between clinicians and researchers – among whom there is often a less than ideal meeting of minds – about a common concept of pervasive developmental disorder. In Italy, ADI-R and ADOS-G are not yet in widespread use, but our clinical experience shows that they provide a great deal of information about the child and a clearer idea of the nature of their problems. ADI-R in particular gives parents the opportunity to rethink their child's difficulties, communicate their concerns and doubts, organize and clarify their ideas about the disorder, and learn about their child's abilities and skills. ADI-R improves our communication with the parents and helps to create a partnership in caring for the child.

References

American Psychiatric Association (1994): Diagnostic and statistical manual of mental disorders, 4th ed. (DSM-IV). Washington, DC: APA.

DiLavore, P., Lord, C. & Rutter, M. (1995): Pre-linguistic autism diagnostic observation schedule (PL-ADOS). *J. Autism Dev. Disord.* **25**, 355–379.

Lord, C., Rutter, M., Goode, S., Heemsbergen, J., Jordan, H., Mawhood, L. & Schopler, E. (1989): Autism diagnostic observation schedule: a standardised observation of communicative and social behavior. *J. Autism Dev. Disord.* **19**, 185–212.

Lord, C., Storoschuk, S., Rutter, M. & Pickles, A. (1993): Using the ADI-R to diagnose autism in preschool children. *Infant Mental Health Journal.* **14**, 234–252.

Lord, C., Rutter, M. & Le Couteur, A. (1994): Autism diagnostic interview – revised: a revised version of a diagnostic interview for caregivers of individuals with possible pervasive developmental disorders. *J. Autism Dev. Disord.* **24**, 659–685.

World Health Organization (1993): ICD-10 classification of mental and behavioural disorders. Geneva: WHO.

Autistic spectrum disorders, D. Riva and I. Rapin (eds.)

Chapter 16

Differential diagnostic features of communication disorders in early childhood

Bruna Molteni, Gloria Airaghi, Santina Magazù, Matilde Prunas, Daniela Sarti and Giovanna Zardini

Department of Developmental Neurology, National Neurological Institute 'C. Besta', via Celoria 11, 20133 Milan, Italy
lingapp@istituto-besta.it

Summary

According to current theoretical approaches, language results from the interaction between perceptual, motor, and cognitive functions (which are mostly innate) and environmental and social factors. In children with developmental language disorders, communication is impaired to a varying degree. On the other hand, a communication disorder may also result from a broad spectrum of childhood developmental disorders. In order to clarify the differential diagnosis between the various communication disorders, it is therefore necessary to apply rigorous diagnostic criteria. The currently used manuals for the classification of mental disorders – that is, the *Diagnostic and Statistical Manual of Mental Disorders*, 4th edition (DSM-IV) and the *International Classification of Diseases*, 10th edition (ICD-10) – are considered by most investigators to be inadequate in childhood as they do not take into account the central role of development in the clinical manifestations of mental disorders and do not consider the tight relations between biological, psychological, and social factors.

This chapter provides an overview of the most recent proposals of classification of the psychopathological disorders of childhood which, in a global and integrated approach, aim to provide symptomatic-behavioural criteria while taking account of both the child's developmental structure and the distinctive environmental features.

Severe impairment in communication is a necessary criterion for diagnosing autistic spectrum disorders; however, the boundaries of this spectrum are still too imprecise, making it necessary to identify early features that allow accurate differentiation between disorders that may evolve in different ways. By reviewing the studies concerning the Theory of Mind and the socio-communicative development in autistic children, we will focus on current knowledge and on the attempts that have been made to integrate the different theoretical approaches such as developmental psychology, neurobiology, and neuropsychology. Most authorities nowadays consider autism to be a neurobiological disorder, rather than a primary inability of parents to establish an adequate relationship with their child. However, genetically determined factors interact with environmental factors in the pathogenesis of this disorder. We will present a specific method of clinical observation, tailored for children younger that 4 years of age, focused on the assessment and analysis of communicative behaviours.

Introduction

According to the classification manuals currently in use, namely the *Diagnostic and Statistical Manual of Mental Disorders*, 4th edition (DSM-IV) (Andreoli *et al.*, 1996) and the *International Classification of Diseases*, 10th edition (ICD-10) (Kemali *et al.*, 1996), a qualitative impairment of verbal and non-verbal communication is regarded as a necessary criterion for the diagnosis of autistic disorder. Rather than a mere description of the characteristics of language and communication in autistic children, our aim is to analyse the diagnostic criteria and instruments developed to assess communication disorders in early infancy.

From an interactionist standpoint, language is regarded as the end point of an extremely complex process presupposing an adequate level of biological and psychic maturation and, most of all, it reflects the desire of each human being to share thoughts, emotions, and desires with others, as well as the awareness of being separate from the rest of the world.

Language results from the integration of a genetically determined predisposition with interactive and social factors. Environmental modifications may therefore modify the phenotype. Verbal language is a specifically human skill, but it is not the only instrument humans use to communicate efficiently. Gestures and language are strictly interconnected: we move our hands to communicate, and emphasize essential words and phrases with gestures performed synchronously with word articulation. By contrast, gestures sometimes betray our real intent, contradicting our words. The experimental abolition of gestures has a negative influence on the production of words, and the production of gestures together with words also takes place when blind people speak to other blind people. In normal development, the first gestures develop at the same age as the first words. Moreover, the emerging of pointing predicts the acquisition of the first words, while the development of the word+gesture combination predicts the emergence of the first association of words.

The clinical observation of gestures may therefore be an important index of the development of language and communication. In infancy, impairment of communication may be a symptom of a wide range of developmental disorders including autistic spectrum disorders, disorders secondary to severe early global deprivation, severe mental retardation, deafness, and specific language impairment.

Aims of diagnosis and currently used classifications

Formulating a diagnosis does not just mean labelling a child, but rather using a definition that is common to different operators – thus allowing shared knowledge – and identifying the strong and weak points of the child in order to apply the best therapeutic strategies. The diagnosis informs the prognosis, creating expectations and reactions in the child's environment which in turn may affect the evolution of his clinical symptoms. The use of one diagnostic label instead of another is therefore a particularly ticklish question when dealing with a child younger than 3–4 years of age, as in this age span the resources driven from the environment may dramatically change the clinical picture.

The diagnosis of developmental disorders in infancy according to the DSM-IV or the ICD-10 classification manuals is categorical, being based on the presence or absence of a given symptom. Such a diagnosis does not take into account the possible adaptive nature of a symptom or its modification over time, and does not consider the role of development and the fact that the same symptom may have different functions and meanings.

According to the classifications currently in use, autism is a developmental disorder characterized by a triad of symptoms: qualitative impairment in social interaction and communication; lack of imaginative play; and stereotyped behaviours with restricted patterns of interests. This categorical definition is nowadays considered insufficient, as it does not allow for an early diagnosis and does not delineate the boundaries of such a complex syndrome. Different investigators have addressed the uncertainties that persist in defining the autistic syndrome, and various classifications have been proposed that are partly overlapping. The terms 'autistic spectrum' and 'pervasive developmental disorder' refer to a wide range of cognitive and behavioural disorders in which the above mentioned triad of symptoms may have different clinical expression, from classical to occult forms. Many terms have been used to refer to such disorders: atypical autism, pervasive developmental disorders-NOS (Not Otherwise Specified), psychotic disharmonies – as referred to by the French authors – and, according to the *Classification Zero-to-Three* (Diagnostic Classification: 0–3, 1994), multisystem developmental disorders.

The French workers have proposed a classification of mental disorders in childhood and adolescence which is based on symptoms and behaviours but also on clinical and structural criteria (Misès, 2000). This classification has not been much adopted outside France, but has the merit of considering the child's developmental structure and of attempting a more accurate distinction between the various developmental disorders. Misès distinguishes psychotic disharmonies from autistic and neurotic syndromes and stresses the convergence between such disorders and the developmental multisystem disorder proposed by the *Classification Zero-to-Three*.

Palacio-Espasa and the investigators from the Geneva group also emphasize the need to consider the pathogenic aspects and the structure of personality in order to reach a diagnosis that is useful for therapeutic purposes (Palacio-Espasa & Dufour, 1995).

The *Classification Zero-to-Three* (Diagnostic Classification: 0–3, 1994) was created to remedy the limits intrinsic to the DSM-IV and ICD-10 classifications, as, apart from the evident signs and symptoms, it also considers the constitutional and maturational features of a given child, the operation of the family system, the individual characteristics of parents, and the relationship and patterns of interaction between the adults and the child. This classification stresses the concept that the child's clinical symptoms take shape within relationships.

In relation to language disorders, the DSM-IV and ICD-10 diagnostic classifications are also oversimplified, as they do not consider that different language disorders of varying degrees of severity may be observed even within the same category.

Among the classifications based on clinical-linguistic criteria stands the one proposed by Rapin & Allen (1983) and recently revised by Rapin *et al.* (1996). However, as stated by Leonard (1998), this classification also includes among the primary language disorders clinical categories that characterize pervasive developmental disorders-NOS. This clearly shows how difficult it can be to establish a neat border between specific language impairment and the autistic spectrum disorders.

Finally, it is worth noting that none of these classifications considers the category of language delay, which is one of the most frequent reasons for seeking medical advice in children younger than 3 years of age.

The identification of reliable diagnostic indices to differentiate between simple (that is, transient) and persistent language delay remains problematic. In a recent study, Chilosi *et al.* (2002) discuss the early diagnostic and prognostic criteria for diagnosing and differentiating specific language impairment. They stress the importance of the age variable with respect to the different language achievements: a delay in language comprehension and lexical development is considered a reliable risk factor in children aged 24 to 36 months, while from 36 months of age the dissociation of grammatical from lexical development becomes the most important index for predicting clinical evolution. These investigators suggest a classification system based on both the clinical features of the language profile and the severity of symptoms, considering this latter in terms of *extension* (number of language domains that are involved) and *entity* (the degree of involvement in different areas) of the disorder. In view of the importance of an early diagnosis in terms of therapeutic outcome, it becomes necessary to differentiate as soon as possible between the wide range of relational, communicative, and language difficulties that may be present in children with a delay in the development of communicative skills; this is also necessary to identify prognostic factors.

Criteria for an early diagnosis of autism

Starting from the 1980s, a new trend in research on autism has developed focused on cognition, leading to the formulation of the Theory of Mind. The Theory of Mind is an evolutionary hypothesis that tries to explain the origin and development of mental states – that is, how the mind emerged from the non-mind.

The Theory of Mind allows one to impute mental states to oneself and to others, and to predict other people's behaviour. This theory argues that mental states are recognized rather than just lived, thus presupposing a reflexive and metarepresentational capacity. Metarepresentation is the ability to manipulate the link between internal representations and external reality, laying the foundations whereby a child will differentiate the objective from the subjective field, and facts from values and opinions. In contrast to the hypothesis of a primary affective disorder or an impairment of affection secondary to mental insufficiency, the Theory of Mind argues that autism is a specific cognitive disorder impairing the child's representational skills (Leslie & Frith, 1988).

Several studies have documented that autistic children do not develop some of the precursors in the Theory of Mind, such as joint attention and declarative pointing (Landry & Loveland, 1989; Abrahamsen & Mitchell, 1990). These children use requesting gestures but cannot perform declarative gestures and, while talking, never volunteer comments or ask for information. Different studies have documented the ability of autistic children to comprehend and perform requesting pointing while being unable to understand and perform declarative pointing (Mundy *et al.*, 1986; Baron-Cohen *et al.*, 1992; Baron-Cohen *et al.*, 1996; Muratori *et al.*, 1992; Bernabei *et al.*, 1997; Camaioni *et al.*, 1997; Muratori *et al.*, 1997). Declarative pointing in fact presupposes a metarepresentational comprehension of attention. When showing a declarative intent, the adult becomes to the child not just the 'means' to obtain something, but rather the 'aim'. The child intends to influence the adult's behaviour, his internal mental state. It is therefore necessary for the child to perceive the adult as having mental states.

Research on the Theory of Mind has initiated the integration of traditionally separate sectors such as cognitive psychology, psychopathology, and psychoanalysis. Back in 1991, some of the first studies had demonstrated the positive relation between metacognitive skills and infant attachment patterns (Main, 1991). Ensuing research sought an integration of developmental psychoanalytic theories with the Theory of Mind (Fonagy *et al.*, 1997; Meins, 1997; Meins *et al.*, 1998; Symons & Clark, 2000; Liverta Sempio & Marchetti, 2001), converging on the need to adopt a perspective that considers the quality of relationships.

According to Fonagy and co-workers (1997), the development of the Theory of Mind depends on the degree of coherence and confidence of the first objective relationships, which provides the child with a solid basis for exploring the caregiver's mind, in which he will find an image of himself as an individual provided with intentions and therefore able to think. Other investigators – Siegel (2001) and Schore (1994, 2001a, 2001b) in particular – argue that complex bonds exist between the relationship experiences and brain maturation. In the initial stages, the development of the nervous system could be influenced by the stimuli provided by the caregiver. Tactile, visual, and auditory sensory stimulation, proper to the mother-child interaction during the first months of life, could be a decisive factor in addressing neural growth and synaptic connections, mainly within the amygdala and hippocampus. Sharing arguments and joint attention, which defines the mother-child relationship in the second semester of life, could facilitate the integration processes between the orbitofrontal and the limbic structures. These cerebral areas are considered to be the most important in establishing, generalizing, and inhibiting affective stimuli (Dawson *et al.*, 2002). The medial temporal cortex seems to play a crucial role in social perception – that is, in recognizing the affective meaning of facial expressions, body movements, and eye gaze – and therefore for the establishment of joint attention.

Given that autistic children may show subtle signs of developmental and behavioural derangement earlier than 18 months of age, the issue to address is the identification of clinical features that are specific, predictive, and recurrent. Quite often, parents become aware of something strange in their child as early as the first months of life; in other circumstances this happens only when the child is 2 to 3 years old. Different retrospective studies have shown that non-specific symptoms, such as lack of initiative, hyperactivity, sleep problems, and feeding difficulties, are common to various developmental disorders (Gillberg, 1989). Many research studies carried out in the last 10 years (Baron-Cohen *et al.*, 1992, 1996; Muratori *et al.*, 1992, 1997; Bernabei *et al.*, 1997; Franco & Butterworth, 1996; Gillberg, 1996; Gillberg & Coleman, 2000; Camaioni, 1997; Mundy *et al.*, 1993, 1994; Mundy, 1995, Stone *et al.*, 1999) have confirmed the most specific predictive signs of autism, which can be identified by 18 months of age. These are: lack of declarative pointing; lack of gaze monitoring; and lack of imaginative play.

Declarative pointing

With respect to the predictive value of declarative pointing, back in the 1930s Vygotskij had already differentiated between requesting imperative pointing and communicative referential pointing. He suggested that the shift from one to the other is fostered by social intervention and that the pointing gesture contains the rudiments of denomination (Vygotskij, 1934).

According to psychoanalytical theories, pointing stands for a turning point in the process of separation-individuation, and marks the achievement of intersubjectivity in the development of Self (Stern, 1995).

Cognitive theories based on the Theory of Mind consider declarative pointing as a precursor of the Theory of Mind because it presupposes the possibility of perceiving and understanding other people's mental states. Requesting pointing expresses the expectation of an action by the adult, while declarative pointing expresses the intention to communicate.

Gaze monitoring

In the healthy child, pointing temporally coordinates visual checking with the social partner. At 12 months, visual checking occurs right after pointing, whereas by 16 months of age it occurs immediately before the gesture. This shift suggests that pointing relies on some awareness by the child of the sequence 'perception-attention-interest' as a psychological process occurring in the other and in the self (Franco & Butterworth, 1996). The direction of the gaze associated with the gesture, which stands for joint attention, is commonly considered as evidence for a communicative intent. According to Baron-Cohen and co-workers (1992), being aware of attention in others is one of the precursors of the Theory of Mind.

Imaginative play

Symbolic play, language, and deferred imitation are the first forms of mental representation – that is, the ability to remind and represent to oneself aspects or events that are not immediately present. In autistic children, as in mentally retarded children it is difficult for symbolic play to emerge, as it is actually based on representative skills that such children have not yet achieved.

Diagnostic criteria for language delay or language disorders

The diagnosis of a specific language delay or disorder rests on exclusion rather than on inclusion criteria. Exclusion criteria are as follows: hearing impairment, mental impairment, neurological diseases, structural anomalies of the phono-articulatory organs, and disorders affecting social interaction.

When dealing with children who do not speak or speak very little, the first diagnostic issue to address does not relate to the type of language disorder (delay *vs* impairment), but to the presence of a specific language problem in contrast to a more general developmental disorder. In our opinion, the only useful diagnostic criterion for differentiating between these two possibilities is the quality of social interaction and of communicative behaviour: the differential diagnosis between communication disorders in the context of a specific language impairment from those secondary to mental insufficiency or autistic spectrum disorders lies in the possibility of pointing out, quantifying, and analysing selected clinical features such as the use of eye gaze, gesture modes, behaviours of joint attention, play activity, and parent-child interaction habits, and on the possible modifications to such features over time.

Clinical assessment of communication disorders

Following from the above mentioned topics, the proper assessment of language and communication must also involve consideration of the pragmatic and social aspects.

Whatever instruments one may choose to evaluate a child – whether they be tests, interviews, or narrative reports – these must be used in the context of a global and integrated approach, considering the child's overall performance within the relationship with the parents and the specific life context. As a result, the clinical observation of socio-communicative behaviours becomes the most valuable instrument for differentiating among the different communication disorders. We will focus on the characteristics and purposes of these observations, leaving out all other aspects of the diagnostic work-up such as the history, neurological evaluation, laboratory and instrumental examinations, parental interview, and neuropsychological evaluation.

The direct and systematic clinical observation of a child and their patterns of interaction allows one to collect two different types of information: *objective data*, the observed behaviours revealing the child's level of development and mental status; and *subjective data*, the experience and fantasies of the parents regarding their child (Cammarella *et al.*, 2001).

Various recent studies of developmental psychology have shown that the Self of an individual has a genetically determined internal organization thanks to which the child is, from the very beginning, active, competent, able to autoregulate, and able to have intentions and expectations within an organized, continuous, and predictable context of cares and exchanges with his parents (Stern, 1995; Fonagy *et al.*, 1997; Zeanah *et al.*, 2000; Riva Crugnola, 2002). As a result, in evaluating the development of a given child and even when focusing on the individual behaviour, one must take into account the parent-child relationship, because any observed behaviour is part of an interactive system in which every component influences and regulates the behaviour of others.

Characteristics of the clinical observation

The evaluation of language and communication may be carried out through observations of the child's play in the presence of the parents, in free or semi-structured situations and, when possible, using standardized testing material. The setting in which the clinical observation occurs must take account of the child's age and level of cognitive and emotional development. The use of prearranged settings allows an easy longitudinal analysis of clinical data and the evaluation of the results of rehabilitation projects. Moreover, it is of fundamental importance to videotape the clinical observations in order to allow accurate analysis of the verbal and gestural communicative behaviours.

The purposes of the clinical observation are as follows:

(1) *The assessment of verbal and non-verbal comprehension*, derived from the analysis of all behavioural and linguistic responses.

• Very often, parents and clinicians take for granted that the child understands, and may misinterpret a lack of response to verbal and gesture communication as a sign of opposition or disinterest towards the communicative exchange.

• The strict comprehension of verbal language may be revealed only when a child understands words or phrases in the absence of contextual facilitations, which may be supported by facial mimicry and gesticulation.

(2) *The assessment of verbal and communicative production* through the analysis of communicative means – that is, the behaviours revealing the child's intentions, emotions, and psychological states (how the child communicates), as well as the communicative functions – the purposes of communication (why the child communicates).

The communicative means include the following:

• in very young children of preverbal age, as well as in children with very low developmental level: different non-verbal and vocal behaviours such as body postures, facial expressions, eye contact, active avoidance of gaze contact, focusing eye gaze on the same object as the social partner, vocalization, babbling;

• in older, yet still pre-verbal, children: undifferentiated gestures such as taking the other's hand; deitic, emphatic, symbolic or referential, routine gestures; and vocalizations or isolated words;

• in talking children: samples of spontaneous or solicited verbal production are analysed in order to assess phonology, morphosyntaxis, lexicon, and semantic and pragmatic competences. In addition, one must evaluate whether vocal productions are associated with gestures and what the preferred communicative mode may be.

Communicative functions may be expressed through verbal or non-verbal modes, and include the following:
– communication to satisfy one's needs;
– communication to obtain attention, to drive the attention of others on selected objects or events, and declarative communication.

(3) *The evaluation of play*. Within the diagnostic work-up, observation of play is a useful tool for assessing the development of symbolic abilities in children with sparse or absent language production and in those to whom structured tests cannot be administered. In addition, playing allows one to share affective experiences with the child and to assess the quality of the emotional experiences which, if inadequate, may hamper capacity for thought.

There have been many theories and research contributions to the study of the development of imaginative play which have had important applications in the clinical context (Camaioni *et al.*, 1976; Lombardino & Sproul, 1984; Lombardino *et al.*, 1986).

During the diagnostic work-up, it may be useful to address the clinical observation of playing behaviour according to the following three indices: (1) decontextualization (reducing subordination to the object in favour of imagination); (2) ability to integrate separate actions in coordinate behavioural sequences; and (3) decentralization (the ability to involve in play activity with other characters besides oneself).

In order to achieve a correct differential diagnosis between communication disorders, it is necessary to assess the variety of levels in the child's play, the length and variability of its sequences, the changes in the levels of play according to the models supplied by the adult, and the level of social participation (solitary, parallel, or cooperative).

It is also necessary to provide the child with toys that facilitate imaginative play on familiar themes, which promote social participation, and which allow one to identify even minimal representative abilities such as the 'peekaboo' game.

In order to collect samples of playing behaviour that reflect the child's best performance but still ensure consistency among different observers, there are certain observational instruments which, although not standardized, remain the most useful for clinical evaluation. Examples of such instruments are the sequence of symbolic play by Lombardino and co-workers (1984, 1986), and the observational setting used in the 'Interact' rehabilitation approach by Bonifacio & Stefani (1998). Once the toys and contexts have been adapted to the particular case, this kind of setting – originally conceived for children who are late talkers – can also be useful for assessing children with marked representative and communicative difficulties. In such cases, as observed by us, the evaluation of the parental communicative style in the interaction with their child may help both in assessing the quality of parental function, which is quite often difficult to do, and in correcting it, so that faulty environmental interventions are not perpetuated.

Conclusion

Qualitative and quantitative assessments of communicative functions, play activity, and the style of the parent-child interaction are the most useful tools for establishing the diagnosis in early-onset communication disorders and in selecting the most suitable rehabilitation treatments.

References

Abrahamsen, E.P. & Mitchell, J.R. (1990): Communication and sensorimotor functioning in children with autism. *J. Autism Dev. Disord.* **20**, 75–85.

Andreoli, V., Cassano, G.B. & Rossi, R. (1996): *DSM-IV. Manuale diagnostico e statistico dei disturbi mentali*, p. 958. Milan: Masson.

Baron-Cohen, S., Allen, J. & Gillberg, C. (1992): Can autism be detected at 18 months? The needle, the haystack, and the CHAT. *Br. J. Psychiatry* **161**, 839–843.

Baron-Cohen, S., Cox, A., Baird, G., Swettenham, J., Nightingale, N., Morgan, K., Drew, A. & Charman, T. (1996): Psychological markers in the detection of autism in infancy in a large population. *Br. J. Psychiatry* **168**, 158–163.

Bernabei, P., Campioni, L., Levi, G., Di Falco, M. & Paolesse, C. (1997): Lo sviluppo socio-comunicativo nei primi due anni di vita di bambini con autismo: possibilità di una diagnosi precoce. *Psicologia Clinica dello Sviluppo* **2**, 245–259.

Bonifacio, S. & Hvastja Stefani, L. (1998): *L'interazione comunicativa e linguistica nel bambino con ritardo nel linguaggio*. Tirrenia (Pisa): Edizioni Del Cerro.

Camaioni, L., Volterra, V. & Bates, E. (1976): *La comunicazione nel primo anno di vita*. Torino: Boringhieri.

Camaioni, L., Perucchini, P., Muratori, F. & Milone, A. (1997): Brief report: a longitudinal examination of the communicative gestures deficit in young children with autism. *J. Autism Dev. Disord.* **27**, 715–725.

Cammarella, A., Lucarelli, L. & Vismara, L. (2001): L'osservazione del bambino nel contesto di sviluppo. In: *Manuale di Psicologia dell'Infanzia*, ed. M. Ammaniti, pp. 39–89. Milano: Raffaello Cortina Editore.

Chilosi, A.M., Cipriani, P. & Fapore, T. (2002): I disturbi specifici del linguaggio. In: *I disturbi dello sviluppo. Neuropsicologia clinica e ipotesi riabilitative*, eds. S. Vicari & M.C. Caselli, pp. 59–76. Bologna: Il Mulino.

Dawson, G., Munson, J., Estes, A., Osterling, J., McPartland, J., Toth, K., Carver, L. & Abbott, R. (2002): Neurocognitive function and joint attention ability in young children with autism spectrum disorder *versus* developmental delay. *Child Dev.* **73**, 345–358.

Diagnostic Classification: 0–3. (1994): *Diagnostic classification of mental health and developmental disorders of infancy and early childhood*. Arlington, VA: Zero to Three/National Center for Clinical Infant Programs.

Fonagy, P., Redfern, S. & Charman, T. (1997): The relationship between belief-desire reasoning and a projective measure of attachment security (SAT). *Br. J. Dev. Psychol.* **15**, 51–61.

Franco, F. & Butterworth, G. (1996): Pointing and social awareness: declaring and requesting in the second year. *J. Child Lang.* **23**, 307–336.

Gillberg, C. (1989): Early symptoms of autism. In: *Diagnosis and treatment of autism*, ed. C. Gillberg, pp. 23–32. New York: Plenum Press.

Gillberg, C. (1996): Early detection of autism. Diagnostic instruments for clinicians. *Eur. Child Adolesc. Psychiatry* **5**, 67–74.

Gillberg, C. & Coleman, M. (2000): Diagnosis in infancy. In: *The biology of autistic syndromes*, 3rd ed., eds. C. Gillberg & M. Colemann, pp. 53–62. Cambridge: Cambridge University Press; London: MacKeith Press.

Kemali, D., Maj, M., Catapano, F., Giordano, G. & Saccà, C. (1996): *ICD-10. Classificazione delle sindromi e dei disturbi psichici e comportamentali*, p. 404. Milan: Masson.

Landry, S. & Loveland, K. (1989): Communication behaviours in autism and developmental language delay. *J. Child Psychol. Psychiatry* **29**, 621–634.

Leonard, L. (1998): *Children with specific language impairment*, p. 339. Cambridge (Massachusetts): MIT Press.

Leslie, A.M. & Frith, U. (1988): Autistic children's understanding of seeing, knowing and believing. *Br. J. Dev. Psychol.* **6**, 315–324.

Liverta Sempio, O. & Marchetti, A. (2001): [Comprensione degli stati mentali e relazioni affettive nel contesto familiare e scolastico.] In: *Teoria della mente e relazioni affettive. Contesti familiari e contesti educative*, eds. O. Liverta Sempio & A. Marchetti, pp. 168–213. Torino: UTET.

Lombardino, L.J. & Sproul, C.J. (1984): Patterns of correspondence and non-correspondence between play and language in developmentally delayed preschooler. *Educ. Train. Ment. Retard.* **19**, 5–14.

Lombardino, L.J., Stein, J.E., Krikos, P.B. & Wolf, M.A. (1986): Play diversity and structural relationship in the play and language of language-impaired and language-normal preschoolers: preliminary data. *J. Commun. Disord.* **19**, 475–489.

Main, M. (1991): Metacognitive knowledge, metacognitive monitoring, and singular (coherent) *vs* multiple (incoherent) models of attachment. In: *Attachment across the life cycle*, eds. C.M. Parkes, J. Stevenson-Hinde & P. Marris, pp. 127–159. London: Tavistock/Routledge.

Meins, E. (1997): *Security of attachment and the social development of cognition.* Hove, UK: Psychological Press.

Meins, E., Fernyhough, C., Russell, J. & Clark-Carter, D. (1998): Security of attachment as a predictor of symbolic and mentalising abilities: a longitudinal study. *Soc. Dev.* **7**, 1–24.

Misès, R. (2000): Les dysharmonies psychotiques: une approche nosographique. *Neuropsychiatr. Enfance Adolesc.* **48**, 396–401.

Mundy, P. (1995): Joint attention and social-emotional approach behavior in children with autism. *Dev. Psychopathol.* **7**, 63–82.

Mundy, P., Sigman, M., Ungerer, J. & Sherman, T. (1986): Defining the social deficits of autism: the contribution of non-verbal communication measure. *J. Child Psychol. Psychiatry* **27**, 657–669.

Mundy, P., Sigman, M. & Kasari, C. (1993): The theory of mind and joint-attention deficits in autism. In: *Understanding other minds: perspective from autism*, eds. S. Baron-Cohen, H.S. Tager-Flusberg & D.J. Cohen. Oxford: Oxford University Press.

Mundy, P., Sigman, M. & Kasari, C. (1994): Joint attention, developmental level, and symptom presentation in autism. *Dev. Psychopathol.* **6**, 389–401.

Muratori, F., Bernazzani, I., Cerri, B. & Conti, P. (1992): L'organizzazione preverbale del linguaggio nelle psicosi precoci. *Giorn. Neuropsich. Età Evol.* **12**, 91–101.

Muratori, F., Milone, A., Camaioni, L. & Perucchini, P. (1997): Valore diagnostico e prognostico nell'indicare dichiarativo nell'autismo. *Psicologia Clinica dello Sviluppo* **2**, 261–273.

Palacio-Espasia, F. & Dufour, R. (1995): *La diagnosi strutturale in età evolutiva.* Milano: Masson.

Rapin, I. & Allen, D.A. (1983): Developmental language disorders: nosological considerations. In: *Neuropsychology of language, reading, and spelling*, ed. U. Kirk, pp. 155–184. New York: Academic Press.

Rapin, I., Allen, D.A., Aram, D.M., Dunn, M.A., Fein, D., Morris, R. & Waterhouse, L. (1996): Classification issues. In: *Preschool children with inadequate communication: developmental language disorders, autism, low I.Q.*, ed. I. Rapin, pp. 190–213. London: MacKeith Press.

Riva Crugnola, C. (2002): Regolazione e comunicazione affettiva nelle prime relazioni tra bambino e genitori. *Psicologia Clinica nello Sviluppo* **3**, 359–395.

Schore, S.N. (1994): *Affect regulation and the origin of the self: the neurobiology of emotional development.* Mahwah, N.J.: Erlbaum.

Schore, S.N. (2001a): Effects of a secure attachment relationship on right brain development, affect regulation, and infant mental health. *Infant Ment. Health J.* **22**, 6–66.

Schore, S.N. (2001b): The effects of early relational trauma on right brain development, affect regulation, and infant mental health. *Infant Ment. Health J.* **22**, 201–269.

Siegel, D.J. (2001): Toward an interpersonal neurobiology of the developing mind: attachment relationships, 'mindsight', and neural integration. *Infant Ment. Health J.* **22**, 67–94.

Stern, D.N. (1995): *La costellazione materna.* Torino: Bollati Boringhieri

Stone, W.L., Lee, E.B., Ashford, L., Brissie, J., Hepburn, S.L., Coonrod, E.E. & Weiss, B.H. (1999): Can autism be diagnosed accurately in children under 3 years? *J. Child Psychol. Psychiatry.* **40**, 219–226.

Symons, D.K. & Clark, S.E. (2000): A longitudinal study of mother-child relationships and theory of mind in the preschool period. *Soc. Dev.* **9**, 3–23.

Vygotskij, L.S. (1934): *Pensiero e linguaggio. Ricerche psicologiche.* Bari: Laterza.

Zeanah, C.H., Larrieu, J.A., Heller, S.S. & Valliere, J. (2000): Infant-parent relationship assessment. In: *Handbook of infant mental health*, ed. C.H. Zeanah, pp. 222–235. New York: Guilford Press.

Autistic spectrum disorders, D. Riva and I. Rapin (eds.)

Chapter 17

Variations in developmental trajectories: lessons learned from clinical cases

Wendy Roberts and Tamarah Kagan-Kushnir*

Child Development Centre, The Hospital for Sick Children, 555 University Avenue, Toronto, Ontario M5G 1X, Canada;
* *Bloorview MacMillan Children's Centre, 25 Buchan Court, North York, Ontario M2J 4S9, Canada*
wendy.roberts@sickkids.ca

Summary

Common clinical scenarios are used to illustrate typical developmental trajectories found in children with disorders on the autism spectrum. The paediatric clinician has a major role to play not only in the early diagnosis of ASD but also in the ongoing management. Parents require support in recognizing, understanding and managing nutritional, gastrointestinal, neurological, sleep and psychopharmacological issues in their child with ASD as well as support for family planning.

Introduction

As our understanding of the heterogeneous group of developmental disorders now known as the autism spectrum of disorders (ASD) has increased over the last few years, we realize that there are many different trajectories of development for affected boys and girls to travel along. We have moved from the view of autism as an attachment disorder to one which reflects changes in the development of the nervous system very early in prenatal life (Bauman & Kemper, 2003). We now know that early signs are quite varied and still require careful study, although a reliable diagnosis can be made as early as 2 years of age. However, we are not good at giving a prognosis for the 2-year-old, as we do not yet know precisely what factors determine an individual child's eventual developmental trajectory with or without intervention.

During the last decade in Canada, there has been a major change in the role of the paediatrician in identifying and helping to manage developmental disorders. As a professional who will take time to study a child's behaviour and learning style, the paediatrician is in a unique position to understand the strengths and vulnerabilities arising from a child's developmental, medical, and family history, and to help in the diagnostic and management planning process. The new subspecialty of Developmental Paediatrics has evolved as general paediatricans have been called on to play this role and need academic leaders to educate them and to develop models of effective medical assessment and management. Some of the change has been the result of feedback from parents who experience great anguish as they recognize differences in their child but have felt that the paediatrician's minimizing of problems or attributing them to poor parenting has been disturbing and has resulted in unnecessary waits for intervention.

In this chapter, we review some of our Canadian paediatric experience gathered while working with children with ASD. Typical clinical scenarios are used to illustrate basic principles of developmental paediatric care for children on the autism spectrum of disorders. These encompass the topics of assessment, early intervention, and management of related nutritional, gastrointestinal, neurological, sleep, and genetic issues addressed by the developmental paediatrician.

A typical case

A 17-month-old boy presented with parental concern about language development and play. First concerns at 10 months, related to lack of interest in people, fixation on certain toys that he inspected at close range for long periods, and cessation of babbling.

Early development had seemed normal. Birth weight was 3.2 kg at term. Frequent crying occurred from 2 weeks until 8 months. He smiled at 2 to 3 months and seemed very alert, with babbling and eye contact being coordinated when seen at 7 months by his paediatrician. He sat at 7 months, crawled at 13 months, and walked at 15 months.

At 17 months, he could imitate some sounds but initiated no interaction, did not point or request, and had a limited range of facial expressions. Eye contact was minimal and there was no social smile. He played only with spinning tops and a jack in the box, and would watch toilets flush repetitively for long periods. He looked at objects from unusual angles, watched his fingers wiggling, and tensed his upper body repetitively when anxious or excited. He had severe chronic constipation and an extremely limited diet, consisting essentially of white bagels and frozen blueberries only.

A presumptive diagnosis of ASD was given to his parents in order to initiate early intervention.

Parents were faced with making rapid decisions regarding how to proceed as they dealt with their mourning, guilt, and difficult adjustment to parenting a very atypical child.

Assessment and diagnosis

The first signs of an ASD are typically evident in the first 2 years of life. Current studies suggest that there are signs even at 1 year which can reliably predict a diagnosis of autistic disorder at 3 years. These signs include unusual reactivity, either passivity or irritability often in the same child, reduced eye gaze and social smiling, delayed imitation, and unusual degrees of difficulty with change (Zwaigenbaum *et al.*, 2005). A familiar regression or plateau in social communication is seen between 1 and 2 years of age in at least 30 per cent of children (Goldberg *et al.*, 2003). Unusual hand movements as well as intense interest in shapes, letters, and numbers can be seen as early as 15 months. Some children may improve quickly in social interaction and language development, or, on the other hand, may become more 'sticky' and aversive to change, looking more severely autistic as they enter school at around 4 or 5 years.

Understanding progress in the first few years, the response to experience and treatment, and alterations in behaviour (particularly imaginative and social play) is a critical part of appreciating the basis of parents' concern that something is different about their child. Input from teachers, grandparents, and others who know the child is also very helpful. Particularly in less clear presentations, the use of a semi-structured interview such as the Autism Diagnostic Interview (ADI) can be most helpful (Lord *et al.*, 1994) and many developmental paediatricians now use this tool routinely in clinical assessments. The ADI allows careful analysis of a child's past and present symptoms by the parents and clinician.

Time spent interacting directly with the child is a unique extension of the typical paediatric physical examination intended to cover the area of social communication, much as the extended musculoskeletal examination explores signs of arthritis for a rheumatologist. Observing how the child warms up to an unfamiliar person, shares information, asks questions, and shows social interest can be done in a semistructured way that is standardized and reliable, as in the Autism Diagnostic Observation Schedule (ADOS) (Lord *et al.*, 2000). This instrument has led to a profound difference in the appreciation of autistic features which can be documented in a 1-hour clinical interaction. The 'friendly social world' of the ADOS is quite different from the usual clinical assessment, being systematically created by the clinician to see how the child or adolescent will respond, based on expectations derived from the child's language level. In older individuals, peer perceptions, insight, and curiosity about typical social situations, anxiety and humour, as well as topics of interest and unusual mannerisms or routines are documented. Interpretation is done in the light of the history obtained from parents and others.

Physical examination

The physical examination is an important opportunity for a child's medical needs to be viewed holistically in the broader context of one's developmental, behavioural, and psychosocial needs. At times, anxiety or behavioural difficulties can make it difficult for some children with ASD to cooperate in physical examinations. As such, they do not always undergo routine health maintenance assessments or even proper examinations for specific health concerns. Developmental paediatricians can often overcome these barriers because of their knowledge of ASD, and thus are key persons in ensuring appropriate basic health care, in addition to ruling out any underlying untreated medical conditions (Challman, 2003).

The neurological examination is an integral part of the general physical examination. In addition to ruling out a serious neurological disorder, the examination identifies so called 'soft neurological signs', or findings that are not clearly indicative of underlying structural lesions but rather indicate CNS immaturity. These are commonly found in individuals with ASD and generally include signs of motor overflow and poor coordination as well as problems with motor planning. Identifying these signs can often help to explain a child's motor difficulties and may point to the need for further evaluation or suggest programming strategies (Tupper, 1987).

While in most cases ASD is not associated with any underlying syndrome or genetic disorder, there are conditions that carry a higher risk of autistic features, including fragile X, neurofibromatosis, microdeletion 22, and tuberous sclerosis. The physical examination helps the developmental paediatrician to assess the probability of these disorders. Larger than expected head circumference may be seen in some children with ASD, as well as in neurofibromatosis. Recent suggestions of increasing head circumference in the first 14 months after birth are now being followed up in a North American study through National Institutes for Health (NIH) funded autism programmes (Courchesne *et al.*, 2003). Signs of fragile X that may coexist with ASD include specific facial features such as a long face, prominent jaw, and large prominent ears (Rogers *et al.*, 2001). Characteristics of female carriers and of patients with smaller DNA repeat sizes are more subtle, and screening for fragile X should be considered even in the absence of classic facial features or cognitive impairment, and always when there is a family history of developmental disability. Identifying any underlying organic aetiologies is not simply an academic exercise but may have implications for identifying associated medical problems and determining recurrence risk. Genetic counselling may also be helpful.

Laboratory investigations

The need for laboratory investigations, if any, follows from the discussion above. If any unaddressed health concerns are identified, further laboratory investigations are also used to rule out underlying genetic or metabolic disorders. The history and physical examination may point to specific tests. However, even in the absence of specific concerns, it may still be helpful to study chromosomes (karyotype through cytogenetics) and DNA for fragile X assessment, as research has suggested that these investigations have the highest aetiological yield. Metabolic screens and neuroimaging (brain computed tomography and magnetic resonance imaging) may be done on a case-by-case basis (Filipek *et al.*, 2000).

The parents' choices in intervention

First step: parent education

Hanen, More than Words (MTW) is a manualized (Sussman, 1999), brief (12 weeks), naturalistic intervention to promote communication skills in young children with ASD. MTW builds on existing prelinguistic and linguistic means of communication to develop and enhance intentional communication, as well as to improve play, joint attention, phonology, and adult responsivity to the child.

The method has been adapted for ASD children from the Hanen Early Language Parent Programme that has been shown to help children with language delays (Tannock *et al.*, 1992). Speech and language pathologists spend three sessions in the home with child and family and this is combined with 12 group lectures or a weekend of group teaching for the parents.

The MTW programme is followed by ongoing speech therapy, ideally once or twice a week in combination with other front line workers interacting with the child to reinforce communication skills. Parental sensitivity to the focus of their child's attention has been linked to the child's subsequent development of communication skills (Siller & Sigman, 2002).

Second step: Intensive Behavioural Intervention (IBI)

Based on the principles of applied behavioural analysis, communication skills and social behaviours are taught through 20 to 40 hours each week, spent with instructor, therapists and parents. This programme is supervised collaboratively by a behavioural psychologist and a speech and language pathologist (Maurice *et al.*, 1997).

Many Canadian parents have to find private funds to pay for this IBI treatment as public services only fund small numbers of the most obviously developmentally disabled children.

Third step: peer interaction in nursery school

Social skills are often the most difficult to teach systematically. Many parents start with play dates as part of individual therapy. A consistent session each week is spent either at home or in a nursery school with one other child, as an adult facilitator encourages interactions, prompts speech where appropriate, and helps to enhance the level of play skills.

The goal is to move gradually to larger groups of peers and facilitate the transition into more typical school environments as well as to improve pretend play and spontaneous social interaction.

Is there medical pathology?

The frequency of comorbid medical problems in individuals with ASD has forced researchers to think beyond traditional neurological and psychological boundaries. Exciting research is happening around the world, exploring the effects and interactions of various body systems and the brain. This will hopefully lead to new insights into ASD and other developmental disorders.

Case II

A 7-year-old boy presented with classical signs of high-functioning autism including very repetitive scripted language and behaviour. He had a restricted diet and between two and four loose watery stools each day. He was very irritable and had a distended abdomen on physical examination but no other abnormal physical signs.

Serum ferritin was 11 μg/dl and antigliadin antibody was abnormally raised at 60 U/ml.

A casein- and gluten-free diet was begun after consultation with a gastroenterologist and resulted in rapid improvement in gastrointestinal function, with one bowel movement a day and less abdominal distension and irritability.

Gastrointestinal symptoms and diet

Gastrointestinal symptoms, particularly diarrhoea, are common in children with ASD. Some children experience cycling from diarrhoea to severe constipation, although this has not been documented specifically in ASD. There are published reports of a variety of clinical gastrointestinal symptoms, malabsorption conditions, and enteropathy on biopsy examinations as well as laboratory abnormalities in ASD children. In recent years, there has been increasing interest in the concept and potential importance of a brain-gut axis in ASD, and this has suggested lines of investigation into the pathogenesis and treatment, although much of this currently remains at the theoretical level (White, 2003).

The high prevalence of diarrhoea in ASD individuals has suggested that there may be parallels between ASD and gastrointestinal disorders such as coeliac disease. Some investigators have postulated an opioid theory of ASD which proposes that individuals with these conditions have leaky gut epithelium that allows absorption of opioid-like proteins which then have an affect on the developing brain. These theories have led to the view that dietary interventions, and in particular gluten- and casein-free diets, might be helpful in improving the core symptoms and behaviour in ASD (Knivsberg *et al.*, 1990; Lucarelli *et al.*, 1995; Whiteley *et al.*, 1999).

To date, there is no rigorous evidence for or against dietary intervention. Perhaps because of its relative simplicity, the idea is compelling to many parents, however, and in fact dietary intervention has been attempted for up to one-third of patients with ASD. Unfortunately, this treatment is not without significant risks, including the creation of iron deficiency, serious protein deficiency, and a potential increase in irritability. Careful research (that is, randomized controlled trials) is urgently needed in this area but will be difficult and expensive to undertake rigorously.

In the interim, the role of the developmental paediatrician is to evaluate the nutritional status of ASD children and refer them for further investigations of gastrointestinal symptoms if necessary. In addition, the paediatrician plays a key role in educating patients and their families about dietary interventions, and providing them with support that will minimize potential nutritional consequences should they choose to pursue such interventions (Kagan-Kushnir *et al.*, 2002).

Iron

There is emerging evidence that it is important to check both haemoglobin and ferritin levels in individuals with ASD, as iron deficiency is a common and frequently undiagnosed problem that does not seem to be related to dietary factors alone (Roberts *et al.*, 2004a). The reasons for this association, the degree to which it is related to the increased incidence of gastrointestinal dysfunction, and the implications it may have for pathogenesis and treatment of ASD are not yet clear.

Case III

A 9-year-old boy presented with several grand mal seizures at the age of 7. He had a history of delayed language development, not speaking in sentences until he was 4, and having behavioural and social problems in the early school years. Since developing epilepsy, his behaviour had become more obsessive, always being focused on video scripts and violent themes. Parents questioned if epilepsy caused the increase in autistic behaviour or if there was a common aetiology. Seizures were controlled with sodium valproate. Adverse reactions occurred with all selective serotonin reuptake inhibitors used to treat his obsessive behaviour.

Seizure disorders and anticonvulsant medications

Seizure disorders are common in children in the autism spectrum, occurring in approximately one-third of cases across the life span (Tuchman & Rapin, 2002). The explanation for this high incidence is currently part of an active debate and controversy surrounding the effect of seizures on the developing brain. There are many questions over the extent to which seizure activity – clinical or present on EEG only – causes or reflects cognitive and behavioural changes (Deonna, 1995; Tuchman & Rapin, 2002).

These hypotheses have important implications for understanding the pathogenesis of ASD and the factors contributing to behavioural and cognitive difficulties in children with these conditions. In addition, they create questions as to whether treating clinical or subclinical seizures will have an impact on the core deficits in ASD (Tuchman & Rapin, 2002). To date, case series and case reports suggest improvements in children with ASD treated with anticonvulsants (Nass & Petrucha, 1990; Plioplys, 1994; Childs & Blair, 1997; Burd *et al.*, 1998; Belsito, 2001; Hollander *et al.*, 2001). However, these reports are anecdotal only and rigorous evidence in this area is currently lacking.

Regardless of these factors, the high incidence of seizures in children with ASD creates a need to maintain a high level of suspicion about seizures. The possibility of seizures needs to be a consideration when taking a medical history and carrying out a physical examination. In addition, assessing specific concerns such as staring spells, developmental regression, and sleep problems is vital. Unless seizures are obvious, it may be necessary to conduct an overnight EEG to identify epileptiform abnormalities, as the aetiological yield is generally higher with more prolonged monitoring, and in particular monitoring that includes a long duration of natural sleep (Kagan-Kushnir *et al.*, 2005).

All types of seizures have been described in individuals with ASD and although the literature on the subject remains limited, there has been no suggestion to date that seizures are more difficult to treat in children with ASD than in other children with seizure disorders. Thus seizure management strategies and anticonvulsant choice would not be different in children with ASD, with the initial medication being determined by seizure type (Tuchman & Rapin, 2002). Additionally, anticonvulsants may also be useful in the management of behaviour, aggression, and mood instability because of their affect regulating properties (Di Martino & Tuchman, 2001).

Case IV

A 6-year-old girl was diagnosed with a communication disorder at 4 years of age. Autistic features were noted but were not felt to be sufficiently pervasive to warrant a diagnosis of ASD. Upon school entry, her behaviour deteriorated, repetitive interests were difficult to interrupt without prolonged tantrums, and sleep became increasingly disrupted. She awoke every night between 2 and 4 am and spent two hours jumping and rocking from side to side before going back to sleep. Parents and child were exhausted. Careful evaluation showed that the criteria for a diagnosis of autistic disorder were now met.

Sleep

Sleep difficulties are a common problem in ASD. They include difficulty falling asleep as well as night awakening. Several factors may be contributory, including anxiety, and especially in younger children, poor sleep hygiene (that is, the behaviours and environment surrounding bedtime). Seizures can also disrupt sleep and lead to night awakenings. They may need to be ruled out as a cause of related behavioural concerns. The developmental paediatrician can assess these various factors and offer investigations and treatment recommendations, including education around sleep hygiene, as appropriate.

For some individuals who are having difficulty with sleep onset, melatonin might be helpful. Melatonin is a hormone produced by the pineal gland which regulates sleep-wake cycles. There is emerging evidence that melatonin is beneficial in treating sleep disturbances with secondary improvements in behaviour in children with ASD (Paavonen *et al.*, 2003). If melatonin is given, it is necessary to address any contributing factors concomitantly, particularly sleep hygiene, as it will not be effective on its own in these situations.

The contribution of genetics

At the visit after the one in which diagnosis is shared for the first time, questions are often raised about recurrence of ASD in future pregnancies or features of the disorder seen in a sibling. Research studies are underway in many centres to ascertain genetic linkage of autism within pedigrees as well as to study siblings' development.

In addition to familial recurrence, certain genetic syndromes such as tuberous sclerosis carry an increased risk for ASD. The reason behind these associations is the focus of investigation in various laboratories around the world in order to identify candidate genes which may be involved in the development of ASD.

Research has shown that autistic disorders, as neurobiological disorders, have genetic underpinnings, whether or not a specific genetic syndrome is identified. Evidence for this comes from family and twin studies (Szatmari *et al.*, 1998).

As with diabetes and many other disorders currently under investigation, it is now apparent that the genetics behind ASD are complex. This is very different from disorders such as Down syndrome or muscular dystrophy, where it is clear that a difference in a specific chromosome or gene is the cause of the disorder. In the case of ASD, it is currently believed that simultaneous changes to several genes on different chromosomes are required, perhaps in combination with environmental factors, in order for the neurobiological changes that reflect ASD to occur. Candidate genes are being investigated on several chromosomes, including chromosomes 1, 2, 7, 15, and 16, with the strongest associations being on chromosomes 7 and 16 (International Molecular Genetic Study of Autism, 2001). It is theorized that different individuals may have different combinations of genes affected, and that a certain threshold must be reached for the combination of changes to result in ASD. This view helps to explain the spectrum of severity and range of symptoms seen across ASD. It also helps explain the broader spectrum of related disorders that are seen more often in families of ASD patients, including obsessive-compulsive disorder and language disorders (Rutter, 2003).

In terms of recurrence risk, in the absence of a comorbid genetic disorder most studies have suggested that a sibling of a child with ASD has a five to seven per cent risk of developing an ASD. This is higher than the general population risk of approximately 6 per 1000 for Asperger syndrome and ASD combined. If these numbers are true, this would suggest that the risk of having a second child on the autism spectrum is greater than six per cent (Rutter, 2003). These estimates come from retrospective studies as well as from emerging evidence from prospective studies evaluating infant siblings of children with ASD (Roberts *et al.*, 2004b).

As more information about genotype and familial patterns of inheritance becomes available, it may be possible to be more precise in offering a prognosis for parents as well as in genetic counselling.

Behavioural and developmental trajectories

Over time, behavioural difficulties may increase, particularly after 4 years of age and as increased expectations arise in school environments where many new sensory, social, and learning challenges are experienced. The physician can help to solve problems arising from difficult behaviours, identify contributing factors, suggest interventions, and follow-up the child to evaluate the efficacy of these interventions and suggest next steps.

Anxiety and mood disorders are common in individuals with ASD (Smalley *et al.*, 1995). The presentation of these problems varies depending on a child's age and developmental level, often becoming more frequent at around 8 or 9 years as insight into reality-based fears increases. This recurs in adolescence as societal expectations about independence and the future become more apparent. Both anxiety and mood disorders can affect behaviour, making the early identification of symptoms an important part of planning treatment and intervention, including possible pharmacotherapy.

Inattention can be a complex problem to assess and treat in children with ASD. While some children have primary problems with sustaining attention, other difficulties can contribute to and masquerade as inattention, including language and learning problems, anxiety, obsessions, and behavioural rigidity. Research has shown that children with ASD have difficulty disengaging attention, and this is felt to be a core deficit (Bryson *et al.*, 2003). This, too, can masquerade as inattention to the task at hand. A child who is having difficulty transitioning from the last activity, is anxious because a new teacher is in the class, or is focused on his current obsession, may appear every bit as inattentive as a child with severe primary inattention. However, stimulant medication would be inappropriate in these situations and might even exacerbate the problem.

In the situation where primary inattention is felt to be the underlying problem, in whole or in part, stimulant drugs can be helpful. However, care needs to be taken in their administration, as children with ASD seem to be at higher risk of developing side effects, including increases in anxiety, obsessions, and behavioural rigidity. It has been our experience that doses much lower than typically used in children with attention deficit-hyperactivity disorder can be effective for children with ASD (Aman & Langworthy, 2000).

There are no drugs that have been shown to have an impact on the core symptoms of ASD. However, drug treatment is often useful to help treat symptoms and comorbid problems including anxiety, mood problems, attention problems, aggression, and explosive outbursts. In most situations, medication should be viewed as an adjunct to other interventions, its primary role being to help alleviate symptoms and 'take the edge off' behaviour which may be interfering with learning, both academically and socially.

Conclusions

Our understanding of ASD has changed over the last decade and so has the role of the paediatrician in the diagnosis and elucidation of the medical factors that need to be considered as management is planned. Much work remains to be done as we move forward with colleagues in many disciplines to understand these remarkable disorders. Further research into aetiology, early identification, and intervention needs to be conducted. Political advocacy is needed to allow earlier, more effective, and more available resources for assessment, intervention, and support for children with ASD, as well as for their families.

References

Aman, M.G. & Langworthy, K.S. (2000): Pharmacotherapy for hyperactivity in children with autism and other pervasive developmental disorders. *J. Autism Dev. Disord.* **30**, 451–459.

Bauman, M.L. & Kemper, T.L. (2003): The neuropathology of the autism spectrum disorders: what have we learned? *Novartis Foundation Symposium* **251**, 112–122.

Belsito, K.M., Law, P.A., Kirk, K.S., Landa, R.J. & Zimmerman, A.W. (2001): Lamotrigine therapy for autistic disorder: a randomized, double-blind, placebo-controlled trial. *J. Autism Dev. Disord.* **31**, 175–181.

Bryson, S., Czapinski, P., Landry, R., McConnell, B., Rombough, V. & Wainwright, A. (2004): Autistic spectrum disorders: causal mechanisms and recent findings on attention and emotion. *International Journal of Special Education* **19**, 14–22.

Burd, L., Ivey, M., Barth, A. & Kerbeshian, J. (1998): Two males with childhood disintegrative disorder: a prospective 14-year outcome study. *Dev. Med. Child Neurol.* **40**, 702–707.

Challman, T.D., Barbaresi, W.J., Katusic, S.K. & Weaver, A. (2003): The yield of the medical evaluation of children with pervasive developmental disorders. *J. Autism Dev. Disord.* **35**, 187–192.

Childs, J.A. & Blair, J.L. (1997): Valproic acid treatment of epilepsy in autistic twins. *J. Neurosci. Nurs.* **29**, 244–248.

Courchesne, E., Carper, R. & Akshoomoff, N. (2003): Evidence of brain overgrowth in the first year of life in autism. *JAMA* **290**, 337–344.

Deonna, T. (1995): Cognitive and behavioral disturbances as epileptic manifestations in children: an overview. *Semin. Pediatr. Neurol.* **2**, 254–260.

Di Martino, A. & Tuchman, R.F. (2001): Antiepileptic drugs: affective use in autism spectrum disorders. *Pediatr. Neurol.* **25**, 199–207.

Filipek, P.A., Accardo, P.J., Ashwal, S., Baranek, G.T., Cook, E.H., Dawson, G., Gordon, B., Gravel, J.S., Johnson, C.P., Kallen, R.J., Levy, S.E., Minshew, N.J., Ozonoff, S., Prizant, B.M., Rapin, I., Rogers, S.J., Stone, W.L., Teplin, S.W., Tuchman, R.F. & Volkmar, F.R. (2000): Practice parameter: screening and diagnosis of autism. Report of the Quality Standards Subcommittee of the American Academy of Neurology and the Child Neurology Society. *Neurology* **55**, 468–479.

Goldberg, W.A., Osann, K., Filipek, P.A., Laulhere, T., Jarvis, K., Modahl, C., Flodman, P. & Spence, M.A. (2003): Language and other regression: assessment and timing. *J. Autism Dev. Disord.* **33**, 607–616.

Hansen, R. & Ozonoff, S. (2003): Assessment and therapy options. In: *Autism spectrum disorders: a research review for practitioners*, eds. S. Ozonoff, S. Rogers & R. Hendren. Washington: American Psychiatric Publishing.

Hollander, E., Dolgoff-Kaspar, R., Cartwright, C., Rawitt, R. & Novotny, S. (2001): An open trial of divalproex sodium in autism spectrum disorders. *J. Clin. Psychiatry* **62**, 530–534.

International Molecular Genetic Study of Autism (2001): A genome wide screen for autism: strong evidence for linkage to chromosomes 2q, 7q, and 16p. *Am. J. Hum. Genet.* **69**, 570–581.

Kagan-Kushnir, T., Griffiths, A. & Roberts, W. (2002): Gastrointestinal symptoms in autism spectrum disorders (abstract). Presented at Canadian Paediatric Society Conference.

Kagan-Kushnir, T., Roberts, W. & Snead, O.C.S. (2005): Screening electroencephalograms in autism spectrum disorders: an evidence based guideline. *J. Child Neurol.* Vol. 20. **3**, 197–206.

Knivsberg, A.-M., Wiig, K., Lind, G., Nodland, M. *et al.* (1990): Dietary intervention in autistic syndromes. *Brain Dysfunction* **3**, 315–327.

Kurita, H. (1997): A comparative study of Asperger syndrome with high-functioning atypical autism. *Psychiatry Clin. Neurosci.* **51**, 67–70.

Lord, C., Risi, S., Lambrecht, L., Cook, E.H., Leventhal, B.L., DiLavore, P.C., Pickles, A. & Rutter, M. (2000): The Autism Diagnostic Observation Schedule-Generic: a standard measure of social and communication deficits associated with the spectrum of autism. *J. Autism Dev. Disord.* **30**, 205–223.

Lord, C., Rutter, M. & Le Couteur, A. (1994): Autism Diagnostic Interview-Revised: a revised version of a diagnostic interview for caregivers of individuals with possible pervasive developmental disorders. *J. Autism Dev. Disord.* **22**, 563–581.

Lucarelli, S., Frediani, T., Zingoni, A.M., Ferruzzi, F., Giardini, O., Quintieri, F., Barbato, M., D'Eufemia, P. & Cardi, E. (1995): Food allergy and infantile autism. *Panminerva Med.* **37**, 137–141.

Maurice, C., Green, G. & Luce, S. (1996): *Behavioral intervention for young children with autism: a manual for parents and professionals.* Austin, Texas: Pro-Ed Publishing.

Nass, R. & Petrucha, D. (1990): Acquired aphasia with convulsive disorder: a pervasive developmental disorder variant. *J. Child Neurol.* **5**, 327–328.

Paavonen, E.J., Nieminen-von Wendt, T., Vanhala, R., Aronen, E.T. & von Wendt, L. (2003): Effectiveness of melatonin in the treatment of sleep disturbances in children with Asperger disorder. *J. Child Adolesc. Psychopharmacol.* **13**, 83–95.

Plioplys, A.V. (1994): Autism: electroencephalogram abnormalities and clinical improvement with valproic acid. *Arch. Pediatr. Adolesc. Med.* **148**, 220–222.

Roberts, W., Dosman, C., Drmic, I., Harford, M., Sharieff, W., Smith, R., Moldofsky, H., Zlotkin, S. & Brian, J. (2004a): Serum ferritin and response to iron supplementation in autism (abstract). Presented at Society for Pediatric Research, San Francisco.

Roberts, S.W., Zwaigenbaum, L., Bryson, S.E., Brian, J. & Szatmari, P. (2004b): 12-month-old siblings of children with autism (abstract). Presented at Society for Pediatric Research, San Francisco.

Rogers, S.J., Wehner, D.E. & Hagerman, R. (2001): The behavioral phenotype in fragile X: symptoms of autism in very young children with fragile X syndrome, idiopathic autism, and other developmental disorders. *J. Dev. Behav. Pediatr.* **22**, 409–417.

Rutter, M. (2003): Introduction: autism – the challenges ahead. In: *Symposium on autism: neural basis and treatment possibilities*, eds. G. Bock & J. Goode, pp. 4. Chichester: John Wiley.

Siller, M. & Sigman, M. (2002): The behaviors of parents of children with autism predict the subsequent development of their children's communication. *J. Autism Dev. Disord.* **32**, 77–79.

Smalley, S.L., McCracken, J. & Tanguay, P. (1995): Autism, affective disorders, and social phobia. *Am. J. Med. Genet.* **60**, 19–26.

Sussman, F. (1999): *Hanen, More Than Words*. Toronto. Beacon Herald Fine Printing Division.

Szatmari, P., Jones, M.B., Zwaigenbaum, L. & MacLean, J.E. (1998): Genetics of autism: overview and new directions. *J. Autism Dev. Disord.* **28**, 351–368.

Tannock, R., Girolametto, L. & Siegel, L.S. (1992): Language intervention with children who have developmental delays: effects of an interactive approach. *Am. J. Ment. Retard.* **97**, 145–160

Tuchman, R. & Rapin, I. (2002): Epilepsy in autism. *Lancet Neurol.* **1**, 352–358.

Tupper, D.E. (1987): *Soft neurological signs*. Orlando, FL: Grune & Stratton, Inc.

Wakefield, A.J., Murch, S.H., Anthony, A., Linnell, J., Casson, D.M., Malik, M., Berelowitz, M., Dhillon, A.P., Thomson, M.A., Harvey, P., Valentine, A., Davies, S.E. & Walker-Smith, J.A. (1998): Ileal-lymphoid-nodular hyperplasia, non-specific colitis, and pervasive developmental disorder in children. *Lancet* **351**, 637–641.

White, J.F. (2003): Intestinal pathophysiology in autism. *Exp. Biol. Med.* **228**, 639–649.

Whiteley, P., Rodgers, J., Savery, D. & Shattock, P. (1999): A gluten-free diet as an intervention for autism and associated spectrum disorders: preliminary findings. *Autism* **3**, 45–65.

Zwaigenbaum, L., Bryson, S., Rogers, T., Roberts, W., Brian, J. & Szatmari, P. (2005): Behavioral manifestations of autism in the first year of life. *Int. J. Dev. Neurosci.* **23**, 143–152.

Autistic spectrum disorders, D. Riva and I. Rapin (eds.)

Chapter 18

Autism: an operational model for diagnosis and for planning interventions in a hospital setting

Paola Visconti, Roberta Truzzi, Marcella Peroni, Francesca Ciceri and Giuseppe Gobbi

Ambulatory of Autism, Operative Unit of Child Neurology, largo Nigrisoli 2, 40133 Bologna, Italy
Paola.Visconti@ausl.bologna.it

Summary

We present an outline of the operational model developed by Autism Clinic at the Ospedale Maggiore in Bologna and the diagnostic and clinical records of the patients examined at the service in 2001–2002. We studied the link between neurological pathology and pervasive developmental disorders (PDD), and compared our results with data from published reports. We considered two groups of patients: those with PDD and those with mental retardation without social abnormalities.
The results showed that 10.5 per cent of children with PDD had associated neurological pathology (epilepsy, epileptic encephalopathy, genetic syndromes). This increased to 32 per cent if we included less specific abnormalities that were not part of a defined neurological syndrome, such as EEG abnormalities (10.8 per cent) or magnetic resonance imaging (MRI) abnormalities (25.8 per cent). For mental retardation without social abnormalities, 28.6 per cent had associated neurological pathology, and this increased to 60.7 per cent if EEG and MRI abnormalities were also considered. Neurobiological factors were more common in patients with PDD and mental retardation with moderate to severe cognitive impairment. Among PDD subtypes, neurobiological factors were more common in children with atypical autism or childhood disintegrative disorder with a higher degree of cognitive impairment.
Finally, we present preliminary data on our treatment model results, examining the relations between the medical protocol, functional-neuropsychological evaluation, and type of intervention.

Introduction

In this chapter we outline the operational model developed by Autism Clinic at the Ospedale Maggiore in Bologna, and explain the results of the diagnostic and clinical records of the patients examined at the service in 2001–2002. The services provided include an comprehensive diagnostic evaluation following an autism-specific medical protocol, and the development of individualized psycho-educational projects in collaboration with the family and school. These programmes are based on a specific neuropsychological evaluation, taking into account the severity of the pathology, the patient's age, and the level of functional development.

The clinical assessment involves the following:

• *unstructured clinical observation*; mainly focused on the child's relationship with the parents and with the examiners, to explore possible differences;
• *diagnostic assessment* according to clinical criteria and validated scales [Childhood Autism Rating Scale (CARS), Behavioural Summarized Evaluation (BSE), Diagnostic and Statistical Manual of Mental disorders, 4th edition (DSM-IV), and the International classification of diseases, 10th edition (ICD-10)];
• evaluation of *cognitive development* and *visual-motor integration profile* [Wechsler Intelligence Scale for Children, Revised (WISC-R), Leiter International Scale, Raven Standard Progressive Matrices (SPM), Bayley Scale, and the Visual-Motor Integration Test (VMI)];
• evaluation of the *functional development* [Psycho-Educational Profile, Revised (PEP-R), Adolescent and Adult Psychoeducational Profile (AAPEP)];
• evaluation of *executive functions* (high-functioning subjects) (Wisconsin Card Sorting Test (WCST), Verbal Fluency Test) ;
• evaluation of *metacognitive abilities* [Sally and Ann Test, Howlin's pictures (Howlin *et al.*, 1999)];
• evaluation of the child's *play abilities* (Symbolic Play Test);
• evaluation of *social adaptation* (Vineland Adaptive Behaviour Scales).

This assessment is carried out over 2 days and its aim is to formulate a multidimensional individualized profile and provide a psycho-educational and neuropsychological project report. The evaluation and the interviews take place with the child's parents being present, in order to familiarize the child with the environment and to observe possible changes in behaviour determined by the new setting. The principal aim is to share ideas about the child, to formulate a therapeutic strategy, and to achieve a 'therapeutic alliance'.

At the meeting when the project is finalised, the presence of the professional workers who support the child (teachers, neuropsychiatrists, psychologists, speech therapists and so on) is formally requested. The intervention is composed of periodic follow-up evaluations and meetings between parents and therapists with the aim of achieving a unified approach and sharing the positive and negative elements of the individualized project.

In presenting an overview of our work we have summarized the preliminary results in three different fields: neuropsychology, neurobiology, and the intervention approach.

Preliminary results of the neuropsychological data

This section presents the results of our preliminary analysis of some cognitive elements based on the data processing.

We studied a sample of 12 children from a larger series of PDD patients (mean age 11 years, range 8 to 14), all of whom had been tested using the WISC-R scale. We did not observe any significant inhomogeneity in the cognitive profile between verbal and performance IQ, though we found particular profiles with significant differences in selected subtests.

The average profile included positive peaks in performances tests such as *Block Design* and *Object Assembly*, and negative peaks in verbal subtests such as *Arithmetic* and *Comprehension* and the *Coding Task* subtest.

The positive peaks can be attributed to the ability of these patients to organize the task in a perceptive way – that is, they tend to concentrate more on details rather than on the whole picture (deficit of central coherence). On the other hand, weaknesses are evident in coding and arithmetical tasks in which integrity of abstraction abilities, working memory (executive functions), motor abilities, and visual-perceptive integration is required. The negative peak in the comprehension subtests is probably related to the difficulty in understanding social rules that characterizes this syndrome.

Similar results are reported in the literature. Recent studies show that the *Block Design* task constitutes a strong point in autistic and Asperger subjects, whereas these patients have greater difficulties in arithmetical and coding subtests (Ehlers, 1997; Marjiviona & Prior, 1999).

According to the cognitive theory that relates PDD with a deficit of executive function, patients functioning at a good intellectual level are currently given the WCST. This is used to evaluate executive functions and to measure flexibility, as it requires subjects to shift their cognitive set on up to six occasions during the task, each time changing the implicit rules. The primary index used to analyse executive dysfunction is the number of perseverative responses that the child continues to give despite the feedback.

Different studies have shown that this test can be used in autistic patients (Ozonoff, 1995), and all support the hypothesis of a specific deficit of executive functions in PDD subjects, in whom the results are consistently below average compared with normal controls.

The sample was composed of 14 PDD subjects. Statistical analysis of the data has not yet been carried out. However, we present a single case report to provide an example of the peculiar functioning of a 'typical' autistic boy.

A. was 14 years old with an IQ of 83 (evaluated using the Raven Standard Progressive Matrices). He presented qualitative abnormalities of intersubjectivity and communication, and stereotyped and obsessive behaviours. He had special abilities in calendar calculation and music. He had difficulties in completing the WCST: of the 128 items administered, he could answer correctly on 46 occasions (64 per cent error). In particular, he gave perseverative responses in 75 per cent of the cases. His results place him in the first percentile, consistently below average for normal subjects of the same chronological age. He completed only two categories, and gave conceptual level responses in a low percentage (17 per cent). On the other hand, when he understood the underlying rule, he was able to maintain the same and correct set of answers, further showing his tendency to persevere in the responses.

Preliminary results of the neurobiological data

The data reported here refer to 140 patients (108 male and 32 female), divided into two groups. The subjects included in the first group were affected by PDD (n = 104; mean age 7 years, range 1 to 20), while those in the second group had a diagnosis of mental retardation without social abnormalities (n = 28; mean age 8 years, range 3 to 18). Both groups underwent a thorough medical evaluation to determine whether there were associated organic disorders or EEG and/or MRI abnormalities. The differences between the two groups were then analysed.

A definite neurological disorder could be documented in 11/104 patients with PDD (10.6 per cent) and in 8/28 patients with mental retardation (28.6 per cent), including genetic abnormalities, epileptic encephalopathies, Landau–Kleffner syndrome, and other forms of epilepsy.

EEG abnormalities without epilepsy were documented in 10.8 per cent of PDD patients (irrespective of the degree of mental impairment) and in 20 per cent of patients with mental retardation (showing moderate to severe mental impairment).

MRI abnormalities were found in 19/104 PDD patients (25.3 per cent) and in 13/104 patients with mental retardation (59 per cent), including the following:

- mild periventricular white matter signal abnormalities;
- periventricular leukomalacia;
- enlargement and asymmetry of the lateral ventricles;
- posterior fossa arachnoid cysts;
- hippocampal hypoplasia;
- cortical dysplasia;
- Chiari malformation type 1;
- delayed myelination of peritrigonal white matter;
- hypoplasia of the cerebellar vermis.

In both groups, the degree of delay was moderate to severe.

In conclusion, the neurobiological factors associated with PDD and mental retardation included definite neurological disorders, EEG abnormalities, and MRI abnormalities. The respective percentages of these in the two groups were 32.7 per cent (34/104) in PDD, and 60.7 per cent (17/28) in mental retardation.

Summary of the preliminary neurobiological results

Neurological disorders (epileptic encephalopathies, genetic syndromes) conceivably play an important role in the pathogenesis of PDD. A definite neurological disorder was documented in 10.6 per cent of our PDD patients, and the percentage increased to 32.7 per cent with the co-occurrence of qualitative abnormalities on EEG (10.8 per cent) or MRI (25.3 per cent). These results are in line with previously reported data: 5 to 30 per cent of PDD patients are affected by another neurological disorder, which is aetiologically relevant in 11 per cent (Dykens & Volkmar, 1997).

No cases of metabolic disorders, fragile X syndrome, or phacomatosis were documented in our series of patients.

In relation to mental retardation without social abnormalities, 28.6 per cent of our patients were affected by a neurological disorder, increasing to 60.7 per cent if EEG or MRI abnormalities were also considered.

When comparing the two groups, these data show how neurobiological factors can be documented in patients with moderate or severe mental impairment, irrespective of the diagnosis, as already reported by other investigators (Rutter *et al.*, 1994). Considering the PDD subtypes, the strongest association was found between neurobiological factors and atypical autism and childhood disintegrative disorder (see *Table 1* for details). On the other hand, as recently reported by other investigators, Asperger syndrome and high-functioning autism are not usually associated with structural abnormalities, even though some degree of dysfunction may be documented by PET or functional MRI studies. Abnormal functioning of the fusiform gyrus (recognition of faces) and of the left medial frontal cortex (deficit of the Theory of Mind) appear particularly intriguing in this scenario, as these structures seem to be involved in specific neuropsychological abilities (Fletcher, 1995; Schultz *et al.*, 2000;).

Many studies have focused on high-functioning autism and Asperger syndrome. Given the absence or the mild degree of mental impairment encountered in these syndromes, such studies could address and clarify the cognitive aspects and social peculiarities of these disorders. Further research is needed to provide more insight on this issue.

Table 1. Neurobiological factors in relation to the different types of pervasive developmental disorder

Diagnosis	Associated neurobiological factors
Atypical autism	80%
Childhood disintegrative disorder	60%
PDD-NOS	30%
Multisystemic developmental disorder (diagnostic classification *Zero-to-Three*)	36%
Autistic disorder	29%
High-functioning autism and Asperger syndrome	0%

PDD-NOS, Pervasive Developmental Disorder-Not Otherwise Specified.

'Intervention' aspects

We analysed a group of 20 patients (19 male, 1 female; mean age of 73 months, range 37 to 110; mean functional developmental age 23.3 months (PEP-R), range 13 to 48 months) followed up for 1½ years. We evaluated the effects of our cognitive-behavioural approach based on different methods and strategies tailored according to the age, functional level, and family needs.

Projects for habilitation: 'No one size fits all' (Schreibman, 2000).

In this section, we report the key points and references for our different intervention approaches, which are modified according to the child's age and developmental level. In toddlers, we suggest that the intervention should be focused on intersubjectivity; with increasing age and developmental level, we propose more structured activities to implement independent work and social abilities *(Fig. 1)*.

Clinical evaluation using the CARS and PEP-R scales was carried out at the time of the first observation and after 18 months of follow-up, in order to verify the sensitivity of these tools for identifying modifications induced by treatment. The influence of selected clinical variables on the CARS and PEP-R scores before and after treatment was also determined.

Methods

The following variables were considered: chronological age; functional developmental age; degree of mental impairment; neurological factors; diagnostic categories; language abilities.

To undertake statistical analyses, variables were grouped in clusters as follows:

Sample in relation to language abilities (n = 20):
1 = absence of language (n = 10);
2 = word-phrase or combination of two words (n = 5);
3 = sentences with at least three words (n = 5).
Sample in relation to neurological factors (n = 20):
Absent (n = 15);
Minor = EEG abnormalities (n = 3);
Greater = cerebral MRI abnormalities (n = 2).

Intersubjectivity
- Exchange and development therapy (TED) (Barthelemy *et al.*, 1995)
- Communication prerequisites (Dawson), 1991)

functional developmental age ↓

Self-independent teaching:
- Portage (Bluma *et al.*, 1990)
- TEACCH Program (Treatment and Education of Autistic and Communication Handicapped Children; Schopler *et al.*, 1971 Schopler & Olley, 1982)
- Structured teaching

functional developmental age ↓

Social Abilities Teaching
(Mesibov, 1986; Lord, 1995)

Meta-cognitive competence teaching
(Jordan & Powell, 1995; Howlin *et al.*, 1999)

Employment of educational software to implement cognitive, communicative, and social abilities
(Trehin, 1997; Bernard-Opitz *et al.*, 2001)

Fig. 1. Interventional approach modified according to the child's age.

Sample in relation to degree of mental impairment (n = 20) (degree of delay evaluated in respect of the chronological age):
1 = under 2 years 'mild' (n = 5);
2 = under 4 years 'moderate' (n = 5);
3 = more than 4 years 'severe' (n = 10).
CARS items were subdivided into three areas according to Di Lalla & Rogers (1994):
1. Social impairment (SI);
2. Negative emotionality (NE);
3. Distorted sensory response (DSR).

These variables were subjected to analysis of variance with repeated measures and independent groups.

Conclusions

Our preliminary conclusions were as follows.

(1) PEP-R and CARS assessments before and after treatment

• PEP-R: there was a significant difference in the scores achieved before and after treatment (in each area $F(1,19) = 23.19$; $p < 0.0001$).

• CARS: there were globally significant differences in the scores achieved before and after treatment ($F(1,19) = 6.42$; $p = 0.02$). Considering the three different areas, a statistically significant difference was documented only in the Social Impairment area ($p = 0.011$).

(2) Variables assessed for differences in the scores achieved before and after treatment

There were no significant differences in chronological age, age of functional development, 'index delay', diagnostic categories, or neurological components.

For language ability there was a significant correlation with the improvements documented by PEP-R ($F [2.17] = 8.38$; $p < 0.0029$).

(3) Methodological strategies

The most effective strategies common to the different interventions were as follows: planning proposed activities; providing predictable and clear activities; use of structured spaces, daily schedules, and job systems; providing a calm and clean environment; teaching one to one, then by tutor, then in a group; supplementary and alternative systems of communication; and strategies based on the neuropsychological results.

According to our experience, and as a result of this study, we emphasize that linking the different agencies involved with the child seems to play a central role in ensuring the effectiveness of the intervention.

In summary, the core features of this net appear to be well trained professional operators, periodic interviews (at least every 3 months), videotaped school visits and observations, and compliance and partnership with the family.

References

Barthelemy, C., Hameury L. & Lelord, G. (1995): *L'autisme de l'enfant. La thérapie d'échange et de développement.* Paris: Expansion Scientifique Française.

Bernard-Opitz, V., Sriram, N. & Nakhoda-Sapuan, S. (2001): Enhancing social problem solving in children with autism and normal children through computer-assisted instruction. *J. Autism Dev. Disord.* **31**, 377–384.

Bluma, S.M., Shearer, M.S., Frohman, A.H. & Hilliard, J.M. (1990): *Il metodo Portage. Guida pratica per l'educazione precoce.* [Italian translation]. Torino: Omega Edizioni.

Dawson, G. (1991): A psychobiological perspective on the early socio-emotional development of children with autism. In: *Rochester Symposium on developmental psychopathology*, vol. 3, eds. D. Cicchetti & S. Toth. Rochester, NY: University of Rochester Press.

DiLalla, D.L. & Rogers, S.J. (1994): Domains of the Childhood Autism Rating Scale: relevance for diagnosis and treatment. *J. Autism Dev. Disord.* **24**, 115–128.

Dyckens, E.M. & Volkmar, F.R. (1997): Medical condition associated with autism. In: *Handbook of autism and pervasive developmental disorders*, 2nd ed., eds. D.J. Cohen & F.R. Volkmar, pp. 388–407. New York: Wiley.

Ehlers, S. (1997): Asperger syndrome, autism and attention disorders: a comparative study of the cognitive profiles of 120 children. *J. Child Psychol. Psychiatry* **38**, 207–217.

Fletcher, P., Happè, F., Frith, U., Baker, S., Dolan, R., Frackowiak, R. & Frith, C. (1995): Other minds in the brain: a functional imaging study of 'theory of mind' in story comprehension. *Cognition* **57**, 109–128.

Howlin, P., Baron-Cohen, S. & Hadwin, J. (1999): *Teoria della mente e autismo. Insegnare a comprendere gli aspetti pschici dell'altro.* [Italian translation]. Trento: Erickson Editore.

Jordan, R. & Powell, S. (1995): *Autismo e intervento educativo. Comunicazione, emotività e pensiero.* Trento: Erickson Editore.

Lord, C. (1995): Facilitare l'inserimento sociale. Esempi di un programma di intervento tra coetanei. In: *Apprendimento e cognizione nell'autismo*, eds. E. Schopler & G.B. Mesibov, pp. 253–274. New York: McGraw-Hill.

Marjiviona, J. & Prior, M. (1999): Neuropsychological profiles of children with Asperger syndrome and autism. *Autism* **3**, 327–356.

Mesibov, G.B. (1986): A cognitive program for teaching social behaviors to verbal autistic adolescents and adults. In: *Social behavior in autism*, eds. E. Schopler & G.B. Mesibov, pp. 265–281. New York: Plenum Press.

Ozonoff, S. (1995): Executive function in autism. In: *Learning and cognition in autism*, eds. E. Schopler & G.B. Mesibov, pp. 199–220. New York: Plenum.

Rutter, M., Bailey, A., Bolton, P. & Le Couteur, A. (1994): Autism and known medical conditions: myth and substance. *J. Child Psychol. Psychiatry* **35**, 311–322.

Schopler, E., Brehm, S.S., Kinsbourne, M. & Reichler, R.J. (1971): Effect of treatment structure of development in autistic children. *Arch. Gen. Psychiatry* **24**, 415–421.

Schopler, E. & Olley, J.G. (1982): Comprehensive educational services for autistic children: the TEACCH model. In: *The handbook of school psychology*, eds. C.R. Reynolds & T.R. Gutkin, pp. 629–643. New York: John Wiley & Sons.

Schultz, R.T., Gauthier, I., Klin, A., Fulbright, R.K., Anderson, A.W., Volkmar, F., Skudlarski, P., Lacadie, C., Cohen, D.J. & Gore, J.C. (2000): Abnormal ventral temporal cortical activity during face discrimination among individuals with autism and Asperger syndrome. *Arch. Gen. Psychiatry* **57**, 331–340.

Trehin, P. (1997): *L'uso dell'informatica nel processo educativo dei soggetti autistici. Atti del convegno Autismo le nuove frontiere della riabilitazione*. Nola (NA).

Autistic spectrum disorders, D. Riva and I. Rapin (eds.)

Chapter 19

Current issues in the behavioural treatment of children with autism

Laura Schreibman

Psychology Department, University of California, San Diego, 9500 Gilman Drive, La Jolla, California 92093–0109, USA
lschreibman@psy.ucsd.edu

Summary

There are few childhood disorders more resistant to treatment than autism. Behavioural treatment remains the only form of treatment that has been shown empirically to be effective with this population. The first demonstrations of the value of the behavioural model were provided in the 1960s when highly structured operant learning programmes were employed to improve the behaviour of these children. Such programmes were successful in increasing language, social, and academic skills, as well as in reducing many of the severe behavioural problems often associated with the disorder. As effective as these early demonstrations proved to be, enthusiasm was tempered when generalization and follow-up results indicated limitations to this effectiveness. To address these limitations the field has evolved and broadened to include not only refinements to the discrete trial strategy but also behavioural strategies that are more 'naturalistic', more loosely structured, conducted in a wider range of environments, and by a wider range of treatment providers.

Although behavioural treatment is considered to be the most effective form of treatment now available, clinical researchers have long reported a great deal of variability in outcome. Thus some children improve substantially while others improve to a lesser degree or not at all. This variability suggests the operation of several important variables that must be considered when designing a treatment programme. It is now apparent that treatments must be designed on an individualized basis taking into account important child, family, treatment, and behavioural variables.

Introduction

The severity of autism, its resistance to treatment, and the failure of other treatment approaches have all contributed to the acceptance of the behavioural approach for the treatment of autism. Before the application of behavioural treatment there were very few available treatment options for these children and such treatments were generally ineffective.

This rather bleak situation was improved greatly with the development of treatments based upon a behavioural model. Essentially, these treatments involve the systematic application of the principles of learning to human behaviour. The treatment was developed through the methodology of applied behaviour analysis, which focuses on the understanding of how the environment affects behaviour. Knowledge of these environment-behaviour principles allows for their use to change behaviour. Importantly (and in contrast to previous treatments based on psychodynamic theory) these treatments emphasize data collection, experimental analysis of these data, empirical verification, and self-critical analysis. Such an objective, data-driven methodology ensures rigorous demonstrations of effectiveness. Also, such methodology allows the identification of treatment strengths and weaknesses. The latter serve to inform further research and continual improvement and refinement of the treatment methodology.

Early development of behavioural interventions

The initial demonstrations of the use of behavioural principles ('behaviour modification') were conducted in the early 1960s and were the first to show that autistic children could learn if the systematic application of operant discrimination learning techniques was employed (Ferster & DeMyer, 1961; Ferster & DeMyer, 1962). These early investigators showed that the youngsters could indeed learn new behaviours under conditions where correct responses to a discrimination task (pressing a key) were followed by contingent applications of reinforcement (for example, food, candy, or trinkets). While the discrimination taught was simple and not very functional in terms of an academic curriculum or social interaction, it did indicate that the children could learn and this was in a prevailing atmosphere where many doubted the ability of the children to benefit from educational programmes.

Building upon this early work, behavioural researchers developed procedures to teach more functional behaviours, focusing on communication, social behaviour, toy play, academic skills, and so on. The most important contribution in this work was the application of operant discrimination learning principles to teach these behaviours. This form of treatment, Discrete Trial Training (DTT), involves breaking down complex target behaviours into smaller components and teaching these components individually in a systematic manner. Thus vocal speech is taught by first gaining the child's attention, rewarding the child for eye contact, rewarding the child for spontaneous vocalizations, shaping imitative vocalizations, putting vocalizations together into words, teaching the verbal referents to the words, and so on until a larger repertoire is built. The training is accomplished by presenting the child with a series of individual trials which are presented in blocks of 10, 20, or more trials per block. Each trial comprises a question or instruction, a response by the child (or failure to respond), followed by an appropriate consequence. After an intertrial interval, the next trial is presented. For a comprehensive description of this treatment, the reader is referred to Maurice *et al.* (1996). *Figure 1* presents the basic components of DTT training.

The first demonstrations of DTT were very impressive. Indeed, here for the first time was a treatment strategy that proved to be effective in establishing a wide range of significant behaviours in children with autism (for example, Lovaas *et al.*, 1981). In fact, this form of treatment has led to substantial improvement in many children with autism. While not a 'cure' for the disorder, the prognosis for some is certainly more hopeful, particularly if the treatment is implemented when the child is very young (2 to 4 years of age). The importance of this form of therapy in revolutionizing autism treatment cannot be overstated. DTT principles have provided the basis for all behavioural treatments that have followed it. However, while DTT provided the first systematic, empirically validated form of treatment for these children, the news was not uniformly good. The fact remained that there was (and is) substantial variability in outcome – some children improve a great deal while some improve minimally or not at all.

BASIC COMPONENTS OF DISCRETE TRIAL TRAINING

Instruction > Response < Consequence

Presenting Instructions and Questions

- Child attending
- Easily discriminable
- Short and consistent

Child responds (correctly or incorrectly) or fails to respond

Consequences

Types of consequences (*e.g.* positive reinforcement)

Manner of presenting consequences

- Contingent and consistent
- Appropriate to child's response

Easily discriminable

Fig. 1. The basic components of Discrete Trial Training.

COMPONENTS OF PIVOTAL RESPONSE TRAINING

Motivation

- Child choice
- Reinforce attempts
- Direct reinforcement
- Intersperse maintenance tasks
- Frequent task variation
- Turn taking

Responsivity to Multiple Cues

- Tasks involve conditional discriminations

Fig. 2. The components of Pivotal Response Training.

In addition to the heterogeneity in treatment outcome, other limitations were discovered over the years as follow-up assessments of the children suggested that additional significant problem areas existed. These include the following:

(1) *Limitations to stimulus generalization.* Behaviours taught in certain environments or by certain trainers were not shown in other situations. Thus a child who could correctly identify the colour red in the clinic might fail to identify a red car in a parking lot.
(2) *Limitations to response generalization.* Changes in specific behaviours may not also lead to changes in other, untrained behaviours. A child's screaming may be reduced but self biting may not.
(3) The children may *lack spontaneity* in their responding, requiring an initial instruction or question before responding.
(4) As the highly structured nature of DTT typically involves training specific responses, often the children tend to be *robotic* in their response, responding in exactly the same way on each occasion rather than with normal, natural variation of behaviour.
(5) The children tend to remain *dependent on prompts*, thus waiting for assistance before responding.
(6) *Progress can be very slow*, requiring many trials and a great deal of time and effort.
(7) The treatment is *difficult to implement* in that it requires the treatment provider (parent, teacher, clinician) to be carefully trained. Also, it is not a natural form of interaction so it may not come easily to the therapist.
(8) The children and the treatment provider *may not like the treatment.* This may lead to child tantrums and other escape motivated behaviours and a failure of the treatment provider (especially the parent) to implement the treatment.

While these limitations to DTT are of concern, they did inform and help to guide the development of improved treatment strategies.

Increasing effectiveness of behavioural interventions

In response to the problem of variability in treatment outcome and other limitations evident with DTT, behavioural treatments that were more 'naturalistic' were developed. Interestingly, these treatments arose independently and almost simultaneously from various different laboratories in the USA – a fact suggesting that the movement to more naturalistic strategies was the right course. These naturalistic treatments have different names depending on the laboratory; these include 'Incidental Teaching' (Hart & Risley, 1980; McGee *et al.*, 1985), 'Pivotal Response Training' (Koegel *et al.*, 1989), 'Natural Language Paradigm' (Koegel *et al.*, 1987a), 'Milieu Treatment' (Kaiser *et al.*, 1992), and so on. Importantly, all of these treatments share many of the same components. They are all child directed, introduce variability in training stimuli and responses, and use natural consequences and programme generalization in the training.

A description of one of these naturalistic strategies, Pivotal Response Training (PRT), will illustrate how these procedures work. As discussed above, a main issue in the treatment of children with autism is the generalization of treatment effectiveness. Thus we seek to develop treatments that will be expressed, first, in a wide variety of stimulus situations; second, across a range of individual behaviours; third, over extended periods of time; and fourth, will promote a spontaneous and naturally variable response. We also seek to develop treatments that are more pleasant for the child and the treatment provider, thereby increasing the likelihood the treatment will be implemented. Focusing on 'pivotal' behaviours means a greater economy and efficiency in our efforts because we assume a greater overall impact as a function of targeting a few (pivotal) behaviours. The pivotal behaviours chosen are *motivation* and *responsivity to multiple cues*. Both these areas have proven to be very difficult for children with autism, and the basic premise behind PRT is that improvement in motivation and responsivity will lead to widespread collateral changes in other behaviours, thus obviating the need to teach all of these behaviours separately. The components of PRT are shown in *Fig. 2*.

Increasing motivation

Treatment providers are taught to increase the child's motivation by using several individual strategies that have each been shown to increase motivation and enhance learning (Turner, 1978; Koegel & Egel, 1979; Koegel & Williams, 1980; O'Dell & Koegel, 1981; O'Dell *et al.*, 1983; Koegel *et al.*, 1987b). The strategies include the following:

(1) *Child choice*. To maximize the children's interest in the learning situation, they are given a great deal of input in determining the specific stimuli and the nature of the learning interaction. Various materials (for example, toys, games, snacks) are presented and the child is allowed to select an activity or object about which the learning interaction will take place. The treatment provider is encouraged to be alert to the child's changing interests and to allow the child to change to another preferred activity.

(2) *Reinforcement of attempts*. To maximize reinforcement and therefore enhance the child's motivation to respond, treatment providers are trained to reinforce all reasonable attempts made by the child to respond. Thus reinforcers are contingent upon attempts that may not be completely correct, and may not be quite as good as previous attempts, but are within a broader range of correct responses.

(3) *Direct/natural reinforcers*. Direct rather than indirect reinforcers are used. Direct reinforcers are consequences that are directly related to the response they follow. A direct reinforcer for the verbal response 'car' might be access to a toy car as opposed to a food or token reinforcer. Access to a toy car is a direct and natural consequence of saying 'car', whereas food is not.

(4) *Interspersed maintenance tasks*. In order to enhance motivation by keeping the overall success and reinforcement level high, previously mastered tasks are interspersed frequently among more difficult tasks.

(5) *Frequent task variation*. Tasks are varied often to reduce boredom and to allow the child to sample a variety of antecedent stimuli and a variety of appropriate responses. This reduces the robotic responding and the overly restricted stimulus control often associated with the more highly structured DTT-type treatment.

(6) *Turn taking*. The therapist takes turns while interacting with the child such that the child learns to respond and also to enable the therapist to respond. This allows the therapist multiple opportunities to model a variety of appropriate language, play, and social behaviours as well as to allow the child to practice the natural give-and-take nature of social and conversational discourse.

Increasing responsivity to simultaneous multiple cues

Previous research has identified an attentional deficit, *stimulus overselectivity*, found in many children with autism. This pattern of attention is characterized by a failure to respond to simultaneous multiple cues as they typically occur in a learning situation (see Schreibman, 1988 for a review). This deficit has been implicated in a wide range of behavioural deficits including failure to generalize (Lovaas *et al.*, 1979; Schreibman, 1988). We also know that for many of these children overselectivity may be remediated by training the children on a series of successive *conditional discriminations* (Koegel & Schreibman, 1977; Schreibman *et al.*, 1982). A conditional discrimination is one that *requires* response to multiple cues. For example, asking a child to go and get her red sweater is a conditional discrimination task. This is because the child undoubtedly has more than one red item of clothing and more than one sweater. Correct responding depends on attention to both colour *and* object. Treatment providers are taught to present their children with tasks involving conditional discriminations. As the children learn to respond on the basis of multiple cues their attention is more normalized, allowing additional environmental cues to become functional. As stimulus control of behaviour is no longer as restricted, enhanced generalization should and does result.

The results of naturalistic treatment strategies have been most impressive. In fact many studies have presented data suggesting the superiority of these strategies over the more highly structured behavioural formats such as DTT in terms of the acquisition and generalization of behaviours in children with autism (see Delprato, 2001, for a review). Thus the goal of addressing some of the limitations of the highly structured treatments looks as though it has been realized.

Further, naturalistic strategies seem to be more enjoyable for both the children and the treatment providers. Koegel and his colleagues (1992a) found that children in the naturalistic training were rated as having more positive affect (that is, they were happier) than the children in the DTT training. Further, the researchers found that the children in the naturalistic training showed fewer escape-motivated behaviours such as tantrums and attempts to leave the teaching situation. Schreibman *et al.* (1991) showed naive observers similar videotapes of autistic children working with their parent. Some of the child-parent dyads were engaged in the naturalistic PRT training and the other dyads were engaged in the highly structured DTT training. The observers were asked to rate the parent in terms of enthusiasm, happiness, and interest. As with the children in the earlier study, the parents in Schreibman's 1991 study were rated as having more positive affect. Looking at videotapes of home (dinner time) interactions, Koegel *et al.* (1996) found that naive observers rated the home interactions of families where the parents had been trained in PRT to be more positive than those of families where the parents had been trained in DTT. Taken together, these studies do indeed suggest that naturalistic strategies hold potential for being more positive and pleasant for the child and for the treatment provider.

In order to affect significant improvement in the maximum number of children with autism other extensions and enhancements of behavioural treatment have been developed. These include broadening the range of treatment providers to include parents (for example, Albert & Kaiser, 1992; Schreibman & Koegel, 2005), siblings (Celiberti & Harris; 1993), and peers (Pierce & Schreibman, 1995; Pierce & Schreibman, 1997) into the treatment programmes, and teaching self management to the autistic children as a means of increasing independence (for example, Koegel & Koegel, 1990; Pierce & Schreibman, 1994).

Other recent developments

In more recent years, behavioural treatment research has emphasized the inclusion of functional analysis to identify more precisely any potentially appropriate treatment options. Functional analyses occur when experimental manipulation allows for the determination of the function of a behaviour on the environment. Such information helps to ensure that the best treatment is applied. For example, a child's tantrums might serve different functions. For one child the tantrums may serve to gain attention from others in the environment. For another, the tantrums may serve to escape or to avoid an aversive situation such as participating in an educational activity. The treatment to reduce tantrums in the first case might involve denying the child attention until the tantrums cease. However, the treatment for the second case might involve continuing the educational demands until the tantrums cease. Obviously the treatment procedures are very different and an understanding of the function of the behaviour helps ensure we are right the first time. Of course a better option in both cases would be to teach the child another way to communicate their desires. Learning a socially acceptable alternative to tantrums (for example, saying or using a manual sign to indicate 'I want a break') would allow these more appropriate forms of communication to serve the same function as the tantrums. This is typically referred to as 'functional communication training' and has served to reduce or eliminate need to use more aversive procedures to reduce severely disruptive behaviours (for example, Carr, 1994).

Early intervention

One of the most exciting findings to come from the research in behavioural intervention in autism is the work pointing to the potentially dramatic effects of providing intensive behavioural treatment to children who are very young. Lovaas (1987) studied three groups of very young autistic children (under 41 months of age at the start of treatment). One group, the experimental group (n = 19), received more than 40 hours a week of one-to-one DTT treatment delivered by trained student therapists in the children's home, school, and community. This treatment also included the systematic application of physical aversives for some of the children. In addition, the parents were also taught to work with their children as part of the intensive treatment. A second group of children, control group 1 (n = 19), received the same treatment but at a lesser intensity (fewer than 10 hours a week) and without the application of aversives. A third group, control group 2 (n = 21), did not receive any behavioural treatment. After 2 years the groups were evaluated. The results were quite impressive. Forty seven per cent of the children receiving the intensive treatment achieved 'normal functioning' defined by IQ scores in the normal range and successful passage through first grade in a regular public school classroom. Forty three per cent of the experimental group showed substantial progress although not to the level of 'normal' functioning. Thus fully 90 per cent of the children receiving the intensive early intervention were reported to have had very positive outcomes. This is in contrast to the poor outcome for the children in the control groups. Only one child in control group 2 and no children in control group 1 achieved the criteria designated in the study as 'normal functioning'. Further, the children in the experimental (high intensity) group were followed up at between 9 and 19 years of age and it was reported that they maintained their gains in IQ and were said by their parents to have normal adaptive behaviour and personality functioning.

As can be imagined, the impact of this study was dramatic. However, the study has been subjected to a great deal of criticism because of some rather serious methodological and interpretive flaws (for example, the lack of random assignment to the groups, limited outcome measures, and questions over the representativeness of the samples). While these concerns are significant, and the overall very high optimism of the findings may not be well founded, the fact remains that early intervention is obviously very important. What we do know is that with the development of improved forms of DTT and with the advent of more naturalistic behavioural strategies, there are more options for intervening with effective treatments at an early age. This should lead to an increase in treatment impact.

Individualization of treatment

Despite the continual development of more and more effective and efficient behavioural treatments, the fact remains that no matter which treatment is applied to children with autism, there is still a good deal of variability of treatment outcome. In fact no single form of intervention can realistically boast substantial success in more than 50 to 70 per cent of children. This variability in child response indicates that there are variables that serve to affect treatment outcome, and an understanding of these variables is necessary if we are to develop maximally effective interventions. Once the influence of these variables is understood we should be in a position to tailor treatments to the individual needs of a specific child. Our goal would be to be able to individualize treatment and thus greatly increase the overall effectiveness of treatment for this population.

What types of variables would be important to consider? Such variables would probably include child characteristics, parent and family characteristics, cultural factors, and treatment-behaviour interactions. The ultimate goal is to be in a position to determine *a priori* which treatment procedures will be most effective and efficient with a particular child and a particular family situation, at a particular point in treatment.

Child characteristics

Research on the child characteristics that best predict treatment outcome for a particular intervention is just beginning (Ingersoll *et al.*, 2001; Anderson, 2002). For example, one study has identified a behavioural profile of children who are likely to respond well to PRT, and a separate profile of children who are likely to have a poor response to this treatment (Sherer & Schreibman, in press). These findings can help determine which children are appropriate candidates for PRT. Also, the findings should promote additional research to determine which alternative treatment options are most appropriate for children who meet the profile of a 'non-responder' to PRT (Schreibman *et al.*, 2001). As a field it is important to continue to fine tune this line of research, thus deriving the most benefit from early intervention.

Caregiver characteristics

In addition to child characteristics, it is also important to consider the individual characteristics of the child's caregivers, especially the parents. The field is just beginning to examine how family variables interact with treatment effectiveness. The effects of culture, ethnicity, marital status, parental attitudes, parental age, level of education, socioeconomic status, and other factors may all affect how treatment is best delivered and the ultimate effectiveness of the treatment. For example, research has shown that children of more responsive and educated parents are more likely to benefit from prelinguistic milieu teaching, while children of less responsive and less educated mothers benefit more from responsive small group instruction (Yoder & Warren, 1998). Also, training in self management may be more successfully implemented by parents for whom child independence is important (Schreibman & Koegel, 1996). However, certain cultures may not place a strong emphasis on child independence; thus, the parents may not choose to use self management with their child or may use it ineffectively. Another example is the effect of stress. It has been shown that parents of children with autism report being under high levels of stress (for example, Koegel *et al.*, 1992b). Perhaps parents who are under a good deal of stress at a particular time would be poor candidates to implement training with their child; a clinician may then be the treatment provider of choice. At a later time, if the stress is reduced, these parents could perhaps implement the treatment very effectively.

Treatment/behaviour interactions

It is also important to consider treatment/behaviour interactions. Certain behaviours may be best addressed by one form of treatment as opposed to another. As toileting is perhaps not a behaviour that is intrinsically reinforcing (as toy play might be), it is likely that depending upon child choice as a motivator is unrealistic. Therefore it may be more successful to address this behaviour through more highly structured behaviour training as opposed to a naturalistic strategy.

Conclusions

In response to increased attention on individualization of treatment, many researchers and service providers have come to recognize that multiple behavioural methodologies have a place within a comprehensive treatment programme. Although there are still strong proponents of particular behavioural intervention strategies, researchers and service providers must challenge themselves to explore multiple options for individual children. The combination of improved behavioural technologies plus a focus on identifying important variables for individualization suggest that the future of behavioural intervention for children with autism is most promising. In fact the combination of individualized treatments and early intervention may prove to be our most effective weapon to date in the war against this devastating child disorder.

Acknowledgments: Preparation of this chapter and some of the research reported herein were facilitated by USPHS. Research Grant N° MH39434 from the National Institute of Mental Health.

References

Alpert, C.L. & Kaiser, A.P. (1992): Training parents as milieu language teachers. *J. Early Intervent.* **16**, 31–52.

Anderson, A.E. (2002): Augmentative communication and autism: a comparison of sign language and the picture exchange communication system. (Doctoral dissertation, University of California, San Diego, 2001). *Dissertation Abstracts International* **62**, 4269-B.

Carr, E.G. (1994): Emerging themes in the functional analysis of problem behavior. Special issue: functional analysis approaches to behavioral assessment and treatment. *J. Appl. Behav. Anal.* **27**, 393–399.

Celiberti, D.A. & Harris, S.L. (1993): Behavioral intervention for siblings of children with autism: a focus on skills to enhance play. *Behav. Ther.* **24**, 573–599.

Delprato, D.J. (2001): Comparisons of discrete-trial and normalized behavioral intervention for young children with autism. *J. Autism Dev. Disord.* **31**, 315–325.

Ferster, C.B. & DeMyer, M.K. (1961): The development of performance in autistic children in an automatically controlled environment. *J. Chron. Dis.* **13**, 312–345.

Ferster, C.B. & DeMyer, M.K. (1962): A method for the experimental analysis of the behavior of autistic children. *Am. J. Orthopsychiatry* **32**, 89–98.

Hart, B. & Risley, T.R. (1980): *In vivo* language intervention: unanticipated general effects. *J. Appl. Behav. Anal.* **13**, 407–432.

Ingersoll, B., Schreibman, L. & Stahmer, A. (2001): Brief report: differential treatment outcomes for children with autistic spectrum disorder based on level of peer social avoidance. *J. Autism Dev. Disord.* **31**, 343–349.

Kaiser, A.P., Yoder, P.J. & Keetz, A. (1992): Evaluating milieu training. In: *Causes and effects in communication and language intervention*, eds. S.F. Warren & J. Reichle. Baltimore: P.H. Brookes Publishing Co.

Koegel, R.L. & Schreibman, L. (1977): Teaching autistic children to respond to simultaneous multiple cues. *J. Exp. Child Psychol.* **24**, 299–311.

Koegel, R.L. & Egel, A. (1979): Motivating autistic children. *J. Abnorm. Psychol.* **88**, 418–426.

Koegel, R.L. & Williams, J. (1980): Direct *vs* indirect response-reinforcer relationships in teaching autistic children. *J. Abnorm. Child Psychol.* **4**, 536–547.

Koegel, R.L. & Koegel, L.K. (1990): Extended reductions in stereotypic behavior through self-management in multiple community settings. *J. Appl. Behav. Anal.* **23**, 119–127.

Koegel, R.L., Dyer, K. & Bell, L.K. (1987): The influence of child preferred activities on autistic children's social behavior. *J. Appl. Behav. Anal.* **20**, 243–252.

Koegel, R.L., O'Dell, M.C. & Koegel, L.K. (1987a): A natural language teaching paradigm for non-verbal autistic children. *J. Autism Dev. Disord.* **17**, 187–200.

Koegel, R.L., Schreibman, L., Good, A., Cerniglia, L., Murphy, C. & Koegel, L.L. (1989): *How to teach pivotal behaviors to children with autism: a training manual.* Santa Barbara: University of California.

Koegel, R.L., Koegel, L.K. & Surratt, A. (1992a): Language intervention and disruptive behavior in preschool children with autism. *J. Autism Dev. Disord.* **22**, 141–153.

Koegel, R.L., Schreibman, L., Loos, L.M. & Dirlich-Wilhelm, H. (1992b): Consistent stress profiles in mothers of children with autism. *J. Autism Dev. Disord.* **22**, 205–216.

Koegel, R.L., Bimbela, A. & Schreibman, L. (1996): Collateral effects of parent training on family interactions. *J. Autism Dev. Disord.* **26**, 347–359.

Lovaas, O.I. (1987): Behavioral treatment and normal educational and intellectual functioning in young autistic children. *J. Consult. Clin. Psychol.* **55**, 3–9.

Lovaas, O.I., Koegel, R.L. & Schreibman, L. (1979): Stimulus overselectivity in autism: a review of research. *Psychol. Bull.* **86**, 1236–1254.

Lovaas, O.I., Ackerman, A.B., Alexander, D., Firestone, P., Perkins, J. & Young, D. (1981): *Teaching developmentally disabled children: the ME book.* Austin, Texas: Pro-Ed Publishing.

Maurice, C., Green, G. & Luce, S.C. (1996): *Behavioral intervention for young children with autism: a manual of parents and professionals.* Austin, Texas: Pro-Ed Publishing.

McGee, G.G., Krantz, P.J. & McClannahan, L.E.S. (1985): The facilitative effects of incidental teaching on preposition use by autistic children. *J. Appl. Behav. Anal.* **18**, 17–31.

O'Dell, M.C. & Koegel, R.L. (1981): *The differential effects of two methods of promoting speech in non-verbal autistic children.* Paper presented at the American Speech-Language-Hearing Association, Los Angeles, California, USA.

O'Dell, M.C., Dunlap, G. & Koegel, R.L. (1983): *The importance of reinforcing verbal attempts during speech training with non-verbal children.* Paper presented at the Annual convention of the American Psychological Association, Los Angeles, California, USA.

Pierce, K. & Schreibman, L. (1994): Teaching children with autism daily living skills in unsupervised settings through pictorial self-management. *J. Appl. Behav. Anal.* **27**, 471–481.

Pierce, K. & Schreibman, L. (1995): Increasing complex social behaviors in children with autism: effects of peer-implemented pivotal response training. *J. Appl. Behav. Anal.* **28**, 285–295.

Pierce, K. & Schreibman, L. (1997): Multiple peer use of pivotal response training social behaviors of classmates with autism: results from trained and untrained peers. *J. Appl. Behav. Anal.* **30**, 157–160.

Schreibman, L. (1988): *Autism.* Newbury Park, California: Sage Publications.

Schreibman, L. & Koegel, R.L. (1996): Fostering self-management: parent-delivered pivotal response training for children with autistic disorder. In: *Psychosocial treatments for child and adolescent disorders: empirically based strategies for clinical practice*, eds. E.D. Hibbs & P.S. Jensen, pp. 525–552. Washington, DC: American Psychological Association.

Schreibman, L. & Koegel, R.L. (2005): Training for parents of children with autism: Pivotal responses, generalization, and individualization of interventions. In: *Psychosocial treatment for child and adolescent disorders: empirically based strategies for clinical practice*, 2nd ed, pp. 605–631, eds. E.D. Hibbs & P.S. Jensen. Washington, DC: American Psychological Association.

Schreibman, L., Charlop, M.H. & Koegel, R.L. (1982): Teaching autistic children to use extra-stimulus prompts. *J. Exp. Child Psychol.* **33**, 475–491.

Schreibman, L., Kaneko, W.M. & Koegel, R.L. (1991): Positive affect of parents of autistic children: a comparison across two teaching techniques. *Behav. Ther.* **22**, 479–490.

Schreibman, L., Stahmer, A. & Cestone, V. (2001): *Turning treatment nonresponders into treatment responders: development of individualized treatment protocols for children with autism.* Paper presented at the 1st annual meeting of the International Meeting for Autism Research, San Diego, California, USA.

Sherer, M.R. & Schreibman, L. (in press): Individual behavioral profiles and predictors of treatment effectiveness for children with autism. *Journal of Consulting and Clinical Psychology.*

Turner, B.L. (1978): *The effects of choice of stimulus materials on interest in the remediation process and the generalized use of language training.* [Unpublished master's thesis, University of California, Santa Barbara.]

Yoder, P.J. & Warren, S.F. (1998): Maternal responsivity predicts the prelinguistic communication intervention that facilitates generalized intentional communication. *J. Speech Lang. Hear. Res.* **41**, 1207–1219.

Autistic spectrum disorders, D. Riva and I. Rapin (eds.)

Chapter 20

Psychotherapy: epicrisis of the past and future perspectives

Filippo Muratori

Pisa University – IRCCS Stella Maris, via dei Giacinti 2, 56018 Calambrone (Pisa), Italy
f.muratori@inpe.unipi.it

Summary

In recent years, the role of psychotherapy in the treatment of children with pervasive developmental disorders (PDD) has been questioned. Progress in neuropsychiatry, neuropsychology, and genetics, combined with improved behavioural and educational techniques, has relegated discussions about psychotherapy mostly to reviews dealing with the history of treatment of autism. Even when psychotherapeutic work is suggested, only very structured supportive counselling for older and higher-functioning children and adolescents is usually considered. On the basis of recent changes in the definition and role of psychotherapy in developmental psychopathology, it is argued that there is still a role for psychotherapy for children with PDD and that psychotherapeutic interventions should begin at a younger rather than an older age. Different types of psychotherapy for different types and needs of children and their families will be considered, focusing on the role of psychotherapeutic interventions in an integrated treatment project.

Introduction

The relation between psychotherapy and autism over the last 60 years shaped the history of modern child psychiatry and also represents a paradigm of its difficulties. When Kanner (1943) described his 11 children with autism, there was a general trend to search for the psychogenetic nature of mental disorders and a too hurried shift from observing difficult child-parent relationships towards considering such difficulties as the cause of the disorder. At the same time psychotherapy was considered a powerful instrument capable of acting on the original causes of mental disorders, to remove them, and to allow the individual to regain a state of normality. Historically, the ascent of psychoanalysis was a time of tremendous optimism (some might now say grandiosity) in this respect. Psychotherapy was readily considered to be an instrument for recovery instead of a type of care to be adapted to individual cases.

The psychogenetic theories of autism sprang from this double historical happening, as for many years did the idea that psychotherapy was really the only treatment that could affect the evolution of this disorder. Mistakes resulting from the acceptance of this point of view were serious, but nowadays we consider them past history. Many years ago Francis Tustin (1977) stated: 'In the past much unnecessary hurt has been caused by attributing undue blame to mothers of psychotic children. Sadly, this has often come from psychotherapeutic quarters, where the aim should be to understand rather than to blame. Parents, and particularly the mothers, are often in a state of acute distress due to years of living in close proximity to a psychotic child, a far more upsetting condition than living with any other sort of handicap. In my opinion, phrases such as "refrigerator mothers" and "schizophrenogenic mothers" have distorted our approach to psychotic patients. It has been my experience that there are many varied factors which can cause a breakdown in the early attachment processes. Some of these factors are possible organic, cognitive, muscular, sensory or affective defects in the child.'

It seems that we have now moved to a new and opposite paradigm (Eisenberg, 2001). The fact that autism (as for many if not all psychiatric disorders) can be better understood as a biological dysfunction of the brain leads increasingly to a denial that psychotherapy has any role as a therapeutic tool in this condition. Generally speaking, research in psychotherapy has been poor; in the field of autism it is almost absent (Kasari, 2002; Ruberman, 2002). In other words it seems that, as knowledge of psychiatric and neurobiological disorders is widening, at the same time the field of psychotherapy is narrowing, almost to zero. According to this new paradigm, which is just as pseudoscientific as the previous one, the more autism is seen as a neurobiological disorder, the more unsuitable psychotherapy appears as an intervention. No serious attempt to study the role of psychotherapy in treating autism has been carried out; behavioural treatments (also called 'surface interventions', as opposed to treatments that try to modify the emotional-affective patterns by insight) have been considered more consistent with the nature of the disorder and were progressively developed. I shall try to show that this paradigm is deeply wrong and risks leading psychiatry into an amentalistic drift which could make it insensitive and mechanistic.

A new background for psychotherapy

Nancy Andreasen (2000) recently wrote that the enormous progress in psychopharmacology, molecular biology, imaging, and genetics which characterized the last part of the 20th century has sparked concern that the focus of psychiatry might become exclusively biological, with the consequent risk of losing any human implications of the discipline. A result of such biological reductionism is the fragmentation of psychiatric care, and the risk that psychiatrists lose their listening and observing skills, becoming only 'diagnosis makers' and 'pill prescribers'. As recently indicated by Leon Eisenberg (2001), in a brief but incisive paper on the modifications of child psychiatry in the USA during the past 50 years, the moment has come to invent paradigms that will give new meanings to the old term 'psychogenetic': a term that, far from being the expression of a psychological reductionism, indicates the need to create bridges between neurobiology, human behaviour, emotion, and social context, on which new foundations for developmental psychopathology and child psychiatry can be established. Neurobiological research on the role that experience plays in shaping brain anatomy seems a suitable basis for such a challenge. Early brain development (neuron differentiation and migration to the proper area of the brain, the growth of axons, synapse development, apoptosis) – which in the very first stages of development is based on intrinsic factors that are largely independent of the environment – becomes heavily experience-dependent after birth (Schore, 1996); this means that experience plays a decisive role in refining connections between neurons and in developing their functional specialisation (Hockfield & Lambroso, 1998). According to Kandel (1998), one of the basic principles of the 21st century psychiatry concerns the complex relation between genes and the environment. As stated by this principle, behaviour is able to modify gene expressivity, and gene alterations are not able, alone, to explain all the variations that a major mental disorder may assume. According to these principles, social relationships, conversational sequences, and development-specific behaviours need to be considered as factors affecting the brain by feedback mechanisms capable of modifying gene expressivity and brain cell function. As stated by Eisenberg (2000), psychotherapy may literally modify brain structure by altering brain function.

Psychotherapy and autism

Kanner described children with autism as 'children that come to the world with an inborn disorder in affective contact with people, just as other children come to the world with a physical or intellective handicap'. Kanner's great intuition is today widely confirmed both by clinical studies signalling a defect in joint attention skills as early cues for autism, and by imaging studies indicating dysfunction in the complex cortical networks of areas assigned to sensory, motor, social, affective, and emotional regulation. From this point of view psychotherapy, which is easy to describe as a technique capable of supporting the development of affect and relationships through the contact between two minds, appears to be a pertinent intervention for autism, as physiotherapy can be for motor disorders or speech therapy for language disorders. In disorders such as autism, where the core dysfunction involves cortical areas deputed to the child's entrance to the world of social relationships, it is necessary to think about interventions aiming to augment children's social functions.

The role of psychotherapy could assume even greater importance if the concept of autism as an innate disorder is further clarified. In the development of humans, 'innate' does not mean not modifiable and chronically stable, as it is often easily interpreted; it does on the other hand mean that there is a dysfunction which can become a chronic deficit if no environmental factor intervenes to modify the relation between genetic programming and clinical expression. Research on the first years of life in children with autism through home video recordings has led us to the view that autism is also an innate disorder. In fact research in this field confronted us with infants and toddlers without any clear symptomatic organization and in whom the autistic disorder is organized around fluctuating and 'soft' deficits in intersubjective skills (Maestro *et al.*, 2001). Among these, children with autism fail to orient according to naturally occurring social stimuli (Dawson *et al.*, 1998) and it is suggested that impairments in social orienting may contribute to the difficulties in shared attention found in autism. In our research on the first 6 months of life in children with autism through home videos, infants with autism also showed a specific qualitative pattern of attention, highly consistent with theories predicting that such children have a specific deficit in responding to social stimuli, while attention paid to objects does not distinguish autistic from normal infants (Maestro *et al.*, 2002). This probably means that attention is not implicated as a primary function but as an elective function only towards social stimuli. But a second study (Maestro *et al.*, 2005) has produced some unexpected findings: the first consists of a decrease in differences during the second semester of life between normal and autistic children as far as attention to social stimuli is concerned; the second consists of an increase in behaviour involving attention to non-social stimuli, which is present in both groups but more evident in infants with autism, so that at the end of the first year these children are significantly more attracted by objects than normal children. A confirmation of this early disconnection in attention directed to objects and humans has been proposed recently by Schultz *et al.* (2000). Using functional magnetic resonance imaging to study face and object perception, they found that during face (but not object) discrimination, the autism group had significantly different activation from controls in some cerebral areas and they concluded that individuals with autism have a pattern of brain activity during face discrimination that is consistent with the pattern more typical of object perception.

This decreased or distorted interest in the human face has a devastating effect on the brain, which is programmed to assume that the face (of the mother) is the most powerful visual stimulus for development of infant intersubjectivity, which in turn plays an essential role for the development of parenting. This defect in the early dyadic social system seems to represent a core feature of autistic disorder on which psychotherapy can maintain its appropriate role as a technique capable of sustaining interpersonal emotional-cognitive circuitry. Paraphrasing Carver & Dawson (2002), it is possible to believe that, if children with autism are not capable of developing a specialized system for face recognition, a focus of early intervention would be to motivate children to look at and take an interest in human faces; changing the environmental input by training children to become face experts might provide an important stimulus to this neural system that could have a remedial effect. Moreover, we know that, in normal development, interest in faces is associated with specific attention provoked in the infant by the very distinctive manner of an affectionate adult's vocalisations in the presence of a baby. 'Motherese' or infant-directed speech has well-defined rhythmic and melodic features as well as voicing qualities. It is organized in repeated phrases with higher pitch, larger range, and longer pauses, and tends to create slowly changing cyclical narratives of emotion. Comparison of parent's speech to infants in different languages confirms that there are universal rhythmic and prosodic features in the expression of human feelings and sympathetic interest (Fernald, 1989; Fernald & Mazzie, 1991). Fernald has also found that when infants listen to recorded words addressed by the mother to an absent child, the strong attention and increased sucking that occur when the mother talks directly to the child are absent; he also showed how the typical prosodic peaks were absent in the recorded voice, and that this was the reason why the infant showed so little interest in the mother language. Trevarthen & Aitken (2001) have recently focused their attention on the child's strong aptitude to motherese and on its central role not only for language development but also for emotional development and infant intersubjectivity. In home videos of children it is clear that when an adult voice has the characteristics of motherese, infants and toddlers with autism show focal attention: their faces seem to light up and they show unexpected interactive skills. The observation of empathic interactive sequences aroused by the motherese demonstrates their important role in supporting early integrative functions that are otherwise defective, and indicates how far we are from those psychotherapeutic techniques that use verbal language as the main tool of communication with these children. For a long time such children have been treated on the basis of a false hypothesis that verbal interpretations explaining past events could help them, without considering the severe impairment in their mental functioning. By contrast, Alvarez (1992), one of the most advanced psychotherapists treating children with autism, signals the following as essential for psychotherapy with such children: a preverbal musical language; minor attention to the past in favour of prompt attention to the quality of the current relationship; an active search for visual contact and for appropriate physical distance; attention to voice tone, speed, and grade of intensity; and one-trace simplified comments taking account of the specific difficulties that children with autism show in retaining two ideas in the mind simultaneously (Bruner's two-trace thought).

Psychotherapeutic interventions should begin at a younger rather than an older age

Research on the development of autistic disorder, both through observation of home videos and through early screening (for example, using the checklist for autism in the toddler (CHAT; Baron-Cohen *et al.*, 1992), revealed the difficulties in early diagnosis. Such difficulties were highlighted by a 6-year follow-up study of the population of children screened at 18 months with the CHAT. This study (Baird *et al.*, 2000) revealed a large false-negative group (over 50 per cent), composed of children who were not recognized as autistic at 18 to 24 months of age because they showed behaviour at that age considered to represent theory-of-mind precursors (such as pointing and joint attention). The fact that these children were later diagnosed as having autism or PDD suggests that there are different types of onset and in particular a late-onset form which requires more sophisticated diagnostic tools. Another problem connected to early diagnosis emerged from a study by Stone *et al.* (1999) which showed a variable proportion (15 to 30 per cent) of children initially diagnosed with autism in whom the diagnosis was no longer considered to be correct after two years. This latter evidence persuaded the diagnostic classification (DC) 0–3 (Zero-to-Three Classification Task Force – National Centre for Clinical Infant Programs, 1994) to introduce a new diagnostic category called Multisystemic Developmental Disorders, which are severe but curable disorders of relationship and communication characterized by a disturbance of sensory regulation which results in a non-permanent disorder of interaction. For the majority of these children, the relationship problem is not evident in the first year of life but occurs later in connection with difficulties in processing sensations (Muratori *et al.*, 2001). The link that DC 0–3 poses between disorders of sensory and emotional regulation and autistic disorders is of particular interest in light of recent work by Casanova *et al.* (2002) on the specific minicolumnar pathology in some prefrontal and temporal areas of autistic subjects. Based on necropsy findings showing more numerous, smaller, and less compact cell columns in brains of autistic patients, Casanova argued that the basis of autism is a disorder of the arousal-modulating systems of the brain. According to this theory, children with autism experience a chronic state of overarousal and show abnormal behaviour to diminish it. This arousal theory is of interest because it is consistent with a reduction of inhibitory interneuronal activity, which would affect the ability to discriminate between competing types of sensory information. Such evidence on the complex underlying neurobiological network seems to suggest a dynamic view of autism, but in spite of this, the approach in the majority of children is still based on obsolete and static theories, both psychotherapeutic and behavioural. This dynamic perspective on autism is well represented by Mundy's hypothesis (Mundy & Crowson, 1997; Mundy & Neal, 2001), that autism has its root in an initial pathological process which only later leads to a secondary neurological disorder. The hypothesis of an initial pathological process (which in my view could be partially modifiable through early treatment) seems to suggest that autism reflects early dysfunction in a complex cortical-subcortical network, congruent with clinical expression which clearly emerges from the research on home videos.

Treatment of core symptoms

An original form of treatment is that proposed by the CHAT Group (and in parallel by Sigman's group in Los Angeles). On the basis of the centrality of joint attention deficit, Drew *et al.* (2002) defined a model of treatment based on parent training of joint attention sequence stimulation and its precursors. They have tried to assess the efficacy of such a treatment through a randomized clinical study on a sample of 24 children (mean age 23 months) reassessed after one year of treatment. The improvement shown by the treatment group involved language development but not social interaction or non-verbal communication, as anticipated at the start of the study. It is interesting to note that preliminary results of Bono's study (Bono *et al.*, 2002) reported meaningful progress in linguistic development of children treated by similar joint attention early stimulation. To focus the therapeutic work on joint attention is of particular importance because it is now considered to be a pivotal skill in normal development and a deficit in joint attention is considered to be a core symptom of autism (Charman, 2003). Dawson *et al.* (2002) hypothesized that a deficit in joint attention was primary and was followed by the executive function deficit. These investigators found that 3- to 4-year-old children with autism did not show differences in executive function compared with normal children or with children with mental retardation, but were equal in mental age in this respect; they did, however, show differences in joint attention tasks. They concluded that the neurocognitive theory of autism, based on the presence of a primary deficit of executive function, could be a false notion derived from a knowledge of older children; older children indeed have a deficit of executive function but it should be considered secondary to the early primary deficit of joint attention. From this point of view the social deficit is not secondary to a basic cognitive problem, and the cognitive hypothesis of autism seems rather to be a source of misunderstanding, considering both the characteristics of normal social development (Stern, 1985) and other recent research which points out clear differences in early development between children with autism and children with mental retardation (Osterling *et al.*, 2002).

Along these lines, Trevarthen & Aitken (2001) proposed – contrary to many theories that place the physical object awareness as the central problem in early development – that purposeful intersubjectivity is fundamental for human mental development. The infant is thus proved to possess an active and immediately responsive conscious appreciation of the adult's communicative intentions (primary intersubjectivity). The baby's increasing interest in objects is observed to grow in competition with the earlier developed motives for protoconversational play, leading, around the middle of the first year, to the elaboration of more lively games with objects. Just before the end of the first year, there was a rather sudden development of joint interest of the mother and her infant in their surroundings. An important stage in mental activity is represented by the development of joint mother-infant attention towards external objects. The development of these joint attention sequences is, according to Trevarthen, an expression of secondary intersubjectivity (or person-person-object awareness), and has major consequences for the way the adult acts and talks to the child. The development of this intersubjectivity should be the focus of any therapy of autism, and the attention paid to it could bring about a developmentally oriented therapeutic approach. Psychotherapy should be conceived as a method for increasing the links between emotional-affective and cognitive skills in the context of human interactions and considering the child's developmental level. That psychotherapy must be heavily oriented to child development is a mandatory acquisition for anybody aiming to undertake psychotherapeutic work; in contrast to behavioural programmes, psychotherapeutic programmes need to increase the cognitive-emotional integrative circuitry.

Psychotherapy and the DIR model

Among the approaches involving a model based on the increase of such circuits rather that on behavioural conditioning, the Developmental, Individual Differences, Relationship Based (DIR) model (also called 'Floortime Approach') has to be considered (Greenspan & Wieder, 1998; Greenspan & Wieder, 1999; Greenspan, 2000). The theory underlying this programme is that affective development is not separate from cognitive and language development. Moreover, it considers affect as the organizing principle of development. The treatment is developmentally organized, taking affect and the capacity for relationships into account. It is a kind of treatment that underlines the importance of identifying, first, the level of functional and emotional development reached by the child; second, the individual differences in the modality of sensory and motor information processing; and third, the kind of relationships and interactions that the child establishes with adults. The core of this treatment is the functional development (where 'functional' means the child's ability to use their own skills to reach an emotional object or to satisfy a need) of interactive modalities appropriate for the child's developmental level, affective tone, motivation, and the specific difficulties in information processing. Such interactive modalities aim to establish and to increase more circuits of communication, expanding both the range of emotional states and the skills for communication and symbolisation in the child. It begins at the point where the child starts to turn away from the parents' smiles and from their attempts to make contact. It is a therapeutic tool which implies engagement by a relevant parent or other adult caregiver; it further implies that much of the time at the child's disposal is spent in the following interactive aims:

- to undertake a multisensory affective experience and at the same time keep a state of regulated calm (looking at, listening to, and following the other's movements);
- to express pleasure when relating to a caregiver and to show an affective preference towards the caregiver;
- to initiate and respond to mutual gestures and presymbolic communication (smiles, sounds);
- to integrate affective polarities and show the start of self/other representations (take Daddy's hand to take a toy from a shelf);
- to use ideas in a functional way as a basis for creative thinking (pretend play);
- to build bridges among ideas as a basis for a reality test;
- to facilitate sensory modulation (hypo- and hyper-reactivity to touch, sounds, smells, sight, or movements), sensory processing (verbal-auditory and visuospatial), sensory-affective processing, motor planning, and language.

In the course of treatment, meaning is given to actions through their connection to emotions, intentions, and affect. Throughout this work on the role of affect in mental development, both in terms of individual differences and for processing mechanisms, DIR has been shown to be more effective than cognitive models in building cognitive and affective patterns.

Conclusions

Greenspan (2000) is careful to contrast his floor time method with psychotherapy or play therapy. Traditional psychotherapeutic efforts tend to engage the child in a type of parallel play where the child feels the clinician's warmth and support but is not mobilized into types of interaction that are likely to lead to growth in the critical areas of development. Historically this type of psychotherapy has not proven especially helpful for the majority of children with autistic patterns. But present-day psychotherapists may be well informed both psychodynamically and developmentally. We are certainly very far from a 'defences and transfer interpretation' centred psychotherapy, and we can safely say that it does *not* work in autism. The capacity for internalisation in these children is so poor and selective, and their cognitive skills so peculiar, that the time needed to engage in mental representations and defences is often impossibly long. What we are facing in such situations is not any resistance to making contact from a dynamic point of view, but the incapability of making contact from a different way of incorporating the world around.

Kanner's description of the phenomenology of autism included lack of imagination and of an inner creative life, which is in direct contrast to the idea of psychic drive taking refuge in a fantasy as a consequence of an early negative experience. This part of Kanner's original description seems to have been lost for many psychotherapists, who proceed along lines of tremendous optimism, diametrically opposed to Freud's pessimistic view at the end of his life when he raised questions about the possibility of recovering from neurosis. On the other hand, psychotherapists have long thought that an unconditioned experience of love and containment could allow the autistic child to emerge from their shell as if by magic.

However, we are also far from the idea presented in the practice parameters of the American Academy of Child and Adolescent Psychiatry Society (Volkmar *et al.*, 1999), that psychotherapy may be particularly appropriate for older and higher-functioning children. On the other hand, the observations discussed here support the importance of early work conducted on integrational and regulatory processes that imply emotions and affect. It could be argued that what I have tried to describe as psychotherapy is in fact a simple, warm affective relationship based on play and a fair knowledge of development. This question can be left open for the moment, but we should remember that the psychotherapeutic formula may allow augmentation of empathic skills which are essential when dealing with children affected by an empathy disorder. Shapiro (2000) suggests some central points for psychotherapy in such clinical situations:

(1) The language and verbal play of the child with autism are more likely to be related to sound and phonetic similarities than to meaning streams.
(2) Play requires understanding for its repetitiveness, but we must not reach too quickly for unconscious fantasy as the mediating mental force. Indeed, repetitive rigidity may instead derive from need for mastery, pleasure in repetition, and positive reinforcement for pleased adults.
(3) Insofar as children with autism incorporate schemes of action, such as imitative behaviours, they tend to remain like foreign bodies within and are only gradually assimilated as unique parts of well-functioning self and ego systems.
(4) As increasing self-consciousness is apparent, these children may be vulnerable to emotional hurt and personal injury as they are excluded and not recognized. The humane quality of the therapeutic relationship must be maintained and the therapist be available both to contain the emotions and to reflect on social skills with an eye toward better adaptation.

Many of the positions stated in this chapter are not new, but they may be new for some psychotherapists, either psychoanalytic or cognitive or behaviourally oriented. The chapter is designed more to inform than to criticize, hoping that this point of view will enable us to use the appropriate therapeutic tools at our disposal effectively. In this manner we will best serve our patients and our profession and not extend our therapy beyond the limits of what we know.

References

Alvarez, A. (1992): *Live company*. London: Tavistock/Routledge.

Andreasen, N.C.A. (2000): Prediction in clinical psychiatry: what does the future hold? *Am. J. Psychiatry* **157**, 1373–1374.

Baird, C., Charman, T., Baron-Cohen, S., Cox, A., Swettenham, J., Wheelwright, S. & Drew, A. (2000): A screening instrument for autism at 18 months of age: a 6-year follow-up study. *J. Am. Acad. Child Adolesc. Psychiatry* **39**, 694–702.

Baron-Cohen, S., Allen, J. & Gillberg, C. (1992): Can autism be detected at 18 months? The needle, the haystack and the CHAT. *Br. J. Psychiatry* **161**, 839–843.

Bono, M.A., Daley, T., Travis, L. & Sigman, M. (2002): Response to joint attention moderates the relation between amount of intervention and gain in language age in young children with autism. In: *Proceedings of the IMFAR Congress*, Orlando, Florida.

Carver, L.J. & Dawson, G. (2002): Development and neural bases of face recognition in autism. *Mol. Psychiatry* **7**, S18-S20

Casanova, M.F., Buxhoeveden, D.P., Switala, A.E. & Roy, E. (2002): Minicolumnar pathology in autism. *Neurology* **58**, 428–432.

Charman, T. (2003): Why is joint attention a pivotal skill in autism? *Phil. Trans. R. Soc. Lond.* **358**, 315–324.

Dawson, G., Meltzoff, A.N., Osterling, J., Rinaldi, J. & Brown, E. (1998): Children with autism fail to orient to naturally occurring social stimuli. *J. Autism Dev. Disord.* **28**, 479–485.

Dawson, G., Munson, J. & Estes, A. (2002): Neurocognitive function and joint attention ability in young children with autism spectrum disorder *versus* developmental delay. *Child Dev.* **73**, 345–358.

Drew, A., Baird, G., Baron-Cohen, S., Cox, A., Slonims, V., Wheelwright, S., Swettenham, J., Berry, B. & Charman, T. (2002): A pilot randomised control trial of a parent training intervention for pre-school children with autism: preliminary findings and methodological challenges. *Eur. Child Adolesc. Psychiatry* **11**, 266–272.

Eisenberg, L. (2000): Is psychiatry more mindful or brainier than it was a decade ago? *Br. J. Psychiatry* **176**, 1–5.

Eisenberg, L. (2001): The past 50 years of child and adolescent psychiatry: a personal memoir. *J. Am. Acad. Child Adolesc. Psychiatry* **40**, 743–748.

Fernald, A. (1989): Intonation and communicative interest in mother's speech to infants: is the melody the message? *Child Dev.* **6**, 1497–1510.

Fernald, A. & Mazzie, C. (1991): Prosody and focus in speech to infants and adults. *Dev. Psychol.* **27**, 209–221.

Greenspan, S.I. (2000): Children with autistic spectrum disorders: individual differences, affect, interaction, and outcomes. *Psychoanalytic Inquiry* **20**, 675–703.

Greenspan, S.I. & Wieder, S. (1998): *The child with special needs: Intellectual and emotional growth*. Reading, MA: Addison Wesley Longman.

Greenspan, S.I. & Wieder, S. (1999): A functional developmental approach to autism spectrum disorders. *Journal of the Association for Persons with Severe Handicaps* **24**, 147–161.

Hockfield, S. & Lombroso, P.J. (1998): Development of the cerebral cortex. IX. Cortical development and experience. *J. Am. Acad. Child Adolesc. Psychiatry* **37**, 992–993.

Kandel, E. (1998): A new intellectual framework for psychiatry. *Am. J. Psychiatry* **155**, 457–469

Kanner, L. (1943): Autistic disturbances of affective contact. *Nerv. Child* **2**, 217–250.

Kasari, C. (2002): Assessing change in early intervention programs for children with autism. *J. Autism Dev. Disord.* **32**, 447–461.

Maestro, S., Muratori, F., Barbieri, F., Casella, C., Cattaneo, V., Cavallaro, M.C., Cesari, A., Milone, A., Rizzo, L., Viglione, V., Stern, D. & Palacio-Espasa, F. (2001): Early behavioral development in autistic children: the first two years of life through the home movies. *Psychopathology* **34**, 147–152.

Maestro, S., Muratori, F., Cavallaro, M.C., Pei, F., Stern, D., Golse, B. & Palacio-Espasa, F. (2002): Attentional skills during the first 6 months of age in autism spectrum disorder. *J. Am. Acad. Child Adolesc. Psychiatry* **41**, 1239–1245.

Maestro, S., Muratori, F., Cavallaro, M.C., Pecini, C., Cesari, A., Paziente, A., Stern, D., Golse, B. & Palacio-Espasa, F. (2005): How young children treat objects and people: an empirical study of the first year of life in autism. *Child Psychiatry and Human development* **35**.

Mundy, P. & Crowson, M. (1997): Joint attention and early social communication: implications for research on intervention with autism. *J. Autism Dev. Disord.* **27**, 653–676.

Mundy, P. & Neal, R. (2001): Neural plasticity; joint attention, and autistic developmental pathology. *Int. Rev. Res. Mental. Retard.* **23**, 139–168.

Muratori, F., Cosenza, A. & Parrini, B. (2001): Disturbi multisistemici dello sviluppo. In: *Manuale di psicopatologia dell'infanzia*, ed. M. Ammaniti. Milan: Raffaello Cortina.

National Center for Infants, Toddlers, and Families (1994): *Zero to Three, Diagnostic classification 0–3*. Washington DC.

Osterling, J.A., Dawson, G. & Munson, J.A. (2002): Early recognition of 1-year-old infants with autism spectrum disorder *versus* mental retardation. *Dev. Psychopathol.* **14**, 239–251.

Ruberman, L. (2002): Psychotherapy of children with pervasive developmental disorders. *Am. J. Psychother.* **56**, 262–273.

Schore, A.N. (1996): The experience-dependent maturation of a regulatory system in the orbital prefrontal cortex and the origin of developmental psychopathology. *Dev. Psychopathol.* **8**, 59–87.

Schultz, R.T., Gauthier, I., Klin, A., Fulbright, R.K., Anderson, A.W., Volkmar, F., Skudlarski, P., Lacadie, C., Cohen, D.J. & Gore, J.C. (2000): Abnormal ventral temporal cortical activity during face discrimination among individuals with autism and Asperger syndrome. *Arch. Gen. Psychiatry* **57**, 331–340.

Shapiro, T. (2000): Autism and the psychoanalyst. *Psychoanalytic Inquiry* **20**, 648–659.

Stern, D.N. (1985): *The interpersonal world of the infant.* New York: Basic Books.

Stone, W.L., Lee, E.B., Ashford, L., Hepburn, S.L., Coonrod, E.E. & Weiss, B.H. (1999): Can autism be diagnosed accurately in children under 3 years? *J. Child Psychol. Psychiatry* **40**, 219–226.

Trevarthen, C. & Aitken, K.J. (2001): Infant intersubjectivity: research, theory and clinical applications. *J. Child Psychol. Psychiatry* **42**, 3–48.

Tustin, F. (1977): Psychotherapy with psychotic children. *Child Psychotherapist* 232–250.

Volkmar, F.R. (2000): Understanding autism: implications for psychoanalysis. *Psychoanalytic Inquiry* **20**, 660–674.

Volkmar, F., Cook, E.H., Pomeroy, J., Realmuto, G. & Tanguay, P. (1999): Practice parameters for the assessment and treatment of children, adolescents and adults with autism and other pervasive developmental disorders. American Academy of Child and Adolescent Psychiatry Working Group on Quality Issues. *J. Am. Acad. Child Adolesc. Psychiatry* **38** (Suppl.), 32S–54S.

Autistic spectrum disorders, D. Riva and I. Rapin (eds.)
© 2005 John Libbey Eurotext, pp. 197–205.

Chapter 21

Semi-residential treatment of autism in young children: past choices and future prospects

Carla Marzani and Rita A. Montoli

UONPIA, Niguarda Hospital, piazza Ospedale Maggiore 3, 20162 Milan, Italy
rita.montoli@iol.it

Summary

The experience of a working group, which from the 1980s onwards has been conducting research on forms of infantile psychosis, has been transferred to the Lombardy Region's Service on Mental Health in Children (UONPIA), operating at the Niguarda hospital.
At the outset the theory and practice of infantile psychoanalysis formed the basis of this work, adapted where necessary for treating severe cases. This approach has also been included in the activities of the Regional Rehabilitation Centre, whose semi-residential work aims at dealing with the most difficult cases of psychosis, those of autistic children in particular.
In the last few years, recently acquired knowledge and further experience gained on the causes of developmental disorders in children – as well as a clearer understanding of autistic core functions – has greatly altered our approach to diagnosis and treatment. Importance is attached to integration between the cognitive-relational and psychodynamic approaches.
The semi-residential centre at present offers a service for assessing and treating children between the ages of 3 and 6, often referred by paediatricians or by other professionals working in this field, in whom autism is suspected. Starting from the paediatrician's opinion of the child, the basis for diagnosis is a case history drawn up after observation of parent-child interaction and rating scales (PEP, CARS, and so on) over a period of about 15 hours spread over several days. In addition to this, eight children are treated at the centre, each for three mornings a week, with the primary aim of forming an attachment and recreating a 'social loop' as rapidly as possible by applying intensive educational programmes. Close contact is also maintained with parents so that a clearer understanding of the child's difficulties may be gained and support given to assist with subsequent development.

Introduction

The work now being done at Lombardy Region's Service on Mental Health in Children (UONPIA) is a continuation of the many years of experience gained since the 1980s in the semi-residential treatment of psychotic children with severe cognitive disorders. The present organization is one of the few of its kind in Lombardy considered essential by the Region and forming part of the UONPIA plan.

The child guidance clinic in Via Cherasco was set up in 1975 at the initiative of Dr. M.E. Berrini, and later became the Milan municipality's Mental Hygiene Service for Children

(SIMEE), formerly the Italian Society for Infantile Neuropsychiatry (SINPI). From its earliest days, the new service was organized as a centre for treating these types of serious disorders in young children, taking a holistic view that included the child's family and environmental relationships.

Staff training was based on psychodynamic psychoanalytic theory, of great interest at that time, later followed by practical work, taking as an example the psychiatric services for children set up in France.

The semi-residential work, which started in 1980, was for some years open both to psychotic cases and to children with biologically based cognitive disorders. However, after a few years of inactivity, work was resumed in 1990 specifically directed towards psychotic and autistic cases.

The basic idea, fully accepted by the staff and with psychodynamic psychotherapeutic supervision, was to create a warm and welcoming atmosphere where friendships could be formed, and a homely environment in which the children could live through the main activities of the day (arrival, play, visit to the bathroom, mealtime, rest hour). In this way a new primary relationship could be developed, with the potential to re-establish sensorimotor and perceptive experiences, along with greater independence.

In support of the environmental effect, individual programmes of education, psychotherapy, or rehabilitation were added according to specific needs, as well as concentrated work with the parents and with the school, which was attended for a few hours each day by all the children.

Educational practice was based on techniques adopted by well known psychotherapists (Tustin, Corominas, Alvarez) in their work with autistic children – namely the provision of a structured and safe environment offering consistent stimulation of a selective nature.

A clearer understanding of the probable physical causes of infantile autism, as well as the development of treatment techniques based on learning theories, were at this time providing the stimulus for a partial revision of the educational programmes for such children. The need was felt for a more precise appreciation of the significance of the autistic process and of the child's level of perception and awareness. The Psychoeducational Profile (PEP), the Child Autism Rating Scale (CARS), and later the Vineland rating scales were thus included in routine treatment, revising the content of some educational sessions and introducing methods derived from psychoeducational approaches such as TEACCH.

Only in the schoolyear 2000–2001, however, was a decision taken for a radical change in the work of the clinic, and for setting up a specific module for evaluating and treating development disorders in young children from 3 to 6 years of age (Table 1). Alongside this, the usual activities were continued for the older children who were still attending the clinic.

Summary of recent experience

The new work we have been undertaking is based on the positive results – and therefore their social utility – achieved by the early intervention programmes carried out in the USA and summarized by Guralnick (1988). These programmes were applied to children with problems of late development, prematurity, autism, and others, and to families which faced difficulties in looking after them. As the author himself says, the programmes lacked homogeneity, which makes comparisons difficult, but the fact emerges that intensive treatment – both when concentrated over several hours and when spread out over a longer period – enables progress to be made in development without causing any great delay in the acquisition of functions. For details of the content see Table 2.

Table 1. Project for intensive early treatment at the UONPIA semi-residential unit, Niguarda Hospital, Milan

Dr. R.A. Montoli, coordinator and scientific adviser for the project Dr. E. Brunati, chief, and child psychiatrist Dr. C. Marzani, former chief child psychiatrist
Team: 2 professional educators (D. Acerbi, P. Incoronato); 4 psychologists (D. Biunno, organizational coordination, A. Bottani, C. Carenzi, A. Gernone), each working about 4 hours a week
Project, March 2002 to March 2004, financed by the Cariplo Foundation.

Table 2. USA early intensive psychoeducational treatment

Since the 1960s in the U.S. early intensive psychoeducational treatment is being provided (Lovaas, 1967; Dawson & Osterling, 1997): • early (from 2–3 years of age) lasting 2–3 years • intensive (at least 20 hours a week) • educational (based mainly on *Applied Behavioural Analysis*) • integrated (focusing direct imitative stimulation, social play, intersubjectivity, communication, autonomy, language) • specific for a precise diagnosis of the different areas

One programme that appeared to be of particular educational interest, which was not mentioned by Guralnick, is the Denver Model initiated in 1981 and supported by the US Department of Education Handicapped Children's Early Education Programs and by the University of Colorado. This was planned by Dr. Sally J. Rogers and her collaborators. Dr. Montoli attended a series of Rogers' seminars and was therefore able to make direct contact with the application of this method. The theoretical basis of Rogers' work was described in 1991 (Rogers & Pennington, 1991).

Rogers supports a theory of autistic development based on the psychology of development, following the stages of evolution of self by Stern in *The interpersonal world of the infant* (1985) (Table 3).

Table 3. Stages of evolution of self according to Stern (1985)

Stage 1 (0–2 months) *self-emerging*: exchanges of imitation and talking, start of social representation and exchange Stage 2 (2–6 months) *self-focal*: child now a socially organized and motivated partner; exchange, regulation, and modulation takes place mainly on affect and excitement Stage 3 (6–9 months) *self-subjective*: child now aware of own and other's minds, mental states become object of the relationship (affect tuning). Intersubjectivity (shared attention, referential gestures, declarative pointing) Stage 4 (10–24 months) *self-verbal*: symbolic communication, language and play

Rogers sees (Fig. 1), as an essential core of autistic development, an inborn deficit in the ability to *imitate* in the early months of life; later on (or perhaps the basis for this is also inborn) this turns into a difficulty in *synthesizing emotional conditions* and therefore in achieving *intersubjectivity* (impaired 'theory of mind'), all of which leads to withdrawal from social contact and from there towards autistic isolation (Fig. 2).

She states with great clarity the differences between her hypothesis of autistic development and those propounded by Hobson and Baron-Cohen in the late 1980s, in the sense that Hobson considered a 'deficit of innate ability to interact emotionally with others' to be of prime importance, while Baron-Cohen preferred 'an innate deficit of metarepresentation'.

The Denver model treats this precocious 'derailment' of functions, which leads to intersubjectivity and therefore to symbolization and to language, with a programme based on two essential elements:

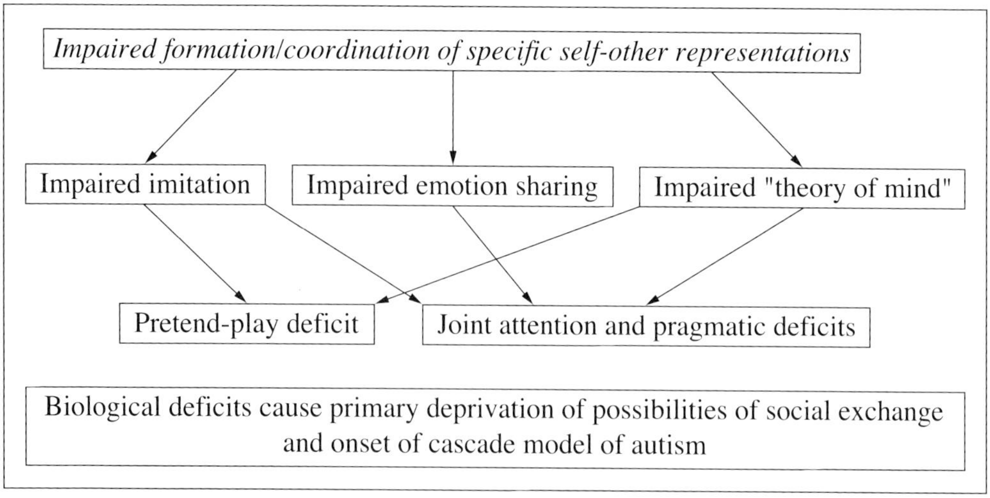

Fig. 1. Theory of intersubjectivity (Rogers & Pennington, 1991).

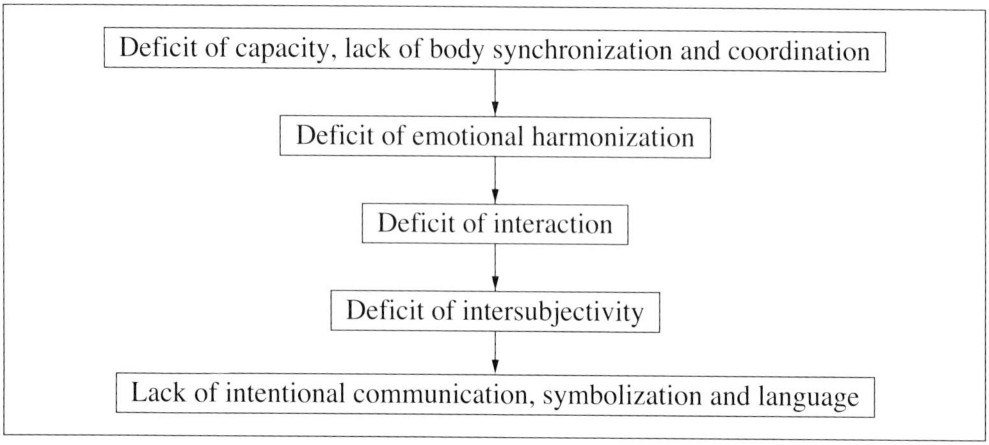

Fig. 2. Cascade disorganization (Rogers & Pennington, 1991).

(1) keeping the child for as great a part of the day as possible in a situation of coordinated interactive relations, favourable to imitation and to symbolic and interpersonal communication, and to a perception of this social experience; and
(2) intensive teaching to make up for backwardness in learning owing to previous lack of communication (because even at home the child's condition leads to an impaired level of social exchange).

The Denver programme proposes intensive treatment for a total of at least 20 hours a week (both in the home routine and at nursery school).

As will be explained later, the intensive treatment we offer closely follows Rogers' theoretical and practical concepts: for each child there is a specific individual and group programme, allied to cooperation with the school and with the parents – a normal aspect of our work. This form of treatment is used for children suffering from disorders of development which, at the ages of 2 or 3 years, cannot with any degree of certainty be classified as 'pervasive developmental disorders' (PDD).

In agreement with Dr. Brunati, head of the Cherasco Clinic, the Marzani-Montoli *Guidelines for Internal Use* (Marzani & Montoli, 2002) have been adopted for evaluating and treating infantile autism in children of preschool age (to which reference is made in Table 5). In replanning the diagnostic process for children aged from 2 to 6 (Table 4) we have made every effort to apply as much scientific guidance as possible, gained from both the Italian and the international literature, not only to avoid an approach too closely based on 'clinical subjectivity' but also to ensure adoption of best practice. We believe that an initial diagnosis based on DSM-IV or ICD-10 should be followed by a diagnosis of development to discover how far basic interactive patterns can function in the areas of primary and secondary intersubjectivity as, according to our model of reference, these are the priority focuses of stimulation.

The process of case evaluation we are now presenting (Table 5) was worked out in collaboration with Dr. Anna Dallavecchia and with a team from the Autism Clinic at the Reggio Emilia health centre.

Table 4. Which diagnosis for which treatment?

At our clinic:
- the psychopathological and neuropsychological aspects derived from observation and evaluation are integrated in the semi-structural and structural contexts;
- clinical observation in early infancy, paying attention to child-family relationships and exchanges, is integrated by formal evaluation of the various aspects of development.

↓

Differential diagnoses can therefore be formed, such as:
- impaired attachment and relationships with/without delayed development
- Pervasive developmental disorders (PDD)
- retarded cognitive development

Table 5. Guidelines for internal use in diagnosing children aged from 2 to 6 years

Interviews with parents:	**Formal evaluation:**
• case histories	• PEP-R
• collection of details about behaviour and habits	• CARS
Observation with parents and staff; areas of observation:	• Vineland questionnaire
• intersubjectivity	• Camaioni questionnaire
• imitation	• Denver checklist
• emotional functioning	
• symbolic play	**Observations and evaluations are recorded on video**
• preverbal and verbal modes of communication	
• social cognition	

CARS, Child Autism Rating Scale; PEP-R, Psychoeducational Profile-Revised.

We thus arrived at a diagnostic method capable of bringing to light not only the child's emotive and cognitive potentials and limitations but also those of the family, following the model adopted by the Cherasco Child Guidance Clinic. The method includes supportive consultations which, from the outset, aim at sustaining parent-child interaction and related emotional bonds, in full realization of the fact that, where severe biological pathology is suspected, the anxiety felt by the parents will generate difficulties in maintaining communication. This alone will adversely affect evolutionary processes and risk provoking a state of total emotional confusion in the child.

Objections appear to be raised against the belief that this also applies to children affected by some form of autism which – in view of the mainly organic nature of their disorder – may make them seem unaware of the troubled family atmosphere around them. To our way of thinking this cultural attitude may in itself lead to a child's confused and repetitive behaviour becoming chronic (a secondary form of autism, induced by unsuitable or incorrect treatment), tending as it does towards estrangement between parent and child, hindering the establishment of those primitive bonds created by emotional exchange.

To use a clinical expression coined by Selma Freiberg for a normal child (Freiberg, 1980), an autistic child also is a 'transference object', as the baby re-enacts memories and experiences of the past, of grandparents and parents (fantasies), that often exert a negative effect on development. We have summarized in *Table 6* the line of action our clinic is proposing for involving parents and schools in the treatment of these cases.

Table 6. Parallel action

By individual or group discussions we offer:	
Parents	**The school**
• an understanding of the child's mental and neuropsychic processes • an explanation of painful feelings and encouragement to undertake the experience of treatment in alliance with the team • practical suggestions, analysis of the behaviour problem • talks on periodical evaluations of the child's development and on the checks made by the NPI specialists	• monthly discussion groups to agree with teachers on focus for work Weekly verifications have been begun for each child along the lines of 'Infant Observation' adapted to the context, and aimed at observing any anxiety shown when separated from the parent, and on moments of emotional and cognitive disorganization, so as to note how any autistic defences operate.

Indications for treatment

The outline given in *Table 7* was followed initially. At present we are looking for more specific indicators and are researching the psychological and behavioural subtypes based on the CARS scale of development and linked to an evaluation of alterations to various courses of treatment.

Table 7. Indications for treatment (Guralnick, 1998)

- 12 months overall retardation
- or 33% retardation in a functional area
- or 25% retardation in two areas
- or 2 standard deviations below average in one area
- or 1.5 standard deviations below average in two areas

The structure of treatments in the year 2002–2003 is given in *Tables 8 and 9*.

Table 8. Structure of treatment in the year 2002–2003 (stage 1)

A	B
Applied to: 2 girls, 1 boy Diagnosis: pervasive developmental disorders (PDD) Average chronological age: 4 years Average age of development: 21 months Frequency: $2^1/_2$ hours on 3 days a week (total $7^1/_2$ hours weekly) Activity in a small group context (2–3 children)	Applied to: 2 girls, 1 boy Diagnosis: mental retardation Average chronological age: $4^1/_2$ years Average age of development: 19.6 months Frequency: $2^1/_2$ hours on 2 days a week (total 5 hours weekly) Individual and small group activity (2–3 children)
The children receive regular neuropsychiatric treatment and a course of training is provided for parents and teachers	

Table 9. A typical day

Welcome: semi-structured play and circle time with mimed songs (about 20 min) First activity (about 40 min) Visit to the toilet followed by mid-morning snack Structured group play (about 20 min) Second activity (about 40 min) Leave taking: circle time with mimed songs
First and second activity alternate with imitation, intersubjectivity, symbolic play, movement stimulation

Particular attention was paid to planning play activity with the aim of stimulating imitation (series of small movements, facial/mouth movements, gestures, simple and sequential movements), joint attention, and turn taking. For this area special psychopedagogic attention is needed, with the use of applied behavioural analysis (ABA) qualifications *(Table 10)*.

Table 10. Applied Behavioural Analysis (ABA)

- use of educational techniques applying psychological learning principles
- presentation of foreseeable and structural activities (TEACCH)
- evaluation of results
- assessment of how far learning has become generalized in different contexts, and monitoring follow-up
- use of *discrete trials, mass trials*
- programmes based on more naturalistic methods using stimuli linked to the child's environment and to daily activities (school, at home)
- *incidental teaching* and *pivotal response*

Evaluation of treatment

In view of the small size of our sample and the impossibility of basing our research on the use of control groups, we decided to use the single case method comparing the results of treatment with the periods of non-treatment to see if these could produce a stable change in the rate of development *(Table 11). Table 12* summarizes the recommendations deduced from a wide range of cases that have been the subject of scientific study.

Table 11. Evaluation of treatment results

Frequency • once a year
Method • PEP-R • Vineland questionnaire • Camaioni questionnaire • CARS scale • Comparison between rate of development with/without treatment, using a method modified by single case research

CARS, Child Autism Rating Scale; PEP-R, Psychoeducational Profile-Revised.

Laura Schriebman (2000) offers a full examination of the problem of evaluating treatment and of the risk of irresponsible or unguarded interference. There are no standards applicable to all children or to all the services available; effective action can apply even to the individual child.

Table 12. Criteria for ensuring effectiveness of the treatment

Recommendations derived from studies recently published in the USA (Dawson & Osterling, 1997)
• content of the curriculum
• environment providing great support to natural learning
• routine and predictability
• functional approach for understanding and modifying dysfunctional behaviour
• close integration with school syllabuses (at least 20 hours a week)
• good involvement of parents at all times, especially during periodical evaluations

Conclusions

The experience at present in progress has involved a great deal of work in the way of preparation and training of personnel and, regrettably, a similar effort to secure the necessary funds. Much room for improvement remains, both in extending our work to cover a larger number of children and in the amount of time devoted to each child; the same applies to the need for further study of the tools and techniques used in checking results. The question may perhaps be posed as to why it was decided to choose a type of treatment based on teaching theories by a working group that had always preferred a psychoanalytically orientated educational method. Compared with others of a more behaviourist bent, we believed this to be the right choice because it is based on a theory of development closer to our previous one (psychoanalytical theory *versus* that of Stern); that is, an attempt to prevent autistic development at least partially, starting from a close observation of how the primary representative relational and sensorimotor experiences became distorted, causing the onset of autism – though it is now understood that the educational method must also be used for treating a basic cognitive deficit.

An important point on which we feel absolutely convinced – although we are as yet unable to support it with our own data – is the need to oppose a tendency to autistic distortion by early application of intensive treatment, including the establishment of cooperation with the parents and, if possible, with the school as well. We are of course fully conscious of the obstacles to be faced over setting up health and educational projects that work together for the same purpose and are allowed to carry on for a suitable period of time.

The experience at present being gained by the UONPIA semi-residential unit at Niguarda Hospital, with its almost 30 years of service, has in spite of some inevitable failures produced a great deal in the way of positive results in the field of infantile autism. This provides encouragement not only to the specialists concerned but above all, we hope, to administrative staff regarding the vital need to create suitable environments for autistic children (as well as others), where real success can be achieved; in other words, the paramount need is to ensure that funds are allocated to really useful projects! The present work has been made possible by financial help from the Cariplo foundation to which we express our grateful thanks.

Finally, we feel that ongoing discussion on how autism should be treated – even now being conducted in warlike tones – should allow for the fact that *treating this condition*, especially in very small children, means accepting its aetiological multifactorial nature and planning treatment on the basis of learning, while making full allowance for the importance of emotional bonds. Basically therefore, even if the cause is biological, present research shows that psychoeducational treatment is currently the only type available to us.

References

Dawson, G. & Osterling, J. (1997): Early intervention in autism. In: *The effectiveness of early intervention*, ed. M.J. Guaralnick, pp. 307–326. Baltimore: Brookes Publishing Co.

Freiberg, S. (1980): *Clinical studies in infant mental health: the first year of life*. London: Tavistock Publications.

Guralnick, M.J. (1998): The effectiveness of early intervention for vulnerable children: a developmental perspective. *Am. J. Ment. Retard.* 102–104, 319–345.

Lovaas, D.I. (1967): A behaviour therapy approach to the treatment of childhood schizophrenia. *Minnesota Symposia in Child Psychology* **1**, 108–159.

Marzani, C. & Montoli, R.A. (2002): Linee-guida interne: una proposta evidence-based per la diagnosi dei disturbi pervasivi di sviluppo in età precoce. In: *Interventi intensivi precoci per costruire insieme il futuro del bambino autistico*, pp. 5–17. Milan: Rotary International Distretto 2040.

Osterling, J., Dawson, G. *et al.* (2001): Autism. In: *Handbook of clinical child psychology*, 3rd ed., eds. M.C. Roberts & H. Walker, pp. 432–542. New York: John Wiley and Sons.

Rogers, S.J. & Pennington, B.F. (1991): A theoretical approach to the deficits in infantile autism. *Dev. Psychopathol.* **3**, 137–163.

Schreibman, L. (2000): Intensive behavioral/psychoeducational treatment for autism: research needs and future directions. *J. Autism Dev. Disord.* **30**, 247–256.

Stern, D.N. (1985): *The interpersonal world of the infant*. New York: Basic Books.

Autistic spectrum disorders, D. Riva and I. Rapin (eds.)

Chapter 22

Day care treatment of preschool age children with pervasive developmental disorder: 10 years' experience at the Dosso Verde Institute in Milan

Luisa Salvini*, Paolo Manfredi* and Giovanni Lanzi°

* *Psychotherapy Center, Institute Dosso Verde, Pavia, Milan;*
° *Department of Neurologic and Psychiatric Clinic of Developmental Age, Fondazione 'C. Mondino', University of Pavia, via A. Ferrata 6, 27100 Pavia, Italy*
glanzi@unipv.it

Summary

The Dosso Verde Institute's day care was opened in 1991. This chapter describes the experience – including that acquired at the Dosso Verde Institute in Pavia before the opening of the day care in Milan – which led operators working at the day care to adopt an integrated approach to the treatment of pervasive developmental disorders (PDD).
The history of the centre is recounted briefly, as are the reasons and thinking that led to the development of the current methodology. The way the teams are structured is also explained, looking both at individual skills and at the way work is organised. These aspects are based on the development of a concept of the therapeutic-rehabilitative group, and a particular viewpoint on the type of environmental relationships most suitable for children affected by PDD and their families; they form the framework, which has now been in place for 25 years, of the work carried out at the Dosso Verde. The strength of this framework has allowed the method to be flexible and open, ready to attempt and to assimilate – with the necessary adjustments – the rehabilitative ideas and approaches that have emerged from difference sources in recent years. The method has thus been altered and gradually refined over the years. The chapter ends with a brief description of one patient, underlining the importance of the dialectical relationship between the *stable part* of the method, verified and constant, and the *variable part*, which is in a state of permanent evolution.

Background

In this chapter we outline the method used by the Dosso Verde day care in Milan for the 'enablement' and rehabilitation of children affected by pervasive developmental disorder (PDD).

It seems illogical to try and paint a single picture, however detailed and precise, of a service whose very peculiarity is its capacity to evolve.

When, in 1991, I was asked to organise and coordinate this centre in Milan, I had already been working as a psychotherapist at the Dosso Verde Institute in Pavia for over ten years. It was a period of reassessment within the organisation. Professor Lanzi, in collaboration with the nuns of the 'Maria Consolatrice' order, had founded the Dosso Verde Institute in Pavia at the start of the 1960s. This had come about as a result of needs emerging in the outpatient and inpatient treatment of child neuropsychiatry patients and of the possibility, at the time still regarded as innovative, of using individual psychoanalytical psychotherapy to treat severe psychiatric disturbances in children.

A residential centre for children with infantile psychosis was set up where they were able to receive psychotherapy and to benefit from an environment, including a school, that was tailored to their needs.

It was not long before an outpatient service was added and hospital admission – at the time mainly in a residential-type centre – was restricted to cases presenting with more severe social-environmental problems, some of whom were referred by the juvenile court.

Initially, each therapist had overall responsibility for the patients they were following. In all, we had five therapists and a total of 30 children; not only did we look after the therapeutic side, we were also involved with educational aspects, teachers, families, and referring physicians. The set-up was similar to that of a department in a hospital, where the department physician is almost entirely responsible for his own patients. Thus on Monday mornings we would 'do the rounds' of our own educational groups.

The background pathologies and situations encountered were very diverse and this made the task of the staff extremely complex and difficult. Indeed, when I took up my post at the Dosso Verde Institute, I was replacing not one but two colleagues who, discouraged by the disruptive behaviour of several of the patients, had one after the other handed in their notice and gone back to less demanding work.

However, it is possible, providing one is able to last the course, to learn from this kind of adversity, and the contribution of others was a great help – for example, studying the experiences of others and visiting the various institutions growing up in Europe, and also following the evolution of neuropsychiatry and psychoanalytical thinking over those years.

Team meetings were organised to discuss specific cases, with all the operators regularly getting together to verify results, and plan and coordinate courses of action; conversely, the intervention of the various specialist teams (the psychotherapists, the educators, the school teachers, each with their own demands and often in conflict, both with each other and with the other teams of specialists) was initially organised in an entirely informal manner.

I still recall some general meetings of the Dosso Verde staff that, had it not been for the conciliatory presence of the Scientific Director, could easily have degenerated into 1970s-style political assemblies. They were certainly highly charged situations, but they were also a valuable mine of ideas and proposals.

It became increasingly clear that the main problem to be solved was how to organise these moments of contrast and reflection among operators: how to transform the problems and demands of individuals and of groups of professionals into workable proposals and the start of a therapeutic approach that could not, and indeed should not, be allowed to remain a rigid system.

This was our only hope of evolving and of creating a thoughtful and collaborative environment in which to take care of our patients – the only way in which we could prevent the difficulties encountered in educating and caring for these children, and the frustrations generated by what was a very difficult job, from heightening the personal problems and professional demands on each of us, and leading us into the sort of institutional impasse which, unfortunately, has been typical of psychiatric organisations in the past.

The early 1980s, the period in which, among other things, the Dosso Verde Institute became affiliated with the National Health Service and extended its outpatient department considerably, brought a progressive definition of the working set-up, the educational groups, and the various spheres of competence, and the need emerged both for psychoanalytical supervision of each individual group (of its internal dynamics and of its relations with the other groups) and for consultancy, again from outside the institution, on the working methods adopted.

There also emerged the figure of a Coordinating Neurologist-Psychiatrist – the most competent and experienced member of staff, who was called upon to chair meetings on individual cases and to gather the ideas and demands of each operator and each team. Supported by another neurologist-psychiatrist with particular expertise in paediatric rehabilitation, and working as well in collaboration with the Scientific Director, the Coordinating Neurologist-Psychiatrist gained an overview of the work of the institution.

This period saw an increase in the professional awareness of all the operators, thanks in part to the development of rehabilitative techniques for communication and learning disorders; diagnoses became increasingly specific and the programmes in each of the various ambits richer in potential.

The original proposal, that individual psychotherapy should be of central importance, was verified on different levels. The psychoanalytical approach had allowed us:

• to acquire in-depth knowledge of the structural and relational dynamics of children with severe disorders of mental development;

• to experience the relational problems to which the operators and the institution are exposed and to organise working methods geared at the overcoming of conflicts, allowing the latter instead to become a source of new ideas and proposals;

• to develop better defined therapeutic indications (by taking the results of some 15 years' work and linking them with neuropsychiatric diagnoses that, from a phenomenological perspective, were becoming more and more precise).

While we had achieved satisfying results in the sphere of disorders deriving from situations of deprivation, and in personality, behavioural and emotional disorders, those obtained in subjects with PDD were less encouraging. It was a painful realisation – after all we had expended considerable energy and had required the families and other operators to do likewise – but we had to acknowledge that what we had done was present a model for decoding the internal and external world to patients who simply did not possess the instruments needed to decode these worlds – to attribute them with some meaning, however basic. Often, not even words could be understood.

That is not to say that we did not establish good relations with these children. They were happy to be with us, and they often became calmer and happier in other environments too, but this was not enough. For one thing, we were often able to sense a potential for communication and autonomy which our instruments had not been able to bring out and which, with the new techniques available, we felt we should by now be able to exploit. We welcomed with great enthusiasm the rehabilitative ideas that were emerging at this time and it was this enthusiasm that prompted Professor Lanzi and the Congregation of Nuns running the Dosso Verde Institute to found the day care in Milan – a small organisation devoted to the care of preschool-age children affected by PDD.

Organisation of the service

I will now describe how the day care service is organised.

The working protocol is based on the following:

• Close attention to relations among operators, and to relations with the child and their family, drawing on the experience and knowledge, acquired over many years, in the clinical practice of neuropsychiatry and psychoanalysis, experience that led us to consider fundamentally important the management of the intra- and interpersonal dynamics of each operator involved in the project, paying particular attention to the difficulties and frustration that can easily trigger destructiveness and omnipotence.
• Operators who have shown professionalism, coherence, and openness to the model proposed, as well as an interest in and readiness to respond to fresh stimuli (new methods and techniques).

The day care can accommodate 12 children who are admitted between the ages of 2 and 5 years and who can stay, if necessary, up to the age of 12 years. The day care service occupies an entire floor of a complex owned by the Congregation, which also houses officially recognised nursery and primary schools. The arrangement of the rooms and space – the premises were renovated in 1996 – was planned according to indications contained in the Treatment and Education of Autistic and related Communication Handicapped Children (TEACCH) model.

Adjacent to the day care, but quite independent of it, is the small Dosso Verde state primary school, which is also attended by some of our patients.

The working group is made up of the following teams:

The medical team

This comprises: the director, a doctor specialising in neuropsychiatry, who fulfils a coordinating role, also being required to manage relations with referring services; a neurologist-psychiatrist who looks after neurological, pharmacological, and rehabilitative aspects and supervises, with the parents, the child's course of treatment; a rehabilitative therapist specialising in psychomotricity; and a psychotherapist. The latter two administer individual treatments.

The pedagogic-educational team

This team comprises four professional educators and a nun in a supervisory capacity. Two of the educators are specialists in psychopedagogy, and experts in the TEACCH method and in alternative communication. The educators intervene on two fronts:

• Each educator follows, preferentially, the progress of three children, and looks after their integration into the day care, into the nursery school, and subsequently into the primary school; whe also pursue relations with their parents (being available to see them upon request and for regular meetings); aspects relating to the child's personal and social autonomy; and application of the PEP-R and related tests;
• In the afternoons, the educators run rehabilitation workshops in their specific areas of expertise: cognitive rehabilitation, graphic expression, verbal expression, drama, manual activities, 'girls' workshop', facilitated and other forms of alternative communication, guided motor activities, sensory stimulation, and relaxation.

In small groups, the children are also taken to the games room, into the playground for group games and bike riding and, in the spring and summer, out on recreational and sports trips.

The structuring of a preferential relationship with one educator gives each child an opportunity to experience an important relationship. The various workshops are the places in which the child-educator pair can really become aware of, and learn to know, describe, and use their relationship, in all its aspects. For example, a rehabilitative activity (using the 'theory of mind' model) focusing on understanding the mental states of others seems, to us, to work far better if conducted in a situation of empathy within which the relationships being formed are the ones used to achieve the objective. In this case, it is possible to talk of understanding the mental state of another person through identification.

Overall, the day, the various spaces and the rehabilitative and daily living activities are organised and planned taking into account the peculiar characteristics of the autistic child, which usually include limited and unusual language skills, unusual sensory processing, particularly of multiple stimuli, difficulty with associating and integrating ideas, difficulty in interpreting the underlying meaning of events and experiences, and intolerance to change and unexpected events.

The educators take part in fortnightly meetings overseeing the work of the group, as well as weekly and daily meetings of an organisational nature.

The team of teachers

The picture as regards this team is more varied:

At nursery level, the children, accompanied by their educator, have so far always been integrated into the officially recognised nursery school, which is located in the same complex as the day care and is made up of one prenursery and two mixed classes. We are also now beginning to work in collaboration with the local municipal nursery school.

When the children reach primary age, we can choose from two options, according to their individual needs: we have our officially recognised primary school, located in the day care complex, and the Dosso Verde state primary school (situated, as we have said, adjacent to the day care). The latter has specialised teachers who liaise with the internal primary school over didactic and socialisation aspects, and with whom we have long collaborated. The children are also supported during all the hours they spend at school (the entire morning), by a special needs teacher.

For each child, meetings are held every three months and attended by all those involved (internally and externally) in their care. Each operator presents, in writing, their aspect of the work being carried out, and this is discussed and verified with the others. Twice a year, the Director and the neurologist-psychiatrist, often in the presence of the educator responsible for the child, meet the local health service neurologist-psychiatrist who first referred the child.

The children and their families

Let us now take a look at how the service is organised from the point of view of the children and their families. The child is usually referred by a child neurologist-psychiatrist or psychologist working for a local health authority or child and adolescent neuropsychiatry department, with a request for assessment or sometimes even for admission.

Although we have found, in recent years, that the children's neurological status has already been evaluated by the time they are referred to us, further investigations can sometimes be necessary, in which case arrangements are made with the referring physician and with the family. There then follows a stage during which the child and his family get to know us and our organisation, and *vice versa*.

I will clarify later the reason why I refer to the child's 'family' rather than only to their 'parents'. This stage, the duration of which can vary, comprises informal interviews, observations, the administration of assessment scales, visits to our centre, and meetings with the professionals who work here.

If admission to our institute is deemed practicable and appropriate (by the family as well), then the next phase begins, during which the child is introduced to his new environment: for quite an extended period (a fortnight on average) the child, together with one or both parents, will get acquainted with the person designated to be the principal educator, spending a few hours a day in this person's company. When the child is sufficiently familiar with the educator, the time spent at the institute each day, without the parents being present, is progressively extended. In the meantime, the child neurologist-psychiatrist who is following the parents has frequent meetings with them to hear their suggestions and to discuss how the work is proceeding. After around 6 weeks, the child is accompanied by their educator to the nursery school.

The educators have become a fully integrated part of the teaching staff at the schools, share in the programming of activities, and work both with the children, the patients from the day care, and the other children in small groups. The morning is thus spent at school and ends with lunch, eaten in the company of the educators and the other children.

At around 1 p.m., all the children leave the nursery/primary school canteens and return to the day care, where they all gather in the kitchen to eat some fruit. Then, following a short break for relaxation, they are taken to their workshops. The day ends at 4 p.m. with an afternoon snack, eaten together.

Going back to the introduction period, a decision is usually made over the first two months on the areas in which it appears most appropriate to begin the cognitive and pedagogic rehabilitation programme. Only later is the decision taken regarding the possible need for psychomotor therapy (individual or in small groups), for mother-child psychotherapy, or for individual psychotherapy.

The autistic spectrum covers widely heterogeneous pictures, and the planned rehabilitation must necessarily be personalised and dynamic, in such a way as to allow the operators to 'adjust their aim' continuously according to the evolution of the child and the environment.

I would point out that, in our rehabilitative experience, it is more functional to talk of a spectrum of autistic severity rather than to attempt to formulate different subclassifications as a means of differentiating between different autistic pictures: to highlight the individual differences within a continuum is more useful than subclassifying patients into different groups on the basis of diagnosis or intervention, which risks creating the illusion that we are faced with homogeneous pictures to which a uniform, and thus by definition generic and rigid, type of rehabilitation can be applied. For treatments such as speech therapy and rehabilitative physiotherapy, we have to date benefited from the support of the referring departments of child and adolescent neuropsychiatry.

And now a word about our work with the 'families' – I say families because we often meet the grandparents and siblings of children in our care and, in order to ensure a global intervention, we work with these members of the family too. Indeed, one of the first children admitted to our centre had only a grandmother looking after him. It would be more modern and scientific to refer to this child's 'caregiver', but the woman in question became so important and so dear to us that we do not feel right calling her anything other than his 'granny'.

Our normal working protocol makes provision, in stable periods, for monthly updating and planning meetings with the main family members; these are in addition to the regular meetings with the educators. In recent years, stimulated by our excellent and active educators, we have tried out a more lively form of participation, which started with a few meetings (dealing with topics selected from among several proposed) with a social worker with particular expertise in the field. The families of youngsters already discharged from our day care and the parents of children awaiting admission were invited to take part in these meetings. The idea seemed to work well, and the parents, of their own accord, subsequently met again in rooms at the day care put at their disposal by the nuns. The wish of some of the family members to share their particular skills both in the day care and in the nursery school became apparent and these initiatives have been a considerable success this year.

Case examples

I wish to end with a brief look at the eight children we have discharged to date. For ease of presentation, they are divided into three groups:

Group 1

The first group comprises five children, each of whom was admitted with a diagnosis of autistic-type PDD. Their mean age at admission was 5 years and their mean duration of their stay in our centre was 6 years. In the years spent at our day care they thus had 1 year at the nursery school and 5 years at the primary school (3 in the internal one and 2 in the external one).

Their rehabilitation reflected globally what might, according to reported standards, be expected; two of the children also had individual psychomotor therapy and in three cases, around 3 years after admission – that is, when it was felt that conditions were ripe for this kind of treatment – individual psychotherapy was started.

We have lost touch with one of the children in this group, who was already the most severe case upon admission, presenting severe auto- and hetero-aggressive behaviour and a particularly complex global and social situation. Nevertheless, some improvements were noted in the areas of verbal communication and autonomous function, but there were also several admissions to departments of child neuropsychiatry for episodes of destructive violence.

Of the other four children, one, having gone on to another day care for patients with PDD, has continued to show improvement in communication and autonomous function, but has still not developed any verbal language; the child has adapted well to these new surroundings and family relations are excellent.

Two of the youngsters are now in secondary school, where they are doing well. They are continuing in our centre, with psychotherapy started during their stay with us.

The final member of this group, after leaving us, attended lower secondary school, where he fitted in quite well. After this, upon the wishes of the family, he entered a residential centre.

Group 2

The second group comprises two girls with diagnoses other than PDD, one of whom remained at the day care for only 1½ years owing to the fact that her family moved abroad.

The second, affected by Angelmann's syndrome, and whose social situation was particularly complex (her parents were both minors and gypsies) stayed at our centre for 2½ years, before being discharged at the age of 6. We managed to follow this child's progress as far as her acquisition of the ability to walk and of basic personal autonomy. She gradually opened up and began recognising the main figures around her and her relationship with her mother settled down. This little family group now lives independently and the girl attends a special school.

Group 3

Group 3 comprises a single case, a 9-year-old boy, admitted at the age of 3 years with a diagnosis of autistic-type PDD. His clinical picture was rather severe, although some progress was observed in the sphere of language, albeit non-communicative. An attempt had already been made to introduce this child to a nursery, but he had responded with a heightening of his isolation and stereotyped behaviours.

Marco was an extremely selective eater and refused any activity proposed to him. While with us, he attended the nursery school and then, for 3 years, the primary school. He gradually became attached to his educator and began to show an interest in certain cognitive-type activities, demonstrating, however, an extreme intolerance of any frustration, the manifestations of his distress being so intense as to create real difficulties both for his educators and his parents.

Marco demanded to be called 'the first child'. Thus, when he was around 6 years old, we started mother-child psychotherapy, geared precisely at modifying the mechanism that made it impossible for adults, out of fear of regression (given that the child was giving excellent results overall), to propose new activities to Marco.

Marco's integration into the external primary school strengthened everyone's faith in the stability of the results attained, so much so that we, together with Marco's parents, took the decision to discharge him at the end of his third year in primary school (June 2002), but to continue, on an outpatient basis, the psychotherapy that had been begun. We were all rather worried, as this return to his home town would mean Marco changing schools, teachers, and friends.

Only the psychotherapist was totally convinced that we had made the right choice and, just a few days ago, read to me Marco's first half yearly report from his new school:

The arrival of this friendly child has brought a healthy breath of fresh air and a new outlook.

His integration into the class has been happy and trouble-free, thanks to the openness of and welcome extended by his new classmates, who seem to understand and respect his moments of detachment and extravagance, such as his tendency to immerse himself in the pages of the Monday sports paper, and to roll around on the floor when thwarted or temporarily unable to do something.

He has followed with diligence the activities on the curriculum. Despite often being worried when encountering new situations, Marco is nevertheless able to tackle them easily and overcome them with brilliance.

Articulate and endowed with a rich vocabulary, Marco is very good at problem solving and at arithmetic; he has also made a valuable contribution to the work done in history, geography and science, expressing the knowledge he has acquired with exceptional clarity and demonstrating a critical spirit.

He has taken part, albeit with fluctuating enthusiasm, in workshop activities, physical education, and music, and he has even finally managed to convince himself that he is not hopeless at drawing; on the contrary, his drawings are always expressive and sometimes particularly detailed.

At the present time we have 10 children in the day care, five at the nursery school, four at our internal primary school, and one who is at the external primary school. All the children attend the planned workshops, at different ability levels, and seven have individual psychomotricity sessions.

In recent years, we have received requests for the admission of younger and younger children, whose families have only just leaned of their child's diagnosis and who are anxious about the idea of sending their children to such a specialised centre, fearing that this will exclude the possibility of them ever having a normal education and worried about the effects of excessive proximity with other affected children. This concern is sometimes shared by referring physicians, too, having understandable difficulty supporting these families, who are only just beginning to take on board their child's diagnosis and prognosis. This can lead to a referral that lacks sufficient conviction and support, or to a referral that is delayed until the child reaches primary school age – a stage at which the clear lack of results prompts the decision to try something else, but also a stage at which symptoms are undoubtedly more entrenched.

Conclusions

The course of action proposed by the Dosso Verde Institute is certainly not the only possible option, but it could become, in a climate of greater spread of our clinical experiences – a climate that we have attempted to create here – a sufficiently adaptable model of global intervention, suitable for use in different situations and settings, even in schools, and also as the basis for the organisation of afternoon sessions aimed at youngsters once they start secondary school.

Autistic spectrum disorders, D. Riva and I. Rapin (eds.)
© 2005 John Libbey Eurotext, pp. 217–218.

Chapter 23

The public health services: reality, efficacy, and agenda for the future

Giovanni Marino

President of the National Association of the Parents of Autistic Subjects
melat@libero.it

On behalf of the ANGSA Association (in Italian, National Association of the Parents of Autistic Subjects), I wish to thank the Mariani Foundation for inviting me to contribute. I have been asked to make the closing remarks, which endows me with an authority I do not think I possess. Nevertheless, I shall do my best.

The experiences of families bringing up autistic children are very different from those found with other types of disability: an aetiological diagnosis is often missing; many 'specialists' continue to place responsibility for the syndrome on the mother; many family paediatricians still lack specific experience in dealing with autism; and the success of pharmacological treatment is often less than optimal. These are only the first of a series of difficulties that parents have to face through the years: from the choice of proper rehabilitation treatment to the problems related to the child's schooling, we parents then have to cope with the more general issues of disability in adult life and after we have passed on, unless an effective treatment can be identified in the meantime.

At present, the population of individuals affected by syndromes included in the autistic spectrum (autism proper and other developmental disorders) appears to be nearly two cases per thousand. However, this number may easily increase to three per thousand if the most recent epidemiological data collected in the USA are confirmed.

Most autistic subjects are far from being self-sufficient. When they are adults, they are usually excluded from the labour market. The various treatments that were so popular in Italy up to a few years ago – including systemic, dynamic, aetiological, and family therapy – did not succeed in bringing out the true potential of affected individuals to the same extent as current special educational methods within a comprehensive strategy of interventions and neobehavioural treatments. With these latter methods, it can be shown that a large proportion of autistic subjects may in fact reach good levels of self-sufficiency, as well as the ability to integrate themselves in a normal working environment. On this basis, the heavy responsibility borne by the health services becomes evident.

Even if scanty scientific knowledge of autism could once have justified the poor management of this condition, it is nowadays not acceptable that autistic people and their families should continue to pay for the health professionals' ignorance and stubbornness. Patients' associations can no longer be silent on this issue; they demand that health care providers assume full responsibility for providing the best care.

It is necessary that nationally validated guidelines appropriate for all stages of life are approved; these range from early diagnosis to rehabilitation and treatment in adulthood. Child neurologists have a great responsibility for the early clinical manangement of autistic subjects but necessarily have to abandon them when they come of age. This is clearly unsatisfactory and, as currently happens in some countries, it would be much better if the same health care personnel looked after autistic subjects throughout their entire life from the time of the diagnosis.

Nowadays, when autistic people come of age, their classification changes and they are lumped with different categories of mentally disabled individuals; even among the elderly. In Italy, the National Health Service does not provide for entails structures capable of ensuring proper care for these individuals – care that provides both continuity of treatment and respect for the specific problems posed by autism. Schools are not equipped to receive autistic children. Though there are laws relating to the care of such children, they are apparently too good to enforce, though they feed many illusions. The prestige of special needs teachers, who are usually not proud of their professional specialty, is often below that of a regular teacher, and their ambition is to become the latter. Their recognition needs to be increased so that they can have a successful career and gain advancement in this work.

Parents should seek assistance in enabling their child to gain a greater degree of integration and self-sufficiency, rather than chasing erudition in mathematics or geography; I nearly wrote 'literature' – a subject that many parents have at heart, still expecting too much from facilitated communication methods.

We are now venturing into an area that involves emotions, social issues, politics, and ethics. Autistic subjects need optimal assistance in all aspects relating to their upbringing, and this must be provided by Society. We must not forget that disabled adults are often handicapped as much by being born disabled as by the fact that they did not receive proper treatment at critical times.

Given the current national laws and, more recently, the local laws that govern matters of assistance, the scenario remains confused and lacking in homogeneity, with the exception of a few 'happy' islands. Some of the more powerful associations for disabled people, which benefit from greater political support or a more developed organization, do not acknowledge associations such as ANGSA, and lobby for resources to be assigned through the network of services put in place by general Italian law. One can theoretically be in agreement with such an approach, which focuses on the social integration of disabled people.

For our children, and for all severely disabled people, we should not hesitate to demand that resources be assigned directly to the families as soon as the diagnosis of a severe disorder is made. These resources can then be spent on local facilities once they have become fully operative. Currently, the only applicable source of funding is that provided for disabled subjects who are not self-sufficient.

The role of patients' associations becomes more and more crucial, and their claims need to be sustained by strength of numbers and by the credibility of their initiatives. Unfortunately, not enough parents of autistic children join our association, many being shy of making this commitment or ashamed to admit that their child has this disability. We ask the experts in this field to help us consolidate the meagre resources available, in order to achieve the best results for our children.

Achevé d'imprimer par Corlet, Imprimeur, S.A.
14110 Condé-sur-Noireau
N° d'Imprimeur : 85101 - Dépôt légal : octobre 2005
Imprimé en France